Arcadian Visions

Pastoral Influences on Poetry,
Painting and the Design of Landscape

Allan R. Ruff

WINDgather PRESS

Windgather Press is an imprint of Oxbow Books

Published in the United Kingdom in 2015 by
OXBOW BOOKS
10 Hythe Bridge Street, Oxford OX1 2EW

and in the United States by
OXBOW BOOKS
908 Darby Road, Havertown, PA 19083

Hardback Edition: ISBN 978-1-909686-66-3
Digital Edition: ISBN 978-1-909686-67-0

A CIP record for this book is available from the British Library

Printed in Malta by Melita Press Ltd.

For a complete list of Windgather titles, please contact:

United Kingdom
Oxbow Books
telephone (01865) 241249
Fax (01865) 794449
Email: oxbow@oxbowbooks.com
www.oxbowbooks.com

United States of America
Oxbow Books
telephone (800) 791-9354
Fax (610) 853-9146
Email: queries@casemateacademic.com
www.casemateacademic.com/oxbow

Oxbow Books is part of the Casemate group

Contents

List of Illustrations, Sources and Credits

Plates

1. Arcadia today. Author's photograph.

2. Pan teaching the shepherd Daphnis to play the panpipes. Haiduc.

3. Virgil mosaic. I, Cybjog.

4. The Canopus, at Hadrian's villa near Rome. Author's photograph.

5. English or German fifth century book illustration. PD-Art Yorck Project.

6. The ruins of Virgil's tomb, Naples. Armando Mancini.

7. Simone Martini: Petrarch's *Virgil*. Biblioteca Ambrosiana, Milan.

8. Villa Careggi. Sailko.

9. Apollonio di Giovanni: The *Eclogues*. Riccardiana ms. 492, fol.1r. By permission of the Biblioteca Riccardiana, Florence.

10. Signorelli: The Realm of Pan. Vasari, G., *Lives of the Most Eminent Painters Sculptors and Architects*, Vol. 4. The Project Gutenberg EBook 28420. 2009.

11. Giovanni Bellini: *St Francis in Ecstasy c.*1475–8 © The Frick Collection.

12. Giorgione: *Fete Champetre c.*1510. © RMN (Musée du Louvre)/Hervé Lewandowski.

13. Boldrini after Titian: *Landscape with a Milkmaid c.*1530–1550. Courtesy National Gallery of Art, Washington.

14. The Villa Borghese on the Pincian Hill. The Elisha Whittelsey Collection, The Elisha Whittelsey Fund, 1961, www.metmuseum.org

15. Claude: *Pastoral Landscape: The Roman Campagna c.*1646–7, www.metmuseum.org.

16. Castle Howard: the Temple of the Four Winds with Mausoleum and bridge in the distance. www.digilibraries.com.

17. Frans Hals: *Isaak Abraham Massa and Beatreix van der Lean c.*1622. Rijksmuseum, Amsterdam.

18. Cornelis Troost: *Blindmans Buff c.*1740. Purchase with the support of: Vereniging Rembrandt 1939 Museum Boijmans Van Beuningen, Rotterdam.

19. Claes Jansz Visscher: *Bleaching Fields beyond Haarlem Woods c.*1611–12. Los Angeles County Museum of Art. www.lacma.org.in.

20. Adriaen van der Velde: *Family in Landscape c.*1667. Rijksmuseum, Amsterdam.

21. Jan van Goyen: *View of Haarlem. c.*1646. Metropolitan Museum of Art, New York. www.metmuseum.org.

22. Paulus Potter: *Young Bull c.*1647. *Century Magazine* 48(6) Old Dutch Masters Paul Potter.

23. Rembrandt van Rijn: *View of Omval c.*1645. © Victoria and Albert Museum, London.

24. Dryden's *Georgics of Virgil.* © Andybrill.

25. Autumnal Richmond Hill and Thames. © Colin Smith licensed for reuse under this Creative Common License.

26. Ruins of seventeenth century Southdean Parish Church. © Walter Baxter.

27. Hagley Hall today. Author's photograph.

28. Kent (and Tardieu): *Spring* – from James Thomson, *The Seasons c.*1730. © Royal Academy of Arts.

29. Rousham: Kent's drawing for the gothic farmhouse and the ruined classical arch. Courtesy of C. Cottrell-Dormer.

30. Rousham: view from the gardens today. Source unknown.

31. Rousham: William Kent: *Vale of Venus.* Courtesy of C. Cottrell-Dormer.

32. Rousham: the Vale of Venus today. © www.gardenvisit.com.

33. Thomas Gainsborough: *Major John Dade, of Tannington, Suffolk c.*1755. Yale Center for British Art, Paul Mellon Collection.

Arcadia and the Pastoral Landscape

This book is about Arcadia and the Pastoral tradition; what it has meant for successive generations and their vision of the landscape, as well as the implications this has had for its design and management. But, at the outset there needs to be a word of explanation as to why a landscape architect who is neither an art historian nor a classical scholar, should have felt the need to write this book.

Like many mentioned on the following pages I spent my most formative years roaming the fields and woods, in my case near Bedford learning the common names of wild flowers before I could read or write. My career as a gardener was never in question, only its direction. This was determined during my time as a student at the Royal Botanic Garden, Edinburgh. One afternoon, when standing under a Zelkova tree, I was given a slim volume of selected writings by Henry Thoreau, a person completely unknown to me at the time. I was drawn immediately to an extract entitled *On Beauty* in which Thoreau asks "what are the natural features that make a township beautiful". In his opinion "a river, with its waterfalls and meadows, a lake, a hill, a cliff, or individual rocks, a forest and ancient trees standing singly were beautiful". Looking at Edinburgh, with the wild landscape of Arthur's Seat brooding over the city, and the Waters of Leith threading its way though the Georgian New Town, it was possible to see the wisdom of Thoreau's words. But looking at more recent developments in the city's suburbs, it was obvious that the natural features had been neglected. Throughout the western world the post-war development of towns and cities had seen the landscape become no more than endless acres of close mown grass dotted with flowering cherry trees, and decorated with interludes of colourful annuals and shrubs. The very reverse of Thoreau's belief that ornamental beauty should "be like the lining of a shell, inward looking and essential of which the inhabitant is unconscious and not mere garnishing". Thoreau's words helped direct me towards landscape architecture and to academic research as the most obvious way to bring about changes in the urban landscape. To that end I spent a large part of my career at Manchester University, England, participating in the development of an ecological approach to landscape design, involving the use of native plants to create a nature-like landscapes for people's use and enjoyment, what was described as 'nature on the doorstep'.

The Issue

Ecological landscapes were a departure from the usual practice of landscape architecture. Few landscape architects looked to the landscape as an exemplar, even fewer attempted to re-create it, and most were making gardens on a large or small scale. It seemed as though there was a dichotomy at the heart of the profession. One of the first landscape architects, the American Frederick Law Olmsted, took pains to distinguish himself from gardeners. He saw his work as the art of creating landscapes and was heavily influenced by the rural landscape. "Nothing", he said, "can be written on the subject in which extreme care is not taken to discriminate between what is meant in common use of the words garden, gardening, gardener, and the art which I try to pursue". It was unfortunate that in Britain one of the first persons to call himself a landscape architect was the garden maker, Thomas Mawson, first president of the Institute of Landscape Architects in 1929. Was this the beginnings of a confusion between garden and landscape?

By the 1980s the development of ecological ideas and approaches had led me to a conviction that landscape design needed to adopt a 'design through management' approach and education needed to respond to that change. What followed was a Masters in Landscape Management at Manchester University. When designing the programme I was aware of the need for a module on landscape history. Not the chronology of parks and gardens, the customary history for landscape architects; nor the history set out by geographers or ecological historians but an appreciation of how our ideas about the cultural landscape have evolved, and as a result, how we perceive the landscape around us, and, why we see it in the way we do. From this stemmed the module entitled 'Man and the landscape' that has been the inspiration for this book.

It was my belief that designers of landscape, those nature-like landscapes, were a part of a much larger coterie of artists, writers and composers who also took the landscape as their inspiration. By restricting history to that of gardens not only excluded landscape architects from this rich heritage but also reduced greatly their significance. If a distinction could be drawn between garden making and landscape design – the former involving the manipulation of nature and the arrest of natural development, and the latter harmonising with nature and allowing natural processes to evolve – was there also a distinct landscape tradition? I was vaguely aware of many apparent past kindred spirits who seemed to be a part of such a tradition; besides Thoreau and Olmsted there were artists like Giorgione, Claude and Constable, along with writers as diverse as Petrarch, Wordsworth and William Gilpin.

At this point two simple questions stood out: firstly, who were these people and what did they have in common; and secondly was there a single, linking thread running through history?

Through identifying those artists, writers, poets, as well as designers of the landscape, I discovered the common thread was the concept of Arcadia, first given form by Theocritus and the Roman poet Virgil. This ran throughout the ages providing the unifying link, but it was not a static tradition. As people's perception of nature changed, so the interpretation of Arcadia and the pastoral shifted through time, and with it our view of landscape, its design and management.

Today the concept of Arcadia, and way it has shaped our landscape, is dimly perceived, little understood by landscape architects and those responsible for the management of land. This is in marked contrast to previous centuries when the vision of Arcadia and the pastoral was implanted by education among the more privileged in society. Young men, and it usually was the male of the species, spent many hours translating and learning by rote the words of Virgil and other classical authors and on the Grand Tour they would be introduced to the work of painters like Poussin and Claude and their interpretations of the Ideal pastoral landscape. Even in the nineteenth century, a new translation of Virgil was considered sufficiently important to be advertised in a nineteenth century gardening magazine. But though our knowledge of Virgil has diminished, the pastoral remains embedded in our collective memory. And as more and more of world's population are forced to adopt an urban lifestyle, the urge to escape and return to a simpler, rural existence remains undiminished. It underlays the desire to own a country retreat, to become a new age traveller, or take a holiday in the Mediterranean sun. Today Arcadia holds as powerful an influence as at any time in the past. For that reason alone it is important that we plan our urban environment in ways that harmonise with the natural world.

The reason for writing this book is to provide an alternative landscape history for all those involved with the landscape – either through its design, management, use or enjoyment. It begins by examining the origins of Arcadia and the pastoral in the classical poetry of Theocritus and Virgil, and the effects of, and on, Christianity before outlining its development in renaissance Italy and subsequently in the Netherlands, America and England. It concludes by looking at how arcadian ecology is bringing about a re-appraisal of the pastoral in the twenty-first century. In each chapter the implication of Arcadia and the pastoral on the design and management of the landscape is considered wherever relevant.

I am aware that many will criticise what will inevitably be a simplistic, simplified and selective account. To those critics I can only apologise and say that such criticism in no way diminishes what I regard as a legitimate attempt at trying to trace the cultural history of landscape. My motives for undertaking this task can be expressed simply in the words T. S. Eliot's, it is so "we might better understand the place from whence we start". For I believe it is important to understand how Arcadia and the pastoral tradition has shaped, and continues to influence, our design and appreciation of the landscape.

Allan R. Ruff
July 2014

CHAPTER ONE

The Classical Origins of Arcadia

Arcadia – the reality and the myth

We have all dwelt in Arcadia. Experienced lying in the summer sun, with the perfume of wild flowers carried by warm soft breezes, with a gentle hum of insects filling the air, a picnic enjoyed with friends, all recalled as a time suffused with a sense of happiness and well-being. So it is important to start by asking: 'where is Arcadia, and how has this word come to define those moments of perfect bliss?' Arcadia (in Greek *Arkadia*) is a region of Greece located in the central finger of the Peloponnese, and is a land of mountains and plains (Figure 1). In ancient times its fascination lay in its remoteness and distance from the civilised society of Athens. Such remote places were regarded as the home of simpletons and murky goings on. The ancient Greeks saw Arcadians as "hunters and gatherers, warriors and sensualists, inhabiting a landscape, notorious for its brutal harshness, trapped between arid drought and merciless floods".[1] Arcadians were believed to dwell in caves or crude shelters subsisting on acorns and the meat and milk of their goats (Plate 1). The presiding divinity of Arcadia was Pan, half man, half goat with woolly thighs and cloven feet, who could appear at any place and at any time. He was the god of shepherds and their flocks, fields and the wooded glens of Arcadia. Ordinary people throughout Greece believed the mischievous, fun-loving Pan was the incarnation of nature which meant he could found anywhere in the countryside. The one quality that softened the brutishness of Arcadian life was music, whether performed by the goatherds or played by Pan. The sound of his pipes, the syrinx, (seven reeds of unequal length held together by wax and string) with "its woodland and wilderness melodies" could "bewitch the hearer into states of pan-ic or pan-demonium".[2] The simple, moving music of the shepherds gained a wide appreciation over all the Greek world. In time, this pastoral (in Latin *pastor* = shepherd) music began to inspire highly educated poets who developed verses in which shepherds exchanged songs in beautiful natural settings, preserved pristine from any incursions from a dangerous outside world. The beginnings of this pastoral verse, with its visions of Arcadia, occurred in the Greek city of Alexandria.

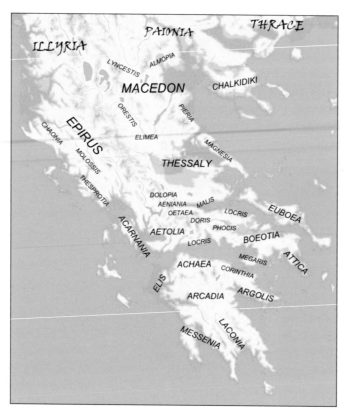

FIGURE I. Regions of ancient Greece: Arcadia in the Peloponissos region.

The City of Alexandria

The city had been founded by Alexander the Great and was carefully planned with parks, theatres and squares, with one of the finest libraries the world had seen. Merchants, bureaucrats and industrialists flocked to the city from Egypt, Greece, Syria and even Italy and by the third century BC Alexandria had become a vast sprawling, impersonal metropolis with a population of more than a million people. After Alexander's death in 323 BC the religious and political ties that once bound people to a small city state were loosened and the sense of community that arose from a shared democracy, was replaced by a growing emphasis on the individual and self-interest. The middle classes enjoyed both increasing levels of education and the opportunity to indulge in the material pleasures of life; parties, courtesans, comfortable houses and the purchase of country estates. But there was also a growing sense of unease; as affluent Alexandrines became aware of their greed and the widening gap between the rich and poor. They could also see the pollution, filth and disease of the hostile city that enveloped them. Humanity had emerged finally as an urban animal in Alexandria and for the first time in history, people felt trapped by their urbanised surroundings. Alexandrines began to appreciate what had so recently been lost and this fostered a growing nostalgia for the simpler, less civilised life of the countryside. It could not be found in the environs of the

PLATE 1 *(left)*. Arcadia. Today the Province can be easily reached by fast motorways – but the way of life has altered little over the centuries – some things never change, except for fashions.

PLATE 2 *(right)*. Pan teaching the shepherd Daphnis to play the panpipes. Second century AD Roman copy of Greek original *c.*100 BC attributed to Heliodorus (found at Pompeii).

city where the streams had become turgid and insect-filled, and vast numbers of peasants laboured to provide the city's food. Instead their nostalgia was for the mountains and clean air of Greece, described by Homer and long associated with escape and refreshment of the spirit. But it was more than just a physical place, it was also metaphysical, a time when man and the spirits had lived a simple life together, in harmony with nature. Personifying this nostalgic dream was the deity Pan in his mountainous, Arcadian home. (Plate 2). As Homer said:

> Muse, tell me about Pan, the dear son of Hermes, with his goats feet and two horns – a lover of merry noise. Through wooded glades he wanders with dancing nymph who foot it on some sheer cliff edge, calling upon Pan, the shepherd god, long haired unkempt. He has every snowy height and the mountain peaks and rocky crest for his domain; hither and thither he goes through the close thickets, now living by soft streams, and now he presses on amongst towering crags and climbs to the highest peaks that overlook the flocks.
>
> Homer: *Homeric Hymn 19 to Pan* (trans. Evelyn White)[3]

Theocritus

The poet who first gave form to this longing for a return to the simple life was the Sicilian-born poet Theocritus (316–260 BC). Born in Syracuse, Theocritus spent his early years roaming the hilly landscapes, enjoying the pleasures of the countryside and learning the songs and improvisations used by shepherds to pass the time. When he came to create his own, imaginary bucolic landscape his experience of clear springs, mossy rocks, carpets of soft grass and shepherds would all be evident.

In Greek literature there was no precedent for bucolic/pastoral poetry, it seems to have arrived, fully formed in the ten *Idylls* Theocritus wrote for the enjoyment of an educated urban audience who longed to escape to the countryside but nevertheless, wished to retain all their urbanity. In his nostalgic, bucolic poetry[4] (in Greek *bukolos* = herdsman) the landscape is filled with herdsmen who could speak words of sophistication for the delight of tired and jaded Alexandrines. Theocritus raised the herdsmen above their humble position by a love of beauty, both for young girls and adolescents, and for music and poetry which gave rise to endless musical contests and poetic challenges. Theocritus also shifted Arcadia away from the harsh realities of the Peloponnese, to the more amenable landscape of his childhood home in Sicily.

The most evocative description of the arcadian landscape comes at the end of *Idyll* vii *The Harvest Home* which contains a variety of natural detail, as well as a great deal of sensory perception. It describes how two friends and the narrator, most probably the poet himself, steal away from the city to enjoy a day in the country, and once there they join in the harvest festivities. There is an overwhelming sense of well-being, of harmony between man and nature, and pleasure in the fecundity of harvest:

> But Eucrite and I and pretty Amyrituas
> Turned towards Phasidamos' farm, there we lay down
>   rejoicing
> On deep beds of sweet-smelling rushes and freshly stripped
>   vine leaves.
> Overhead rustled many black poplars and elm trees,
> And Sacred water chuckled and gurgled nearby
> As it trickled forth from the caves of the nymphs.
> Dusky locusts were hard at their chirping on shady
>   branches,
> And from afar the tree frog crooned in a dense thorn bush,
> And the crested larks and the linnet sang, and the turtle
>   dove mooned,
> And the yellow bees buzzed as they hovered around the clear
>   spring.
> All was fragrant with rich summer, the odours of fruit
>   time.
> Pears lay by our feet, by our sides apples
> In lavish abundance were rolling, and the boughs
> Of the plum trees, heavy laden drooped to the ground.
> And the four-year seal was loosened from the head of the wine
>   jars.

Theocritus (trans Sargent): Idyll vii The Harvest Festival[5]

This timeless description of a picnic enjoyed in the warm afternoon sun of Kos is what many people would describe today as 'idyllic', the dream of escape and release in Arcadia. For the first time in poetry, Theocritus conveys a feeling both for nature and of man's place within nature, in so doing, he goes beyond the written word into a world of shared experience with the reader. The Idyll is full of the sights and sounds, even the scents, of a hot summers day; the gentle breeze rustling the leaves of the trees, the sound of gurgling water and the noises of the frog, the melodious song of the birds and the buzzing of the bees. There is an unwritten sense of soporific pleasure as one is absorbed into the landscape, in the heavy, sleepy atmosphere enhanced by the wine.

But unlike the later English Romantic poets, Theocritus was not a nature poet. There is no affinity with nature and the shepherds, neither worship nor offer sacrifices to deities or sacred places. In consequence, the landscape derives its beauty not from any divine grace but from the fact that it is free from any restrictions, obligations or associations. The pastoral landscape is the perfect human setting for love and music, the *locus amoenus*, a place free from all jarring elements whether insects that bite or gaudy brash flowers – or in modern times, unwanted noise. Such feelings of freedom and unalloyed pleasure have characterised the pastoral and the love of the countryside ever since, even by those unaware of Theocritus and his Idylls. But there is more than just sensual pleasure. There is the duality of town and country, "idealization and realism, celebration and regret",[6] escape and return, that serve to establish the tension which is the very essence of pastoral. Man can return to nature, a place where he feels at home, and where he is free to indulge and express his feelings about himself and nature, but he has to return to the city.

Virgil and his formative years

The *Idylls* of Theocritus may have remained obscure Greek verse, if it had not been for Publius Vergilius Maro, known simply as Virgil, who brought the pastoral to its fullest and most enduring form. Virgil (70–19 BC) was born into a family of modest landowners in Andes, the modern town of Pietole. The family farm was watered by the rivers Po and Mincius in the very fertile region of Cisapline. The geographer Strabo, a contemporary of Virgil, noted the production of the region surpassed the rest of Italy. Large quantities of wheat were exported across Europe and grapes and other fruit trees produced abundant yields. In his youth Virgil was able to wander freely in this diverse and luxuriant landscape, taking a keen interest in both farming practice and the natural world. Later he described the family estates;

> ... all the land, from the place where
> That spur with its gentle slope juts out from the recessive
> Hill-line, as far as the water and the old bench trees with
> Their shattered tops ...
>
> Virgil: *Eclogues* 9, lines 7–10[7]

> And the place where;
> ...in the green meadows I'll build a shrine of marble
> Close to the waterside, where the river Mincius wanders
> With lazy loops and fringes with delicate reed.
>
> Virgil: *Georgics* 3, lines 16–18

His father wanted Virgil to join the elite of Roman society and so after exhausting the limited offerings of Mantua, Virgil was sent at the age of 12 to Cremona for advanced studies, and on to Milan. On attaining manhood he moved to Rome to study law but Virgil transferred his studies to philosophy. During his time in Rome the storm clouds of civil war were gathering. Though Cisalpine Gaul was not part of the Roman empire, its inhabitants were demanding their rights from Rome. Their champion was Julius Caesar who granted them citizenship and made his home there during ensuing the civil war It is not certain what part, if any, Virgil played in the war. Though he may have been conscripted by Caesar only to be discharged as medically unfit after the first hard winter, it is also possible he remained in Rome throughout the conflict. What is certain is that in 48 BC, at the time of Caesar's victory at Phasarlus, Virgil left Rome and settled permanently in the Campagna. Shortly after moving to Naples, Virgil was overwhelmed by events that were to cast a shadow over the remainder of his life. A bitter struggle had broken out after Caesar's death in 44 BC between rival groups anxious to secure the succession. Two years later an alliance between Mark Antony, Lepidus and Octavian, the future Augustus and Caesar's adopted son, defeated their rivals Brutus and Cassius at Philippi. Before the battle Augustus promised his troops a share of Italian farmland as the spoils of war and to meet the demands of some 200,000 soldiers he confiscated estates and land in Cisalpine Gaul. Among them the rich properties of Virgil's father which was divided into 60 allotments for resettlement. Virgil was now an exile from the land he had loved so dearly as a child and though part of the estate may have been restored to the family later, he never returned. These events greatly affected Virgil and exerted a strong influence on his writing and strengthened his desire to escape from the chaos, violence and disorder of war, into the serenity and peace of an Arcadian dream.

Virgil's philosophy

In Naples Virgil was part of a philosophical circle known as 'The Garden' in which the inspired teaching of Philodemus and Siro gave him a knowledge and sympathy for Epicurean and oriental philosophies. The more usual philosophy in Roman society was stoicism but epicureanism enjoyed a brief popularity during Virgil's lifetime. Both the philosophies had emerged in Alexandria when the collapse of the city state saw the old religions and social allegiances replaced by more rational, personal religions. Stoicism, with its practical and logical reasoning, appealed to the Romans because it matched their sense of dignity, loyalty, steadfastness of will and moral leadership. The fashion for Epicureanism may have developed because it offered some respite from this "excessive consciousness of responsibility".[8] Epicureans believed pleasure was the greatest good, and the way to attain this was to live modestly and gain a knowledge of the workings of the world. This would lead to a state of tranquility and freedom from fear, as well as an absence of bodily pain. Epicureanism

PLATE 3. Virgil: this mosaic of the poet seated between Clio, the muse of history and Melpomene, muse of tragic and lyric poetry, is his only known portrait. Sousse, third century AD. Bardo Museum, Tunis.

obviously appealed to Virgil's temperament and its philosophy was to have a strong influence on his writing.

Epicureanism also contributed to Virgil's inner, moral conflict. Epicurean ideas, it was said, "detached men from an obedience to authority by diverting their attention from politics and the State". Under the Republic, Epicureans were regarded as anti-social, even revolutionary, and during his time in The Garden, Virgil experienced a growing sense of resentment towards authority. The events in Cisalpine had fuelled his feelings of injustice, bitterness and despair, and bred a desperate hope for the future well-being of the country he loved so passionately. In making himself the mouthpiece for many who shared these emotions, Virgil was faced with a dilemma: "how could he express his indignation in a form that would be accessible and understood by his readers, but without alienating the authorities in Rome"? His solution came through the adoption of the obscure Greek form of poetry, the pastoral. Under Augustus the myth of Rome was being perfected and citizens, in all spheres of cultural activity, were expected to look first to Greece before showing how Roman's had surpassed their achievements (Plate 3). Authors had to adopt one of the classical Greek styles of literature – epic, comedy, history, oratory – not in the manner of plagiarism, but to fulfill the heroic task of creating a Latin literature that could stand alongside, and surpass the glorious achievements of Greece. Not to have done so was considered unbearably uncouth.[9] In Theocritus Virgil found not only a Greek poet whose work was of the highest technical elegance but one who had not been hackneyed by earlier Latin imitators. In the lines of the *Idylls*, he discovered a shared interest and love for the countryside, along with detailed observations of nature. But there was also a sense of suspended reality in the *Idylls*, nothing was entirely what it seemed at first glance. This hint of complexity and subterfuge, implicit in the poems but never fully explained, offered Virgil the possibility of handling complex and dangerous material without making his own position explicit or unambiguous.[10]

The *Eclogues*

In his first long poem, the ten *Eclogues* (Latin = Fragments) or *Bucolics*, Virgil set out to establish himself as the Roman Theocritus, and wanted others to see him in that way. In the first *Eclogue* Virgil presents the image of the idyllic countryside, the home of sophisticated shepherds, but it contains a deeper, darker message. The two Sicilian shepherds, Meliboeus and Tityrus are located in a familiar pastoral landscape but clearly all is not well, it is not the ideal, untroubled Arcadia of Theocritus;

> Tityrus, here you loll, your slim reed pipe serenading
> The woodland spirit beneath a spread of sheltering beech,
> Whilst I must leave my home place, the fields so dear to me.
> I'm driven from my home place; but you can take it easy
> In shade and teach the woods to repeat 'Fair Amaryllis'.

Virgil: *Eclogues* 1, 1–5

In referring to the land confiscations of 41 BC Virgil introduced the reality of Roman politics and events. For this reason the first *Eclogue* has been seen as an allegory of Virgil's own circumstances but it is ambiguous and offers an insight into how the poet used the pastoral form to criticise without commitment. The fragment appears to be about two dispossessed shepherds; Meliboeus, for whom there was no miraculous deliverer and Tityrus whose lands have been restored by the "gay, young prince in Rome". This seems to refer to Octavius (Augustus) but reading further, Virgil makes it clear that Tityrus had not gone to Rome to seek the restoration of his land but as an old slave, to beg freedom from his master. So although Virgil appears to be using contemporary Roman events, he avoids direct criticism by retreating back into the fictional Greek world of Theocritus. As Lyne points out, in the introduction to the C. Day Lewis's translation, there is no resolution to the question of whether this is an allegory of contemporary events or an entertaining fiction based on Theocritan slave shepherds. Oscillating between the two alternatives without committing himself, Virgil probes the moral and political issues of the day but declines to tie his poetry to something as imprudent as reality.[11]

This ambiguity was Virgil's lasting achievement in the *Eclogues*. The pastoral form is established as a vehicle through which contemporary moral and political issues might be explored without criticism. In essence the pastoral form presents the reader with a contrast between the idyllic harmony of an alternative world, in which man lives in harmony with nature, and the reality which threatens to destroy it. This is the continuing fascination of the pastoral which has afforded generations of translators, as well writers of their own pastorals and artists of many kinds, the opportunity to use the same ambiguity to comment on society and the issues of the day, whilst hiding behind the guise of a simple pastoral poem.

Virgil's other great achievement in the *Eclogues* was the invention and naming of the place known as Arcadia. Theocritus set his herdsmen in a Sicilian landscape and his obscure reference to Arcadia was by association with Pan and the occasional Arcadian shepherd. But by the time Virgil was writing his pastoral, Sicily had become a Roman province and the shepherds had become the slaves of large landowners. As such they could not be regarded as free, independent spirits, idling the day away with love and music, so Virgil had to find a new home for his shepherds. He may have been alerted to the possibility of Arcadia, as a place far away from everyday realities and unlikely to have been visited by his readers, by the writings of the historian Polybus, a native of that hostile, remote region. The region's one redeeming feature were its inhabitants, renowned for their musical accomplishments, rugged virtues and rustic hospitality.[12] In idealising Arcadia, Virgil not only made much of these human virtues but gave the landscape charms it had never possessed – a luxuriant vegetation, an eternal spring and for its inhabitants, unlimited time to enjoy music and love.

So through the imagination of Virgil, the bucolics of Theocritus were transferred to the place he gave to the world as Arcadia. But it is not a place to be found on any map. In the first *Eclogue* the Arcadian shepherds are near a small town, close to Rome, and in the seventh, a singing concert takes place on the banks of the Mincius, Virgil's own river, though both contestants are Arcadians. Arcadia is a landscape of the imagination, accessible to all and a place in which all its inhabitants – divine, human, animal, even vegetable – live in mutual harmony and sympathy. A place where even the rocks and mountains are able to share in the emotions of joy and sadness. Virgil's Arcadia is like some half-remembered memory of childhood, in which endless sunlit days remain undisturbed by the harsher realities of the adult world, a vision which can only be glimpsed and never sharply focused, before it recedes once more.

The *Georgics*

The second of Virgil's long poems, the *Georgics* (Greek 'to farm') was altogether different in intent. In comparison to the dreamlike state of his first poem the *Georgics* draws on Virgil's childhood observations and describes in extensive and accurate detail, the management of a farm.It was not that Virgil had forgotten the expulsions or turned his back on Arcadia but he had matured as a person. The Eclogues were the work of a young aspiring poet, anxious to establish his reputation, and once his position was assured Virgil could focus his critical attention on something very important to him – the Italian farming landscape. Childhood experiences had left him with a passionate love of the countryside and he had come to see the small farmer as a metaphor for all that was good in the nation. But all was not well, in the aftermath of the civil war small farmers had deserted the countryside leaving the land to be managed increasingly by absentee landlords who resided in Rome and other cities. The result was an inevitable decline in the farming landscape and the state of the countryside was a matter of great concern to Virgil. So though the Georgics appear to be a treatise on farming, their underlying message is directed at the imperial circle in Rome. Virgil wanted to restore a sense of pride in the work of the small farmer and the plough. He argued that the true Italian way of life, when things were better, had been an agricultural one; "such was the life the Sabines lived in days of old, and Remus and his brother".[13] Virgil suggests that the glories of the city were dependent on the hard work of small farmers.

Virgil's message went further than just encouraging absentee landlords to patriotism and the restoration of a way of life that had become moribund and demoralised. Just as he had created the powerful image of Arcadia in the Eclogue, so in the *Georgics* Virgil sets out a powerful vision of the farmer and farming as part of an organic whole, dignified and beautiful in its own right and in close accord with nature. This, the poet believed, was the only true form of existence. To establish his ancient credentials Virgil used the work of the Greek writer Hesiod, a small farmer in northern Greece and minor poet who had written two poems: *Works and Days* and *Theogony*.[14] The first was a sort of handbook for farmers and the other, an explanation of nature and the history of the Gods. Both were written in pre-literary verse and only occasionally rose to the level of real poetry. Virgil's debt to Hesiod was less than it had been to Theocritus but he did take up the poet's didactic form, that is to say, a work that appears to convey instruction:

> What makes the cornfield happy, under what constellation
> Its best to turn the soil, my friend, and train the vine
> On the elm; the care of cattle, the management of flocks,
> The need for keeping frugal bees: –
> All this I'll begin to relate.
>
> Virgil: *Georgics* i, 1–5

In the *Georgic's* four books Virgil sets out detailed instructions for every conceivable aspect of farming practice, from the tillage of the soil, the cultivation of the vine, the husbandry of sheep and other animals, to the keeping of bees for their "heavenly gift of honey". But in spite of the *Georgic's* authoritative tone, few in Virgil's own lifetime regarded it as simply a farming manual. His descriptions were those of a poet drawing on what he had seen as a child on the family farm and by the time the *Georgics* were written, many practices had been improved. These changes had been described a short time before by Varro, in his treatise on farming, another source used by Virgil. So though the *Georgics* were valued as a delightful evocation of farming, its message was in the lessons Virgil drew from rural life.

One of the constant themes was the value of hard work. Virgil takes up Hesiod's lines that the farmer should observe justice and piety, as well as follow the rhythms of hard work which accompany the seasons of the year. Men are forced to practice the skills of hard work because:

> ... the father of agriculture
> Gave us a hard calling; he first decreed it an art
> To work the fields, sent worries to sharpen our moral wits
> And would not allow his realm to grow listless from
>   lethargy.
>
> Virgil: *Georgics* i, 123–7

This is a very different picture from the earlier vision of Arcadia with its pastoral calm, idleness and plaintiff love songs. However, Virgil does hark back to a golden age when there had been no need for such toil:

> Before Jove's time no settlers brought the land under
>   subjection
> Not lawful even to divide the plain with landmarks and boundaries:
> All produce went to a common pool, and the earth unprompted
> Was free with all her fruits.
>
> Virgil: *Georgics* i, 124–32

But such Arcadian dreams had been left behind in the harsher realities of everyday life and Virgil suggests God had imposed unremitting toil on man so as to induce him to strain for survival and civilisation by his art. Whereas earlier

Greek philosophers had been concerned with ideas of Man's painful progress from primitive ignorance to civilised power, and the ancient association between the culture of the land and culture of the mind, Virgil accentuated the pleasures associated with such labour. First comes the joys of harvest:

> ... the year teems with orchard fruit, or young
> Of cattle, or sheaves of corn,
> Brimming the furrows with plenty, overflowing the barns.
> Winter comes, when olives are crushed in the press, and
> pigs
> Return elate with acorns, and woods give arbutus berries:
> Autumn drops her varied fruits at our feet, while far
> Above on sunny rocks the vintage basks and mellows.
>
> Virgil: *Georgics* 2, 516–22

Virgil's message is clear, if man does his bit, then nature will respond in overflowing measure, and the farmer can take his pleasure:

> The farmer himself keeps holidays when, at ease in a
> meadow,
> A fire in the midst and friends there to crown the flowing
> bowl,
> He drinks the health of the Wine-God and arranges for his
> herdsmen
> A darts match, setting the target upon an elm tree,
> And the labourers bare their sinewy bodies for country
> wrestling.
>
> Virgil: *Georgics* 2, 529–36

However this was not simply a description of the contented farmer and his happy rural life but a metaphor for the state of Rome. Virgil makes it clear that whilst others might "dare the season their oar, or dash on the sword or insinuate themselves in royal courts" all such activities result in pain and suffering, the farmer who furrows the land with his curving plough is not only content but keeps his native country. For Virgil, the poet and patriotic countryman, happy the man who is:

> ... friends with the country gods –
> Pan and old Silvanus and the sisterhood of nymphs:
> The fasces has no power to disturb him, nor the purple
> Of monarchs, nor civil war that sets brother at brother's
> throat,
> Nor yet the scheming Dacian as he marches down from the
> Danube
> Nor the Roman Empire itself and kingdoms falling to ruin.[15]
>
> Virgil: *Georgics* 2, 494–502

Here in essence is Virgil's personal creed borne of bitter personal experience and education as an Epicurean who has a supreme indifference towards a life of politics, of power, even of Rome itself. What does it matter if the barbarian hordes are massing, even the rule of Rome must one day pass away. What truly matters is the landscape itself; this is what makes the country and gives it strength and character. And for the citizen, it is not the pleasures of court, travel or the thrill of war, but the simple rural life, upright and robust, enjoyed with ones family and friends, lived in essential harmony with nature and the passing seasons. Virgil's idealising the countryside and country values in this way was very important to the later development of the pastoral.

One further aspect of Virgil's writing that was to have a profound influence came from the poet's capacity to describe the landscape. In the *Eclogues* there are few of what Wilkinson termed, "pictorial glimpses",[16] only perhaps in the first *Eclogue* where there is a description of the farm restored to Tityrus:

> Ah fortunate old man, here among hallowed springs
> And familiar streams you'll enjoy the longed-for shade, the
>   cool shade
> here, as of old, where your neighbour's land marches with
>   yours,
> The sally hedge, with bees of Hybla sipping its blossom,
> Shall often hum you gently to sleep.
>
> Virgil: Eclogues 1, 51–4

As a young poet Virgil did not seem interested in conjuring up word pictures, or even in using those he found in Theocritus, but there was a poet, known to him, who did, Lucretius. His only known work is *De rerum natura* (trans. *On the Nature of Things*) which is about the beliefs of Epicureanism. Though his aim was to reinforce his scientific doctrine, Lucretius, "ranged freely over all nature choosing his illustrations from a great variety of observed phenomena".[17] It is Wilkinson's contention that Virgil, through reading Lucretius, discovered how an accumulation of detailed observations, however commonplace in themselves, could create a great panoramic picture, and the framework for this could be a didactic treatise. So by the time an older Virgil wrote the Georgics there were many examples of pictorial glimpses:

> But when the west wind calls and the exquisite warm season
> Ushers them out, both sheep and goats, to glade and pasture,
> At the first wink of the Morning Star let us wend away
> To the frore fields, while the morning is young, the meadow
>   pearly,
> And dew so dear to cattle lies on the tender grass
> Then, when the fourth hour of the sun has created a thirst
> And the plantations vibrate with the pizzicato of crickets,
> I'll bring the flocks to water by wells and by deep ponds,
> I'll bid them drink the water that runs through the troughs of ilex
> But now it's the noonday heat, make for a shady combe
> Where some great ancient-hearted oak throws out its huge
> Boughs, or the wood is black with
> A wealth of holm-oak and broods in its own haunted shadow.
> Then give them runnels of water again and let them browse

About sundown, when the cool star of evening assuages
The air, and moonlight falls now with dew to freshen the glades,
And the kingfisher's heard on the shore and the warbler in
   woody thickets.

Virgil: *Georgics* 3, 321–38

This sophisticated nature poetry makes the Georgics the first poem in all literature wherein a description may be said to be the chief *raison d'être* and source of pleasure. This innovation would resonate down the ages, influencing European culture in literature, painting and the design of landscape.

Arcadia and the Pastoral

So to answer the questions which opened this chapter, Arcadia refers to a vision of pastoralism and harmony with nature. And though Arcadia is an actual region, it was appropriated by Virgil in the Eclogues as the perfect location for a poetic paradise, a literary construct of a past Golden Age. Its dream-like presence is in sharp contrast to the kind of recognisable realism within which the Georgics are to be read, prompting one commentator to called the work a description of a "humdrum Arcadia".

The term 'Pastoral' has been used to describe a poem describing the life and manners of shepherds, their flocks and herds; whereas 'pastoral' is any poem or picture describing a simple country life. A rural 'Idyll' meaning a little picture or a little poem would seem to be about more than pastoral but all three terms, Eclogue, Pastoral and Idyll have generally been used synonymously. Added to these is the term 'Bucolics' which Virgil used to call his imitations of Theocritus. 'Georgic' meaning literally 'earth-work' or field-work applies to work in the fields, of husbandary or more broadly, rural occupations. It therefore accords with pastoral; both have the same background and a shepherd's life may be depicted in both and together there is a delight in country life. There is however one important distinction. The shepherd of Virgil's Eclogues is abstracted from the reality of country-life and the idea of toil is not suggested:

The soil will need no harrowing, the vine no pruning knife
And the tough ploughman may at last unyoke the oxen

The shepherd, free of responsibility, ownership and the cares of family life, can pass his time joyously in comparative ease, like Tityrus reclining under the shade of a spreading beech, meditating on the woodland muse, Pan, and playing his slender reed. The Georgics are the very opposite and are a guide to the practicalities of daily farm life, written in the guise of a didatic poem. Taken as whole the Georgics are not truly a pastoral, but they have become a generic name for writing that primarily details rural work. Together 'the Pastorals' reveal the process by which a natural enjoyment of working in harmony with the seasons can become an idealisation of stability which in turn implies criticism of turbulent city affairs. However, the *Eclogues* are not purely nostalgic, as some critics suggest for the fourth *Eclogue* is set in a future where the Golden Age has been restored. This *Eclogue* is important in underpining utopian Arcadias that predict an idealised future, wherein rural values, lost to the earth by urbanisation, industrialisation or technological innovation are restored. All of these visions would play their part in the development of the European landscape tradition.

Notes and References

1. Schama, S., *Landscape and Memory*. Harper Collins, London, 1995, p. 526.
2. *Ibid.*
3. Evelyn-White, H. G., *Hesiod: The Homeric Hymns and Homerica*. Loeb Classical Library: Revised edition 1914. Harvard University Press, Cambridge, Massachusetts.
4. Theocritus was under the patronage of a Greek general who colonised Egypt in the third century. Gifford, T., *Pastoral*. Routledge, London, 1999, p. 15.
5. Sargent, T., trans. *Theocritus*. W. W. Norton, New York, 1986. The word 'idyll' derives from the greek *eidyllion* meaning a small picture, and characterises a short poem of idealised description. "It is used in a general way, rather than of a specific poetic form. So for example not having to harvest fruit or even reach up to pick a plum from the tree would, indeed be idyllic." Gifford, T., *Pastoral*. Routledge London, 1999, p. 16.
6. Gifford, T., *op. cit.,* p.17.
7. Day Lewis, C., (trans.) *Virgil: The Eclogues, The Georgics*. Oxford University Press, London, 1983. This is the source of all quotations from the *Eclogues* and the *Georgics* in this chapter.
8. Knight, W., *Roman Vergil*. Faber and Faber, London, 1944, p. 24.
9. Griffin, J., *Virgil*. Oxford University Press, Oxford, 1986, p. 9.
10. *Ibid.*, p. 10.
11. Lyne, R. O. A. M., 'Introduction' in Day Lewis, C., *op. cit.*, p. xix.
12. Panofsky, E., *Meaning in the Visual Arts*. Anchor Books, New York, 1955, p. 343.
13. *Georgics* 2: 237. Remus and Romulus were regarded as the founders of Rome.
14. Griffin, J., *op. cit.*, p. 37. Tandy, D. W. and Neale, W. C., *Work and Days*. University of California Press, Berkeley, 1997.
15. 'Silvanus': an Italian rural deity; 'scheming Dacian': the Dacians, invading across the Danube from modern Romania caused much trouble to Rome during the 30s BC.
16. Wilkinson, L. P., *The Georgics of Virgil*. Cambridge University Press, Cambridge, 1969, p. 7.
17. *Ibid.*, pp. 9–10.

CHAPTER TWO

Virgil: the house, garden and landscape

Virgil was an instant success and his place in history was secured during his own lifetime. His poetry was the subject of school textbooks and quotations and even appeared as graffiti on house walls in Pompeii, hardly surprising as he was the local poet, from nearby Naples. Virgil's popularity was due in large measure to the fact that he was writing about the familiar and his understanding of countryside and the simple rustic life, gave his sophisticated Roman readers something entirely new to contemplate. But Virgil's poetry did not just remain on the printed page. From the very beginning the notion of Arcadia and the pastoral was a major influence on how people saw themselves in relation to nature, and on how that relationship was expressed in their homes, estates and gardens. His readers would have had considerable first hand experience of gardens, paintings of gardens and cultivated areas. In Pompeii, as in other Roman towns, house walls were decorated with pastoral scenes. Vitruvius records in *De Architectura*, that public rooms in houses and villas were decorated with paintings of "rivers, springs, straits, temples, groves, hills, cattle and shepherds and other country features, designed to imitate landscape".[1] Elsewhere more satyric landscapes featured caves, mountains, woods and cloven footed Pan.

Landscape and the Romans

FIGURE 2. The Villa Urbana – Settefinestre, Tuscany.

Though Virgil's influence can be seen in the decoration of the peristyle houses of Pompeii, it was country villas of the more wealthy aristocrats that added something new to an understanding of what the pastoral represents. The Romans lacked a fully fledged notion of landscape, countryside or nature. For them the world was comprehended as the City, the surrounding 'Other'[2] whose outer boundary was obscure, and 'Beyond', the wilder regions. The author Tacitus made the distinction between the wild and tame countryside; the wood and empty spaces, *solitudines*, which the Romans did not care much for, set against the scenes of agricultural activity. Where town gave way to countryside in close proximity to the city, wealthy citizens built their country houses, the *villa urbana* (Figure 2) a defining feature of the ruling class in the late Republican and Imperial periods.[3] As Frazer observed in *The Roman Villa and the Pastoral Ideal*, the *villa urbana* was "a setting for country life artistically considered, that is, in part the subject of pastoral poetry".[4] There the wealthy could indulge in the new found pleasure of *villeggiatura*, sojourning in the countryside, as an escape from the city with its stresses, political intrigue and the clamour of war. The appeal of rural retirement, *villeggiatura*, lay in the fact that the pastoral landscape was between city and wilderness; as Leo Marx said of Virgil's first *Eclogue*, "nothing makes the mediating character of the pastoral ideal so clear as the spatial symbolism in which it is expressed. The good place is a lovely green hollow. To arrive at this haven it is necessary to move away from Rome in the direction of nature. But the centrifugal motions stops short of unimproved, raw nature".[5] Country life – *re rustica* – became the distinguishing, if not the only cry, of the Roman gentleman.

At the *villa urbana* the owner could live the life of the 'happy husbandman', in the poetic imagination at least. With the *Georgics* in mind, the villa owner, or his guests, could overlook from the pleasure buildings or one of the many benches in the garden or parkland, the productive area and imagine the slaves to be bucolic natives wrapped-up in their own lives, blissfully unaware of their master's proximity.[6] In their minds eye the countryside was populated by rustics engaged in pruning the vines, shearing sheep, ploughing the soil, looking after bees and enjoying the harvest festival – the *dramatis personnae* of pastoral and bucolic poetry. But for the pastoral to be appropriated in this way, it had first to undergo a fundamental shift in meaning. Coming from the city, the villa owner found himself surrounded by the mystique of agrarian life and he needed to make sense of the mysteries of rural life. The countryside was not the untrammelled nature described by Theocritus or Virgil: "earthy by nature yet capable of nymph-inspired song". The Roman countryside was very different, as Ruskin observed, it was characterised by the "evident subservience of the whole landscape to human comfort, to the foot, the taste, or the smell".[7] The conversion of nature into the pastoral landscape involved the necessity of human toil but the servile labourers whose work and presence was necessary, were antithetical to the poetic discourse on the freedom and spontaneity of country life. So "the human staffage of the pastoral landscape" had to be banished and those servile workers regarded as essential, became an anonymous part of the countryside. Only then could the country landowner use the intellectual and poetic framework of the Pastorals to justify his own position in the countryside. It was argued, that just as Theocritus was a poetically-inclined city man wayfaring in the guise of Symichidas (*Idyll* 7), then so to was the owner of a Roman villa. And the widely-read *Georgics* could both be a metaphor for *villeggiatura*, living the simple life, and an undemanding way of seeing the countryside.

The Pastoral offered an acceptance of the human condition as part of nature, and allowed the garden, or what should more accurately be described as a landscape, to be created wherein man was in harmony with the natural world, and ultimately, attuned to the rhythms of life and death. The *Georgics* in particular were attuned to such natural processes, and the annual cycle that led to harvest, with its sense of natural and human completion. By this simple act of association the entire world of the Pastoral became available to the Roman elite, as part of their wider expropriation of Hellenistic culture.

The location and layout of the *villa urbana*

The location of the *villa urbana* (the country villa) was of critical importance. In siting the buildings of the villa, elevation, and the importance of the vantage point, was of paramount importance. Through capturing the view, the whole of the wider landscape was made subservient to the villa and could be thought of as serving the purpose of its owner. Likewise the villa owner and his architect were very concerned about the view others had of their villa and the vantage points from which it could be seen. Nothing could be further removed from the inward looking concept of the old Italian domus – as seen in the older houses at Pompeii. The grand scenery of the Sabine and Umbrian Hills was a particular attraction, and in his letters Pliny shows how conscious a Roman villa owner was of the surrounding landscape:

> The character of the country is exceedingly beautiful. Picture to yourself an immense amphitheatre, such as nature only could create. Before you lies a broad, extended plain bounded by a range of mountains, whose summits are covered with tall and ancient woods, which are stocked with all kinds of game. The descending slopes of the mountains are planted with underwood, among which are a number of little hills rising with a rich soil, on which hardly a stone is to be found. In fruitfulness they are equal to a valley, and though their harvest is rather later, their crops are just as good. At the foot of these, on the mountainside, the eye, wherever it turns, runs along unbroken stretch of vineyards terminated by a belt of shrubs. Next, you have meadows and the open plain. The arable land is so stiff that it is necessary to go over it nine times with the biggest oxen and the strongest ploughs. The meadows are bright with flowers, and produce trefoil and other kinds of herbage as and tender as if it were just sprung up, for all the soil is refreshed by never-failing streams. But though there is plenty of water, there are no marshes; for the ground being on a slope, whatever water it receives without absorbing runs off into the Tiber. This river, which winds through the middle of the meadows, is navigable only in the winter and spring at which seasons it transports the produce of the lands to Rome: but in summer it sinks below its banks, leaving the name of a great river to an almost empty channel: towards the autumn, however, it begins again to renew its claim to that title. You would be charmed by taking a view of this country from the top of one of our neighbouring mountains, and would fancy that not a real, but some imaginary landscape, painted by the most exquisite pencil, lay before you, such an harmonious variety of beautiful objects meets the eye, whichever way it turns. My house, although at the foot of the hill, commands as good a view as if stood on its brow, yet as you approach by so gentle and gradual a rise that you find yourself on high ground without perceiving you have been making an ascent.
>
> Pliny the Younger: Letter To Domitius Apollinaris[8]

From the villa, the garden and the grounds, the Romans liked to frame the view by natural features, such as the view up a narrow valley or best of all, out of a cave. Where there was not a natural cave, an elaborate nymphaeum would often be cut into the rock or otherwise constructed. But since the villa, its garden, grounds, surrounding countryside and even the sea were regarded not as discrete units but as an aesthetically integral entity, divisions between all these features were blurred. Open air colonnades adorned with shrubs served as a transition from house to terraced gardens, which contained shrines, grottoes and arbours, and beyond to the artificially created meadows and framed views of farm landscape. Pliny provides a graphic account of such an arrangement in his description of his villa at Tusculum:

> The greater part of the house has a southern aspect, and seems to invite the afternoon sun in summer (but rather earlier in the winter) into a broad and proportionately long portico, consisting off several rooms, particularly a court of antique fashion. In front of the portico is a sort of terrace, edged with box and shrubs cut into different shapes. You descend, from the terrace, by an easy slope adorned with the figures of animals in box, facing each other, to a lawn over spread with the soft, I almost said liquid, Acanthus: this is surrounded by a walk enclosed with evergreens, shaped into a variety of forms. Beyond it is the gestatio laid out in the form of a circus running round the multiform box-hedge and the dwarf trees, which are cut quite close. The whole is fenced in with a wall completely covered by box cut into steps all the way up to the top. On the outside of the wall lies a meadow that owes as many beauties to nature as all I have been describing within does to art; at the end of which are open plain and numerous other meadows and copses.
>
> Pliny the Younger: Letter To Domitius Apollinaris[9]

A recurring theme in pastoral poetry is the taking of a simple meal out-of-doors and *al fresco* dining was a frequent practice in Roman *villeggiatura*. The lines of Theocritus' *Idyll* 7 provides the starting point in understanding the Roman approach to *al fresco* dining both in the setting and its provision. The *Idyll* speaks a meal taken reclining on "a soft bed of scented rushes and new-stripped vine leaves" and the presence of "a nymphs cave from which splashed sacred water". In the *villa urbana* diners would take their meals in front of the grotto or cave, overgrown or overlain with an accretion of pebbles, shells and pumice stone. As to the actual arrangement of the diners, the simple semicircle seems have become a fixed concrete form by the first century AD on which was laid a mattress, called a *stibadium* – a term derived from the Greek verb meaning to strew – that is to strew rushes for a rustic couch of the sort encountered in Theocritus. At Hadrian's villa near Tivoli, Rome, the semicircular *stibadium* is set within an elaborate, vaulted grotto once sheathed in marble and mosaic (Plate 4). At Laurentium Pliny describes a more simple arrangement:

> At the upper end is an alcove of white marble, shaded by vines and supported by four small Carystian columns. From this semicircular couch, the water, gushing up through several little pipes, as though pressed out by the weight of the persons who recline themselves upon it, falls into a a stone cistern underneath, from whence it is received into a fine polished marble basin, so skillfully contrived that it is always

PLATE 4. The Canopus, at Hadrian's villa near Rome.

full without ever overflowing. When I sup here, this basin serves as a table, the larger of dishes being placed around the margins, while the smaller ones swim about in the form of vessels and water fowl. Opposite this is a fountain which is incessantly emptying and filling, for the water which it throws up to a great height, falling back again into it, is by means of consecutive apertures returned as fast as it is received.

Pliny the Younger: Letter To Domitius Apollinaris[10]

The enjoyment of *villeggiatura*, and the accompanying *otium* – what today would be understood as working from home – afforded the more affluent Romans the opportunity to enjoy a golden age:

I enjoy here a cosier, more profound and undisturbed retirement than anywhere else, as I am at a greater distance from the business of the town and the interruption of troublesome clients. All is calm and composed; which circumstances contribute no less than its clean air and unclouded sky to that health of body and mind I particularly enjoy in this palace, both of which I keep in full swing by study and hunting. And indeed there is no place agrees better with my family, at least I am sure I have yet not lost (may the expression be allowed) of all those I brought here with me. And may the gods continue that happiness to me, and that honour to my villa.

Pliny the Younger: Letter To Domitius Apollinaris[11]

As memories of ancient Rome faded with the rise of Christianity, at the beginning of the fourth century AD, the *villa urbana* and joys of rural life were forgotten. It would be many centuries before the writings of Pliny and other classical authors were rediscovered, inspiring a resurgence of interest in the pastoral landscape.

Notes and References

1. Vitruvius, *On Architecture* 5.6.9. quoted in McKenzie, J., *The Architecture of Alexandria and Egypt c.300 BC to AD 700.* Yale University Press, Princeton, 2007, p. 393. Of the trees and shrubs mentioned by Virgil only five species have not been identified in physical remains or paintings, these are *Abies* (fir), *Alnus* (Alder), *Ornus* (Rowan), *Salictus/Salix* (willow) and *Taxus* (Yew). There is evidence in wall paintings of *Arbutus* (strawberry tree), *Corylus* (hazel) as a tree and nut, *Laurus* (laurel), *Malus* (apple) as fruit in a basket and on a tree, *Pinus* (pine), *Pyrus* (pear in fruit and tree), plum (in fruit and tree), *Quercus* (oak as branches, leaves and acorns), and walnuts. The shrubs myrtle, ivy and the geulder rose are also found in paintings and there is evidence of chestnuts in gardens. (Jones, F., *Virgil's Garden.* Bristol Classical Press, London, 2011, p. 29).
2. Jones, F., *op. cit.*, p. 135.
3. Late Republican up to 30 BC Imperial period 27 BC–AD 565.
4. Frazer, A. (ed.), *The Villa Urbana.* University of Pennsylvania Museum, Philadelphia, 1998.
5. Marx, L., *The Machine in the Garden.* Oxford University Press, Oxford, 1964, p. 20.
6. Jones, F., *op. cit.*, p. 144.
7. Quoted in Calhoun, B., *The Pastoral Vision of William Morris.* University of Georgia, Athens, 1975, p. 79.
8. Pliny the Younger, *Letter To Domitius Apollinaris.* Harvard Classics, 1904–14, p. 14. www.bartleby.com/9/4/1052.
9. *Ibid.*
10. *Ibid.*
11. *Ibid.*

CHAPTER THREE

The Christian World and Arcadia

The creation myth of the Israelite tribes which came to dominate European thought was very different from the Arcadian vision of landscape and nature created by Theocritus and Virgil. As one of several nomadic tribes roaming the harsh deserts of Mesopotamia, they did not find their God in such barren places. They did not worship nature nor did they need to placate the spirits of natural places, for their God was outside of nature and omnipresent, which was appropriate for the deity of a nomadic peoples. In place of Arcadia the Judaic creation myth described how God created a garden cooled by the sparkling waters of a river, in which He planted every tree that was pleasant to look at and good to eat. An oasis garden, the contrast between the fertility of the Garden of Eden and the barrenness of the desert serving as a metaphor for the distance between God and humanity. And after the FALL, when Adam and Eve succumbed to temptation, Man was sent forth to subdue the earth and the whole of creation, finding God wherever the Jews roamed.

When the whole of Europe first came under the influence of Christianity, following the conversion of Constantine sometime after AD 305 no reference was made to the FALL. But when a power struggle, during the fourth century AD, resulted in the teachings of Augustine being adopted, the way nature was seen in western theology was irrevocably changed. Augustine argued that Adam's sin had brought about moral corruption, not only in man but throughout the whole of nature. Where once there had been only things that were good to eat and see, nature now brought forth thorns and thistles. From the time of St Augustine until the renaissance, the medieval world would share the belief of St Paul, that the whole of creation groaned in travail. By the FALL, the earth had become a heap of ruins and living things were poisoned by their nature. For six centuries nature was regarded as evil and man's vices were an expression of his base, animal instincts. In church art these vices were frequently represented symbolically in animal form and following a decree by Pope Gregory, it was understood that the sole purpose of the decorative arts was to remind people of the biblical message, and the evil warnings of nature. The Satyric landscape was used to warn people of the frailty of human nature and the dangers that lurked within nature, both real and imaginary. Beasts were the army of Satan and it has been suggested that the image of Pan was transformed into that of the devil. Whilst the hedonistic landscape with all its sensory and sensual pleasure was equally banished. Medieval theologians, like Bernard of Clairvaux condemned everything that was beautiful to the eye, soft to the ear, agreeable to the smell, sweet to the taste and pleasant to touch. As a consequence, Cistercian monks sort out the most inhospitable places to found their settlements and for nearly a millennium Christianity regarded nature as a hostile force with which to do battle, man against nature. The harshness of this teaching contrasts with that of ancient Rome where Saturn was the god of Agriculture and whose reign was depicted as a Golden Age of abundance and peace. In The *Georgics* Virgil tells how the Father of agriculture gave humans 'a hard calling' so man's ingenuity and hard work might restore the Golden Age to the earth:

> He first decreed it an art
> To work the fields, sent worries to sharpen our mortal wits
> And would not allow his realm to grow listless from lethargy.
> Before Jove's time no settlers brought the land under subjection;
> Not lawful even to divide the plain with landmarks and boundaries:
> All produce went to a common pool, and earth unprompted
> Was free will all her fruits.
> Jove put the wicked poison in the black serpents tooth,
> Jove told the wolf to ravin, the sea to be restive always,
> He shook from the leaves their honey, he had all fire removed,
> And stopped the wine that ran in rivers everywhere,
> So thought and experiment might forge man's various crafts
> Little by little, asking the furrow to yield the corn-blade,
> Striking the hidden fire that lies in veins of flint.
>
> Virgil: *Georgics* I, 121–35[1]

Virgil and Christianity

That a love of nature was kept alive throughout the Middle Ages was due in part to the tradition of pre-Christian art from northern Europe and to the writings of Virgil. As noted in the previous chapter, Virgil's poetry became a standard text in schools and this continued after the decline of the Roman Empire (Plate 5). Augustine told how Virgil was instilled in the young, so they could not forget its language, full as it was of Roman gods: "Little boys are made to read him, to insure that this great and most famous and best poet of all, drunk into impressionable minds, can never be drained into forgetfulness".[2] Augustine remained deeply influenced by Virgil, his own writing style was heavily indebted to the *Aeneid*, the third of Virgil's great works. Even so he found he could not admire his poetry because of its pagan subjects and he deplored the effect of Virgil who clothed the pagan gods in such haunting images and beguiling language. In the Confessions written after his conversion, Augustine was forced to reject the poet because of his new Christian beliefs.

Virgil's undoubted popularity ensured his poetry was read throughout medieval Europe, even though the survival of latin literature, as Butterfield expressed it, was "a process fraught with difficulty, ever at the mercy of transient cultural tastes and unpredictable vicissitudes of fate".[3] Butterfield was writing specifically about the classical manuscripts held at the monasteries St Gall and Reichenau where the promulgation of ancient literature was a core feature of monastic life. Though the monks devoted their primary attention to religious scripture, many pagan authors of the classical period enjoyed considerable influence in monastic education, and at the forefront of their teaching and activity was the work of Virgil.

The reason why Virgil of all pagan (*i.e.* non-Christian) writers should continue to be read by devout Christians was due, in large measure, to a most fortuitous literary coincidence. In the fourth *Eclogue*, (often termed the *Messianic Eclogue*) Virgil appears to predict the birth of a child saviour:

> Ours is the crowning era foretold in prophecy:
> Born of a Time, a great new cycle of centuries
> Begins. Justice returns to earth, the Golden Age
> Returns, and its first-born comes down from
> heaven above.

Virgil: Eclogues 4, 4–7

The idea of a baby heralding a Golden Age was recurrent theme in middle eastern religions and Virgil's prophecy had much in common with Isaiah, the Old Testament prophet. However there is no evidence to suggest Virgil had access to Hebrew literature, even though he would have known Jews in Naples. The Hebrew bible was little known in Italy at the time and it is more likely Virgil was influenced by the eastern Greek religion of Zoroastrian. This played a formative part in both Judaism and Stoicism to which, as we have seen, Virgil owed a certain debt. His strong sensitivity to the past and present undoubtedly led Virgil to choose the image of a baby as the herald of a new Golden Age, in much the same way as the early Christians contemplated the Babe in Bethlehem. Much debate continues around whose child this would be, but it is most likely Virgil was referring to his patron Octavius who had recently married. There would, said Virgil, be a return to primeval simplicity as the child grew to manhood, wars and their causes would die away and be replaced by peace and unlimited leisure in which Gods and men would freely associate. This could be a metaphor both for an age in which Octavius, as the Emperor Augustus, would bring peace to a country ravaged by civil war and, the birth of a son and heir. In the event there was no baby but Virgil's prediction led to his adoption as a proto-Christian. It is said that St Paul wept over his grave and lamented the fact that he had died before the Light came into the world.[4] The veneration of Virgil led an unknown hymn writer to include lines describing St Paul stopping at Virgil's tomb in Naples (Plate 6) on his way to Rome, in a Mass celebrating the feast of the conversion of St Paul:

> The Apostle led to Virgil's tomb,
> grieving at his untimely doom,
>   let fall a reverent tear;
> had I but met thee face to face,
> blest wouldst thou be in Paradise.
> poet without a peer.[5]

PLATE 5. *Georgics* Book
3 Shepherd with Flocks.
English or German
c. fifth century.

From the third century AD the pastoral began to be interwoven with Christian teaching. The Emperor Constantine made strong use of the fourth *Eclogue* in a decree establishing Christianity as the religion of Rome. For this reason it has been suggested that Virgil bridged the ancient and modern worlds in a way that made possible what finally emerged as Christian orthodoxy. The four Gospels were no more than historical narratives that provided little to feed the imagination whereas the *Eclogues* helped foster the pastoral vision of Christ the shepherd tending his flock of disciples. And in a world totally dominated by the harsh doctrine of St Augustine with its rejection of nature, it was Virgil's Arcadian vision that kept alive an alternative view of life lived in harmony with nature, a prerequisite to the enjoyment of the natural world.

Petrarch – the prophet of the new age

With medieval society in Christian Europe dominated by St Augustine any change in attitude towards nature had first to be preceded by a shift in the theological perspective. By the twelfth century there were growing signs in the

PLATE 6. Reputed site of Virgil's tomb, Naples.

old Roman world of an increasing mistrust of medieval scholasticism and other worldliness. The person who did much to bring about a new attitude, and with it a rediscovery of nature, was the scholar and poet Petrarch (1304–1374). Though Petrarch loved Italy, it was said that he never had any fatherland other than the dreamland of antiquity. The son of a Florentine banker, Petrarch was born in exile and, like Virgil, spent much of his life away from his home. In 1312 the family moved to Avignon, France, then the papal residence, where Petrarch pursued legal studies but he preferred the classical poets to the study of law. When his father discovered some hidden books, he began to burn them and it was only Petrarch's pleading that saved a copy of Virgil from the fire. After the death of his father in 1330 Petrarch took ecclesiastical orders to help the depleted family income.

Petrarch made his home at Vacluse, a valley close to Avignon, a place that had attracted him as a child and it remained, "the dearest spot on earth", throughout his life. There he led a life of solitude and simplicity but, unlike the Cistertian monks who renounced life on earth and the pleasures of nature, Petrarch lived in a rather more modern way. He himself said he felt as though he stood between antiquity and posterity. In a letter to a friend he expressed his enjoyment of the countryside; "would that you could know with what joy I wander free and alone among the mountains, forests, and streams." Petrarch was perhaps the first person in the modern world to restate the desire of Theocritus, to escape the turmoil of the city and escape into the tranquillity of the countryside.

Petrarch's admiration for Virgil could have inspired him to become the first person to a climb a mountain for pleasure. In the Eclogues, Virgil praises "Father Apennine, when through his glistening Holm oaks he murmurs low, and, lifting himself with snowy peak to the winds of heaven, rejoices".[6] Such rapture for mountains had not been known in the intervening centuries, medieval poets had spoken of forest fears and mountain panics. Petrarch recounts that on 26 April 1336, with his brother and two servants, he climbed to the top of Mount Ventoux (6273 ft/1912 m). At the summit he was dazed and stirred by the view of the Alps, the mountains around Lyon, the Rhone, the Bay of Marseilles.[7] But at the very moment of his triumph, in spite of his pleasure or most likely because of it, Petrarch was filled with guilt, he could not overcome his monastic education. Petrarch opened the tiny copy of St Augustine's *Confessions* he carried at all times, and later recounted what happened after after his eyes fell upon the passage:

> 'And men go about to wonder at the heights of the mountains, and the mighty waves of the sea, and the wide sweep of rivers, and the circuits of the ocean, and the revolution of the stars, but themselves they consider not.' I was abashed, and asking my brother (who was anxious to hear more) not to annoy me, I closed the book, angry with myself that I should still be admiring earthly things, who might long ago have learned from even pagan philosophers that nothing is wonderful but the soul, which, when great itself, finds nothing great outside. Then, in truth, I was satisfied that I had seen enough of the mountain; I turned my inward eye upon myself, and from that time not a syllable fell from my lips until we reached the bottom again.[8]

Petrarch was clearly troubled by the conflict between his sensual love of nature and his intellectual mistrust of the outside world. His response was to turn from the outer world of nature to the inner world of 'soul'. James Hillman argues that this rediscovery of the inner world is the real significance of the Ventoux event. The renaissance begins, he argues, not with the ascent of Mont Ventoux but the subsequent descent: "the return ... to the valley of the soul".[9]

Petrarch's garden

Though nature as a whole was still disturbing, the landscape vast and fearful, and "lays open the mind to many dangerous thoughts",[10] it was possible to enclose a garden. In the garden there was no such problems, for the garden was a man-made creation and there Petrarch's love of nature and the classics could be combined to the greater glory of God. Petrarch seems to have made gardens where ever he lived, taking his inspiration from the classical world of Pliny the Younger. Pliny referred to his villa near Rome, the *Laurentum*, with its close association between garden, landscape, sea and shore, as his Helicon "an endless source of inspiration".[11] Acknowledging his debt to Pliny, Petrarch described to his own more modest property at Vacluse, as his "transalpine Helicon". And though the gardens were laid-out in the style of the medieval garden, there was something more, for Petrarch's gardens were a place of learning and poetry, just as Plato's had been:

> Then with fresh shoots our Helicon shall glow;
> Then the fresh laurel spread its sacred bough;
> Then the highest intellect and docile mind

Shall renovate the studies of mankind-
The love of beauty and cause of truth
From ancient sources draw eternal youth.[12]

Petrarch: Sonnet from Africa

And, so closely did Petrarch associate gardening in his mind with Virgil and his classical studies, that once, when he was unable to follow the precepts of the Georgics in grafting vines, he feared they might die. His surprise was all the greater when the vines flourished.

Petrarch and Virgil

New humanists, like Petrarch, regarded worldly and classical beauty as reflections of the divine; and truth was embodied in a perfection of form that could only be grasped by a study of ancient writers. Petrarch associated himself completely with the ancient writers, identifying himself with Virgil. This identification implied something more than veneration, as can be deduced from his favourite copy of Virgil's poetry. Petrarch asked his friend, the painter Simone Martini, prepare a pastoral frontispiece for the book (Plate 7). Since Martini was known to paint from natural sources, this scene is perhaps the first time since antiquity that the real pursuits of country-life were represented in art as a source of happiness and poetry. In the painting Virgil is seated in the shade of a flowery orchard, adopting a pose of rural leisure that made writing possible.[13] In the lower half of the painting there is a shepherd and a vine tender, on the left, a military figure so completing the triple allusion to the Eclogues, Georgics and Aeneid. The figure with the outstretched arm is Servius, a grammarian and teacher of rhetoric in Rome at the end of AD 4. The two epigrams added to the painting, it is said by Petrarch himself, make clear the significance of the manuscript and the function of the interpreter:

> Italy, kind country, you feed famous poets. So this one (Virgil) allowed you to attain Grecian goals. Here is Servius, recovering the enigmas of high-spoken Virgil, so they are revealed in generals, shepherds and farmers.

Petrarch and Martini included Servius in the painting because they recognised what the grammarian had seen in the Eclogues, namely the relationship between the writer and political power. It was the Servian assumption that Virgil himself was present in the *Eclogues* in the figurative form of Tityrus, and the shade under which he reposes, represents the power of Augustus. Thus the Pastoral was not simply a pleasing tale of shepherds and country life but a commentary on the relationship between the poet and political power, whether that power was vested in the individual or the State. As Patterson observed, what Servius had seen in Virgil and Petrarch in Servius became part of the genetic structure of pastoral and could never be completely unwritten.[14] Therefore what the Martini frontispiece represents is Servius taking that tradition from Virgil and by implication, passing it on to Petrarch.

PLATE 7. Simone Martini
(1285–1344): Petrarch's
Virgil, title page *c.*1336.

Petrarch had seen that Virgil's *Eclogues* and *Georgics* were not simply about
the natural world, fact or fiction, but were metaphors for the social and political
worlds. As such, he saw parallels between Virgil's world and his own decadent
society, divided as it was between the authority of the papacy and the so-called
Holy Roman Empire. The church was hopelessly corrupted by secular power,
the city of Rome was left with no central authority and feuding between two
great dynasties, as well as the Hundred Years War between France and England,
had deferred any question of Italian unity. It is not difficult to see an analogy
between Virgil's objectives at the end of the civil war and Petrarch's own hopes of
a regenerate empire that was both Roman and holy, in which classical beauty and
meaning had been restored. In his first folio of Virgil's *Eclogues*, Petrarch wrote:

PLATE 8. Villa Careggi, Florence.

Poet: you are permitted to write the history of Rome and what ever you wish; for us it is not so. We are outcasts from our country, that is, the history of Rome which is our common patrimony, and the sweet fields, that is, our studies and our songs, in which, after the custom of farmers, poets are employed in labour and cultivation.[15]

Petrarch made the pastoral a metaphor for the condition of the intellectual, humanist scholar and poet in the middle of the fourteenth century. In so doing he established the relevance of Virgil and the *Eclogues* to the social, political and aesthetic thinking of the Italian Renaissance, ensuring they would have a considerable influence during the coming century and beyond, as the impact of the renaissance spread into northern Europe.

Florence and the Medicis

By the time Petrach died in 1374 the centre of civilisation was moving away from the abbey and church into large urban centres, like Florence and Milan, where a more middle class society emerged, comprising merchants, bankers and lawyers. Their concerns with the accumulation of wealth and civic affairs heralded a more worldly view of life and this increasingly secular society had a growing mistrust of medieval scholasticism and other-worldliness, and a renewed appreciation of the ancient civilisation. This new attitude was expressed in the *Humanisti Salutati* which warned in a letter around 1390:

> Do not believe that to avoid the sight of beautiful things, to shut oneself up in a cloister is the way to perfection. In striving and working at caring for your family and friends and your city, you cannot but follow the right way to God.

The humanist revolution, known as the Renaissance, took the form of a renewed belief in Man's ability to guide his own destiny and control the natural forces of his world. This meant expanding the boundaries of human knowledge, both scientific and aesthetic. At the beginning of the fourteenth century the question was how to achieve this as quickly as possible. It was widely believed that the Middle Ages, those centuries between the Roman Empire of AD 4 and their own, had been barbarous with little significant culture. The solution, as Petrarch had shown, was to return to classical sources. Libraries throughout Europe, including those at the monasteries of St Gall and Reichenau, were ransacked for any available literature, including treatise on medicine, farming, architecture, art, and any other conceivable subject.

Foremost in this search for knowledge were the Medici family of Florence, wealthy bankers who were among the most successful and influential of collectors. For three generations, they gathered around them the most outstanding cultural figures of the day, creating a culture to rival that of ancient Rome and Greece. The Medici dynasty was founded by Giovanni, chief executive of Florence under whose patronage the city sponsored architecture and sculpture but the genuine, enthusiastic patron was his son, Cosimo. He followed the example of Plato in establishing an Academy at the Villa Careggi (1462) (Plate 8) which was situated on a hillside overlooking the Tuscan countryside, just as Virgil's estate had overlooked the Mincius. Here the most successful writers, philosophers, doctors, architects, scientists, and many others, gathered to discuss emerging ideas.

The great aim of humanism was to recapture the spirit of the classical world with its ideals of beauty allied to knowledge and the perfection of the human personality – the complete man. Cosimo Medici instructed his librarian Marcilo Forcino to collect and translate ancient texts and through his translation of the Greek philosopher, Plato, he helped bring about an all important shift in medieval theology. Neo-platonist studies did much to free men's minds from the rigid Aristotelian philosophy of the past. No longer was man under any higher authority, now "everything God had expressed was expressed in Man". This helped to bring about a liberation from medieval strictures and the feeling that "God was sitting on the world with Man quietly padding around down below making sure he wasn't giving offence". With the lifting of the cloud of medieval religious oppression came a renewed interest in all spheres of human activity. The fear of nature receded and as Bronowski expressed it in *The Ascent of Man*, there was, "a rainbow in the sky, the world was beautiful and men could enjoy a transcending vision of beauty". For the first time since Virgil, Renaissance man was free to observe and enjoy nature. There was an understanding that God had designed nature for man's benefit and it was argued that to know God, you had first to find out how creation worked. The study of the natural world was seen as an extension of theology.

Lorenzo the Magnificent

The Platonic Academy at Careggi was expanded by Lorenzo the Magnificent (1449–1492), grandson of Cosimo. Lorenzo was scarcely 20 years old when he assumed full responsibility for the Medici empire on his father's death in 1469 but already he was a gifted statesman, a generous host and above all else, a devoted patron of the arts and sciences. Under his guidance life at Careggi was based around Virgil, characterised by a fusing of the Arcadian pastoral and the *Georgics*, both in the iconography devised by him and for him. He practised careful and diversified husbandry on the estate, after the manner of Virgil's *Georgics*, whilst much of the iconography surrounding Lorenzo was based on the fourth *Eclogue* and the ideal of the Golden Age. He was associated with this throughout his life and there is much evidence to support the suggestion that he actively encouraged this image and took its implications seriously. The earliest association of Lorenzo with the iconography of Virgil appeared in an illustrated manuscript of Virgil's work, published by the scribe Niccolo Ricci in 1460. At the opening of The *Eclogues*, the illustration by Apollonio di Giovanni is a beautifully observed and detailed study of Tityrus and Meliboeus in a landscape. But the interest focuses not on the principle subjects but the small figure standing between them dressed in aristocratic clothes with an elegant little dog at his feet (Plate 9). There is no explanation as to who he is, and no other illustration contains a figure who cannot be accounted for, even more intriguing is the absence of a name which elsewhere identifies each of the figures. The most plausible explanation is that this was an idealised representation of Lorenzo, then aged thirteen, whose presence in the pastoral world of Careggi was confirmed by his tutor Landino.

The second *Eclogue* yielded material for mystic cult of Pan Medicus, derived from Virgil "Pan looks after sheep and shepherds" (*Eclogue* 2, 23) and was associated with a sense of cosmic unity and harmony. It was used as a symbol of the numinous, or spiritual power, of the Medici's and Lorenzo, in his diplomacy, strove to create a climate of peace in which the arts and sciences could flourish. As a youth Lorenzo had jocularly been called Pan as a result of his love of hunting, music and pretty girls but the Cult of Pan that developed around Lorenzo was not because of these happy associations but from his desire to escape from the harsh political realities of daily life. In the first half of the 1480s Lorenzo and his circle became disillusioned with political intrigue – a hostile Pope, endless rivalry between Italian States and intermittent wars of attrition led to a desire to escape the city and return to the countryside. There they wished to pursue rural pleasures and write *Eclogues* based on Virgil and

Theocritus; and celebrate Pan, the God of flocks and shepherds who preferred to live in Arcadia rather than among the Olympians.

PLATE 9. Apollonio di Giovanni (1414–1465): *The Eclogues.*

The mystic cult of Pan was definitively attached to Lorenzo by the artist Luca Signorelli in his painting *The Realm of Pan* (Plate 10), painted in 1492, two years before Lorenzo's death. It showed a goat-legged figure who was clearly Pan, sitting at the centre of the composition, with his eyes fixed longingly on a young female, a nymph or goddess, who in turn gazes at a young reclining male. Both are making music on long reed pipes, whilst another male dances before Pan and plays on a pipe. An older man seeks to turn Pan's loving gaze in the direction of an aged man who leans on a stick and watches the scene sadly. In the background are two female figures, one seated hanging her head with eyes downcast. Signorelli derived the main elements of the painting from Ovid's *Metamorphoses* in which there is an account of how Pan fell in love with a chaste Arcadian nymph, Syrinx. He pursued her a long days journey from Mount Lycaeum to the river Ladon and there, in response to her own prayer, she was turned into a reed. Pan, unable to distinguish her from all the rest, cut several reeds at random and made the first musical instrument – the Pan pipes. All these elements are combined in the painting. The female holding the reed pipe is Syrinx in her dual role as nymph and reed. The male dancer playing the flute is Pan as the master of music, song, and inspired poetry – the arts that derive from unfulfilled love. The seated Pan is too forlorn to hear the flute and its hopeful message and the figure beside him indicating the aged man, is calling his attention to the passing of time. Something Pan, as a mortal, can appreciate. The message would seem to be that as life is so short, let Pan, or Lorenzo, cease to pine for his lost nymph. He should play his pipe, sing, and dance and through his love, rediscover the prophecy that is God-given inspiration.

Lorenzo's love of nature was not confined to either the garden or iconography but in a very modern desire it extended to a repeated and meaningful contact with the natural world, which he needed in order to function as a person. He personally supervised the cultivation of the farm and was particularly adept at grafting and pruning vines. This he did for 2 hours each day before settling down to read a religious text. Much of his life was spent in a search for solitary or shady places where he might recreate himself. At a time when his contemporaries were seeking a more aristocratic lifestyle, Lorenzo was expressing a contempt for the city. His own poems are full of the sites, sounds and smells of the countryside, all of which indicate an acute observation of nature:

> Let all who will, seek grandeur and fame:
> Piazzas, temples and magnificent buildings,
> Enjoyment, treasures always following
>   green meadow with beautiful flowers
> A flowing stream circling the growing grass,
> A little bird sadly singing of love,
> Will far better appease every desire;
> The shady woods, the rocks, and high mountains,
> The dark caverns and fugitive wild beasts
> Maybe a charming, fearful nymph.[16]

At no time do these poems descend into a self-indulgent academic pastoralism, for Lorenzo had a very modern desire for re-creation in the solitude of the countryside whether in reality or metaphysically, in order to return refreshed to the social world.

The revival of pastoral poetry created a cultural climate that was particularly receptive to the possibilities of secular meaning and effect in the natural scene. At the Medici Academy Lorenzo helped to bring about a change in the attitudes of painters and their patrons. Artists were encouraged not to rely solely on the representation of religious subjects but develop an art that represented secular or human values. But in Florence expression of a personal enjoyment of the countryside was confined to literature, as Kenneth Clark observed, landscape had no part in the pictorial tradition of Florence.[17] The extraordinary step of translating the rural atmosphere of bucolic pastoral verse into a visual form took place in Venice which had become a city of power and wealth, commanding trade and ideas, from both east and west.

PLATE 10. Luca Signorelli (1445–1523): *The Realm of Pan* c.1490.

Notes and References

1. Day Lewis, C. (trans.) *Virgil: The Eclogues, The Georgics*. Oxford University Press, London, 1983.
2. Wills, G., in *A Companion to Vergil's Aeneid and its Tradition*. Edited by J. Farrell and M. Putnam, Wiley-Blackwell, Chichester, 2010, p. 209.
3. Butterfield, D., *Classical Manuscripts at St Gall and Reichenau*. The Carolingian Libraries of St Gall and Reichenau. www.stgallplan.org
4. Valentine, T. W., The Medieval Church and Vergil. *Classical Weekly* 25 (1931), pp. 65–7.
5. Falconer, R. Sir, *St Paul at the Tomb of Virgil*, University of Toronto Quarterly. University of Toronto Press, Toronto 6(1), October 1936, p. 18.
6. Petrarch claimed he was inspired by Philip V of Macedon's ascent to Mount Haemo.
7. Plumb, J. H., *The Italian Renaissance*; Chapter XI by Morris Bishop 'Petrarch' American Heritage New York, 1961, pp. 161–75.
8. Petrarch, *Epistolae familiares* iv. i. (trans.) Robinson, J. H., *The First Modern Scholar and Man of Letters*. G. P. Putnam, New York, 1898.
9. Hillman, J., *Revisioning Psychology*. Harper Row, New York, 1992, p. 197.
10. Clark, K., *Landscape into Art*. John Murray, London, 1952, p. 7.
11. Millar. F. J., (trans.) *Ovid: Metamorphoses*. Loeb Classical Library, London, 2008. In antiquity the natural home of the nine Muses was at Mount Parnassus and nearby Mount Helicon. There the Muses, symbolising poetry and those other intellectual activities fostered by solitude and tranquility of nature, dwelt among "the ancient woods, the grottoes, and the grass, spangled with countless flowers".
12. Ellis, E., *Petrarch's Africa I–IV: a translation and commentary*. Baylor University, Waco, Texas, 2007.
13. Patterson, A., *Pastoral and Ideology*. University of California Press, Berkeley, 1987, p. 20.
14. *Ibid.*, p. 14.
15. *Ibid.*, p. 43.
16. Hook, J., *Lorenzo de Medici: a historical biography*. H. Hamilton, London, 1984, p. 141.
17. Clark, K., *Landscape into Art*. John Murray, London, 1952, p. 22.

CHAPTER FOUR

Venice and the Pastoral Landscape

The importance of Venetian painters to the pastoral tradition was in developing the idea of painting as a kind of poetry. All classical minded humanists subscribed to the dictum of the Roman poet Horace that *Ut Pictura Poesis* 'as poetry so is painting' and this opened the door to a new range of subjects with themes drawn from classical mythology. Once this idea became universal, the association between painting and "a 'pastoral' kind of poetry must have associated itself to many".[1] Venice was a city less intellectual than Florence and though it nurtured a new spontaneous approach to painting, no treatise on Art would be written. As Venturi observed, no Venetian artist was an intellectual and to regard them as deep thinkers or philosophers would be to misjudge them. Above all Venetian painters, like Bellini and his follower Giorgione, loved life, both in nature and the city, and in so doing they reflected a society that regarded sensation as the fountainhead of knowledge. Sensations, such as the light of the Veneto which Bellini described as, "the soft, palpable air of a summers evening, when the buildings and trees seem to give back the light they have absorbed during the day"[2] were more basic than form.

Giovanni Bellini

This can be seen in one of the first great landscape paintings, Giovanni Bellini's portrayal of *St Francis of Assisi in Ecstasy*, a natural choice to display man's new found accord with nature (Plate 11). St Francis was in the tradition of Adam and Eve before the FALL, a time when man and nature were in harmony and not a reminder of his bestial nature. Though the figure is shown with arms outstretched towards the sun rather than the landscape, it is evident that Bellini has totally embraced the landscape. The detail of every twig, stone, fern and ivy leaf has been carefully observed and rendered whilst the whole landscape glows in the warmth of a new day's sun. As with Theocritus, the landscape provides the setting which fills the space around the figure, directing attention to the virtues of St Francis and the landscape. Not since Virgil had the farmed landscape been so carefully observed; ploughing and seed sowing, sheep in the meadow, a coppiced tree are all depicted in careful detail. Bellini's concern with the rediscovery of nature was not for any scientific purpose but a desire to place his subject in as natural setting as possible with all its sensuous colour and light. In so doing Bellini established the notion of the religious pastoral;

the poetry of the classical pastoral is made subservient to general sense of calm and security provided by the Georgic landscape.

Whereas Bellini's painting was religious in content, his pupil Giorgione would secularise the new art. Today, when perception is not determined by religious dogma, it is possible to regard Bellini's religious subjects and Giorgione's pagan themes as no more than artistic preference. Both hang side by side in art galleries and visitors do not give a moments thought to the apparent incongruity. In doing so they overlook the most fundamental and far reaching change that had taken place in man's relationship to nature. The achievement of the Renaissance was to make it possible for man to come to terms with the natural world, within the context of existing medieval theology. This had been achieved by a return to classical antiquity, and in particular, by severing the new Golden Age from its religious and messianic associations and returning it to

PLATE 11. Giovanni Bellini (1430–1516): *St Francis in Ecstasy* c.1475–1480.

the pastoral utopia of Theocritus and Virgil. In this atmosphere the essentially pagan landscape tradition could flourish and before long it would absorb the Christian message, in the wonderfully ambiguous paintings of Titian.

Though this secular change had begun in Florence, it reached its zenith in Venice with the publication in 1480s of *Arcadia* by Jacopo Sannazaro. Written in Italian, and therefore accessible to a large audience, it brought the classical vision of Arcadia into contemporary life. In the poem Sannazaro repeated all the familiar themes of the *Eclogues* and described what this Arcadia looked like, as his shepherd Sincero approaches a mysterious temple where:

> ... above the doorway certain woods and hills of the most delightful beauty, full of leafy trees and a thousand sorts of flowers, among which were seen the many herds at pasture, winding with pleasure through the green fields, with peradventure ten dogs to guard them, ... Of the shepherds, some were milking, some shearing wool, others playing on pipe, and there were a few, who, as it seemed were singing and endeavouring to keep in tune with them. But that which pleased me to regard with most attention were certain naked nymphs, standing half hidden behind a chestnut boll, laughing at a ram who, in his eagerness to gnaw a wreath of Oak that hung before his eyes, forgot to feed upon the grass around him. At that moment came four satyrs, with horns upon their heads and goats feet, stealing through the shrubbery of lentisks, softly, softly to take the maidens by surprise.[3]

In the poem *Arcadia,* Sannazaro combined all four interpretations of the pastoral world; perpetual spring with that of sensual pleasure, the bucolic with the wild untamed Satyric landscape. But though Sannazaro often provided beautiful descriptions of the natural world, a pictorial representation of how the ancients, or rather how Sannazaro envisaged the realm of Pan, was lacking. The giving of form to the Arcadian landscape would be the great achievement of Giorgione, who was widely accepted by his Venetian patrons to be painting Sannazaro, rather than an obscure classical theme.

Giorgione and the *Fete Champetre*

Giorgione was born in 1477 at Castelfranco near Venice, and grew up in a countryside that was half cultivated and half covered by primitive vegetation. Although Giorgione left no written accounts, it is obvious his childhood landscape had a profound influence on him; the fields, groves, streams, hills, farmhouses and the blue distant hills of Castelfranco all feature in his paintings. Another important influence on Giorgione during his youth were the poets of the Arcadia movement centred on the court of Caterina Cornaro, the Queen of Cyprus, who resided at Asolo near Venice. These poets were inspired by Virgil, not only his evocation of scenery but also the myth of rural rusticity. In 1495 Aldus Manulus, one of Giorgione's patrons, produced a translation of Theocritus's *Idylls,* one of the first to be published during the renaissance. At the poetic centre of this movement was Cardinal Pietro Bembo (1470–1547) who composed *Gli Asolani*, a book devoted to the power of love, in which:

... with primeval beauty be renewed
The Golden Age, the old beatitude.

This sentiment was at the heart of the new romantic poetry. In 1499 the Dominican friar Francesco Colonna published his strange visionary poem *Hypnerotomachia Poliphili* (*The Dream of Poliphilus*) which transposed the pastoral into a medieval context. It describes how Poliphilus pursued the beautiful Polia before being united in the Temple of Venus on the island of Cythera. The work includes detailed accounts of gardens, particularly those on Cythera, and the Venetian spirit of nature is reflected in Colonna's description of the flowers found growing in cultivation and the field:

> It was wonderful to see the greens there of powdered with such variety of sundry sorted clouds and diverse fashioned flowers as Yellow Crowsfoot or golden knop, Oxeye, Satrian, Dogges Stone, the lesser Cenarie, Mellitat, Saxifrage, Cowslips, Ladies Fingers, wild Cherville or Shepherdes Needles, Novens Gentio, Sinquiifolie, Eyebright, Strawberries with flowers and fruites, wilde Columbine, Aqua Casrus, Millefoyle, Yarrow, where with Achilles did heal Telephus ... with the white Muscariolo, beeflowers, and Penetes in so beautiful and pleasant manner, that they did greatly comfort me (having lost myself) but even with looking on them.[4]

In 1498 Giorgione moved to Venice taking with him a compound of pastoral ideas and sentiments. It is hardly surprising that in his hands, arcadian art should have emerged and flourished. One painting in particular, the *Fete Champetre,* gave pictorial substance to the Arcadian landscape and "lingers as the subliminal model of the modern humanist's nostalgic attitude towards nature" (Plate 12).[5] In the painting Giorgione's great achievement was to take the everyday landscape of woods and fields and transform them into the sensual, pagan world of Theocritus, Virgil, and Sannazaro. The medieval fear of nature is replaced by the delight of senses; especially that of sound, the pleasant contrast of sun and shade, rustling leaves, water bubbling from the well mixing with the sound of the lute.

The extent to which Giorgione was taking his inspiration from contemporary poets and Sannazaro in particular, can be appreciated by comparing a present-day description of the *Fete Champetre* with the poet's Prologue to Arcadia:

> Assembled in the shade of a tree near a well, an unlikely quartet dominate the foreground: two young men bracketed by a pair of nude women, set apart from and yet very defiantly within a larger landscape that is the world of the picture. One of the youths, dressed quite fashionable is clearly an urban visitor; his tousled rustic companion just as evidently is a native of this bucolic region. Beyond their shaded retreat in the middle ground, a shepherd leads his flock of sheep, and a goat in sunlight past another grove. In the distance buildings interrupt the horizon, architectural signs of civilization – a man made world on the fringes of – and yet somehow containing – the natural landscape in which the gathering takes place.
> Three of the four figures in the group, those seated on the ground are joined in apparent concert, their common focus on the lingering notes just sounded. To the left, the standing nude turns her attention to the well, into which with grave languor she pours water from a crystal pitcher. As surely as their clothes distinguish

PLATE 12. Giorgione (1477/8–1510): *Fete Champetre c.*1510 (this painting has also been ascribed to Titian). The strong diagonals of the painting converge on the distant town and the contrast between town and country is further emphasised by the central axis between the two youths representing urbanity and rusticity. The architecture, above their heads, reflects this cultural divide; a more classical structure is juxtaposed onto a sagging wooden construction, a *villa urbana*. The tall spreading trees give way to trees cultivated, pruned and thinned by cunning hands. The instruments held by the central figures carry their own connotations. In the foreground a nymph is holding a reed wind instrument, perhaps "the lowly pipe of Corydon, whilst the town youth has just finished playing the more sophisticated lute – an instrument with which to accompany the purity of song and represent Man's highest cultural ambition of uniting the wind with the human voice". Giorgione was a fine lute player and sang beautifully, accomplishments that made him a favourite guest at gatherings of his patrons. On the right a shepherd emerges from the hillside making music. In the foreground are the young nymphs, of whose presence the two youths, engrossed in their music, are unaware – "the nymphs have lent their listening ears".

the two youths from one another, so the two women are distinguished from them by their nudity – as well as their gender. Nudity is their natural state, for they have not disrobed. Nudity signifies their higher status; they are divinities, nymphs of the *locus amoenus* that is the requisite site of such pastoral encounters. This indeed is the world of the pastoral tradition of antiquity, with its nymphs and shepherds, its music and poetry, its natural and unforced eroticism.

Rosand: *Places of Delight*[6]

If this is compared to Sannazaro's own account of Arcadia it is possible to appreciate the world fashioned by Giorgione:

More often than not the tall and spreading tree brought forth by nature on the shaggy mountains are wont to bring greater pleasure to those who view them than are the cultivated trees pruned and thinned by cunning hands in ornamental gardens. And the birds of the woodland singing upon the green branches in the solitary forests give much more pleasure to him who hears them than do those birds that have been taught to speak from within their lovely and decorated cages in crowded cities. For this reason it happens, as I judge, that woodland songs carved on the rugged barks of beeches no less delight the one who reads them than do learned verses written on the smooth pages of gilded books. And the wax-bound reeds of shepherds proffer amid the flower-laden valleys perhaps more pleasurable sound than do through proud chambers the polished and costly boxwood instruments of the musicians. And who has any doubt that a fountain that issues naturally from a living rock, surrounded by green growth, is more leasing to the human mind than all the others made by art of whitest marble, resplendent with gold? Certainly no one, to my thinking. Therefore relying on that, I shall among these deserted places recount to the listening trees, and to those few shepherds that will be there, the rude *eclogues* issued from a natural vein, setting them forth just as naked of ornament as I heard them sung by the shepherds of Arcady under the delightful shades, to the murmuring of crystal fountains. To whom not one time but a thousand the mountain Deities overcome by sweetness lent their listening ears, and the delicate nymphs, forgetful of pursuing the wandering beasts, abandoned quiver and bow at the feet of the towering pines of Maenalus and of Lycaeus. Wherefore I, if it were permitted me, would think it more glorious to set my mouth to the lowly pipe of Corydon, given him long ago as a precious gift from Damoetas, than to the sounding flute of Pallas, with which the unhappily proudful satyr provoked Apollo, to his own misfortune. For surely it is better thing to till a small field well, than to let the large piece wretchedly grow wild through ill government.[7]

Though there is no evidence to link the words of Sannazaro with the painting by Giorgione, it is sufficient to observe that the elements and mood are consistent in both. Together, Giorgione and Sannazaro helped created a timeless pastoral, a dream world, into which the tired, jaded viewer or reader could escape. Giorgione's lasting achievement was to portray all of the elements – earth, sky, clouds, trees, people and buildings – as one unity, a landscape. In so doing the *Fete Champetre*'s established the fundamental elements of pastoral painting which, in the course of the following centuries, would open up entirely new directions in European art.

Titian

In the years after Giorgione's early death[8] representation of the pastoral landscape went in two different but highly significant directions. The artist most associated with both developments was Titian (1488/90–1576), a younger contemporary of Giorgione. He brought about a marriage of pagan Arcadia and Christian belief. Whereas the inspiration for the pastoral in Renaissance art and literature had been classical poets, like Theocritus and Virgil, Christian teaching had its own non-pagan pastoral models, from David, the shepherd and musician, to Christ, the Lamb of God and Good Shepherd. In another poem by Sannazaro *On Virgin Birth,* the pastoral character of the Nativity is reinforced by the poet calling the blessed shepherds of the Nativity, Lycidas and Aegon, names taken straight from the *Eclogues* of Virgil. Sannazaro's pagan shepherds would seem to be referring to the fulfillment of the Virgil's prophecy in fourth *Eclogue,* foretelling the birth of Christ. In the painting *Noli me Tangere*, Titian portrays the epitome of the Christian Arcadian pastoral. In the painting Christ the Good Shepherd meets the Magdalene in a landscape every bit as real as that portrayed by Giorgione in the *Fete Champetre*, but it is rendered innocent and free from pagan forces by the presence of Christ.

It was Titian again who had an influential role in transposing this soft pastoral to a more realistic Georgic image.[9] Giorgione's pastoral landscape represented a world as it might have been, a Golden Age unsullied by work or suffering, even though its apparent naturalness was clearly the result of

PLATE 13. Niccolo Boldrini (1510–1566): *after Titian, Landscape with a Milkmaid and Shepherd Boy c.1525.*

human endeavour. In his simpler woodcuts, like *Landscape with a Milkmaid* (Plate 13), Titian created an image of hard unremitting toil, though ultimately rewarding, as befits the georgic life of the farmer. The basic structure of the landscape, with its distance between the foreground figures and the fortified towns on the horizon, evoke certain pastoral values but the figures have little time to escape from the cares of life. There is no idyllic nostalgia, no music or love, the couple must tend the flocks and cattle, feed the goats and milk the cows. This print was widely disseminated and established a repository of motifs that proved to be very influential on artists like Rubens and Gainsborough, whose own painting *Landscape with a Woodcutter Courting a Milkmaid* (see Plate 36) appears to pay homage to Titian. By the middle of the sixteenth century there was a growing urban taste for scenes of farming life and Jacopo Bossano and his studio would specialise in such paintings.

After the neighbouring states of Padua, Verona, and Vicenza were conquered, the Government encouraged the establishment of new estates on the Veneto to serve cultural and political ends. There newly enriched merchants, anxious to escape the pressures of city life, began to establish their country villas, rediscovering the joys of the ancient Roman practice of *villeggiatura*. And as the first printed editions of Virgil became available, pastoral scenery became the model around which the villa estates were planned. In the words of Horace: "happy is the man far from the cares of business, like the ancient generations of man, work his ancestral fields with his own free of all usury", without the discomfort of toil. And like Pliny and the Roman bourgeois, these country gentlemen began to request what, for the first time in the modern world, were called landscape paintings.[10]

Notes and References

1. Gombrich, E. H., *Norm and Form.* Phaidon, Oxford, 1971, p. 112.
2. Clark, K., *Landscape into Art.* John Murray, London, 1952, p. 22.
3. *Ibid.,* pp. 56–7.
4. Quoted in Thacker, C., *The History of Gardens.* University of California Press, Berkeley, 1985, p. 97.
5. Rosand, D., 'Giorgione, Venice and the Pastoral Vision', in *Places of Delight: the pastoral landscape,* R. C. Cafritz, L. Gowing and D. Rosand (eds). The Phillips Collection and Weidenfeld & Nicolson, London, 1988, pp. 30–9. Today experts at the Louvre in

Paris where the *Fete Champetre* hangs, believe the painting to be by a young Titian or at least, completed by him.

6. *Ibid.*

7. Sannazaro, J., (trans. R. Nash) *Arcadia and Piscatorial Eclogues.* Wayne State University Press, Detroit, 1966.

8. Giorgione died in October 1510 at the early age of 33, a victim of a plague raging in Venice.

9. Rosand, D., *op. cit.*, p. 67.

10. Gombrich, *op. cit*, p. 109.

CHAPTER FIVE

Rome and the Pastoral Landscape

So far attention has focused on the pastoral as a relationship to nature expressed through literature and art. Even though Francesco Colonna's pastoral poem *Hypnerotomachia Poliphili* gave a detailed account of gardens, it had little or no influence on their design. In Florence the gardens of the Medici were little more than an extension of Medieval and monastic gardens and the elaborate pleasure gardens, created by cardinals at places like the Villa d'Este and the Villa Lante, were inspired by humanist thought. That is to say, they sought to demonstrate man's mastery over nature. Substantially different was the villa park at Mondragone, developed by Cardinal Scipione for the Borghese clan between 1606–1633 in which the pastoral influenced conception, design, management and appreciation.

The Borghese and the Villa Borghese

The Borghese were part of a new aristocracy catapulted into prominence and wealth by the election of one their number as Pope. They were, as a contemporary Flemish lawyer Teodoro Ameyden described them, a *famiglia da papi*, families whose status was due to the Pope. The Borghese family had been merchants and bankers in Sienna until Marcantonio came to Rome in 1537. Professional advancement and a successful marriage saw the family become accepted among the lesser aristocracy. Then in 1605, when Marcantonio's son, Camillo was appointed Pope Paul V, at the comparatively young age of 52, there was an opportunity to move into the upper echelons of Roman society. Securing the family's position in this way depended on the appointment of a skillful and reliable member of the family – known as the 'cardinal nephew' – who would take on the public role of the papacy – receiving princes, ambassadors and other official visitors, discussing political matters and entertaining on a lavish scale, whilst the Pope observed a pious life. For the Borghese, Cardinal Scipione Caffarelli, son of the Pope's sister, set about this task with relish. He assumed all the high posts in the Vatican and with increasing access to papal riches, Scipione channelled funds into the advancement of the family's social status; through the acquisition of land and estates, the marriage of secular heirs into old, established aristocratic families and the creation of hereditary titles. He was also a great patron of the arts and poured his wealth into art and architecture and though not given to writing poetry like Lorenzo Medici,

Scipione surrounded himself with men of letters and the arts. Men like Stefano Pignatelli, a recognised authority within the world of arts and letters who became chief administrative officer within his household and poets like Lelio Guidiccione, one of his most faithful courtiers. Scipione also participated in the Rome Academia coming into contact with the leading poetic luminaries of the day, joining-in discussions about pastoral poetry, one of the most popular subjects amongst the group.

The Borghese family purchased farms and titled fiefs mainly in the Roman Campagna, the land acquisitions peaking in the years 1612–14. To understand the significance of these purchases, and subsequent developments, it is important to appreciate that in the early seventeenth century Romans regarded the geography of the city and countryside as a series of concentric rings; three belts of land distinguished by function, topography and distance from the urban centre. The first ring, the *vigne*, was a stretch of green landscape extending for 5 miles (*c.*8 km) from the city. Here even modest Romans cultivated small plots with vines and other crops and the more wealthy citizens developed pleasure gardens and villa parks. Beyond lay the Roman Campagna, a vast plain divided since medieval times into 500 farms, small and large. These were once cultivated for cereals but by the sixteenth century the land was mostly pasture, though much was neglected, poorly drained and abandoned. In 1660, long after Scipione's death, the Borghese family would still own 40 farms in the Campagna comprising a twentieth of all available land. The third ring was the hills that rose at the edge of the Campagna, a lush, green forested region where the ancient Romans located their villas and the elite of early modern Rome rediscovered the ancient Roman practice of *villeggiatura*. For them *villeggiatura* was a time for learned leisure and contemplative recreation, as well as displaying their good taste and good breeding. Twice a year at least, in late spring and at the time of the wine vintage in September or October, wealthy Romans would pour out of the city to visit their country properties and partake in the harvest.

Soon after Paul V's election, Scipione began planning the Villa Borghese on the Pincian Hill, within the *vigne*. With no overnight accommodation, it was a place where the 'cardinal's nephew' could entertain lavishly. His illustrious visitors would be dazzled by the wondrous 'showcase' of rare and exotic botanical specimens, wild animals and birds, displays of antiquities, collections of precious stones and minerals. The park that surrounded the villa, developed between 1606 and 1633, was not solely an ornamental garden. The actual garden was reduced to a small enclosed area at the side of the palace and the remaining area was subdivided into square and rectangular compartments planted with rows of trees, each of a single kind – umbrella pines, fir trees, holm oak – bordered by clipped hedges, separated by long wide avenues (Plate 14). Beyond was open grassland, recalling the landscape of the Campagna, and this *barco* or hunting park was stocked with hare, deer and other game, as well as goats, sheep and cattle.

The Villa Borghese was a carefully considered conceit, associating the family with past nobility. It was the first villa since Roman antiquity to include an

VEDVTA E PROSPETTIVA DEL GIARDINO DELL' ECC.^{MO} SIG.^R PRENCIPE BORGHESE FVORI DI PORTA PINCIANA. *Architettura di Flaminio Pontio seguitata col Palazzo da Gio.Vansantio.*

PLATE 14. Simon Felice (published by Giovanni Giacomo De Rossi): *The Villa Borghese on the Pincian Hill* (from Giovanni Giacomo De Rossi. Li giardini di Roma *c.* after 1677).

artificially landscaped hunting park close to the city centre and was modelled on Emperor Nero's, Golden House. Visitors to the Villa Borghese, conscious of the city's structure, would recognise elements brought in from outside the *vigne* – woodland from the third ring where forests and hunting parks were located, and the small lake and meadow land from the Campagna. These conveyed a double message about power: first it spoke of the wealth of an owner who could afford, like Nero, to have large rural lands close to the centre of the city: and secondly a park with its woods and meadows spoke of the owner's string of landholdings further away in the countryside. And because the Villa Borghese was located at the place where other members of the aristocracy began the journey to their own properties in the hills, its message could not be ignored.

Villa Mondragone and the pastoral image

Scipione looked to the outer ring, the forested Alban hills above Frascati, as the place to create a papal and dynastic palace. A place where architecture, landscape and the rituals of ancient *villeggiatura* could be combined to shape a new identity for the Borghese family. Frascati, and its ancient predecessor Tusculum close by, had been a favoured site for ancient Roman *villeggiatura* – Pliny the younger, Cato, Cicero and Lucullus were among the numerous owners of villas and gardens on its slopes and the area naturally attracted the aspiring nobility who, with their passion for antiquity, wanted to build and live among the ancient ruins.[1] In 1613 Scipione acquired the Villa Mondragone, located on a steep hill overlooking the Roman Campagna. The surrounding estate with its fertile, volcanic soil, had been cultivated since the mid-sixteenth century

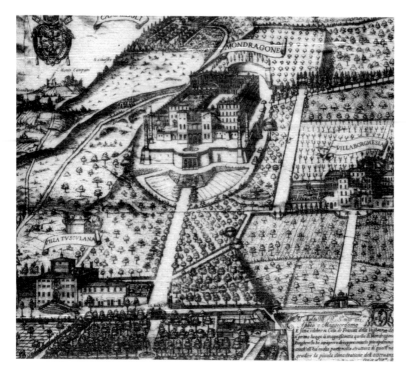

FIGURE 3. Plan of the
Villa Mondragone by
Matteo Greuter *c.*1620
showing many of the
original plantings.

and at the time of Scipione's purchase comprised more than 200 acres (80 ha)
of woods, orchards, vineyards and olive groves. Its extent was doubled almost
immediately by the purchase of a large forest nearby and by the time Scipione
had completed his land purchases in 1620, the estate covered 20,000 acres (8094
ha) of countryside. (Figure 3).

To invent his Roman pedigree, Scipione drew on the classical and medieval
past of Rome, in both the practical management of the estate and its iconography.
He appreciated there was no better way to demonstrate the family's association
with the past than through the use of the classical Pastoral, which could be
used to justify and underline the aspirations of an emerging aristocratic family.
Members of Scipione's circle knew the hillside above Frascati, the ancient *ager
tuscalanus*, had once supported splendid Roman villas and their gardens, and
that their estates extended onto the plains far below. Scipione saw the restoration
of this ancient landscape as essential if the Borghese family was to be accepted
as part of the elite aristocracy. This meant unifying the pastoral farming of the
plains with the mixed economy of the hills, with the villa at centre of the entire
enterprise. Since the middle ages, the planting of forests had always a been part
of feudal practice, so Scipione played-up the medieval features of the landscape
by planting groves of trees behind the villa. In front, to the north, the land was
deforested and transformed into vineyards, creating a panoramic view over all the
woods and cultivated land owned by the Borghese. And like the *villa urbana* of
ancient Rome, this view was carefully orchestrated. The dirt and sweat of labour
was antithetical to elitist *villeggiatura,* the rural life existing only as a poetic ideal.

So working farm buildings were placed at the periphery of the estate and the toiling labourer was removed from the sight of viewers.

From positions high up in the villa, or from its garden portico, the Pope, his 'papal nephew' and visitors could take in this pastoral landscape with its grazing flocks of sheep and goats, herds of cattle, vine dressers, shepherds, and farmers, wooded groves, vineyards and pastureland. Vistas of the mountains and sea offered reminders of the wild forces of nature, underscoring the orderly harmonious forces at work in the pastoral landscape. And the villa itself, together with the silhouette of Rome on the horizon, served to remind viewers of the contrast between town and country; the world they had left behind when entering this world of the imagination.

At the lavish banquets Scipione laid-on at Mondragone for official visitors and gatherings of friends, musical or literary entertainments and activities were modelled on the pastimes of the ancients, On such occasions the poet Guidiccione was employed to entertain and make people aware of the pastoral world. His duty was to impress on the guests the symbolic implications of the landscape and persuade them of the Borghese's nobility. He would do this through his pastoral poem *Tusculanum Amoentatum* (1623), which brought together various sources, mainly the *Idylls* of Theocritus, the *Odes* of Horace, Virgil's *Eclogues* and *Georgics* and Sannazarro's *Eclogues* and *Arcadia*. From these he drew pastoral conventions, stock characters and even direct quotations.

In opening the poem Guidiccione fashioned himself as the shepherd-poet singing his tale of love and despair as he lay, tired, in the grass besides a stream. Around him animals grazed while shepherds sang their songs and played their rustic flutes. The shepherd Aminta sat besides a babbling brook pining for Silva as in a pastoral *Eclogue* but this was combined with the *Georgic*, as Aminta "tills the fields alone, and cultivates the silent woods". Guidiccione's aim was to soothe the audience by convincing them that Frascati was a haven from "the whirlpool of urban cares" and, in the tradition of Pastoral, assure his listeners that they had left the city of Rome behind. It was important for the Borghese to declare to the world that they were living as the ancients and Guidiccione employed archaic language to highlight this fact. The setting for Guidiccione's pastoral was Tusculum, a *locus amoenus* of woodlands and meadows with field and vineyards, and his verse extolled its virtues, its healthy climate, its ancient forests and agricultural riches, its modern villas and the Roman ruins on which they stood. He praised the fertile slopes covered in antiquity, as in modern times, with fruitful vines and pleasing groves. He commended the landscape of Mondragone to those who dedicated themselves to 'hard labour', in the pastoral spirit of the *Eclogues* and the *Georgics*.

Guidiccione provided an artistic structure for his listeners, one familiar to them from their knowledge of Virgil and his renaissance interpreters, so they could reconstruct a living, idyllic landscape in their minds. Exploring more fully the landscape they had seen already from the selected viewpoints. As they moved through the landscape, Guidiccione's poetry offered Virgilian glimpses of the countryside and a sequence of evocative contrasts, characteristic of the pastoral;

the ills of the city and the ease of the countryside, the ruined splendour of the ancients and the towering wonders of the moderns, the madness of spurned love and the joys of reconciliation. Guidiccione suggested that the slopes of Frascati had been transformed into an earthly paradise, its forests protected by gods, its grounds home to satyrs and fauns, the companion of shepherds. Here Guidiccione declared, Arcadians lived by "a happy turn of events joining in on pastoral songs". In heralding the return of a Golden Age, Guidiccione declared that the beauties of modern Tusculum would surpass the Golden Age of the past, for here there was a continual spring and fruit maturing in all seasons. The poem concluded as it had begun with the simple words "the fields are pleasing". Other poets in the Borghese circle described Scipione, not surprisingly, as the new Augustus, responsible for this new Golden Age – a conceit which belongs to realm of hyperbole but one which no doubt suited the aspirations of the Borghese family.

Guidiccione's words were reinforced by epigrams inscribed around the garden portico of the Villa Mondragone declaring that the villa was a retreat from worldly cares and comparing its landscape to the ancient classical sites, the Garden of Hesperides and the valley of the Tempe. For the Borghese, the poet implied, the landscape of the villa was the new Arcadia. This notion, involving the reality of land transformed into an idyllic poetic, pastoral landscape, was reinforced by Scipione's collection of landscape paintings. From the princely apartments, offering an open view of the Campagna, the visitor entered a gallery with its carefully circumscribed vistas. On the walls Scipione displayed Flemish landscapes, still-lives and rustic, genre scenes; and he commissioned several rising landscape painters like Paul Brill and Agostino Tassi to create frescoes. The paintings provided the pastoral images for viewing the landscape, supporting the intellectual flights of fancy. Visitors could compare the painted representations of rural life and landscape with what they had seen on their tour of the villa and garden. Before their eyes were peasants, shepherds, goatherds, cows and goats that were echoed in the grounds of the villa. The gallery presented the very conceit at the heart of the pastoral, for whilst the landscape of the villa appeared natural, it was no less artificial, no less idealised, no less a representation than the painted landscapes and peasants on the gallery walls.[2] Before Pope Paul V died in 1621, Scipione could say of the countryside at Mondragone, just as Pliny the Younger had said of his Tuscan villa at Laurentium, that it was:

> ... very beautiful. Picture to yourself a vast amphitheatre such as could only be the work of nature; the great spreading plain is ringed round by mountains, their summits crowned with ancient woods of tall trees, where there is a good deal of mixed hunting to be had. Down the mountain slopes are timber woods interspersed with small hills of soil so rich that there is scarcely a rocky outcrop to be found; these hills are as fully fertile as the level plain and yield quite as rich a harvest, though it ripens rather later in the season. Below them the vineyards spreading down every slope weave their uniform pattern far and wide, their lower limit bordered by a plantation of tree. Then come the meadows and the cornfields, where the land can be broken up only by heavy oxen and the strongest ploughs ... It is a great pleasure to look down on the countryside from the mountain, for the view seems to be a

painted scene of unusual beauty rather than a real landscape , and the harmony to be found in this variety refreshes the eye wherever it turns.[3]

For those labouring in the fields, looking up at the villa, the pastoral landscape they helped create by working the land and tending the grazing sheep, was a landscape of privilege from which they were excluded. Agriculture for them was not an aspect of *otium* but one of hard work. So whilst the pastoral landscape confirmed the spectators sense of privilege and underscored the elite status of the patron, it also reinforced the hierarchal social order.

Claude Lorrain

A few years after the death of Pope Paul V there arrived in Rome an artist whose paintings would represent the Arcadian landscape on canvas. His name was Claude Gelle (Lorrain) from the French region of the Duchy of Lorraine. Claude's pastoral vision was inspired by the views of the Campagna he had seen from places like the Villa Mondragone. He visited the Alban hills often, from the late 1620s into the 1630s, preparing the studies of trees, shepherds with flocks and landmarks of antiquity he would use later in his large oil paintings. Claude, like all renaissance painters, relied on commissions and his success was dependent on providing the canvases and images his clients demanded. Among his clients were Pope Urban VII, who commissioned four paintings, and the rising papal aristocracy – the Pamphilj,[4] the Ludovisi and Barbarini. Claude was successful because his pastoral paintings represented more than views of an Ideal classical world, they also provided ideal images of the Roman campagna. In the seventeenth century land and its ownership as source of wealth and social status had become a central preoccupation among the papal families. This resulted in a rapid change in the management of the land. Traditionally, Rome's agrarian economy had been balanced between cereal cultivation and livestock but in the seventeenth century there was a major shift towards animal husbandry. Even though there was a shortage of grain in the city, big Roman landowners found there were even greater profits to be made from raising livestock. Harvesting grain was expensive as labour was scarce and costly, making it more profitable to grow hay and rent land to shepherds for grazing. As a result, ploughed land and cultivated fields gradually disappeared and by 1650 only a quarter of the farmland was sown with anything, and that was mainly hay. The remainder of Campagna was grassland which, due to over grazing and the absence of labour to install drainage, was increasingly subject to flooding.

So in paintings like the *Sunrise* Claude portrayed the Campagna as his patrons would wish to see it (Plate 15). A wistful pastoral landscape, with no evidence of cultivation, though in his drawings he had observed such activities. The landscape is populated not with poor itinerant herders and labourers but by well-fed shepherds wending their way with their flocks The shepherds are depicted in ancient dress, a "state of Innocence of that Golden Age, that blessed time, when Sincerity, and Innocence, Peace, Ease and Plenty inhabited the Plains". This ideal occupation had to be joined to the Ideal landscape: "pleasing Meadows, shady Groves, green banks, stately Trees, flowing Springs and the wanton windings of a river fit objects for quiet innocence".[5] Though Claude's paintings do not illustrate any particular text, he lacked a classical education, his landscapes were essentially pastoral paintings, that "depended for their resonance's on a literary tradition – the pastoral poem".[6] It was as though "he painted these pastoral scenes while reading Varro, Pliny the Younger and Horace", to which has to be added Virgil: "the texts his patrons were reading".[7] Though, as Wine points out, Virgil at this time was appreciated more through recent poems such as Sannazaro's *Arcadia* in which the nobleman Sincero became a shepherd and dwells in Arcadia, a poetic land of melancholy. The appeal of this image was the unreality, which allowed the cultivated reader or viewer to identify, with such scenes.[8] In the painting, as in many of Claude's paintings, the cities are far distant, and in the spirit of *villeggiatura*, offer the observer the choice between the ideal life of the country and the squalid reality of the town, with its cares of court and city life.

The fantasy of the pastoral enjoyed by the elite aristocracy was expressed shortly after Claude's death by French writer Fontenelle (1657–1757):

> When someone represents to me the calm that reigns in the country, the simplicity and tenderness with which love is there experienced, my imagination, touched and affected transforms me into the shepherd's condition, I am a shepherd: but when someone represents to me, though with all possible accuracy and justice, the wretched tasks that shepherds do, I cannot envy them, and my imagination remains stone cold.[9]

This did not mean that landscape itself was entirely fictitious. The view widely held in the seventeenth century was that both poetry and painting should represent things not as they were but as they ideally should be. That is to say nature should not be simply imitated but improved upon by selection from its most beautiful parts. This extraction of the Ideal from nature was dependent on an intimate knowledge of nature. The kind of knowledge and understanding that is apparent from Claude's studies of plants, trees, rocks and other natural forms. To create an Ideal landscape that is both familiar and removed from everyday reality, Claude did not copy his drawings from nature but invented landscapes, based on his understanding and observations of nature. Transposing the natural elements of the third ring, into the recognisable landscape of the Campagna; a verdant, pastoral landscape often associated with familiar architectural features, though never in complete archaeological detail. These elements were placed in unfamiliar settings and with other imaginary buildings.

The Grand Tourists

The Ideal harmonious world of Claude's paintings and the actual landscapes of Mondragone, along with others, like the Villas Borghese and Pamphilj, greatly influenced aristocratic young men taking the Grand Tour to Rome. Long after Scipione's death the architectural form of the Villa Mondragone and the garden with its carefully arranged views, evocative epigrams and paintings in the gallery would delight and surprise the visitor. An English visitor Francis Mortoft visited Monte Dragone in 1659 and experienced the landscape as an earthly paradise or *locus amoenus* much as Scipione had hoped. He found the view from the villas "the most pleasant prospect in the world" whilst the hillside below to be planted with "all the blessings of Canaan, Corne, wynee, and oyle growing altogether".

For Mortoft and others, the act of viewing was an occasion for pastoral reveries, to which they readily succumbed: "the extended grounds of the villa are an ideal *locus* for the artistic consumption of rural life and landscape". Forty years later, when a very different attitude to nature prevailed in England, Joseph Addison, the essayist proclaimed, on his return from the Grand Tour, that one could successfully

PLATE 15. Claude (1600–1682): *Sunrise c.*1646–7.

PLATE 16. Castle Howard: the Temple of the Four Winds with Mausoleum and bridge in the distance. In this carefully composed Claudian picture – the eye moves from Vanbrugh's Temple of the Four Winds, modelled in part on Palladio's Villa Rotunda, towards a massive new river bridge, based on another Palladio design, to Hawksmoor's gigantic mausoleum. The whole scene framed by woodland with a pastoral landscape pervading throughout.

make of one's own estate, a garden. This thought must have occurred to Charles Howard, the third Earl of Carlisle, who was so impressed by the imagery of Claude that he laid-out his new estate at Castle Howard, Yorkshire as a three-dimensional painting. Architectural elements, such as Palladio's rotunda at Vicenza, a palladian bridge and a mausoleum designed by Nicholas Hawksmoor, were all disposed within a pastoral landscape (Plate 16).

Carlisle left no written accounts of his intentions but his daughter, Lady Ann Howard (later Irwin), was in no doubt her father was inspired by a vision of the elysium of the antique world. In her poem *Castle Howard,* Lady Ann provides provides an insight into the prevailing ideas of each component of the composition, of the landscape she says:

> From ev'ry Place you cast your wand'ring Eys'
> You view gay Landscips, and new Prospects rise,
> There a Green Lawn bounded by with Shady Wood,
> Here Downy Swans sport in a Lucid Flood,
> Buildings the proper Points of View adorn,
> Of *Grecian*, *Roman* and *Egyptian* Form.
>
> These interspers'd with Woods and Vedent Plains,
> Such as possess'd of old th' *Arcadian* swains.
> Hills rise on Hills: and to complete the Scenes,
> Like one continu'd Wood th' Horizon seems.[10]

The Roman pastoral would provide an exquisite vehicle for wealthy Englishmen to mythologise their own agrarian landscapes.

Notes and References

1. Ehrlich, T. L., *Landscape and Identity in Early Rome: villa culture at Frascati in the Borghese era*. Cambridge University Press, Cambridge in association with American Academy, Rome, 2002, p. 1.
2. *Ibid.*, p. 260
3. Pliny the Younger, *Epistulae* 5.6.7–13.
4. One of Claude's principle patrons was Cardinal Camillo Pamphili, papal nephew of Innocent X (reigned 1644–55) who built the Villa Pamphili on the Janiculum Hill, 1645–70. Between 1645 and 1648 he commissioned six landscapes from Claude and for the next 20 years he collected hundreds of landscape paintings. At least two of the Claudes and more than twelve of the landscapes were hung in the garden room of the of the Pamphili palace. As Wise has pointed out, the landscape paintings, including those by Claude, were hung to complement the views over the garden, rather than to focus attention on the episode shown in the picture frame; exactly the same as the relationship at Mondragone.
5. Wine, H., *Claude: the poetic landscape*. National Gallery Publications, London, 1994, p. 29.
6. *Ibid.*
7. Benes, M. and Harris, D. S., *Villas and Gardens in Early Modern Italy and France*. Cambridge University Press, Cambridge, 2001, p. 110.
8. Wine, H., *op. cit.*, p. 30.
9. *Ibid.*
10. In Hunt, J. D. and Willis, P. (eds), *The Genius of the Place*. Paul Elek, London, 1975, pp. 228–231.

CHAPTER SIX

The Dutch Republic
and the Golden Age of Landscape

In the course of the seventeenth century the newly founded Dutch republic took over from Venice as the trading centre of the world and came to dominate European affairs. With the growing commercial success came an inevitable and rapid expansion of the country's major towns and cities and this, along with improvements in agricultural production, led to fundamental changes in the Dutch landscape. As in classical Rome and renaissance Venice these circumstances were important precursors to the development of the pastoral landscape tradition, but with the important difference that in the Dutch republic the changes were suffused with a spirit of scientific investigation. Microscopes, telescopes and other scientific instruments revealed an hitherto unknown world and for the first time people began to see nature as it really was. So, without any apparent self-consciousness, the culture of the Dutch republic in the seventeenth century combined the classical traditions of ancient Rome with a new world order in art and science. The solid foundation of ancient wisdom combined with new knowledge, gave the Dutch confidence to become one of Europe's leading nations.

The Treaty of Utrecht and its aftermath

The signatories of the Union Treaty of Utrecht (1579) which brought an end to Spain's domination – Holland, Zeeland, Utrecht, Groningen and Guelderland – had no intention of forming a new republic but they were united in their hatred of Spain and recognised the need to co-operate in order to survive. The nation that emerged was a loose association of separate Provinces held together by an adherence to the Reformed Calvinist religion, the authority of the semi-monarchial House of Orange-Nassau, and the domination of the Province of Holland. The confederation was, in large measure, ruled by a strong oligarchy drawn from the wealthiest merchant families. The Regents, as they preferred to be known, numbered around 10,000 and were largely urban in character, though there was a handful of members from an older, landed gentry. The Regents kept the political affairs of the Provinces, and of the country, within their own families and despite the apparent inequality and scope for injustice, people were content to leave matters in "the hands of this burgher aristocracy".[1] At the heart of the Dutch trading empire was the port of Amsterdam which

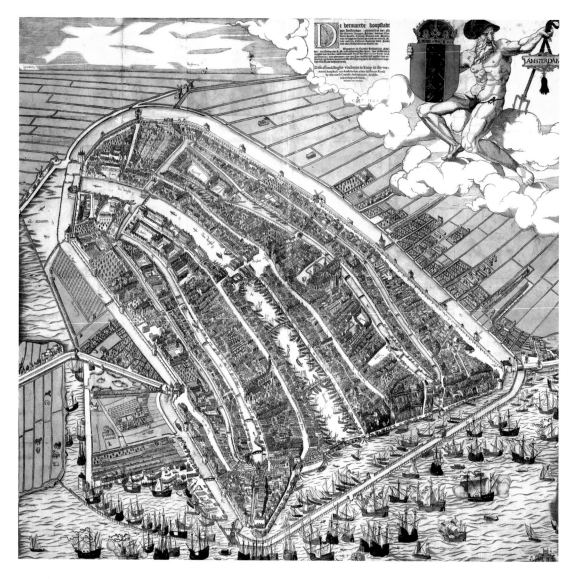

FIGURE 4. Cornelis Athonisz: *Bird's eye view of Amsterdam c.*1544. Woodcut.

was also the country's largest centre of population (Figure 4). At the beginning of the seventeenth century the Dutch nation comprised about one and a half million people, of whom two-thirds lived in the coastal provinces and 100,000 in Amsterdam alone. The population was swollen by people moving to the city from the surrounding countryside and others who had migrated from the southern provinces. Some 60–90,000 Flemings went to Holland in the years after 1585.[2] These migrants were allowed to take money and personal property with them, thus adding greatly to the wealth of the northern Provinces. This wealth, along with an entrepreneurial spirit, made sure the migrants were among the first to engage in new enterprises, including the development of the Port of Amsterdam and the expansion of the old medieval towns. Another highly speculative, and ultimately profitable investment, was the reclamation of land involving the drainage of inland lakes and shallow seas. New farmland was needed to provide food for the growing population, and to create a surplus for export. But reclamation and the improvement of existing farms, resulted in an inevitable and rapid change in the landscape of the seaward provinces. The old informality giving way to the straight lines of the new polders.

The response to change

The Dutch republic came into being without any historical past. To overcome this the Regents drew parallels between their own state and that of ancient Rome. Their country had grown from small beginnings, extending its empire to all parts of the known world and the creation of this republic had been the achievement of a small oligarchy. As in the Rome of Augustus, a prominent position was held by an hereditary leader, the *Stadtholder*, who, though commander of the army and navy, was no more than the first of citizens. Thus the burgher-aristocrats of Holland regarded themselves as the Romans of northern Europe and the humanistic tradition that had prevailed since Erasmus gave life and colour to this perception.

The sense of national superiority was supported by the Calvinist church. The most charismatic preacher of the day, Borstius of Dordrecht, proclaimed the whole meaning of their national existence was a plan that God had for the world. Whether they liked it or not their history was written on the scroll of providential design:

> the almighty had endowed them with the wit and will to conquer waters, and even turn the waters against their enemies; and he had raised them to great riches and power, the better to proclaim His omnipotence, rather than to liberate them from it in this world.[3]

It was even argued with great weight and seriousness by Jan van Gorp, a physician, that Dutch had been the language spoken in the Garden of Eden. In this way the emerging Dutch nation linked itself to classical Arcadia and the biblical Garden of Eden, and both, it was believed, were mirrored in the landscape. Calvinism also played an important part in shaping a new outlook on nature. Its adherents believed a knowledge of creation brought Man closer to knowing God. This encouraged Calvin's followers to turn to the natural world and to study it; using the new scientific methods, inspired by the writings of Francis Bacon.

Arguably, Bacon's most important contribution to scientific theory was in setting aside the dogma of St Augustine by a simple observation that theology and science were concerned with same ends, namely the improvement of the human condition.[4] This, said Bacon, could be achieved in the afterlife through theology and in the here and now by science. Understanding how nature worked, through the steady collection of observed data and a process of experimentation, would give Man power over nature and the knowledge gained could be used to relieve man's temporal estate. Such knowledge would glorify God, and in Bacon's opinion scientists would become the new secular priests:

this view of the professional scientist: objective, undogmatic, internationalist and committed to improving man's lot can easily be equated with that of a priest, replacing the established religious priesthood. He was working, it seemed for a universal good,...This was science's self justification, and it was a powerful one which would appeal to any group wanting to legitimate its own activities.[5]

One Regent who personified this was new attitude was Constantijn Huygens (1596–1687), a fervent classicist and devout calvinist, who embraced the new science with an enthusiasm of someone seeing the world for the first time. The 'eye' was praised by Huygens as among the highest of God's gifts to man; it was the means by which one sees and reports on the new knowledge of the world: "For we are truly as Gods if we can see from the highest point of the heavens to the tiniest creatures on earth". Not surprisingly Huygens was a patron of Leeuwenhoek, the inventor of the modern microscope and extolled this new way of seeing for, he said, it brought an insight into a world antiquity never knew.

Literature and painting

For the Regents intent on re-establishing the glories of Rome anew, literature and art were seen in terms of classical ideals and conventions. The real world, if seen at all, was a private affair. The social elite, from the *Stadtholder* to magistrates and wealthy merchants were patrons of pastoral painting, the form of painting favoured by aristocracy throughout Europe. They were encouraged by Carel van Mander whose important treatise on painting, *Het Schilderboeck* (1604), instructed painters to make landscapes that conveyed humanistic themes: "based on the classical bucolic poetry and idealisations of rural life in Virgil's *Eclogues* and *Georgics*"[6] but van Mander wanted painters to fuse the antique pastoral with contemporary details.[7] So Dutch pastoral paintings often struck a lighter note than those earlier scenes of eternal spring and piping shepherds, and offered the pleasurable, rather than the pensive, aspects of literature. In *The Dutch Arcadia* Kettering suggests Dutch pastoral painters occupied a middle ground between Venetian melancholy, with its desire to escape from the present into the nostalgia of a lost golden age, and later French scenes of frivolity and sensuous pleasure.[8] The Dutch artists were interested in the pleasant possibilities of the pastoral landscape as a diversion – a delightful world into which they might momentarily retreat to celebrate the most agreeable aspects and moments of life and return refreshed and restored. But the landscapes in Dutch pastoral paintings and novels were not entirely imaginary, often they were set in a specifically local setting, or at least an imagined reality. In his marriage portrait of *Isaak Abraham Massa and Beatrix van der Laen*, Frans Hals, who studied with van Mander, depicts the couple in such a world. The newly-weds sit in the bower of an old tree at the edge of an imaginary but instantly recognisable Dutch garden (Plate 17). These painted Arcadian pastoral gardens, a *lusthof,* were populated by happy beings, real or imaginary, set in a realm illuminated by constant but gentle sunlight[9] – a realm not too far away.

Dutch pastoral, despite its local flavour, was an extension of the old order, introduced by a social caste anxious to associate itself with the European aristocracy and whilst it retained the interest of a small minority, a new a vision of reality was already emerging, in drawings, prints and paintings. In the new climate of scientific realism a two way exchange between art and natural knowledge was to be expected, and Huygens, keen to look to the future rather than past, wrote in praise of the new life-like nature of contemporary Dutch painting:

> the crop of landscape painters, as we shall call those who paint woods, fields, mountains and villages, is in our Netherlands so very great and so famous, that if I were to mention them all ... I would fill a small book ... One can say that in the work of these clever men, that as far as naturalness is concerned nothing is lacking except the warmth of the sun and the movement caused by the gentle breeze.[10]

The landscape in poetry

In translating the classics and renaissance emulations, writers like Corneliszoon Hooft, the son of a leading Regent in Amsterdam, Huygens and Jorst van den Vondel sought to revitalise and develop Dutch culture and create a narrative tradition equal to that of Rome. For poets with this outlook and background nothing came more naturally than the writing of Pastoral verse which met the growing sense of nostalgia for a lost countryside and rural life.[11] Writers of Dutch pastoral observed Horace's adage *ut pictura poesis* and used mythological and Arcadian conventions to describe the landscape. But they did not depict nature for its own sake, rather they were concerned with special character of the Dutch landscape. *Hert-speigal* (1600), in which each of the seven books is devoted to one of muses, begins with a "description of nature in a vividly Dutch colour":

> Thalia leads us out by Amsterdamlic streams
> To see the novel rove of the wet fields and orchards
> Whose gaily light-green leaves all of a sudden burst
> From swelling, gravid buds out of dry-skinned branches.
> The grass that in the autumn sank under layers of ice
> Now raises pointed heads that pierce the water's surface.
> The field, a while ago still an abounding lake,
> Shows its rough edges now, its colours returning.
> Where long the darting fish played to their hearts content
> Soon cattle, full of milk, will daily be sent grazing.
> They loath the mussy hay and long for fresh pastures
> That offer better feed, melting to fat and butter.
>
> Speigal: *Hert-speighel*[12]

This wintry Dutch landscape is long way from the warm hillsides of Crete that Theocritus imagined but Speigal maintained that Dutch nature and Dutch art were no less great than the lands, nature and art of antiquity. However, where realistic descriptions of nature are provided, their purpose is to create a setting for some didactic or moralising function. A familiar characteristic of the pastoral

PLATE 17. Frans Hals
(1582–1666): *Isaak
Abraham Massa and
Beatreix van der Lean
c.*1622.

was to extol the virtue of those simple activities found in the countryside, in
contrast to the troubles and turbulence of the city. In *Bauw-heers Welleven* (*The
Good Life of the Farmer*) the writer derives inspiration from the *Georgics*:

> But then his narrow punt speeds through the shallow water
> Towards the fields he shoves or either poles or rows it
> While all the time his eye stays fixed in his own homestead.[13]

The poem continues by meditating on the contrast between city and country
and the farmer's own marital bliss.

Country houses and estates

Early in the seventeenth century wealthy burghers saw the ownership of land
as the ultimate symbol of status, and began to acquire estates in the vicinity
of Amsterdam, Haarlem, Delft, The Hague and other major cities, their villas
forming "an Arcadian landscape ... like a shell enclosing the cities". The luxurious
country house, a beautiful formal garden, with fountains, water gardens, ponds,
statues of classical gods, all offered proof of the owner's classical knowledge. As
with the Medicis in Florence and the *villegiatura* in Rome, the villa represented
the contrast of *otium* – free time, leisure, ease, peace, repose with *negotium* or
business, as well as a retreat into nature and an opportunity to get closer to
God's creation. With typical Dutch pragmatism, many country houses were built
alongside canals and rivers providing not only the benefits of waterside scenery

PLATE 18. Cornelis Troost (1697–1750): *Blindmans Buff* c.1740.

but cheap and easy travel. An important consideration when the entire family and servants, complete with the contents of the house, were transported in the summer to the country estate to avoid the commotion and filthiness of the city. Constantijn Huygens built his country house, Hofwijk[14] sometime after 1639, on the side of the Vliet canal. Some years before he had translated Vitruvius's *De architectura* into Dutch, with his friend Count Johan Maurits van Nassau-Siegen, the owner of the neighbouring Mauritshuis, and the building of Hofwijk gave Huygens the opportunity to realise his ideas of classical architecture.

The country house inspired its own poetic style, the *Hofdicht* (*Country House poem*) regarded as the most important pastoral poetry of seventeenth century Holland. The poems, influenced by the *Georgics* first translated into Dutch by Vondel, rather than the *Eclogues* expressed a genuine feeling for the landscape, inspired by a direct contact with Dutch country life. But the poems also make clear the Regents' renaissance view of nature, that is to say, the landscape outside the town was regarded as imperfect and in need of improvement. In beginning of his Country House poem, about the estate at Diurnal, Conrad Drost described how:

> Man may give nature another face,
> If he is skilled in agriculture,
> Turning the wilderness into useful and fertile land;
> Diurnal ground was strewn with sand:
> Now replaced with entertaining grades.[15]

Like most writers of the *Hofdichten*, Drost stressed the pleasures connected with land and garden; the workings of a well-run estate, the beauty of the property and details of country sports. Important too was the presence of family and discussions with friends about the history of antiquity, mythology or literature, held in the well-stocked library. But Dutch Country House poems differ from comparable poetry in Italy, France or England in their moral and religious view of nature. In poems by Cats or Huygens nature resembles a bible from which such lessons might be learnt. God's greatness, wrote Cats, is revealed in the smallest natural phenomena, a flower, a spider, the leaves of a tree, the shells of a grotto. A more solemn note was struck in the poem *Den Binkhorst* by Borsselen, who used the vagaries of spring frost as an observation on man's frailty:

> Even the most simple flower of thine opulent garden
> Bears on its leaves the praise of its own wise Creator
> And teaches that man too, is like a flowering weed
> That in its Life's fresh April almost passes away
> If its nipping winds just once blow down upon its head.[16]

In this poem Borsselen conforms closely to pastoral principles, praising Jacob Snouckaert, the owner of Brinkhorst, for turning away from the turbulence of city business in favour of a simple country life.[17] Huygens likewise speaks of his friends, entertainments and generous hospitality; at Hofwijck one could engage in archery at the foot of the mountain, pick fruits in the orchard or "bowl on the lawn of the *bolbaen*" along the Vliet. Music and singing were at home in the state room or garden:

> Two Gates speak of more: be I greeting friend or guest
> 'tis not by one door yet by two open doors;
> the spacious entrance shows what is to happen indoors,
> And that friends are welcome to my bread and my wine,
> not half, not whole, not once, but twice.[18]

The *hofdichten* inspired their own pastoral portraits often depicting an intimate family scenes, with husband and wife, numerous children, occasionally with grandparents and servants, shown against a rich landscape background, though by the early 1640s a garden setting was preferred by some fashionable Dutch families. Cornelis Troost's delightful painting *Blindman's Buff* shows a family at ease, playing on terrace of the garden at their country home, with the Dutch landscape of polders and windmills spreading out in the distance (Plate 18). Harmony with nature is implied by the loose, almost casual arrangement of the figures, their relaxed postures and a serenity of expression echoed by the peaceful skies and fertile landscape. In some paintings the affinity with nature is strengthened by children picking flowers or a display of animals killed in the hunt. The whole scene was intended to suggest a parallel between the fruitfulness of the land and the prosperity and fecundity of the family.

Hofdichten poetry and the garden

The *hofdichten* poetry also revealed a general attitude towards gardens as a highly valued part of this culture. Some writers of *hofdichten* poetry were important gardeners themselves, including Jacob Cats and Constantijn Huygens whose poems include ideas on gardening and horticultural practice. So when Jan van der Groen '*gardener to his Illustrious Highness the Lord Prince of Orange*' wrote his treatise on gardening, *Den Nederlandtsen Houvenier (the Dutch Gardener)* (1699), he began by extolling the twin virtues of country life and horticulture.

> Horticulture and life in the country is, according to many learned people, the most *delightful*, the most *advantageous* and *healthiest*, yea oft times the most *blessed* life that one could wish for the person who is not bound by his profession to the town.[19]

In advocating the rural life van der Groen repeated the now familiar arguments of "pleasant gentle air" and on a more practical note "fruits and vegetables from one's own land are not as expensive as in the town". Moreover in the town one is often tempted to eat excessively; whereas in the country people live, eat, drink, sleep and rise with more regularity. And as well as physical health, country life extends its "blessedness" to the moral and spiritual life of man "there are plenty of things that give glory to the name of the great Creator of all these herbs, flowers, fruits, trees, with thanks and praise".

In the *Den Nederlandtsen Houvenier,* van der Groen alludes to the 'Latin poets' though he does not mention them by name and it is unlikely he read them himself. He was however familiar with the ideas of Virgil and others through *hofdichten* poetry, referring to some poems by name and quoting from them, even going so far as to see the Dutch Country House poems as replacing the authority of the classical writers. Like those poets, van der Groen regarded nature, seen in the landscape outside the town, as imperfect. Writing in his introduction he argued that "nature is to be arranged, embellished, put into good order, decorated and made pleasurable by art". The notion that only 'Art perfects nature' was a prevalent idea; only art was capable of adjusting nature and perfecting it so that it could be made more enjoyable and useful to man. For a gardener like van der Groen this meant wild fruits could be domesticated and made tasty by the use of manure, by cherishing and grafting, and infertile ground could be turned into fruitful earth by means of craft and skill. Plants and seeds could achieve optima; grow and produce perfect flowers in greenhouses constructed with the aid of technique and craftsmanship; and the labour and care of the owner. This labour was seen as necessary for the recovery of paradise.[20] However, the making of a garden could only be achieved by subduing natural phenomena to the laws and rules of mathematics and art; geometry and uniformity, taken from the laws of art and architecture. Laying out of a garden was not regarded as an art in the same way as painting, sculpture, or architecture. The design of a garden was seen as a product of science, surveying and mathematics, in combination with horticulture. Moreover the cultivation of herbs, flowers and trees was regarded, along with farming and stockbreeding, as belonging to agriculture; and as with country life, it came under the Virgilian ideal of the *Georgics*. So whereas the Country House poems reveal a delight in country life and the simple, sensory pleasures of nature, wildness can only be glimpsed, very rarely, in the corner of the garden.

Nostalgia and a new realism

As cities like Amsterdam, Haarlem, Delft and Leiden expanded there was growing nostalgia for a world perceived to have been left behind. Excursions to the countryside became an important part of Dutch city life, as the French writer Parival observed in *Les Delices de la Hollande,* the popularity of outings to the countryside among Dutch town dwellers is such that:

> wherever one goes here one finds as many people as would be seen elsewhere in a public procession. All these excursions end up at one of the inns which are to be found everywhere... These are packed with visitors, and the confused murmur of voices is like the sound of a city square. These are inexpensive places which all, even the humblest labourer can share.[21]

People were searching for remnants of the old landscape that could still be found in the dunes stretching along Holland's coastline, or in more distant spots in the east, where winding roads, old rustic farmhouses, irregular lines and an unhurried pace was the rule rather the exception.[22]

On returning home, the excursionists wanted images of these forgotten corners in their homes and the workplace; to transport them, in their imagination, away from the often insanitary, crowded conditions of the town, back to their native village or countryside. This desire for realistic prints and paintings was strongest amongst the new generation of bankers, merchants and trades people who were intensely nationalistic, and hard headed realists, who demanded an "art that was close to nature and the visible world". Increasingly, the affluent middle classes could afford the inexpensive pleasure of a print or painting – no great distinction was made between drawings, prints and paintings – so by 1678, the Flemish artist Samuel Hoogstraten could make the observation that "at the beginning of the century, the walls in Holland were not thickly with painting as they now are".

Naturalistic landscape drawing first emerged in the Antwerp studios of Peter Bruegel the Elder and the print maker Hieronymus Cock in the years before 1579 and made its way to the Dutch republic after Treaty of Utrecht. Among those fleeing north at that time were some 225 painters who were soon offering a variety of paintings – genre, landscape, flower paintings *etc.* As in other fields of cultural activity the northern Provinces had had no distinctive landscape painters – they had been primarily figure painters covering a variety of subjects, including devotional pieces. Carel van Mander (1548–1606) had spent 3 years studying in Rome and was regarded as an established expert by the time he settled in Haarlem in 1577. To encourage young artists, van Mander set-up informal study groups to discuss painting and receive instruction in the classics. Believing all artists should have a familiarity with classical literature, van Mander used his

PLATE 19. Claes Jansz Visscher (1587–1652): *Blekeryen door den Houd't (Bleaching Fields beyond Haarlem Woods) c.*1611–12. The artist himself sits sketching on the fence.

own translation of Virgil's *Eclogues* and *Georgics* (1597) to extoll the virtues of the Dutch countryside and those who worked the land. He transferred the settings to the Dutch countryside and gave them Dutch titles, *Ossen-stal* (*Ox-Stall*) and *Landwerk* (*Land-Work*) and blurred the distinction between Dutch farmers and arcadian shepherds. A poem accompanying the translation, *Oss Abram van Mijll* proclaimed that van Mander "has made his sheep bleat with a Dutch voice and eat Dutch grass and added numerous details from his observation of Dutch life". In his *Schilderboeck* (1604) van Mander encouraged young artists to get up early and go into the countryside with their sketch books and draw from nature. He made specific reference to the watery Dutch landscape "on either side of the winding stream ... we will plant gentle rushes, reeds and sword like irises ... the river with sweeping bends, winding through marshy fields should also be depicted".[23] And it was important, he said, for the artist to master the tree trunk and "show a distinction between the pale thin birches and limes" and for "the wrinkled oak be overgrown with creeper and green ivy". Artists should show:

> little figures ploughing or mowing or loading up a cart, and elsewhere fishing, sailing, catching birds, hunting; show how farm-girls, besides green banks ease out fountains of milk with their hands. Show how Tityrus with his flute, entertains Amaryllis, his beloved among women, resting beneath a beech tree, delights his flock with the pleasant sound. Show the countryside, town and water filled with activity, and make your houses look inhabited and your roads walked on.[24]

Van Mander's intention was to boost pride in the newly formed nation and its landscape, and at one point in his Bucolics, he addresses his beloved Holland in words richly evoking Virgil's praise of rural life in the *Georgics* "You know not, O Land! How fortunate you are". Accordingly, he wanted young painters to be true to what they saw.

By the beginning of the seventeenth century a new generation of writers, artists and graphic designers began to emerge who were not from the aristocracy but the middle and working classes, among them Claus Jansz Visscher (1587–1652), the son of an Amsterdam ships carpenter. In 1605 Visscher began to produce landscape drawings, including scenes of Dutch countryside – villages, farmhouses and inns, often made on the spot. 'Landscapes' had been left previously to expatriate Flemings and Visscher was believed to have trained with the Flemish emigre David Vinkboons, painter, draftsman and occasional print maker. In 1611 Visscher made a series of prints recording the countryside and coastal villages around Haarlem bound into a book titled *Pleasant Places* (Plate 19). The places were well-known to weekend excursionists. Many scenes had historical associations, often with the War of Independence from Spain, and had been described elsewhere by writers. Visscher's intention was, as the verses on the title page made clear, to give "devotees (lovers of nature) who have no time to travel far" images of those Pleasant Places that "here you can contemplate with ease". The latin inscription on the title page describes "the ever delightful roads" and urges readers to let their "eyes roam these open vistas offered by the Sylvan surroundings of Haarlem".[25] For many of Visscher's contemporaries the title *Pleasant Places* would have brought to mind the latin, *locus amoenus*, those pleasant places associated with shady groves, cool streams and verdant meadows celebrated by Theocritus, Virgil and the other poets of the classical age.

The Dutch countryside portrayed by Visscher, and the artists who followed him, differed in one important respect from the *Idylls* of Theocritus. The landscapes were not populated with nymphs, satyrs and the other deities of nature like Pan, for the simple reason that the beauties of the Dutch landscape were considered sufficient. The pastoral tradition could be evoked more simply by a herdsman driving his flock along the road, a piping shepherd at rest, or an occasional milkmaid. These were all that was needed to establish the appropriate bucolic mood. So in Adriaen van der Velde's *Landscape with a Family* (Plate 20) in which an unknown family enjoy a stroll in a peaceful landscape, a reclining shepherd sits by the road piping to his flock. It is highly unlikely such a figure would have been present in the landscape, but the artist was following, in part at least, van Manders instructions for landscape painting "to show how Tityrus with his flute, entertains Amyryllus, his beloved among women, resting beneath a beech tree, and delights his flock with the pleasant sound".[26]

The publication of *Pleasant Places* came at a time when other print publishers were beginning to flood the market with landscape prints of all kinds, but even so the thirst for novelty in landscape views remained undiminished. One of the most prolific artists of this period was Jan van Goyen (1596–1656) based in Haarlem. A near contemporary of Claude Lorrain, van Goyen made many sketches of the scenic countryside around Haarlem, Leiden and The Hague, of which over 800 drawings survive. These were used as the 'raw materials' for his paintings and though like Claude, van Goyen rearranged the buildings, trees, boats and bridges to suit his compositional requirements, the resulting paintings were very different. Instead of portraying 'nostalgic visions' of an Ideal landscape, van Goyen painted ordinary scenes – the grandeur of the Italian renaissance art was replaced by the intimacy and modesty of the Dutch landscape. The landscape was reduced to sand, mud, water, reed and trees painted with a minimalist palette of tonal colours, ochres, browns, metallic greys and aqueous green. Along with other realist artists, van Goyen's achievement was to portray an image of the everyday landscape, populated by people going about their daily lives. Just as Virgil, had discovered how an accumulation of detailed observations, however commonplace in themselves, could create a great panoramic picture, so to did van Goyen. In *Pleasant Places* Gibson suggests the artists were examining the world around them and discovering there was something worth studying, recording and celebrating: "The Netherlands was a new country, like America, discovering itself and in fact making itself". This can be seen in a *View of Haarlem and the Haarlemmer Meer* (Plate 21), a panoramic view which depicts a flat, featureless landscape on the edge of town. Critics like John Ruskin said much later "nothing happens in these pictures" except some indifferent person asks the way of somebody else and who, by "his caste of countenance, is unlikely to know".[27] Closer inspection reveals this to be a pastoral landscape in the making; the mill is pumping water from the meer, exposing the sandy seabed, while cattle graze at the water's edge and hay is cut from newly formed land. Small figures huddle together on the higher ground observing the change and disappearance of the old landscape.

The final stage in the creation of the Dutch landscape was portrayed by Paulus Potter in his many pastoral scenes of the polder landscape. These have no allusions to classical Arcadia or the idealised tradition of Italian landscape painting. In the *Young Bull* the herdsman stands under a pollarded willow with his cattle and sheep, whilst the rest of the animals graze in the reclaimed polder behind (Plate 22). Its location on the edge of town, the church of Rijswijk is just visible on the skyline, establishes the painting's pastoral credentials. Potter was noted for the precise realism in his meticulously finished paintings and would enliven his meadows with frogs, lizards, poppies and butterflies and carefully rendered cloud formations. The sharply focused details in Potter's work stem, in part, from a widespread cultural fascination with advances in the optical sciences. It was specifically the improvement of lenses and the development of the telescope and microscope around 1600 that inspired any number of illustrations analyzing the structure of plants, animals and insects.

The motif of the animal piece became very important during the course of the seventeenth century and Potter was among the most influential of the Dutch artists in developing this genre. Before Potter animals appeared frequently in art as an incidental part of landscapes or history paintings, but rarely as the principal subject of a work. The cow acquired a prominence due to a variety of associations. With new agricultural advances, the development of the dairy industry boomed and contributed to the country's financial prosperity. As a result, cattle were a source of patriotic and economic pride and appear in numerous emblem books and literary works as symbols of fertility, wealth and the earth. The farmers' close contact with nature was regarded as a georgic "emblem of virtue, peace and freedom".[28] In his poem *Hofwijk* Huygens compared the landowner to the "wise and moderate cow". Even Carel van Mander instructed painters to be aware of all the physical details that distinguished various types and breeds. Thus the cow, traditionally the symbol for the earth, came to symbolise the prosperity of the Netherlands.

PLATE 20 *(left)*.
Adriaen van der Velde
(1636–1672): *Family in
Landscape c.1667.*

PLATE 21 *(below)*. Jan
van Goyen (1596–1656):
*View of Haarlem and the
Haarlemmer Meer c.1646.*

PLATE 22 *(above)*. Paulus Potter (1625–1654): *Young Bull* c.1647.

PLATE 23 *(right)*. Rembrandt van Rijn (1606–1669): *View of Omval* c.1650.

Rembrandt – the master of naturalism

Rembrandt was the supreme artist of the naturalism, working in all three mediums, drawings, prints and paintings, combining a pastoral vision with both real and imaginary scenes of the Dutch landscape. His pretty shepherds were a long way from most "Dutch variations on the *Concert Champetre* theme, which were courtly and light hearted in character".[29] They were given an earthy, even crude, realism depicting scenes and situations that could have been encountered anywhere in the Dutch countryside. In *Het Schilderboeck* van Mander had suggested that Titian's woodcuts could provide valuable models for Northern artists and Rembrandt was certainly aware of the Venetian graphic, pastoral tradition. In his etching *View of Omval* (Plate 23), Rembrandt recasts the contrast of town and country in a way that is unmistakably Dutch, in mood and character.

But Rembrandt's vision, like that of other Dutch realist artists, is not all it seems, for the creators of these images were presenting a view of the world their urban patrons wished to see. The major enterprises transforming the Dutch landscape, land improvement and reclamation projects, were not often included in pastoral scenes and the harsh reality of farm life was overlooked. Instead the paintings portrayed a bucolic landscape in which country folk amble along a country lane, lean over a farm gate exchanging the pleasantries of the day or stand idly by a tree. This was the world the town dweller wanted to see and, by extension, imagine himself enjoying these innocent pleasures. The fact that Potter's bull is a composite; with the horns of a 2-year-old, the teeth of a 4-year-old, the shoulders of a fully grown animal and rear of a young bull, would have been of little importance to the urban viewer. The paintings fulfilled the same purpose as the *Idylls* of Theocritus, providing a temporary escape from the pressures of the city and for the more serious, a place of leisure with an opportunity for contemplation and study. As Ann Jensen Adams said "the Dutch attempted to work out their urban anxieties, in political, economic and religious spheres, through landscape painting".[30] The bucolic image of the cow and rural vistas was the perfect emblem of a country at peace and stood-in for an interest in nature, as well as economic prosperity. Dutch realist paintings represented a powerful emotional combination; a satisfaction of the nostalgic desire for the countryside with a patriotic fervour for a country, seeking to establish its identity after the struggles with Spain. Just as Virgil had used the patriotism of the humble farmer, his farm and work in the *Georgics*, as a metaphor for the strength of Rome, so in Holland, the pastoral was broadened into a landscape tradition that stemmed from an intense national feeling of pride for the land and its people.

In so doing, as Edward Norgate painter, musician and writer on art acknowledged, the Dutch had invented *landskip*, as a subject in its own right. "There is", he remarked "an art so new in England and so lately come ashore, as all language within our seas cannot find it a Name but uses a borrowed one from a people that are not great lenders but upon good Securitie, the Dutch".[31] Artists like Van Goyen, and the etchings of Rembrandt were to teach the next and subsequent generations of townspeople to see landscape in terms of the "picturesque in a simple scene". These ideas and images quickly took hold of European imagination and they were to play an important part in the advance of the pastoral tradition in England, influencing both The Picturesque and the early nineteenth century Romantic poets and painters. The homely, simple landscapes of the Dutch realist artists also helped establish the notion of the countryside as a playground for urban recreation and, as the art historian Ernst Gombrich observed "many a rambler in the countryside who delights in what he sees may, without knowing it, owe his joy to those humble masters who first opened our eyes to unpretentious natural beauty".

Notes and References

1. The middle classes, as well as the Regents, were the main beneficiaries of the growing prosperity, profiting from a world-wide trade that saw the Dutch republic emerge as one of the greatest maritime powers in world history.
2. Gibson, W. S., *Pleasant Places*. University of California Press, London, 2000, p. 28.
3. Schama, S., *The Embarrassment of Riches: an interpretation of Dutch culture in the Golden Age*. University of California Press, Berkeley, 1987, p. 45.
4. Bacon, F., *New Atlantis 1626*. In *Ideal Commonwealths*. P. F. Collier & Son, New York, 1901.
5. Pepper, D., *The Roots of Modern Environmentalism*. Croom Helm, London, 1984, p. 56.
6. Cafritz, R., 'Netherlandish reflections of the Venetian landscape tradition', in *Places*

     of Delight: the pastoral landscape. Cafritz, R. *et al.* The Phillips Collection and George Weidenfield & Nicolson, London, 1998, p. 115.

7.   Gibson, W. S., *op. cit.,* p. 131.

8.   Kettering, A., *The Dutch Arcadia.* Boydell Press, Ipswich, 1983, p. 122.

9.   *Ibid.,* p. 82.

10.   Brown, C., *Dutch Landscape: the early years.* National Gallery, London, 1986, p. 44.

11.   Kettering, A., *op. cit.,* p. 22.

12.   Schenkeveld-van der Dussen, M. A. 'Nature and landscape in Dutch Literature of the Golden Age', in Brown, C., *op. cit.,* p. 76.

13.   Kettering, A., *op.cit.,* p. 26.

14.   The word *hofwijk* is a portmanteau word which can be translated as 'place' (*wijck*) with a 'garden' (*hof*), as well as a place where one could 'avoid' or 'retire' (*wijck*) from the 'court' (*hof*) of Orange.

15.   Quoted in 'The Anglo-Dutch Garden in the Age of William and Mary', Hunt, J. D. and de Jong, E. (eds), *Journal of Garden History* 8(2 & 3), 1988, p. 199.

16.   Brown *op. cit.,* p. 77.

17.   Levesque, C., *Journey Through Landscape in Seventeenth Century Holland.* Pennsylvania State University, Philadelphia, 1955, p. 96.

18.   Huygens, C., *Hofwijck* 1653, lines 1064–8.

19.   Quoted in 'The Anglo-Dutch Garden in the Age of William and Mary', Hunt, J. D. and de Jong (eds), *op. cit.,* p. 16. The *Den Nederlandtsen Houvenier* (the Dutch Gardener) was published in 1699 and went through nine printings before 1721, indicating the popularity of ideas about horticulture, garden architecture and 'life in the Netherlands countryside' towards the end of the 17th century.

20.   *Ibid.,* p. 21.

21.   Parival, J. N. de, *Les Delices de la Hollande.* Abraham à Geervliet, Leiden, 1651.

22.   Brown, *op. cit.,* p. 26.

23.   *Ibid.,* p. 39.

24.   Quoted in Gibson, *op. cit.,* p. 118.

25.   *Ibid.,* p. xxvi.

26.   *Ibid.,* p. 131.

27.   *Ibid.,* p. 118.

28.   Quoted in *Shift.* Walsh, A., *Paulus Potter: His Works and Their Meaning,* 1985, PhD diss., Columbia University, NY.

29.   Cafritz, R., *op. cit.,* p. 133.

30.   Quoted by Turnbull, A. in 'The Horse in the Landscape'. *Shift* Issue 3, 2010, p. 8.

31.   Sutton, P. C., *Masters of 17th Century Dutch Landscape Painting.* Herbert Press, London, 1987, p. 119. Edward Norgate made these remarks in *Miniatura,* first published in 1627–8 and substantially revised in 1648.

CHAPTER SEVEN

Changes to the Pastoral Vision in Eighteenth-Century England

In the latter part of the seventeenth century many in England still adhered to medieval theology. In *The Sacred Theory of the Earth* (1681) Thomas Burnett would speak of "man inhabiting a ruin, a deformed, sick senescent world". The damage had been caused by the Deluge as the Almighty's punishment for original sin and restoration would only begin after purification of the earth by fire and a return to the primitive state. Before any wider appreciation of the natural world could take place a fundamental change was required in the way Nature was perceived. That change began 6 years later when Isaac Newton published the *Principia* (1685) accounting "for all the motions of the planets, the comets, the moon and the sea". It was not that Newton disagreed with Burnett, but he argued that the world was full of mysteries and unanswered questions that sensible men did not need to explain. In future men should not concern themselves with the question of 'why' only the practical question of 'how'. In separating science from theology and providing an explanation of nature's workings, Newton helped to finally overthrow medieval cosmology and open the way to a more scientific understanding of the world. After the publication of the *Principia* there was a frenzy of scientific activity and slowly the dogma and suspicion of the older religion was replaced by critical scepticism and openness to new ideas. As Alexander Pope later said:

> Nature and Nature's laws lay hid in Night
> God said, let Newton be! and all was light.

Only 9 years after Burnet's gloomy description, John Ray, the father of English natural history and botany, provided a thoroughly different account of creation. In *The Sacred Theory of Man* (1690) Ray sought to explain the making of the earth within the framework of the biblical account of creation. He accepted the cataclysmic origins of the earth, arguing this was necessary to transform Man from his most abject and stupid behaviour and restore sense and reason. After the Deluge God made the earth niggardly so that man had to labour by the sweat of his brow, so inducing values of frugality, sobriety and discipline. This was in no way a punishment but necessary to bring about the rightness of man's relationship to God and his munificence.[1] What all writers agreed on was the benevolence of Nature which had now come to be seen as an expression of God's goodness to creation and to Man.

The third Earl of Shaftesbury

The enlightened, which included the educated sons of most of the English aristocracy, now sought scientific explanations for everyday phenomena. But whilst this mechanical view of the world led to an increasing mastery over nature, some believed it gave little justification for the arts, or the satisfaction of the artist. Foremost among the critics was Anthony Ashley Cooper, the third Earl of Shaftesbury (1670–1713), and in the *Characteristics of Men, Manners, Opinions, Times* (1711) he sought to establish an entirely new perception of the natural world, and aesthetic of nature, by replacing the analogy of a mechanical universe with a return to the time-honoured Christian analogy of God as the supreme artist. By raising art to the level of divine activity, the artist was akin to God, working in the same way, if at a lower level. In reaching this conclusion, the image of the natural world as an evil, fallen world, came to be replaced by an appreciation of the world as a revelation of the goodness and beauty of the Godhead. Nature was not to be seen as something to be exploited and utilised for man's benefit, but regarded as a work of art, giving onlookers the same kind of pleasure, on a larger scale, as they would derive from contemplating a human work of art.[2] And most important, the natural world was no longer regarded as a conglomeration of meaningless elements but a harmonious whole in which all the parts subserve a totality which is good. In a statement that predates the Gaia theory of the earth by more than two and a half centuries, Shaftesbury stated that:

> All things in the world are united. For as the branch is united with the tree, so is the tree immediately with the earth, air, and water, which feed it. As much as the fertile mould is fitted to the tree, as much as the strong and upright trunk of the oak or elm is fitted to the twining branches of the vine or ivy; so much are the very leaves, the seeds, and fruits of these tress fitted to the various animals; those again to one another and to the elements where they live, and to which they are, as appendices, in the manner fitted and joined, as either wings for the air, fins for the water, feet for the earth, and by other correspondent inward parts of a more curious frame and texture. Thus contemplating all on earth, we must of necessity view all in one, as holding on to a common stock. Thus too in the system of the bigger world. See there what is the mutual dependency of things!, the relationship of one to another, of the sun to this inhabited earth, and of the earth and other planets to the sun! the order, union and coherence of the whole! and know my ingenious friend, that by this survey you will be obliged to own the universal system and coherent scheme of things to be established on abundant proof, capable of convincing any fair and just contemplator of the works of Nature.[3]

Shaftesbury argued that the whole of nature should be an object of contemplation and all its features a source of aesthetic delight, including an appreciation of the awful, the rugged and horrible aspects as well as the more gentle and traditionally admired features. In *The Moralists*, the third part of the Characteristics, Shaftesbury was unequivocal of his own change in outlook:

I shall no longer resist the passion growing within me for things of a natural kind; where neither Art nor the Conceit or Caprice of man has spoiled the genuine Order by breaking upon the Primitive State. Even the rude rocks, the mossy Caverns , the irregular unwrought Grottos and broken Falls of water with all the horrid graces of Wilderness itself … appear with a magnificence beyond the formal mockery of princely gardens.[4]

Shaftesbury's optimistic view of harmony within nature and between man and the natural world was a restatement of the classical, Arcadian understanding of the world.

Joseph Addison – the natural landscape

The person who did much to popularise the philosophical ideas of the *Characteristics* and open the way to a new, wider perception of nature was the essayist Joseph Addison (1672–1719). As C. S. Lewis observed, Addison was very much a man of the new order; he stood at the dividing line between the barbarous past, when man feared the violence of nature he could neither understand nor control and the heyday of Wordsworth when man thought he understood nature and could master it whilst exalting in its beauty.

Addison was born and lived for the first 11 years of his life in the remote Wiltshire hamlet of Milston: "in the muddy bottom of the upper Avon valley".[5] During those years Addison developed a deep rooted love of the countryside and lifelong interest in the wild flowers, trees and birds he would praise later in his essays. This enthusiasm for nature continued at Oxford University where he read whatever works of natural history were available. And at a time when the countryside was still looked upon as crude and nature something to be tamed, Addison's instinct was to draw closer to wild nature whenever the opportunity arose. On one occasion, in 1711, when contemplating a month in the country, Addison expressed a desire to sleep out of doors. To which his friend Wortley, who tolerated Addison's eccentric feelings for nature, humoured him by saying he was "not sure we shall have leave to lodge (sleep) out of the house but we may eat in the woods every day if you like it".[6]

Addison's enthusiasm for the countryside was strengthened at Oxford by reading the *Georgics* and the pastorals, and he regretted there was no English equivalent. This encouraged him to write to John Dryden who had published a translation of the *Georgics* in 1697. After his graduation in 1699, Dryden obtained a government pension for Addison, making it possible for him to go on an extended Grand Tour. During the Tour Addison visited and studied the gardens of palaces and great houses in Italy and France; in Geneva he made excursions around the lake, even climbing mountains, all the while collecting and naming plants. In an essay in the Tatler (1709), Addison recalled those days, referring to a dream vision wherein he wandered through an "alpine landscape enclosing plains which by their beauty and variety surpassed everything he knew".[7] During this time his appreciation of natural scenery, always acute by the standards of the age, underwent a rapid development and showed itself to be far ahead of his contemporaries, with the exception of Shaftesbury:

> If we consider the works of nature and art, as they are qualified to entertain the imagination, we shall find the last very defective in comparison of the former; for though they may sometimes appear as beautiful or strange, they can have nothing in them of that vastness and immensity, which afford so great an entertainment to the mind of the beholder. – The one may be as polite and delicate as the other, but can never show herself so august and magnificent in the design. There is something more bold and masterly in the rough careless strokes of nature than in the nice touches and embellishments of art. The beauties of the most stately garden or palace lie in a narrow compass, the imagination immediately runs them over, and requires something else to gratify her; but in the wide fields of nature the sight wanders up and down without confinement, and is fed with an infinite variety of images without any certain stint or number. For this reason we always find the poet in love with a country life, where nature appears in the greatest perfection, and furnishes out all those scenes that are most apt to delight the imagination.[8]

At the core of Addison's new perception of Nature was Locke's insistence that our physical vision is the agent of our ideas, especially when experiencing a variety of landscapes. In his essay *Concerning Human Understanding* (1690) Locke explained how sense stimuli – notably what we see – provided the mind with simple ideas, which are afterwards compared and combined with more complex ones.[9] Though Locke emphasised that association was an unusual activity which "hinders man from seeing and examining", this did not stop the adoption and application of this psychological theory by painters and designers of landscape gardens. By providing a spectator with certain stimuli, such as images or inscriptions in a garden, one might revive in the mind a whole range of ideas, combining them with ideas already lodged there from previous encounters – with gardens, the paintings of Claude, the classical texts of Virgil and so forth. So in the eighteenth century Augustan age, the defining characteristic of gardens became the elements, incidents and markers designed to trigger such associations. In his essay on the *Imagination*, Addison was quite explicit in making this connection, and in doing so he set out a far-seeing prophesy of how the landscape would eventually be seen by Wordsworth and the Romantics a century later:

> ... a particular Smell or Colour is able to fill the mind, on a sudden, with the Picture of the Fields or Gardens, where we first met with it, and to bring up into View all the Variety of Images that once attended it. Our imagination takes the Hint, and leads us unexpectedly into Cities, or Theatres, Plains or Meadows.[10]

The importance of a varied landscape in stimulating this sequence of mental ideas is a constant theme, "the perpetually shifting" movement of water was a particular preoccupation:

> ... there is nothing that more enlivens a Prospect than Rivers, Jetteaus, or Falls of Water, where every Scene is perpetually shifting and entertaining the Sight at every Moment with something that is new. We are quickly tired with looking upon Hills

and Valleys, where everything continues fixt and settled in the same Place and Posture, but find our Thoughts a little agitated and relieved at the sight of such objects as are ever in motion.[11]

The Kit Kat Club and the pastoral debate

On his return from the Grand Tour Addison fell-in with a group of Whiggish writers and intellectuals and together they established the Kit Kat Club. Its membership included his friend and fellow essayist, Richard Steele and Lord Cobham of Stowe, owner of one of the largest country estates in England, as well the third Earl of Carlisle, owner of Castle Howard. The group fostered the belief that, following the upheavals of the Civil War, the Glorious Revolution of 1688 had seen the absolute monarchy abolished, parliamentary control firmly established and England, like the Rome of the first Augustan age, was embarking on a Golden Age. They described themselves as 'patriots', championing liberalism, and setting a greater stock in private property rather than governmental or monarchic control. These new Augustans were lead subscribers to Dryden's translation of the works of Virgil (Plate 24). Dryden's complete translation of Virgil included an extensive commentary on the *Georgics* written by Addison in which he took pains to point out that critics largely ignored the *Georgics* or confused it with the pastoral. Addison defined the poem as "some part of the science of husbandry put into pleasing dress, and set off with all the Embellishments of poetry".

In the early decades of the eighteenth century the pastoral had become an emotive literary and political subject, much discussed in London coffee houses. One particular argument raged around which was better, ancient or modern scholarship. The debate had been sparked by Dryden whose aim, in his translation, had been "to make Virgil speak such English as he would himself have spoken if he had been born in England, and in this present age".[12] Opposing sides were divided over whether pastoral should include modern English shepherds, set in a typically English environment, speaking in a rustic English dialect in imitation of Theocritus' *Idylls*. This was dubbed the Rationalist theory of pastoral. Or if it should be predominantly an imitation of Virgil's *Eclogues*, having elegant shepherds set in a more traditional pastoral environment speaking simply and elegantly, this was regarded as the Neoclassic theory of pastoral. In this debate, the pastorals of the minor poet Ambrose Philips represented the Rational pastoral theory, and those of Alexander Pope the Neoclassical pastorals, both forms were published in 1709.

Thomas Tickell, a minor poet under the patronage of Addison, was in no doubt that writers of the English pastoral should "introduce certain changes from the ancients" in the interest of probability. "The cornucopia of foreign fruits" which decorates so much pastoral should, said Tickell, "be replaced by kingcups, endives and daisies. The classical Gods must give way to English fays; and superstitions, proverbial sayings, names, customs, sports and language must

Great father Bacchus! to my song repair:
For clust'ring grapes are thy particular care:
For thee large bunches load the bending vine;
and the last blesssings of the year are thine.

Dryden *Georgics* 2, 5–8

PLATE 24. John Dryden's
Georgics of Virgil. First
Subscribers edition – the
illustrations drew heavily
on Dutch paintings.

all be of English peasantry". "How much more pleasing", Tickell asked, "is the
following scene to an English Reader!":

> This Place may seem for Shepherds leisure made,
> So lovingly these Elms unite their Shade.
> Th' ambitious Woodbine, how it climbs to breathe
> Its balmy Sweets around on all beneath![13]

Pope's Pastorals, written when he was only sixteen, transposed Arcadia to
Windsor Forest, a place where he had received "his education as a boy":[14]

> First in these fields I try the sylvan strains, Nor blush to sport on Windsor's blissful
> plains: Fair Thames, flow gently from thy sacred spring, While on thy banks Sicilian
> Muses sing; Let vernal airs through trembling osiers play, And Albion's cliffs resound
> the rural lay.[15]

Pope implies that the English pastoral environment overshadows the traditional
Arcadian locale of previous poets and ancient culture yields to the modern – a
significant statement for a poet considered to represent classical values. But
in explaining his theory of the Pastoral in the *Discourse on Pastoral Poetry*
(1717), Pope argued that any depictions of shepherds and their mistresses in
the pastorals must not be updated shepherds, that they must be Icons of the
Golden Age. "We are not to describe our shepherds as shepherds as at this day
they really are, but as they may be conceived then to have been, when the best
of men followed the employment".

Addison and his colleagues believed modern English writers were the true progeny of the Ancients: "If we look into the Writings of the old Italians, such as Cicero and Virgil", Addison states, "we shall find that the English Writers, in their way of thinking and expressing themselves, resemble those Authors much more than the modern Italians pretend to do".[16] Modern English writers were thought to be part of the proper lineage of pastoral poets: pastoral began with Theocritus, was followed by Virgil, then Spenser, and finally culminated in Pope and Philips. Thomas Tickell expressed this most clearly, in his Guardian essay: Theocritus "left his Dominions to Virgil, Virgil left his to his Son Spencer, and Spencer was succeeded by his eldest-born Philips".[17] The omission of Italian Renaissance poets was not an accident for their artifice was considered contrary to both the Rational and Neoclassic pastoral theories.

Ambrose Philip's Pastorals were not particularly awful poems but they did reflect his desire to 'update' the pastoral and satisfy a contemporary taste. It is easy to understand why promoting Philip's poems over Pope's might suit Addison and his colleagues. Philip's pastorals represented exactly what they wanted to see: all things English over all things foreign. Of course, things are never that simple. A closer comparison of Philip's and Pope's pastorals reveals they have almost as many commonalities as they have differences, and certainly Pope's pastorals cannot be said to promote foreign values and features over native English ones. It is true that Philip's shepherds have the English rustic names Cuddy and Colinet, and Pope's characters have the Italianate names Damon and Daphnis, but both sets of nymphs and swains live in an idyllic English landscape. And whilst Philip's shepherds speak "mummerset"[18] and Pope's swains use simple and elegant modern English, both poets promote an English pastoral concept within an English seasonal environment, with winter and death appearing prominently in both.

However Addison and the Rationalist poets had created a serious literary problem. In making the Pastoral more English they had introduced the very concerns for work and management of the countryside that Virgil's *Eclogues* specifically excluded. As it was not possible to go against the authority of Virgil and the pastoral convention, as understood in England and throughout aristocratic circles in Europe, the way out of this dilemma was to adopt the *Georgics* as the model for the countryside in Georgian England. "The *Georgics*", wrote Addison "(have) given us a collection of the most delightful landscapes that can be made out of the fields and woods, herds of cattle, swarms of bees". Indeed these natural scenes, in reality the farmed landscape, were preferable to the designed landscape:

> ... there are several of these wild scenes that are more delightful than any artificial shows, yet we find the works of nature still more pleasant, the more they resemble those of art,

and

> ... hence it is that we take delight in a prospect which is well laid out, and diversified with fields and meadows, woods and rivers.[19]

The Pastoral as a critique

From the time of William and Mary's arrival in February 1689, the Court in London had ceased to exist and in the ensuing vacuum the English nobility rediscovered the ancient pleasures of villeggiatura. Owners and visitors alike would often describe country estates as idyllic retreats. England was considered not only a legitimate setting for Arcadia, but Arcadia was located in the present, on the country estates of the Nobility. In time honoured fashion the estate created an atmosphere conducive to the patron's relaxation, a place where he could escape the demands of daily city life in favour of enjoying the natural aesthetic, in a variety of ways. And the estate owner, living a relaxed and recreational lifestyle in harmony with his so-called 'natural' surroundings where nature rightfully provides for his every need, was seen as the metaphorical shepherd promoted in pastoral literature. But for Addison, and his fellow patriots, owning these pastoral oases was more than simply a benign expression of wealth and status, pastoral imagery was in essence a very literal expression of political power. In the early eighteenth century agriculture was the primary source of employment and wealth. It was assumed that with financial viability and responsibility came political power and the first Land Qualification Bill in 1696 required every Member of Parliament to have substantial landed property as a condition of taking his seat. But there was more, those who could afford to retire to the country, and yet design or maintain their country estate landscapes in imitation of foreign styles, were perceived by the patriots as supporters of despotism, in the case of French antecedents and the Papacy, for those imitating the Italians.[20] Thus posing a threat to what Addison and his friends perceived to be proper, patriotic English values. Whereas those who adopted a more natural style of garden design were considered friends of civil liberty. And, so the argument ran, if land equals power and pastoral equals the landscape garden, then the type of pastoral environment represented in the design of landscape is a reflection of the symbolic basis of the power of the landowner. As Pope put it:

> But we, brave Britons, Foreign Laws despis'd and let their new landscape
>   garden proclaim their
> freedom from tyranny, oppression, and autocracy.[21]

In 1712 Addison launched an attack on the extent of the foreign influence in English gardens:

> Our British Gardeners, ... instead of humouring Nature, love to deviate from it as much as possible. Our Trees rise in Cones, Globes, and Pyramids. We see the Marks of the Scissors upon every Plant and Bush. I do not know whether I am singular in my Opinion, but, for my own part, I would rather look upon a Tree in all its Luxuriancy and Diffusion of Boughs and Branches, than when it is thus cut and trimmed into a Mathematical Figure; and cannot but fancy that an Orchard in Flower looks infinitely more delightful, than all the little Labyrinths of the [more] finished Parterre.[22]

Addison's critique of those foreign garden in France and Italy was not totally dismissive, as John Dixon Hunt has shown. In fact both Addison and Shaftesbury believed that both the natural and the artificial had their place in garden design:

> On this account our English gardens are not so entertaining to the fancy as those in France and Italy, where we see a large extent of ground covered over with an agreeable mixture of garden and forest, which represent everywhere an artificial rudeness much more charming than that neatness and elegancy which we meet with in those of our own country. It might, indeed, be of ill consequence to the public, as well as unprofitable to private persons, to alienate so much ground from pasturage and the plough in many parts of a country that is so well peopled, and cultivated to a far greater advantage. But why may not a whole estate be thrown into a kind of garden by frequent plantations, that may turn as much to the profit as the pleasure of the owner? A marsh overgrown with willows, or a mountain shaded with oaks, are not only more beautiful, but more beneficial, than when they lie bare and unadorned. Fields of corn make a pleasant prospect, and if the walks were a little taken care of that lie between them, if the natural embroidery of the meadows were helped and improved by some small additions of art, and the several rows of hedges set off by trees and flowers that the soil was capable of receiving, a man might make a pretty landscape of his own possessions.[23]

It has been suggested that Addison's apparent championing of French and Italian gardens was because they were free "from the niceties of Dutch design, which dominated England", and was by inference an attack on the continuing Dutch influence that had arrived with William and Mary.

Addison and the natural garden

Addison's own ambitions were more modest. In 1712 Addison purchased Bilston Hall, near Rugby prompted partly by the political necessity of the Land Qualification Act, and in part, a desire to live a little closer to his ideal of an Augustan statesman, escaping "the heats of Rome in summer". He wanted the pattern of his life to confirm to the Roman concept of virtuous citizenship: "I cannot but think that the very contemplacency and satisfaction which a man takes in these works of nature to be laudable, if not virtuous habit of mind ...". Addison's had a genuine love and knowledge of the English countryside, a dislike of artifice, and believed in the need for Variety to stimulate the mind by association. All of this is apparent from a description of his own garden:

> I have several acres around my house, which I call my garden, and which a skilful gardener would not know what to call. It is a confusion of kitchen and parterre, orchard and flower garden, which lie so mixt and interwoven with one another, that if a foreigner, who had seen nothing of our country, should be conveyed into my garden at his first landing, he would look upon it as a natural wilderness, and one of the uncultivated parts of our country. My flowers grow up in several parts of the garden in the greatest luxury and profusion. I am so far from being fond of any particular one, by reason of its rarity, that if I meet one in a field which pleases me, I give it a place in my garden. By this means when a stranger walks with me, he is

surprised to see several large spots of ground covered with ten thousand colours, & has often singled out flowers he might have met under a common hedge, in a field, or in a meadow, assume of the greatest beauties of the place. The only method I observe in this particular, is to range in the same quarter the products of the same seasons, that they might make their appearance together, and compose a picture of the greatest variety ... I must not omit, that there is a wandering rill, ... I have taken care to let it run in the same manner as it would in an open field, so that it generally passes through banks of violets and primroses, plats of willow or other plants, that seem to be of its own producing.

There is another circumstance of which I am very particular, or, as my neighbours call me, very whimsical: as my garden invites into it all the birds of the country ... I do not suffer anyone to destroy their nests in spring, or drive them from their usual haunts in fruit time; I value my garden more for being full of blackbirds than cherries, and frankly give them fruit for their songs. By this means I always have the music of the season in its perfection.[24]

Nothing remains of the garden at Bilston today, except perhaps for two magnificent evergreen oaks standing near the entrance. Addison loved to plant trees, and perhaps these were intended as a reminder of the sacred grove of oaks that marked the sanctuary of Zeus (*Georgics* I, 149).

Addison's Essays were a part of the literary, pastoral tradition that had begun with Pliny the younger and they would continue to stimulate a preference for more natural gardens in harmony with their surrounding, long after his death in 1719. By then the landscape had become the topic of polite conversion in drawing rooms, coffee houses and at the dinner table. It was a debate that would have far reaching consequences not just for gardens but the whole of the pastoral landscape.

Notes and References

1. Ray. J., *The wisdom of God manifested in the works of the creation.* Facsimile of the 1826 Ray Society, p. 165. Ray is considered the father of English natural history and botany.
2. Brett, R. L., *The Third Earl of Shaftesbury.* Hutchinson University Press, London, 1951, p. 157.
3. Cooper, A., Earl of Shaftesbury., *Characteristics of men, manners, opinions, times.* Indianapolis, Liberty Fund, 2001, 2, pp. 64–5.
4. Quoted in *The Genius of the Place*, Hunt, J. D. and Willis, P. (eds). Paul Elek, London, 1975, p. 124.
5. Smithers, P., *The Life of Joseph Addison.* Oxford University Press, London, 1968, p. 1.
6. *Ibid.*, p. 226.
7. Addison, J., Essay no. 161. *Tatler.* Thursday, 20 April, 1709, p. 157.
8. *Ibid.*
9. Hunt, J. D., *The Figure in the Landscape.* John Hopkins University Press, London, 1976, p. 47.
10. *Ibid.*, pp. 63–4.
11. *Ibid.*
12. Quoted in Williams, R. D. and Pattie, T. S., *Virgil: his poetry through the ages.* British Library, London, 1982, p. 118.
13. Tickell, T., *Guardian* 30. 15 April, 1713.

14. Martin, P., *Pursing Innocent Pleasures: the gardening world of Alexander Pope*. Archon Books, Hamden, Connecticut, 1984, p. xxi.

15. Pope, A., *Spring. The First Pastoral* lines 1–4, 1709. www.humanitiesweb.org

16. Addison, J., *Spectator*. 5 and 6 March, 1711.

17. Tickell, T., *op. cit*. Edmund Spencer (1552–1599) was an Elizabethan poet whose works included the pastoral poem *Shepheardes Calender* (1579)

18. Neufeldt, T., 'Italian Pastoral Opera and Pastoral Politics in England, 1705–1712', in *Discourses in Music* 5(2), Fall 2004.

19. Addison, J., *Spectator* 414. Wednesday, 25 June 1712.

20. Baridon, M., 'The gentleman as gardener: Pope, Shenstone, Mason' in Carré. J. (ed.), *The Crisis of Courtesy: studies in the conduct-book in Britain, 1600–1900*. E. J. Brill, New York, 1994, p. 134.

21. Quoted in Hunt, J. D., *The Figure in the Landscape. op. cit.*, p. 63.

22. Addison, J., *Spectator* 414 Wednesday, 25 June, 1712.

23. Addison, J., *Spectator* 415 Thursday, 26 June, 1712.

24. Addison, J. *Spectator* 477, 6 September ,1712. In reality, Addison's garden may not have been as natural as he described; Addison's daughter said after his death it "preserved all the formality of the old taste".

CHAPTER EIGHT

Arcadia
and the Pastoral Landscape Realised

In the spring of 1719 the poet Alexander Pope took up residence at Twickenham by the river Thames. Until the Tudor period, the Thames landscape between Hampton and Kew consisted largely of quiet riverside villages, orchards and market gardens supplying the capital with food. Then, following the construction of Richmond and Hampton Court Palaces, the landscape began to evolve as successive royal and aristocratic families moved to the area. Up and down the river a series of great palaces, houses, gardens and hunting parks were constructed amid the water meadows and woodland, linked to one another by grand avenues of lime trees. In the eighteenth century, this concentration of wealth and power, together with the area's stunning beauty, attracted the most influential thinkers, poets, artists and landscape designers of the day:

> Heavens! what a goodly prospect spreads around,
> Hills, and dales, and woods, and lawns, and spires,
> And glittering towns, and gilded streams, till all
> The stretching landscape into smoke decays!
> Happy Britannia! where the Queen of Arts,
> Inspiring vigour, Liberty, abroad
> Walks, unconfined, even thy furthest cots,
> And scatters plenty with unsparing hand.

Thomson: *The Seasons – Summer*.[1]

Inspired by the Thames, and in particular by the View from Richmond Hill (Plate 25), a radical new way of perceiving beauty in the landscape was born. For the first time a view was seen as a 'collected' whole where villas, gardens, groves and meadows all formed a perfect picturesque scene. These ideas ushered the end of the formality of Tudor and Stuart gardens in favour of a much more romantic landscape where the boundaries between nature, art, poetry and gardening were merged. These new naturalised gardens were imagined at the time as the dawning of a new Arcadian age – the classical imagery of a simple pastoral life as enjoyed in ancient Greece transferred to the banks of the Thames. These ideas led to the formation of the English Landscape Movement that would ultimately spread across Europe.[2] At the centre of this movement was Richard Boyle, the third Earl of Burlington, 'the Apollo of the Arts' who was to take this Arcadian Dream forward in the second half of the Augustan age.

Lord Burlington

Burlington was 20 when he undertook his first Grand Tour in 1714. On his return from Italy Burlington discovered his true mission as an architect and Man of Taste. Inspired by the renaissance architect Andreo Palladio,[3] Burlington went back to Italy fired with enthusiasm and keen to study Palladian architecture.[4] On his return Burlington designed is own Palladian Villa, Chiswick House. Burlington wanted to emulate the Medici's by establishing his own academy of the arts. A few years before, Lord Shaftesbury had famously lamented that, concerning English academies of painting, sculpture and architecture "we have not so much heard of a proposal; whilst the the Prince of our rival nation raises academys, breeds Youth and sends rewards and Pensions into foreign Countrys, to advance the interest and Credits his own". The foreign prince was Louis XIV who had established two academies of painting and architecture in Paris.[5] Chiswick House was to be Burlington's Villa Careggi, the centre of a British renaissance in the arts and culture. In Rome Burlington had met William Kent, then regarded as the "coming-man" in history painting, and the sculptor Guelfi, in the studio of the leading Roman sculptor Camilla Rusconi. Kent took a prominent role in the architecture of Chiswick House, as well as its interiors and designing the gardens in the new natural style. Burlington's patronage also extended to classical poets, like Alexander Pope, who wrote in praise of his mentor:

> You too proceed! make failing art your care,
> Erect new wonders, and the old repair;
> Jones and Palladio to themselves restore,
> And be whatever Vitruvious was before;
> Till kings call forth th'ideas of your mind,
> Proud to accomplish what such hands design'd …[6]

PLATE 25. Autumnal Richmond Hill and the Thames.

and to the highly influential Scottish poet, James Thomson. At first the academy flourished and Burlington could claim that all the liberal arts were reborn at Chiswick in a spirit that emulated the ancients, but the dream faded. By the end of the 1720s the coterie had dispersed, with the exception of William Kent who remained at Chiswick House.

By the 1730s the Palladian style of architecture was widely accepted as the style for British country houses and public buildings, answering Shaftesbury's call for "a national style of house and gardens", as a place where the so-called natural landscape would flourish.[7] But the appearance of that new landscape was far from being from decided. Burlington, and his coterie, were aware that the new Palladian architecture needed an equally new, landscape setting – one

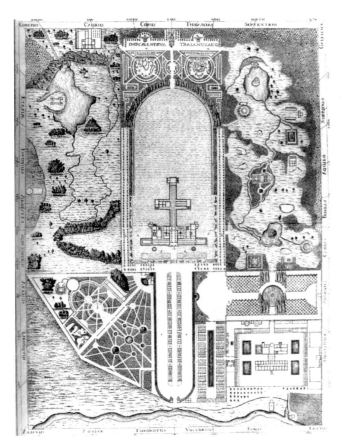

FIGURE 5. Robert Castell: reconstructed plan of an ideal Roman villa, from *The Villas of the Ancients* c.1728.

that carried the imprimatur of traditions derived from modern Italian and ancient Roman antecedents. A pointer towards this new landscape was provided by another member of Burlington's coterie, the architect Robert Castell. His *Villas of the Ancients* (1728) was based on the letters of Pliny the Younger, in which he described the villas at Tusculum and Laurentum.[8] In essence, Castell rediscovered the *villa urbana* surrounded by its georgic landscape (Figure 5). The essential agricultural buildings were dispersed and concealed around a largely informal landscape in which the presence of temples to Ceres, Flora, Bacchus, Luna, Sol, Jupiter, and Venus did not preclude the needs of farming, rather they enhanced it.

Castell's book was widely read and very influential. It helped fuel the imagination of the gentry in Georgian England, many of whom had seen Italian villas, gardens and their surrounding estates, on their Grand Tours to Italy. They believed these villas, ancient and modern, were lived in by a class of people like themselves. And through reading such classical authors as Virgil with his account of farming, Horace's description of his Sabine farm, and Pliny the Younger they developed a vision of villas in ancient Rome. These they saw as unostentatious, on moderately sized country estates, combining an environment of civilised pastoral retreat with a graceful combination of productive agriculture and ornamental horticulture. So by the 1730s, it was popularly believed that the Romans had created their gardens in what was understood to be the natural style.

James Thomson

This vision of a civilised pastoral landscape was given form by the Scottish poet James Thomson; it was "through Thomson that Virgil affected the eighteenth century".[9] Thomson's childhood was spent in the Scottish borders (Plate 26) in a landscape that was to be a major influence on his later life. His biographer, Douglas Grant, believes it was the distinctive upland landscape of gentle rolling hills, that "formed Thomson's eye".[10] When Thomson stood on the high places around his home, and turned his back to the hills, he would have seen laid out before him the long sweep of a delightful pastoral, georgic landscape. While "the English countryside owes its beauty to the cloistered grace of many particulars, a brook, a hedge, a coppice, a beanfield, or a handful of primroses in a hedge", wrote Grant, in:

> the Borders the eye moves down a valley, follows it until it widens and enters another, and continues across a plain which is bounded by the horizon. This landscape is ordered into foreground, middle distance and far distance as though it had been arranged by some great seventeenth century artist, Salvador Rosa or Gaspard Poussin.[11]

These early experiences led Thomson to visualise the landscape as a series of more or less composed pictures. His description of the view from Hagley Park, home of his patron Lord Lyttleton, could almost be description of his childhood landscape (Plate 27):

> Meantime you gain the Height, from whose fair Brow
> The bursting prospect spreads around;
> And snatched o'er Hill and Dale, and Wood and Lawn
> And verdant Field, and darkening heath between,
> And villages embosomed soft in Trees,
> And spiry Towns by surging columns mark'd
> Of rising Smoke, your eye excursive roams-
> Wide-stretching from the Hall in whose kind haunt
> The hospitable Genius lingers still,
> To where the broken Landskip by degrees,
> Ascending, roughens into ridgy Hills;
> O'er which the Cambrian mountains, like far Clouds
> That skirt the blue horizon, dusky rise.
>
> Thomson: *The Seasons – Spring*[12]

Though Thomson was no gardener, he appreciated what these new 'landscape' gardens meant to his poetry, "their usefulness as a means of formulating and shaping his meditations among natural scenery". So much so that garden and landscape experiences become fused, the whole prospect being seen as a 'collected' whole where villas, gardens, groves and meadows all form a perfect picturesque scene, borrowing its grammar and patterns from a Claudian landscape. Christopher Hussey believed Thomson, and his poem *The Seasons,* had a profound effect on the way the landscape was seen and managed. "It was Thomson", he said, along with other "landscape poets", John Gay and John Dyer, who "brought educated men to the stage of landscape appreciation reached by Italian painters".[13] When viewing a landscape, as Hunt explains, "the eye is first hurried hither and thither over a painting, and over a real landscape that painterly tastes have instinctively come to read as paintings, until it either knows the full repertoire of incidents or finds some centre or focus". In Claude's paintings this was often the the horizon and once that has been reached the eye tracks back "lingering over specific items, for their own sakes as well as for their place in the total pattern".[14] Thomson himself gave little indication of having been influenced by any particular painter, but he did acknowledged his debt to Virgil:

There let the Classic Page thy fancy lead
Thro' rural scenes: such as the *Mantuan* Swain
Paints in immortal verse and matchless song.[15]

The Seasons and the Georgic landscape

In *The Seasons* Thomson made use of georgic motives and almost all the georgic conventions but omits the most difficult part of the *Georgics*, the versifying of practical agricultural arts. Instead he describes the occupations of the

PLATE 26. Ruins of the seventeenth century Southdean Parish Church, near Kelso, where James Thomson's father was Church Minister. It is surrounded by the gentle upland landscape familiar to Thomson as a boy.

PLATE 27. A view of Hagley Hall today from the high ground overlooking the park, villages "embosomed soft in in trees" and the distant hills.

farmer in each of the seasons and paints a picture of the fertile, rural, agricultural landscape of England, paying particular attention to rivers, rural pastimes, the diversions of large property owners, inviting retreats, assorted insects, birds, and beasts, both wild and domestic, storms, and a general sense of industry (in the sense of manual labour), improvement, and enlargement in a nation growing in wealth, power and well-being. Throughout he sings the praises of simple country life and in *Autumn,* he describes, in almost Virgil's own words, the existence of the husbandman as being as happy beyond the dreams of the great.

With regard to the natural world there is a change of emphasis however, for whereas Virgil introduced descriptions of nature, chiefly as a background for the husbandman at work, Thomson introduces the farmer and his work chiefly to give life to his descriptions of nature. *The Seasons* is not just one of the first Nature poems, it is an early example of the increasing ability of men and women in the eighteenth century to appreciate and understand Nature scientifically and economically. The microscope, recently developed in the Netherlands, had promoted increasingly careful observation, while words, drawings, and specimens of new plants and animals brought back by wider explorations, were requiring new systems of classification. For Thomson, a son of the Calvinist manse who had studied Divinity, nature was above all else, a manifestation of the power and benevolence of God.

PLATE 28. Kent (and Tardieu): *Spring* – from Thomson's *Seasons c.*1730.

The first complete text of *The Seasons* (1730) was illustrated by William Kent, who was then becoming interested in landscape design. Together, the words and pictures evoke the sensory pleasures of Arcadia in a faintly English setting (Plate 28). The illustration for Spring is a simple Claudian pastoral, the eye is drawn into the landscape by the outstretched arm of a shepherd who points to reed fringed water, like the Mincius river, whilst in the foreground a young swain serenades his lover. The lake is overlooked by a villa which appears to be Palladian extension to an older classical, *villa urbana.* The scene relates more or less to Thomson's verses in, for instance, his description of a walk he took with

Amanda[16] which progresses from "the negligence of Nature, wide and wild" into "the finished garden". In his account Thomson did not follow the Claudian patterns and grammar, but rather he "attempted a new kind of poetry",[17] one that comes closer to the reality of a walk in the English countryside. He conveys detailed impressions of the landscape he was passing through; the Rill oozing through the luxuriant grass, the sweet smell of a bean field and the delights of a flowery mead. All of this Thomson harmonises with the Georgic notion of work, using Virgil's metaphor of the 'fervent bee':

> See, where the winding Vale her lavish stores,
> Irriguous, spreads, See, how the lily drinks
> The Latent Rill, scarce oozing thro' the grass,
> of Growth luxuriant: or humid bank,
> in fair Profusion, decks, Long let us walk,
> Where the Breeze blows from yon extended
> Field of blossom'd Beans.

> Nor is Mead unworthy of thy Foot,
> Full of Fresh verdure, and unumber'd Flowers,
> The negligence of Nature, wide, and wild:
> Where, undistinguished by mimic Art, she spreads
> Unbounded Beauty to the roving eye.

> Here their delicious task the fervent Bees,
> In swarming Millions, tend, Around, athwart,
> Thro' the soft Air, the busy Nations fly'
> Cling to the Bud, and with inserted Tube,
> Suck its pure Essence, its ethereal Soul.
> And oft, with bolder Wing, they soaring dare,
> The purple Heath, or where the Wild-Thyme grows.
> And yellow loads them with luscious Spoil.

> At length the finish'd Garden to the View
> Its Vistas opens, and its alleys green.
> Snatch'd thro' the verdant Maze, the hurried Eye
> Distracted wanders; now the bowery Walk
> of Covert close, where scarce a speck of Day
> Falls on the lengthen'd Gloom, protracted sweeps;
> Now meets the bending Sky; the River now
> Dimpling along, the breezy-ruffled Lake,
> The forest darkening round, the glittering Spire,
> Th'ethereal Mountain and distant Main ....

Thomson *The Seasons – Spring*[18]

In the carefully planned, 'finished' garden Thomson is challenged by the dilemma of making sense of the garden's structure, something familiar to all garden visitors. The eye roams over the various parts, stopping here and there, until, in Thomson's description, it alights, Claude-like, on the distant horizon: "the ethereal mountains and distant main". The elements of nature have been employed, but shaped, to exercise predetermined effects, to elicit, and contain, certain anticipated reactions from visitors as they explore its four-dimensional structure. Thomson suggests the idea of the explorable landscape immediately around them and an inaccessible, "hence ethereal" territory on the horizon.

It was the duty of every artist – whether poet, painter or landscape improver – to reflect the taste of his patron and of the aristocracy in general, in order to maintain the prevailing status quo within society. So it can be assumed that the *The Seasons* reflected the attitudes of the aristocracy towards the landscape in the first half of the eighteenth century. Thomson's landscape is populated with happy haymakers, with swains gathering nuts or ploughing, shepherds and villagers dipping sheep, even a countryman admiring the wonders of the Rainbow.[19] Thomson's message, and that of the ruling oligarchy, was clear – this rural georgic idyll can be achieved by those who work for it. Whether it was the respectable gentleman shooting and fishing for recreation, or the busy citizen who visits the countryside for relaxation or the industrious swain whose rewards are his health guaranteed by the healthy life. And partly because of what it owes to Virgil and partly because the image of the countryside was so refreshing to jaded urban readers, who had never construed a latin line in their lives, it was immensely popular and had a wide influence in England, and beyond in France and Italy, helping to shape the agricultural lore adopted by country gentlemen on their estates and in their gardens.

William Kent and Rousham

The influence of Thomson's descriptive poetry can be traced in the work of his friend William Kent at Rousham, Oxfordshire, a garden which most exemplifies *Ut Pictura Poesis*. Horace Walpole, a near contemporary, described Rousham as "the most engaging of all Kent's works ... it being composed of the sweetest little groves, streams, glades, porticos, cascades and river imaginable". It possesses the same poetic harmony between the world of Arcadia and the apparent reality of the Georgic landscape, as Thomson's verse.

Sir Robert Dormer had bought the estate in the 1630s but the Civil War interrupted the construction of the house. Dormer was a descendent of the Elizabethan courtier and poet Sir Philip Sidney who first "shaped the pastoral vision to his countrymen".[20] Sidney's personal Arcadia was the Wiltshire downs and valleys of the Earl of Pembroke's estates where everything was in harmony and "life itself in a world of beauty is its own rewards":

> Do you not see how all things conspire together to make this country a heavenly dwelling? Do you not see the grassse(s) how in colour they excell the Emeralds, everyone striving to pass his fellow, and yet they are all kept of an equal height? And see you not the rest of the beautiful flowers, each of which would require a man's wit to know, and his life to express? ... Doth not the air breath health, which the Birds (delightful both to the ear and eye) do daily solemnise with the sweet consent of their voices. Is not every *Eccho* thereof a perfect Musicke?[21]

The Dormer family would most certainly have been familiar with Philip Sidney's *Arcadia*; as Royalists they would have known that King Charles the First quoted lines from the poem as he knelt on the scaffold. After Sir Robert Dormer's grandson, Colonel Robert Dormer-Cottrell, inherited Rousham in 1719 he engaged Charles Bridgeman, then the fashionable landscape gardener of the day, to layout the garden in the new and more natural style. After the estate passed to the Colonel's brother General James Dormer-Cotrell,[22] William Kent was commissioned to further enhance and develop Rousham (*c.*1737). Kent was then forty with little experience of garden design but it is likely he was recommended to General Dormer by his friend, and fellow Kit Kat Club member, Lord Burlington of Chiswick House.

Like the villa Mondragone, Rousham was greatly helped by its topography. At rear of the house the land sloped down to the river Cherwell and as the Dormer family could not afford to purchase the land on the far side of river Cherwell, it remained a simple georgic landscape. Kent's genius was to harmonise this wider landscape with the garden, Horace Walpole famous lines "He leapt the fence, and saw that all nature was a garden" continue:

> He felt the delicious contrast of hill and valley changing imperceptibly into each other, tasted the beauty of the gentle swell, or concave swoop, and remarked how loose groves crowned an easy eminence with happy ornament, and while they called in the distant view between their graceful stems, removed and extended the perspective by delusive comparison ... The living landscape was chast'ned or polished, not transformed.[23]

MacClary's tour of the garden

The experience of Rousham was described by the Head Gardener MacClary in a letter to General Dormer-Cotrell. It began as you walked out of the door, on the north side of the Hall where (Figure 6):

> ... you come into a large parterre, the middle of which is a Bowling green, with a Gravel walk all around it, and on each side is a fine Green Terrace Walk, at the end of which is two open groves, back't with two Natural Hillocks planted with Scotch firs, and two Minervas upon terms stand before them, and in the middle stands a lion devouring a horse, upon a very large pedestal, you walk forward to see the Lion nearer, when your eye drops upon a very fine Concave Slope, at the bottom of which runs the Beautiful River Charvell, and at the top stands two pretty garden seats, one on either side, back't with the two Hillocks of Scotch Firs, here you sit down first in one, and then in the other, from whence you have the prettiest view in the whole world, Tho' the most extensive part of it is but short, yet you see from hence five pretty Country Villages, and the Grant Triumphant Arch in Aston Field, together with the natural turnings of the Hills, to let that charming River down to beautify our gardens, and what stops our view is a very pretty Corn Mill, built in the Gothick manner but nothing can please the Eye like our Short View, and their is a fine meadow, cut off from the garden only by the River Charvell whereon is all sorts of cattle feeding, which looks the same as if they were feeding in the garden.[24]

Whilst MacClary describes the unadorned pleasure, and craft of the prospect, the discerning visitor would also have been aware of the garden's allegorical meaning. For though the rich and varied imagery of the farmed landscape is essentially English, it also evokes the Virgilian landscape of the *Georgics* in which the historic virtues of England and King Alfred are melded with Rome's past glories by the presence of a gothicised corn mill and a ruined, classical arch on the skyline. (Plates 29 and 30) This association is reinforced by Scheemaker's copy of the *Lion Attacking the Horse,* placed at the edge of the prospect. This was not an arbitrary eye catcher but a carefully considered statement. Kent would have been familiar with this sculpture in the gardens at the Villa d'Este, Tivoli, where it was positioned to overlook the Fountain of Ancient Rome and across the Campagna to Rome. At Rousham, its position overlooking the countryside beyond the Cherwell, evokes memories of those Italian gardens where garden and campagna were interrelated. As Hunt expressed it Rousham

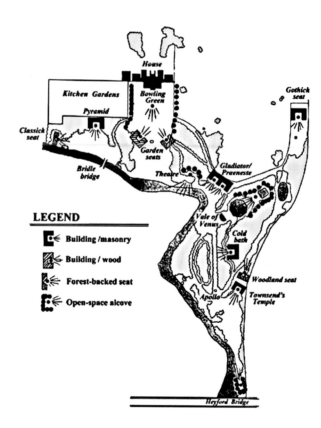

FIGURE 6. A Plan of Rousham

has "so much Italianess" ... "antique Rome, the esteemed variety of modern Roman villas, gardens and groves, garden as theatre, garden as history painting".[25] But Rousham was in no way an imitation, rather it was a transference of Italy into England, and by inference, a passing-on of classical ideals and ideas to the inheritors of the Roman mantle:

> the antique Italian references and the colour of Rousham are accommodated in a purely English scene ... all specific allusions to classical and modern Rome are naturalised: temples designed for groves after the ancient manner are ineluctable Englished when finally sited.[26]

From the Prospect, one walked in quiet contemplation through, what James Thomson described as a "bowery Walk of covert close, where scarce a speck of day falls on the lengthen'd Gloom" until path opens onto the Arcadian scene of the Venus Vale watched over by Pan, lurking at its fringes. MacClary again:

> ... when you come to the end of the grove, you come to two Garden seats, where you set down, but be sure no Tongue can express the Beautiful view that presents itself to your eye, you see a fountain four inches in diameter, playing up fifty feet high, in the middle of a clump of old oaks, and back't with a cascade, where the water comes tumbling down from under three Arches, through Ruff stones, from hence you carry your Eye on, you see on each side unnatural Hillocks planted with large trees of different sorts, and in the middle stands another Cascade, where the

water comes pouring down one Arch, on the right hand of which stands Faun, and on the left stands Pan, upon pedestals, you carry your eye still on you see a fountain playing thirty feet high, and that is five inches Diameter, behind which stands a Figure Venus, on each side stands a Cupid riding upon swans backs, all three upon handsome pedestals, all this back't with very tall Evergreens of Deferent Sorts.[27]

Kent's sketch of the Vale shows the spectators of the scene as actors, taking positions and postures, as though inviting them to both observe "the goddesse's dreams and participate in them" (Plates 31 and 32), in the sure knowledge that they were *Et in Arcadia ego* (*even in Arcadia, there am I*).[28]

North of the Vale of Venus, a new vista opened to the Heyford Bridge, then just outside the grounds, from where the path leads down to the river; in Thomson's words, Virgil's ancient reed-fringed Mincius, the "Latent Rill, scarce oozing thro' the grass, of Growth luxuriant". The path skirts the river throughout the length of the garden, passing the theatre, designed earlier by Charles Bridgeman. The absence of labour is the theme of the theatre; here Kent subtly transferred the viewers attention away from the theatre to the larger landscape by placing three statues, Bacchus, Mercury and Ceres at its edge. The two pastoral deities Ceres and Bacchus[29] are signifiers of the eternal richness and plenitude encompassed in the cycle of nature. They are ritualised intermediaries between Virgil's swains and the dead Daphnis, mythical inventor of bucolic poetry:

> Daphnis shines at heavens's dazzling gate,
>   under his feet sees clouds and planets,
> Shepherds, nymphs and Pan are glad for this,
>   forest and campaign quickened with joy.
> Sheep nor deer have anything to dread –
>   wolf or snare – for Daphnis loves the gentle:
> Wooded hills, crags, orchards cry to heaven
>   jocund hymns – "A god is he!"
>
> Virgil: *Eclogues* 5, 56–63[30]

> These shall be your rites, whenever we
>   honour the nymphs or bless our acres.
> Long as boars love heights and fish love streams,
>   long as cicadas sip at dew,
> Long as bees suck thyme – will you remain
>   praised and famed, our yearly vows receiving,
> Binding us to make them good, the way
>   Corn-god (Ceres) and Wine-god (Bacchus) also do.
>
> Virgil: *Eclogues* 5, 74–81[31]

In the static world of the garden Ceres and Bacchus signify the implicit fruits of nature in a garden where nothing is produced, where nothing will ever be produced, a parody of the self-supporting Pastoral utopia. Yet as representations of natural bounty, both Ceres and Bacchus sanctify and bless the estate, the garden and the landowner by extracting the 'curse of labour'. Within the

confines of the garden, a pseudo-paradise is created that, as noted before, "systematically removes the presence of those who labour consigning all hard agricultural labour to the natural order". The presence of Ceres as spring and Bacchus as autumn invoke an image of perpetual reoccurrence which determines a productive world which is only played out as a masque, as art, in the garden. While Mercury symbolises the passage from death to regeneration; the perpetual return of nature's plenitude and the passage of seasons. At Rousham, Mercury stands ready to transports the onlooker across the river into the countryside beyond – to leap the fence.

Kent's great achievement at Rousham was to unite the make believe world of the soft pastoral, of shepherds and perpetual spring with that of the harder world of the georgic farmer. Rousham was a true pastoral site; it was neither a garden, nor a forest, neither a jungle or a farm, but a pleasance. It was not a rose garden or a *locus conclusus* of Chastity but like the Arcadian world of Giorgione's *Fete Champetre*, it was a *locus amoenus*. An idealised landscape with three fundamental ingredients: trees, grass and water. It offers no criticism of life, of the Enlightenment or of technological and economic progress. It follows Pope's dictum of unreality – "we are not to describe our shepherds as shepherds at this day really are, but as they may be conceived then to have been" – by presenting an idealised image of natural scenery rather than a true representation of working country life, an image in the manner of Sannazarro's Arcadia. Forget, the argument goes, the present reality build instead on how things were or were supposed to be and impose a distance between images and real life. In this the Pastoral creates an image of rural life that ignores its realities. It was an urban dream of the country, the locale indeterminate because the specificity of the setting was not important – Virgil's pastoral place of ease and pleasure that moved from Arcadia to Sicily, to Kos, back to Arcadia, to Italy from the Po valley to the Heel to Thessaly to the Roman campagna and, by inference and with equal ease, to Oxfordshire, via the Thames at Richmond.

PLATE 29 *(above left)*. William Kent (1685–1748) the gothic farmhouse and the ruined classical arch, *c.*1737–41.

PLATE 30 *(above right)*. View from the gardens today with the mill and temple just visible in the trees.

PLATE 31 *(above left)*. William Kent: *The Vale of Venus c.*1737–41.

PLATE 32 *(above right)*. The Vale of Venus today.

Notes and References

1 Thomson, J., *Summer* lines 36–43. www.bartleby.com
2. *Thames Landscape Strategy; The meaning of Arcadia.* www.thames-landscape-strategy. org.uk
3. Colen Campbell praised Palladio in a book on the Roman architect, *Vitruvius* (1715). Campbell, C., *Vitruvius Britannicus,* 3 vols, 1715–1725.
4. Burlington took a copy of Palladio's book *I Quattro Libri dell'Architettura* on his tour of the Veneto (1719) and made copious notes in the margins.
5. Louis XIV founded the academies in 1664 and 1671.
6. Pope, A., *Epistle to Burlington,* lines 191–6.
7. Allinson, K., *Architects and Architecture of London.* Architectural Press, London, 2008, p. 82.
8. Hunt, J. D. and Willis, P. (eds), *The Genius of the Place: the English landscape garden, 1620–1820.* Paul Elek, London, 1975, p. 187.
9. Wilkinson, L. P., *The Georgics of Virgil.* Cambridge University Press, Cambridge, 1969, pp. 303–4.
10. Grant, D., *James Thomson: poet of The Seasons.* Cresset Press, London, 1951, p. 9.
11. *Ibid.*
12. Thomson, J., *The Seasons: Spring.* Clarendon Press, Oxford, 1981.
13. Hussey, C., *The Picturesque.* Routledge, London, 2004, p. 32.
14. Hunt, J. D., *The Figure in the Landscape.* John Hopkins University Press, London, 1976, p. 117.
15. Thomson, J., quoted in Hunt, J. D. and Willis, P. (eds), p. 193.
16. Amanda was a lady of Scottish parentage whose mother forbade her to marry Thompson because she believed she would be reduced to selling penny broadsheets on the street.
17. Hunt, J. D., *The Figure in the Landscape, op. cit.,* p. 111.
18. Thomson, J., *The Seasons: Spring, op. cit.*
19. Drabble, M., *A Writer's Britain.* Thames and Hudson, London, 1984, p. 55.
20. Sir Philip Sidney was an Elizabethan soldier, courtier and poet who composed *Arcadia* towards the end of the sixteenth century.
21. Nicholson, A., *Arcadia.* Harper Perennial, London, 2008, p. 11.
22. James Dormer was Colonel 1st troop of Horse-Grenadier Guards, son of Robert

Dormer, master of ceremonies to Charles 1, Charles11, and James 11 and ambassador at Brussels in 1663.

23. Walpole, H., *The history of modern taste in gardening* (1771–80). Quoted in Hunt, D. H., *Garden and Grove: the Italian Renaissance garden in the English imagination, 1600–1750, op. cit.*, p. 313.

24. Pugh, S., *Garden Nature Language,* Manchester University Press, Manchester, 1998, p. 46. There is considerable debate among garden historians as to whether Kent or the head gardener MacClary had the greater responsibility for the eventual appearance of Rousham, but this matters little when considering the garden's achievements.

25. Hunt, J. D., *Gardens and the Picturesque: studies in the history of landscape architecture.* MIT Press, Cambridge, Massachusetts, 1994, p. 113.

26. *Ibid.*

27. Pugh, S., *op. cit.*, p. 48.

28. Hunt, J. D., *William Kent, Landscape Garden Designer.* W. Zwemmer, London, 1987, p. 86. Horace Walpole believed he could discern the influence of Kent's friend, Alexander Pope, most clearly in the Venus Vale. More recently Kent's biographer Michael Wilson observed that there is "an amalgam of the theories of Pope and Burlington, with (Kent's) own recollections of Italian scenery both natural and artificial and a semi-subconscious assimilation of the Claudian manner in landscape painting". Wilson, M. I., *William Kent: architect, designer, painter, gardener, 1685–1748.* Routledge & Kegan Paul, London, 1984; to which can to be added the influence of Inigo Jones's masque designs.

29. Pugh, S., *op. cit.*, p. 27. Pugh suggests that Bacchus would play a negligible role in the pastoral world, for vine growing and wine making are hard agricultural tasks unsuited to the hedonistic pursuits of the swain or shepherd. However they are very much a part of the Georgic tradition and vines and their culture featured in the pastoral gardens of the Renaissance in Italy and at Painshill Park, created after 1738 by Charles Hamilton.

30. Day Lewis, C. (trans.), *Virgil: The Eclogues, The Georgics.* Oxford University Press, London, 1983, lines 56–63.

31. *Ibid.*, lines 74–81.

CHAPTER NINE

The Happy Rural Life

Dryden's desire to give Virgil a truly English flavour sparked a renewed interest in agricultural poetry and country life among the educated classes. There was also renewed interest in the *Georgics* as a guide to agricultural practice. In 1742 James Hamilton, a schoolmaster of East Calder, near Edinburgh, translated the *Eclogues* and the *Georgics* with the dual object of inspiring the sons of gentlemen to improve agriculture and raise money to buy a farm and, engage skilled ploughmen.[1] Many at this time thought of themselves as practising Virgilian agriculture though it is hard to see the *Georgics* being followed as a manual. In 1724 a William Benson published a book entitled *Virgil's Husbandry* in which he boldly proclaimed "there is more of Virgil's husbandry in England at this instant than in Italy itself". This prompted a sharp reaction from Jethro Tull, one of those responsible for the great change in British agriculture. In his revolutionary book *Horse-hoeing Husbandry* he devoted a special chapter entitled *Remarks on the bad husbandry that is so freely express'd in Virgil's first georgic.* He could not conceive of any practice worse and listed nine points that were wrong and needed correcting. In response Virgil's defenders were quick to say the poet had been misrepresented. Even as late as 1770 Wilkinson notes in the *Georgics of Virgil*, that a Methodist minister in Northern Ireland alleged his father was cultivating a farm according to the rules laid down in Virgil's *Georgics*: "despite the difference in climate from that of Italy, his crops proved not inferior to those of his neighbours, it is clear that his behaviour was by now regarded as eccentric".[2] But the real influence of the *Georgics* had been to inspire an interest in farming and country life. By the middle of the century the ideal of the 'happy rural life', intimated by Virgil and Horace, had become a familiar and persistent theme in literature. Typical was an anonymous poem published in the *Gentleman's Magazine* (1745):

> With plenty bless'd, I lead a peaceful life,
> In rural ease with children, friends and wife.
> My sports are hunting, angling, bowling and shooting;
> I never mind your fiddling and your fluting.
> My business planting and how to drain the mead,
> Or crown the hill with useful shade;
> In the smooth glebe to see the coulter worn;
> And fill the granary with needful corn;
> Curious t'Observe the well fed heifer feed,
> Or mark the paces of the generous steed.[3]

Like the *hofdicht* poems in Holland a century before, the poem describes an idyllic country life, amounting to a Gentleman's creed that expresses an "ideal of human existence to which any respectable Englishman would subscribe, whether he actually owned land or not".[4] It became fashionable for Gentleman to be shown enjoying the country life, as in Gainsborough's portrait, *Major John Dade of Tannington, Suffolk* (Plate 33). In his more celebrated conversation piece, *Mr and Mrs Andrew* (1750), painted on the Auberies estate outside Sudbury, Suffolk, Gainsborough showed the newly married couple seated in their own Arcadia. Mary Andrews was wearing the round-eared cap in imitation of the milkmaids' bonnet that became fashionable after the publication of *The Seasons* and other georgic poems. However, milking is not shown nor is there any other work taking place. In the georgic tradition the labourers have conveniently stepped aside to reveal

PLATE 33. Thomas Gainsborough (1727–1788): *Major John Dade, of Tannington, Suffolk* c.1755

a landscape of recently harvested corn sheaves. In the distance sheep graze in meadows delineated by woven 'quickset' hedges. These were a reminder that enclosure was a recent development, and one that was changing the pastoral landscape irrevocably from openess to the now familiar pattern of enclosed fields. The neat parallel rows of corn, made possible by Jethro Tull's revolutionary and controversial seed drill, all signify that Mr and Mrs Andrews chose to be portrayed against the background of a thoroughly up to date and efficient farm. The painting encapsulates the true spirit of the Georgic landscape, as understood by the landed gentry of the mid eighteenth century, 'peace and plenty' where rich industry sits smiling on the plains.[5]

William Shenstone and the Leasowes

However, William Shenstone (1714–1763) was not interested in profitable farming. After inheriting the Leasowes estate he had given up his academic studies in 1843[6] to pursue the life of a country gentleman. In so doing he embodied the classical ideal of the virtuous wise man choosing a simple pastoral, yet cultured, life in the country, rather than living in the corrupt and corrupting city:

For rural virtues, and for natures skies,
I bade Augusta's venal sons farewell;
Now 'mid trees, I see my smoke arise,
Now hear the fountain bubbling around my cell.

Shenstone, Elegy 1[7]

In 1845 he began to transform his estate into a very different Arcadia, described by Clark as "an elegant expression of that eighteenth century edition of the Ideal".[8] Like his friend, the poet James Thomson, Shenstone was a Virgilian who wanted to recreate the antique landscape in England "as surely as the genius of ancient poetry and politics had been". His aim was to show how an estate of modest extent, might be arranged in ways that exhibited the best possible 'Taste'.

The Leasowes was a small pastoral farm of around one hundred acres (40 ha) possessing a considerable variety and topography, with wooded valleys and small rushing streams. Though as Robert Dodsley, Shenstone's friend and publisher pointed out after his death, the estate was not distinguished until the time of the late owner. It was, said Dodsley, reserved for a person of Shenstone's ingenuity both to discover and improve.[9] Initially Shenstone expressed "no thoughts of laying out my environs"[10] and had begun to lay out a garden in the formal manner, though he had neither the money nor the inclination. Later he regretted these early works and had them demolished. After taking advice from friends, Shenstone decided he wanted a new type of landscape, one that respected and utilised the natural landscape. As funds would allow, he began to lay paths around the farm, at first in an unplanned way, positioning them so they passed a sequence of carefully contrived and constructed views – across both his own property and the surrounding countryside. Eventually the paths encircled the entire estate allowing every aspect to be fully experienced and appreciated. In *Unconnected Thoughts on Gardening* (published posthumously in 1764) Shenstone commented on many points of composition, including the placing of objects and the influence of painters:

> In a scene presented to the eye, objects should never lie so much to the right or left, as to give it any uneasiness in the examination.
>
> No mere slope from one side to the other can be agreeable ground: The eye requires ... a degree of uniformity ... Let us examine what may be said in favour of that regularity which Mr Pope exposes... for a kind of balance in a landskip; and ... the painters generally furnish one: a building for instance on one side, contrasted by a group of trees, a large oak, or a rising hill on the other. Whence does this taste proceed, but from the love we bear to regularity in perfection? After all, in regard to gardens, the shape of ground, the disposition of trees, and the figure of water, must be sacred to nature; and no forms must be allowed that make a discovery of art.
>
> Water should ever appear, as an irregular lake or winding stream. Art, indeed, is often requisite to collect and epitomise the beauties of nature; but should never be suffered to set her mark upon them ...[11]

Shenstone believed the whole of Nature should appear natural; even hedges, then becoming a familiar part of the enclosed landscape, were "... universally bad. They discover art in nature's province". And, in anticipation of the Picturesque movement 50 years later, Shenstone believed the scene could be enriched by variety and in particular, the effect of novelty:

> Variety appears to me to derive good part of it's effect from novelty... Ruinated structures appear to derive their power of pleasing from the irregularity of surface, which is variety: and the latitude they afford the imagination.[12]

The circuit walk and Virgil's grove

Visitors to the Leasowes were invited to take the famous 'circuit walk'. This led past seats and urns carefully positioned to enhance a scene by association, as Addison advised, sometimes affording the opportunity to rest and admire the carefully created views (Plate 34). Some of the seats and urns were dedicated to Shenstone's close friends and many features bore poems to evoke a sense of mood. On one occasion he wrote to a friend, Richard Graves, to ask if he had seen a print or drawing of Poussin's *Et in Arcadia Ego* (see Plate 71) because, he said; "The idea of it is so very pleasing to me, that I had no peace until I had used the inscription ...".[13] A short way into the circuit, a seat beneath a canopy of oaks, was inscribed with carefully selected lines from Virgil's *Eclogues* intended "to establish in the mind of the visitor the arcadian image of the Leasowes as an idealised pastoral world in which Shenstone identified himself with the poetic shepherd of the *Eclogues*, living in rustic retirement among his fields and his flocks":[14]

> Hither, O Meliboeus! bend thy way;
> Thy herds, thy goats, secure from harm repose;
> If happy leisure serve awhile to stay,
> Here rest thy limbs beneath these shady bows.

Though this is the classical translation, C. Day Lewis translates these lines in more immediate and vernacular way;

> Quick Meliboeus,
> Come over here, if you have time to take a breather, and rest
> In the shade with us. Your goat and kids will be safe enough;
> Your bullocks will find their own way across the fields, do
>   they need
> To drink. The grassy banks of the Mincius are fringed
>   here
> With swaying reeds and the sacred oak is a-drone with
>   bees.
>
> Virgil: *Eclogue* 7, 8–13[15]

Water was of great importance in the design of The Leasowes. One inscription placed by a view of a meadow and water was illuminated by Shenstone's only quote from the *Georgics*:

To John Delap Halliday Esq. and the Right Honorable Lady Jane Halliday. this View of the Leasowes & Priory is Inscribed with the greatest respect by their much Obliged & most Humble Servant H. F. James.

PLATE 34. H. F. James:
*View of William
Shenstone' Leasowes and
Priory c.1800.*

Then let the country charm me, the rivers that channel its valleys,
Then may I love its forest and stream, and let fame go hang.

Virgil: *Georgics* 2, 484–6[16]

The climax of the walk was Virgil's Grove on which Shenstone "lavished most attention, perfecting the waterfall and cascades, setting out seats and relaying paths, positioning islands in the streams and carrying out planting to give the grove a sequestered, poetic, pensive air".[17] The entrance was marked with an obelisk announcing that it was dedicated to Virgil, and on entering, the visitor would find the Grove in Shenstone's own description, worked by "surprise" and revealed its charms only gradually (Plate 35).

Shenstone showed it was possible, in Addison's words, to "make a pretty Landskip of (his) own possessions". Working in this way the landscape conveyed the illusion of an idealised Arcadia suited to the poetic temperament of its owner and had very little to do with productive agriculture. Shenstone did not refer to The Leasowes as a garden; he even spoke of a 'garden' as something he wished to avoid creating. He worried that "I have been embroidering my Grove with

PLATE 35. This engraving represents a scene within 'Virgil's Grove', at William Shenstone's estate at the Leasowes, named after the Roman poet. It shows many of the features of Shenstone's 'natural' landscape embellished by 'art'. A winding stream with a waterfall meanders through the scene. Trees are necessary parts of the composition. Visitors walk through the Grove observing its beauties. By the 1750s, the Leasowes was a tourist attraction. R. W. Boodle, *Worcestershire Scrapbook*, Vol. II (1903).

Flowers, till I almost begin to fear it looks too much like a *garden*". He spoke of The Leasowes as "my walks" , "my place" and commonly "my farm". In a letter (1748) he noted that the "French have what they call a *parque ornée*; I suppose, approaching about as near to a garden as Hagley. I give my place the title of a *ferme ornée*".[18] Acknowledging that such naturalness was itself a human construction, Shenstone saw in nature a medium, rather than a given ideal to which he had to aspire.

Reactions to the Leasowes

After Shenstone's death others saw it differently. Thomas Whatley in his *Observations of Modern Gardening* (1770) held that the most natural landscapes were those of a rural farm but because the skills of gardening had hitherto been practiced only on "a small plot appropriated ... to pleasure, while the rest was devoted to profit only, gardeners had sought to make gardens as unnatural as possible, to distinguish them from areas of property devoted to useful cultivation".[19] Whately saw the rise of the natural style as a rejection of that 'vicious taste'. Beginning with the opening of the garden to the country, developing through the 'ornamented farm' and culminating in the truly rural farm, the "idea of a spot appropriated to pleasure only" would finally be superseded by a style in which the landscape's beauties were at their most simple and natural. Whately related Shenstone's *ferme ornée* directly to contemporary ideas of Pastoral poetry, seeing in both a return to simplicity:

> The ideas of pastoral poetry seem now to be the standard of that simplicity; and a place conformable to them is deemed a farm in its utmost purity. An allusion to them evidently enters in to the design of the Leasowes ... the whole is in the same taste, yet full of variety; and except in two or three trifles, every part is rural and natural.[20]

PLATE 36. Thomas Gainsborough: *A Landscape with a Woodcutter courting a Milkmaid c.*1755.

When the travel writer Joseph Heely visited the Leasowes in 1777 he also interpreted the farm as a natural garden, "smiling in all perfection of pastoral beauty":

> ... not in the soft mossy lawn, mown for no other use than to please the eye, or trimmed up in the glare of pompous imagery, shewing the carved vase, or sumptuous temple – but in the chaste humility of domestic and sylvan harmony – in fields glorying in the "milky heifer, and deserving steed" – in groves to give them, cool, refreshing shade.[21]

For several decades the Leasowes was a very popular tourist attraction, many visitors, who were already engaged in improving their own properties, came seeking inspiration. At a time of increasing enclosure of common land, the Leasowes had a profound influence on the appearance of the wider countryside; as one commentator observed England was fortunate that, at the very time the landscape was being transformed, matters of taste and aesthetics in the landscape were at the forefront of gentlemens' minds.

Aristocratic resurgence

During the second half of the century the gentry and the aristocracy parted company in their 'Taste' for landscape. While many of the gentry followed Shenstone's example and sought to improve their estates and harmonise with the surrounding countryside, the aristocracy were retreating into their own private Arcadia. To understand why, it is necessary to appreciate the position of the aristocracy in the middle years of the century. After the Glorious Revolution power had passed to a small number of hereditary landowners and early in the eighteenth century, they sort to justify their elitism through the philosophical concept of *concordia discors*. This was first advanced by Pythagorus who argued

that the cosmos was an harmonious arrangement of various discordant elements
and later it became the Christian doctrine of Divine Providence. The English
aristocracy used this concept to argue that human harmony depended upon
divisions or contrasts within society. The concept of *concordia discors* was also
applied to the aesthetics of landscape. Alexander Pope, in his poem Windsor
Forest (1713), saw the surrounding landscape as a ideal expression of the doctrine:

> Here Hills and Vales, the Woodland and the Plain,
> Here Earth and Water seem to strive again;
> Not Chaos-like together crush'd and bruis'd,
> But as the world, harmoniously confus'd:
> Where Order in Variety we see,
> And where, tho' all things differ, all agree.

Pope: Windsor Forest[22]

The way the aristocracy saw society is revealed in Gainsborough's painting
Landscape with a Woodcutter courting a Milkmaid (1755) (Plate 36) commissioned
by the Duke of Bedford, a prominent member of the ruling oligarchy. Its pastoral
credentials are established by the towers and buildings of a town in the distance,
since identified as Ipswich, whilst in the middle ground is a ploughman with a
team of horses. A ploughman was often used in georgic paintings to depict a
countryman who earnt his bread by the sweat of his brow. The line of a fence
delineates the productive agricultural land from the unenclosed heath and woods.
Here the woodcutter stands with a bundle of sticks and holding a billhook; he has
interrupted the pretty milkmaid in her work and so both are in a state of enforced
leisure. The actual milking is not shown so polite viewers could associate with the
maid, and likewise gentlemen identify with the woodcutter – though not with the
ploughman whose shirt sticks out of his trousers. But even he is not an accurate
portrayal of a countryman, even though his clothes might identify him as one. His
posture conveys a sense of ease and as Barrell observed in the *The Dark Side Of
Landscape* "he trundles his plough through the soil like an empty wheelbarrow".[23]
He is engaged in what the georgic poets described as "happy labour or grateful
toil". Behind the couple is an old gnarled pollard which Barrell suggests is the
only image of unproductive nature in the painting, but this is not strictly true.
Pollarded trees were an important part of the rural economy and ancient trees
were much venerated by georgic poets; perhaps the ancient tree symbolises the old
order against the new represented by the young vigourous tree on the fence line.
Or maybe it reinforces the contrast between classical world of Arcadia and the
reality of the georgic landscape. What Gainsborough has done is create an image
of contrast in the landscape and in the lives of the figures. Between those who are
seen to enjoy the 'idealised rural life' and those in enforced leisure who occupy
the Ideal landscape. And though they ignore each other, they are nevertheless
complimentary as they would be in real life. Most importantly, everyone is in
harmony with nature. The simple message seems to be that if everyone is in
harmony with nature, then everyone is in harmony with each other.

From the middle of the eighteenth century the aristocracy, and their sense of *concordia discors*, was under threat from a new direction. They regarded themselves as the natural leaders of the country, qualified by education in the classical tradition and ownership of large estates, but now they were challenged increasingly by those who had made their money in TRADE. When William Pitt was appointed First Minister in 1756 the government was led, for the first time, not by a person from the landed classes but from a background of TRADE. The response of the aristocracy was to put a renewed effort into reasserting their position as the privileged elite, underlining those qualities that distinguished them from those they regarded as their inferiors. Those qualities included Education, Taste and, the adoption of an even more conspicuous and ostentatious lifestyle. The result has been described as the 'aristocratic resurgence'. One manifestation was the mania for laying-out expensive and expansive landscape parks. After all, it was only the wealthiest and largest landowners who could afford to set aside many acres of often valuable and productive agricultural land as a statement of political power.

From this time the aristocracy saw in ancient Rome a new message; no longer was it the supreme example of a Golden Age but a warning of what could befall a once great empire if it allowed governance to pass into the wrong hands. "Like Rome before her", wrote Henry Fielding, "England is treading a path from virtuous Industry to Wealth; from Wealth to Luxury; from Luxury to some hardy Oppressor, and with the loss of Liberty, loses everything else that is valuable, and gradually sinks into her original barbarism".[24]The answer, according to Fielding, was a return to stronger government and a restoration of the old balance between the nobility and the gentry on the one hand; and on the other, with the commonality. It meant a return to first principles, to the values of a classical education and the goal of a tranquil rural existence, described by Virgil, Horace and other classical writers. To reinforce the sense of a looming catastrophe, ruins became a popular motif in painting and the landscape. Artists like Richard Wilson who had travelled to Rome in 1750, assimilating the work of Claude, returned to paint scenes of a Golden Age overtaken by time. The Arcadian Ideal has retreated beyond reach and ruins abound as a poignant reminder of present fallen Italy and its glorious past. The paintings were intended to emphasise the need to protect the values and wisdom of the past and underline the dangers of the present.

Joshua Reynolds and landscape Taste

Throughout the eighteenth century it had been assumed that ownership of land, and the income it provided, removed the need to work to support oneself or one's dependents and this independence made the aristocracy fit to govern. Without the distraction of having to earn a living, only the aristocracy could grasp the public interest and be wholly impartial in their actions. However, by the second half of the century ownership of land was no longer a criteria as it could be acquired by those who had made their money by work. Instead it was argued that what distinguished the ruling class from their social inferiors was ability to think in abstract terms. To produce abstract ideas from the raw data of experience; the inability to do so was regarded as the result of a lack of education and was characterised by the vulgar; that is to say those who worked, and women. One test of the ability to abstract was the possession of the correct Taste in Landscape. Lack of Taste was regarded as the inability to perform this operation and so take pleasure not in the Ideal representation of an object or landscape but in scenes of an everyday nature. In paintings, Joshua Reynold regarded such scenes, with all their accidental deformities and details, as "unworthy of the attention of a freeman". Those accidents might include natural phenomena, such as storms and rainbows, but were more generally those aspects of nature that suggested the landscape was being viewed at one particular moment, rather than another – the ruffling of trees by wind from a particular direction, clouds forming a particular pattern, seasonal effects and behaviour. In short anything which suggested a view of nature that is anything other than abstract and a typical, permanent phenomena. Such details, he said, were the characteristics of Dutch art, copied initially by Thomas Gainsborough, and which appealed to the new middle, often urban, classes.

In his *Philogical Inquiries* (1780) James Harris noted the vulgar look no further than to such scenes, because all their views end in utility – they "imagine nothing to be real, but that what may be touched or tasted". These "dwellers in the cave of sensuality" he continued, "only remark, that this is fine barley; this is rich clover, as an ox or an ass, if only they could speak, would inform us". By contrast "the liberal have nobler views; and though they give culture its due praise, they can be delighted with natural beauties, where culture was never known".[25] Harris makes a poor effort at explaining what pleasures a liberal might find in natural beauty but he does provide examples what he means: "the great elements of this specific type of beauty are water, wood, uneven ground; to which may be added a fourth, that is to say lawn".

The power to abstract from the elements of nature and to comprehend and organise an extensive prospect, became a testimony of the aristocrats' ability to prefer an art which promoted the public interest – as opposed to ministering to private appetites and interests of particular men. In this way the presentation of a panoramic prospect served as evidence that the landowner was a man of a liberal mind who could abstract from the particular, the public interest from the labyrinth of private interest. The Palladian-style House overlooking a landscape park was a public statement emphasising the right to power and to govern.

Lancelot 'Capability' Brown

The man who understood the requirements of the aristocracy and who possessed both the vision to abstract elements of water, wood, uneven ground and lawn and the technical ability to reassemble them into a 3-dimensional work of art was Lancelot 'Capability' Brown. Of humble origins, Brown was not a theorist

PLATE 37. This affluent of the river Wansbeck valley, 4 miles (6.5 km) from Kirkharle was the way Brown walked to school in Cambo until he was 16.

and he did not go on the Grand Tour, but like Addison and Thomson, his notion of the perfect landscape was influenced by his childhood experiences. Born in the Northumberland village of Kirkharle, Brown spent his formative years in the Wansbeck valley; a landscape of well-rounded hills formed by glacial moraines, topped by clumps of pine and beech. Heavy rains were often followed by long sinuous lakes in the valley bottoms, and these were all features that would find reflection in his later work (Plate 37).

The effects Brown produced were not in any sense a reproduction of any Ideal natural landscape; "talk of Claude and Poussin is beside the mark"[26] but rather they were seen as a vision of an Ideal Pastoral Arcadia from which almost all artefacts had been removed and made timeless, and therefore Ideal, by the removal of all evidence of accident. The grass around the house was regularly scythed or beyond the Ha-Ha, grazed by sheep or cattle; twigs and branches blown down by the wind were removed and reeds fringing the lake were shunned in favour of clear, sharp delineations between land and water.

Whereas in gardens like Rousham the landscape dictated the spectators thoughts and directed his or her feet, with the buildings, statues, inscriptions and other objects more or less compelling the onlooker to follow a predetermined route, on the Brownian estate "the visitor could move freely, look wherever and think whatever they wished, or at least such was the illusion they encouraged".[27] At Blenheim Brown swept away Vanbrugh's Anglo-Dutch Baroque gardens at front of the house and by damming a meagre stream, created a vast serpentine lake to provide a majestic setting for the palace. It remains one the finest compositions of water, landform, woods and architecture on an heroic but highly appropriate scale, a supreme work of art (Plate 38). Brown created parks at over 170 houses from the 1750s until his sudden death in 1783, all characterised by serpentine lakes, clumps of trees and surrounding belts of

PLATE 38. Blenheim Palace, Vanbrugh's bridge – over time the austerity of Brown's landscape with its shaven grass sides to the lake and clear water has been replaced by a more picturesque scene.

woodland and smooth undulating contours of green turf. It was an illusion of nature perfected.

On his death one critic, Sir William Chambers, observed in his *Dissertation on Oriental Gardening* (1772), that "Brown's grounds differ very little from common fields, so closely is nature copied in most of them".[28]

However Chamber's missed the point; the new estate was intended to appear artless and boundless and the larger it was the more natural and free it looked. It was an image captured by Richard Wilson in his painting of *Tabley House* (Plate 39).[29] Wilson is implying, with the approval of the owner Sir Peter Leicester, that the landowner and the rustic family are in an all embracing continuum of ease and contentment – shades of the 'happy rural life'. Wilson is using the iconography of the English georgic to show on the one hand, the pastoral ideal of man in harmony with nature, and on the other, the social ideal of the poor in harmony with the rich. Thus, both Wilson and Brown used the landscape to display the concept of *concordia discors* – a sense of order, tranquility and harmony in society – beneficial to everyone, rich and poor alike. All that is required for this status quo to remain is for the governors to play their part as benevolent paternalists and for the governed to remain in a posture of deferential gratitude.

A changing mood

Though this state of affairs would continue on landed estates for many years to come, it was a vision of England and its society that was already becoming increasingly isolated and difficult to sustain. The effects of emparkment and

PLATE 39. Richard Wilson (1714–1782): *Tabley House, Cheshire* c.1765. The painting's composition derives from two intersecting diagonals, the broad sweep of the river, which gives an impression of calm, and from the tree to the building meeting at a small copse in the lower centre. The trees extend upwards into the broad expanse of sky, reminiscent of Dutch painters like van Goyen and Ruisdael, and cleverly block any view into the distance so diverting the viewers attention to either side. The overall effect is one of massive emptiness punctuated by clumps of trees in the Brownian fashion. The two rustic figures in the foreground though separated from the park by the expanse of water, are linked to the house pictorially by the line of shadow.

the enclosure of common land on rural life and culture, was coming under increasing scrutiny. Oliver Goldsmith's popular poem *The Deserted Village* (1770), was a lament for the charms of rural life and critique of the changing order. In words reminiscent of Virgil's *Georgics*, Goldsmith at first suggests a beautiful relationship between the the two classes "by having the swain, like a traditional shepherd, enjoy both the ease of the rich and the simple honesty of the poor":[30]

> Sweet Auburn, loveliest village of the plain,
> Where health and plenty cheered the labouring swain,
> Where smiling spring its earliest visit paid,
> And parting summer's lingering blooms delayed:
> Dear lovely bowers of innocence and ease,
> Seats of my youth, when every sport could please,
> How often have I loitered o'er thy green,
> Where humble happiness endeared each scene;
> How often have I paused on every charm,
> The sheltered cot, the cultivated farm,
> The never-failing brook, the busy mill,
> The decent church that topped the neighbouring hill,
> The hawthorn bush, with seats beneath the shade,
> For talking age and whispering lovers made.
> How often have I blessed the coming day,
> When toil remitting lent its turn to play,
> And all the village train, from labour free,
> Led up their sports beneath the spreading tree, …

Goldsmith: *The Deserted Village*, 1–18

But now this *concordia discors* was coming under threat, as the landscape was improved:

> Sweet smiling village, loveliest of the lawn,
> Thy sports are fled and all thy charms withdrawn;
> Amidst thy bowers the tyrant's hand is seen,
> And desolation saddens all thy green:
> One only master grasps the whole domain,
> And half a village stints thy smiling plain:
>
> Goldsmith, *The Deserted Village*, 35–40

And the new wealth TRADE had brought had been won at the expense of the poor and was changing England for ever:

> Ye friends to truth, ye statesmen who survey
> The rich man's joys increase, the poor's decay,
> 'Tis yours to judge how wide the limits stand
> Between a splendid and an happy land.
> Proud swells the tide with loads of freighted ore,
> And shouting Folly hails them from her shore;
> Hoards, even beyond the miser's wish, abound,
> And rich men flock from all the world around.
> Yet count our gains. This wealth is but a name
> That leaves with useful products still the same.
> Not so the loss. The man of wealth and pride
> Takes up a space that many poor supplied;
> Space for his lake, his park's extended bounds,
> Space for his horses, equipage, and hounds;
> The robe that wraps his limbs in silken sloth
> Has robbed the neighbouring fields of half their growth;
> His seat, where solitary sports are seen,
> Indignant spurns the cottage from the green;
> Around the world each needful product flies,
> For all the luxuries the world supplies:
> While thus the land, adorned for pleasure all,
> In barren splendour feebly waits the fall.
>
> Goldsmith, *The Deserted Village*, 265–86

For many of the dispossessed, immigration beckoned as Goldsmith foresaw, and their place of destination would be the New World of America:

> I see the rural virtues leave the land.
> Down where yon anchoring vessel spreads the sail,
> That idly waiting flaps with every gale,
>
> Goldsmith, *The Deserted Village*, 398–400[31]

Notes and References

1. Wilkinson, L. P., *The Georgics of Virgil*. Cambridge University Press, Cambridge, 1969, pp. 307–8.
2. *Ibid.*
3. *Gentleman's Magazine* 15, March 1745, p. 161.
4. Solkin, D., *Richard Wilson. The landscape of reaction*. Tate Gallery, London, 1982, p. 24.
5. Waites, I., *Common Land in English painting, 1700–1850*. Boydell Press, Woodbridge, 2012, p. 47
6. Shenstone inherited the estate from his mother's family, along with a small income. The Leasowes is now within the borough of Dudley, close to the western boundary of Birmingham.
7. Quoted in *The Works and Prose of William Shenstone*, edited by C. Cowden Clark. Edinburgh, William P. Nimmo, 1868, p. 1. Augusta was London.
8. Clark, H. F., *The English Landscape Garden*. Alan Sutton, Gloucester, 1980, p. 59.
9. In *The works and prose of William Shenstone, esq*; 2 vols, Dodsley, J., London, 1765, 1, p. 5.
10. 'Letter to Lady Luxborough', 30 August, 1749, quoted in Chambers, D., *The Planter of the English Landscape Garden*. Yale University Press, London, 1993, p. 177.
11. Dodsley, S., *op. cit.*; Shenstone, W., *Unconnected Thoughts on Gardening*, p. 118, p. 125.
12. *Ibid.*, p. 113
13. *Letters*, pp. 534–5.
14. Harrington, R., *Nature Dressed and Redressed: William Shenstone, the Leasowes and the English landscape garden in transition c.1740–c.1763*, Lincoln College, University of Oxford, Oxford, 1994, p. 9.
15. Day Lewis, C. (trans.), *Virgil: The Eclogues, The Georgics*. Oxford University Press, London, 1983, p. 29.
16. *Ibid.*, p. 85.
17. Harrington *op. cit.*, p. 15.
18. *Letters*, 28 August. Quoted in Chambers *op. cit.*, p. 183.
19. Whately, T., *Observations on Modern Gardening*. 2nd edn. London, 1790, p. 161.
20. *Ibid.*, p. 162.
21. Heely, J., *Letters on the Beauties of Hagley, Envil, and The Leasowes*. Garland Publishers, New York, 1982, p. 191.
22. Pope, A. www.poemhunter.com/poem/windsor forest
23. Barrell, J., *The Dark Side of the Landscape*. Cambridge University Press, Cambridge, 1980, p. 49.
24. Fielding, H., *An enquiry into the causes of the late increase of robbers*. A. Millar, London, 1751, p. 762.
25. Harris, J., *The Works of James Harris, esq*. Vincent, J. 1841, p. 525; quoted in Pugh, S., *Garden, Nature and Language*, Manchester University Press, Manchester, 1988.
26. Clifford, D., *A History of Garden Design*. Faber and Faber, London, 1962, p. 158.
27. Solkin, D., *op. cit.* p. 123.
28. Hunt, J. D., *The Figure in the Landscape*. John Hopkins University Press, London, 1976, p. 188.
29. Tabley House was designed by John Carr of York completed in 1769. A landscape park was associated with the new structure in the fashionable style of Lancelot Brown.
30. Marx, L., *The Machine in the Garden*, Oxford University Press, Oxford, 2000, p. 99.
31. www.on-line-literature.com/Oliver Goldsmith

CHAPTER TEN

The Coming of the Picturesque
and the Romantics

From the middle of the eighteenth century a new attitude to nature and landscape had begun to emerge, led not by the aristocracy but the aspiring professional class of doctors, clergymen and country squires. Many of these gentlemen had not experienced the Grand Tour or received a classical education. No longer bound by ideas derived from classical sources, they began to look at landscape as it really was – a purely sensory response to the world around them. In the Age of Reason, though nature had been seen through the eye, its visual qualities were not stressed – the notion of beauty was understood in terms of the Ideal landscape, as seen in the paintings of Claude and Poussin, and by its association with classical writers like Virgil, Ovid and Horace. But throughout the eighteenth century the perception of nature and the landscape continued to evolve. Changes begun by Shaftesbury and Addison, and later by nature poets like James Thomson, gathered momentum. Burke's essay on the *Ideas of the Sublime and Beauty* also contributed to the change. He argued that Beauty was not just determined by renaissance criteria of proportion, scale and so forth, but by a subconscious emotional response. Gradually the serenity and classical nostalgia of Claude lost ground to the wildness of the more rugged Salvator Rosa whose craggy cliffs, broken trees and desolate landscapes were closer to a changing sensibility. The cumulative effect was a loosening of the collective, intellectual understanding of landscape through association with classical precedents, opening the way to a sensory experience of nature that allowed individuals to see the landscape for themselves. Jean Jaques Rousseau further loosened the ties. His emphasis on natural order and the natural state of man ushered in a whole new era of thinking that eventually developed into Romanticism stressing Man's return to life as it can be seen, felt, and experienced, thus encouraging a reliance on emotion, intuition, and instinct as opposed to reason, in guiding human behaviour.

The Picturesque and the Reverend William Gilpin

The mania for the Picturesque at the end of the eighteenth century was an important staging point on the way to Romanticism. It was fostered by a minor clergyman from the Lake District, William Gilpin. Like all educated men in the eighteenth century Gilpin was preoccupied with the landscape and matters of Taste. But Gilpin looked on landscape not in the context of a garden but in nature itself. After visiting Stowe, he spoke of his frustration at the shortcomings of the landscape garden: "the more refined our Taste grows from a study of nature the more insipid the work of art". The answer according to Gilpin was straightforward:

> The connoisseur of landscape gardening must not only be familiar with the appropriate painters, but must be come qualified as a connoisseur of Nature – Nature as she exhibits herself in fine landscapes. In other words he must become a picturesque tourist.[1]

Gilpin was unusual in showing an appreciation for landscape, in particular, the wild and rugged scenery of his childhood; and in believing the landscape was a subject worthy of painting in its own right, not as adjunct to the main subject. He poured scorn on the way the great Claude Lorrain had been forced to add poorly drawn figures to his Ideal landscapes (see Plate 16).

During the late 1760s and 1770s Gilpin travelled extensively, seeking out scenic places in England, Wales and Scotland, making notes and sketches, applying what he called picturesque principles to the landscape.[2] Gilpin defined the picturesque as "that kind of beauty which is agreeable in a picture":

> We precisely mean by it that kind of beauty which would look well in a picture. Neither grounds laid out by art nor improved by agriculture are of this kind. The Isle of Wight is in fact, a large garden or rather a field which in every part has been disfigured by the spade, the coulter and the harrow. It abounds much more in tillage than in pasturage; and of all species of cultivation, cornfields are the most unpicturesque. The regularity of corn fields disgusts, and is out of true with everything else …[3]

Throughout the whole time of the 'picturesque mania' there was no better definition. Gilpin set out to clarify the distinction between Beautiful and Picturesque objects: "between those that please the eye in their *natural state*; and those, which please from some quality, capable of being *illustrated in painting*". Whereas Edmund Burke, in his *Theory of Beauty*, had said beautiful subjects were neat and in particular smooth, the picturesque is identified by opposite properties. Gilpin gave various examples of how roughness or ruggedness of different subjects in nature, like the bark of trees or rocks appeal to the painters eye much more than smooth objects. In place of smooth parkland, the Picturesque artist will prefer "rough pasture; instead of well-worn sheep, the shaggy goat; and instead of the Stubbsian portrait of the "sleek pampered steed", the grooms and jockeys, he will prefer the "wild forester, and worn-out cart-horse".[4] In other words the Picturesque eye was anti-georgic and "must", Gilpin maintained, "find its own beauty". And while nature was good at producing textures and colours, Gilpin argued it was rarely capable of creating the perfect composition. Some extra help from the artist, perhaps in the form of a carefully placed tree, was usually required (Plate 40):

PLATE 40. William Gilpin (1724–1804): *Picturesque composition.*

The blasted tree has often a fine effect both in natural and in artificial landscape. In some scenes it is almost essential. When the dreary heath is spread before the eye and ideas if wildness and desolation are required, what more suitable accompaniment can be imaged than the blasted oak, ragged, scathed and leafless; shooting its peeled white branches thwart the gathering blackness of some rising storm ...[5]

Gilpin urged everyone, not just artists, to go out into the landscape and look for scenes that reminded them of paintings by such masters as Claude Lorraine, not as examples of the Ideal, but as a way of seeing. In so doing he taught a generation to see and appreciate nature, through the mediation of art. In the last decades of the eighteenth century and the early years of the next, hundreds of travellers would set out to discover where scenes of Picturesque beauty might be found in Britain.

Uvedale Price and Richard Payne Knight

The Picturesque provided the background to the theories of Uvedale Price and Richard Payne Knight, estate owners in the Welsh borders. Price initially saw Dutch landscape paintings as a source of instruction and inspiration when creating his own picturesque landscape at Foxley, but as time went by, these were supplanted by direct observations of natural forms and features. When laying out an estate, "it was", said Price, "essential to arrange scenes of intricacy and variety, skillfully divided and arranged in separate compositions, and shown successively in scenes contrasted with each other". The variety is inexhaustible, "especially if to these scenes of beauty in nature, are added the novelty of the seasons, or weather". And, he said, by careful management – if "the proprietor improves, not by a preconcerted plan, but by the more safe and certain method of experimentation and observation".[6]

PLATE 41. B. T. Pouncy after T. Hearn, engravings *c.* 1794 from *The Landscape: A Didactic Poem* in which R. Payne Knight mocked the smooth style of Brown and favoured the roughness of the picturesque.

Richard Payne Knight on the other hand followed his mentor Archibald Alison, in arguing that "all pleasures of the intellect arise from the association of ideas". This being so, he said:

we shall find that much of the pleasure, which we receive from painting, sculpture, music, poetry, etc. arises from our associating other ideas with those immediately excited by them. Hence the productions of these arts are never thoroughly enjoyed but by persons, whose minds are enriched by a variety of kindred and corresponding imagery; ….

Of this description are the objects and circumstances called *picturesque:* (for except in the instances, before explained,) of pleasing colour, light and shadow, they afford no pleasure, but to persons conversant with painting, and sufficiently skilled in it to distinguish, and be really delighted with its real excellences.[7]

And referring to the Pastoral landscape Knight added:

a person conversant with the writings of Theocritus and Virgil, will relish pastoral scenery more than one unacquainted with such poetry. The spectator, having his mind enriched with the embellishments of the painter and the poet, applies them, by spontaneous association of ideas, to the natural objects presented to his eye, which thus acquire ideal and imaginary beauties; that is beauties, which are not felt by the organic sense of vision; but by the intellect and imagination through that sense.[8]

In 1794 Knight published *The Landscape: a Didactic Poem,* as a strongly worded critique of the prevailing fashion for the Ideal natural landscape. Quoting both Virgil and Lucretius as his literary models Knight dismissed the Brownian estate and advocated a rougher, more picturesque beauty of natural landscapes – as seen in the paintings of Claude or the work of the Dutch and Flemish artists he championed (Plate 41). Using words with the precision of a scalpel, Knight surgically dissected landscapes, like those at Tabley House:

Oft when I've seen a some lonely mansion stand,
Fresh from the improver's hand

> Midst shaven lawns, that far around it creep
> In one eternal sweep:
> And scattered clumps, that nod at one another,
> Each stiffly waving to its formal brother;
> Tired with extensive scene, so dull and bare,
> To Heaven devoutly I've addressed my prayer, –
> Again the moss-grown terraces to raise,
> And spread the labyrinth's perplexing maze;
> Replace in even lines the ductile yew,
> And plant again the ancient avenue,
> Some features then, at least we should obtain,
> To mark this flat, insipid, waving plain;
> Some vary'd tints and forms would intervene,
> To break this uniform, eternal green.[9]

Of course what Knight really wanted was a naturalistic landscape and on his estate at Downton Vale, near Ludlow, Shropshire, Knight laid out picturesque walks along the river Teme with caves, hermit cells and an Alpine bridge over the rushing water, prompting Humphry Repton, the leading landscape gardener of the day, to describe Downton Vale as "one of the most beautiful and romantic valleys that the imagination can conceive".

Unfortunately some advocates of the Picturesque strayed into the realms of absurdity and were heavily criticised, most cruelly by William Combe's Dr Syntax in *The Schoolmaster's Tour,* a thinly disguised reference to William Gilpin's tour of the Lakes. Much of the criticism was directed at its concerns for petty details (Plate 42):

> Upon that bank awhile I'll sit,
> And let poor Grizzle graze a bit;
> But, as my time shall not be lost,
> I'll make a drawing of the post;
> And tho' your flimsy taste may flout it,
> There's something picturesque about it.[10]

Given the intense level of satirical criticism, it is hardly surprising that the influence of the Picturesque and the theories of Gilpin, Price *et al.* on the Romantic movement, and in particular on the poet William Wordsworth and artist John Constable, was underplayed. But the satire stemmed from the excesses of the picturesque movement not its central message. As Christopher Hussey wrote in his seminal work *The Picturesque* (1927): "the picturesque interregnum between classical and romantic art was necessary in order to enable the imagination to form the habit of feeling through the eyes".[11]

William Wordsworth and the Picturesque

Wordsworth (1770–1850), was born in Cockermouth on the northern edge of the Lake District and grew up to love the moors and fells, in a mystical as well as physical sense. In his autobiographical poem *The Prelude* Wordsworth

PLATE 42. William Combe/Thomas Rowlandson: *The Tours of Dr Syntax in Search of The Picturesque c.*1809. Dr Syntax 'Losing His Way'. The presence of three animals in the background, with a fourth standing back, is an arrangement advocated by William Gilpin – thus emphasising the object of the caricature.

said as a child he imagined the moorlands breathing down his neck and once, when out on the lake, he had to row in panic when he thought a cliff was pursuing him across the water. As Seamus Heaney observed, every child has its share of such uncanny moments but Wordsworth recognised "by intuition and introspection that such moments were not only the foundation of his sensibility, but also the clue to his identity".[12] In 1790, whilst an undergraduate at Cambridge, Wordsworth went on a tour of the Swiss Alps of Europe with a friend, walking 20–30 miles (*c.*32–48 km) a day to seek out places renowned for the beauty of their landscape. A friend of later life, Thomas De Quincy, author of *Confessions of an English Opium-Eater,* said that for Wordsworth walking was a mode of exertion, which "stood in stead of wine, spirits, and all other stimulants whatsoever to the animal spirits, to which he has been indebted for a life of unclouded happiness, and we for much of what is excellent in his writing".[13] Five years later Wordsworth met Samuel Taylor Coleridge and in need of money, the two friends prepared a collection of poems, the *Lyrical Ballads,* published anonymously in 1798. Three years later the revised edition included Wordsworth's famous definition of poetry: "the spontaneous overflow of powerful feelings: it takes its origins from emotion recollected in tranquility". This, said Wordsworth, was a new type of poetry, in a "language really used by men".[14]

In the summer of 1798 Wordsworth revisited Tintern Abbey, a picturesque ruin made famous by William Gilpin. Choosing not to locate himself at the ruins, recently painted by Turner, he selected a place from where he could see the landscape spread out before him. In the poem Wordsworth describes the mental journey he has made; from seeing the landscape in purely picturesque terms to an appreciation through feeling. In the opening lines Wordsworth describes the scene in picturesque terms:

> The day is come when I again repose
> Here, under this dark sycamore, and view
> These plots of cottage-ground, these orchard tufts,
> Which, at this season, with their unripe fruits,
> Among the woods and copses lose themselves,
> Nor, with their green and simple hue, disturb
> The wild green landscape. Once again I see
> These hedge-rows, hardly hedge-rows, little lines
> Of sportive wood run wild; these pastoral farms
> Green to the very door; and wreathes of smoke
> Sent up, in silence, from among the trees,
> With some uncertain notice, as might seem,
> Of vagrant dwellers in the houseless woods,
> Or of some hermit's cave, where by his fire
> The hermit sits alone.

Wordsworth, *Lines written a few miles above Tintern Abbey*, 9–23

The sycamore frames the picturesque elements – the wood run-wild, pastoral farms echoing the *Georgics*, "green to the door and wreathes of smoke sent up in silence, from among the trees" – and that most picturesque of figures, the Hermit. But Wordsworth goes on to explains how his perception of landscape has changed since he first looked on this scene as young man:

> For I have learned
> To look on nature, not as in the hour
> Of thoughtless youth, but hearing often times
> The still, sad music of humanity,
> Not harsh or grating, though of ample power
> To chasten and subdue. And I have felt
> A presence that disturbs me with the joy
> Of elevated thoughts; a sense sublime
> Of something far more deeply interfused,
> Whose dwelling is the light of setting suns,
> And the round ocean, and the living air,
> And the blue sky, and in the mind of man,
> A motion and a spirit, that impels
> All thinking things, all objects of all thought,
> And rolls through all things.

Wordsworth, *Lines written a few miles above Tintern Abbey*, 89–103

Wordsworth has added to his sensory appreciation of the pastoral landscape, a spiritual dimension that borders on the pantheistic:

> Therefore am I still
> A lover of the meadows and the woods,
> And mountains; and of all that we behold
> From this green earth; of all the mighty world
> Of eye and ear, both what they half-create,
> And what perceive; well pleased to recognise
> In nature and the language of the sense,

The anchor of my purest thoughts, the nurse,
The guide, the guardian of my heart, and soul
Of all my moral being.

Wordsworth, Lines written a few miles above Tintern Abbey, 103–112[15]

Grasmere

In the autumn of 1798 Wordsworth and his sister Dorothy travelled to Germany with their friend Coleridge. Left on their own in Goslar, Germany, at the foot of the Harz mountains, they endured a bitterly cold winter, and Wordsworth, depressed and homesick, began to write what would become *The Prelude*. On returning they were desperately in need of a place to call home and during a walking tour of the Lake District, with Dorothy and Coleridge, Wordsworth came across an old, uninhabited inn, the *Dove and Olive*, at Grasmere. Wordsworth rented the cottage and moved in with Dorothy on a frosty December morning in 1799 (Plate 43). Since childhood Wordsworth had looked upon the Vale of Grasmere as paradise and saw in Dove Cottage the place he could fulfill his childhood dream of living a simple life, close to nature, surrounded by all he held dear – people, places, even the local animals and wildlife:[16]

Something that makes this individual Spot,
This small abiding place of many men,
A termination, and a last retreat,
A centre, come for wheresoe'er you will,
A Whole without dependence or defect,
Made for itself, and happy in itself,
Perfect Contentment, Unity entire.

Wordsworth, Home at Grasmere[17]

Wordsworth was now at the height of his powers, his personal idiom summed up in the words 'nature' and 'imagination'. As Seamus Heaney expressed it, by his late 20s "he knew one big truth, and for the next ten years he kept developing its implications with intense excitement, industry and purpose".[18] In his poetry Wordsworth would adapt the criteria of picturesque aesthetics, adding an emotional dimension offered by the associative value of word, memory and subjective response.

Wordsworth and the hard Pastoral

Though Wordsworth, like the other Romantic poets, no longer saw the landscape through the eyes of classical deities and images, that is not to say the pastoral image was no longer relevant. In his poem *Home at Grasmere*, Wordsworth examined the essence of his craft – pastoral verse – and found it wanting:

PLATE 43. Grasmere: Dove Cottage (in the foreground) from the garden – Wordsworth's "domestic slip of mountain". The much-loved garden was made by William and his sister Dorothy. (The large house obscuring the view of Grasmere was built after Wordsworth left the cottage). From this seat Dorothy wrote in her journal:

6TH May Thursday 1802. A sweet morning ... & here we are sitting in the orchard. It is one o clock. We are sitting upon a seat under the wall ... It is a nice cool shady spot. The small Birds are singing – Lambs bleating, Cuckow callin –The Thrush sings by Fits, Thomas Ashburner's axe is going quietly (without passion) in the orchard –Hens are cackling, Flies humming, the women talking together at their door – Plumb & pear trees are in Blossom, apple trees greenis – the opposite woods green, the crows are cawing. We have heard Ravens. The Ash Trees are in blossom, Birds flying all about us. The stitchwort is coming out, there is one budding Lychnis. The primroses are passing their prime. Celandine violets & wood sorrel for ever more – little geranium & pansies on the wall.

> ... is there not
> An art, a music and a strain of words
> That shall be life, the acknowledged voice of life?
> Shall speak of what is done among the fields,
> Done truly there, or felt, of solid good
> And real evil, yet be sweet withal,
> More grateful, more harmonious than the breath,
> The idle breath of sweetest pipe attuned
> To pastoral fancies?

Wordsworth, *Home at Grasmere*, 401–9[19]

Every schoolboy knew where sheep grazed in Theocritus and Virgil but now it was Wordsworth's intention to re-site the Pastoral on the fells of the Lake District. But it was necessary first to make an essential readjustment to the image. In his semi-autobiographical poem, *The Prelude,* Wordsworth contrasted the old pastoral with the harsh realities of daily life he saw around him. To make his point he littered the poem with references to Virgil's *Georgics*:

> Smooth life had flock and shepherd in old time,
> Long springs and tepid winters, on the banks
> Of delicate Galessus; and no less
> Those scattered along Adria's myrtle shores:
> Smooth life the herdsman, and his snow-white herd
> To triumphs and to sacrificial rites
> Devoted, on the inviolable stream
> Of rich Clitumnus; and the goat-herd lived
> As calmly, underneath the pleasant brows
> Of cool Lucretilis, where the pipe was heard
> Of Pan, the invisible God, thrilling the rocks
> With tutelary music, from all harm
> The fold protecting.

Wordsworth, *Prelude* Bk 8, 173–85[20]

Most revealing are the allusions to the two rivers; Clitumnus which Virgil described as "continual spring and a summer beyond her season"; a place where cattle bear twice a year, apples give a second crop, there are no wild beasts and "no monkshood grows to deceive and poison the wretch who picks it".[21] And at Galaesus, where an old man, a Corycian, owned a few acres of land once useless for arable, grazing cattle and the growing of vines, which he transformed into a kitchen garden. "He could go indoors at night to a table heaped with dainties he never had to buy" along with "contentment equal to the wealth of kings".[22] Wordsworth paints an idyllic scene of a smooth, leisured life, of gentle winters, of festivals, all under the protection of Pan. How very different was the Lake District, where Wordsworth's own father had perished after becoming lost on the fells; not that the pastoral idyll was unattainable, for Wordsworth had seen it in Goslar:

> In manhood then, have seen a pastoral tract
> Like one of these, where Fancy might run wild,
> Though under skies less generous, less serene:
> There, for her own delight had Nature framed
> A pleasure-ground, diffused a fair expanse
> Of level pasture, islanded with groves
> And banked with woody risings; but the Plain
> Endless, here opening widely out, and there
> Shut up in lesser lakes or beds of lawn
> And intricate recesses, creek or bay
> Sheltered within a shelter, where at large
> The shepherd strays, a rolling hut his home.
> Thither he comes with spring-time, there abides
> All summer, and at sunrise ye may hear
> His flageolet to liquid notes of love
> Attuned, or sprightly fife resounding far.

Wordsworth: *Prelude*: 186–201[23]

In those circumstances it was possible to attain the soft pastoral, marked only by "unlaborious pleasure, with no task/More toilsome to carve a beechen bowl", – a reminder of the beechwood cups in Virgil's third *Eclogue* – but Wordsworth rejoiced in his own, harsher environment:

> Yet, hail to you
> Moors, mountains, headlands, and ye hollow vales,
> Ye long deep channels for the Atlantic's voice,
> Powers of my native region! Ye that seize
> The heart with firmer grasp! Your snows and streams
> Ungovernable, and your terrifying winds,
> That howl so dismally for him who treads
> Companionless your awful solitudes!

Wordsworth: *Prelude*: 216–23[24]

Here since childhood, Wordsworth had vicariously experienced the hard pastoral, and:

> There, 'tis the shepherd's task the winter long
> To wait upon the storms: of their approach
> Sagacious, into sheltering coves he drives
> His flock, and thither from the homestead bears
> A toilsome burden up the craggy ways,
> And deals it out, their regular nourishment
> Strewn on the frozen snow. And when the spring
> Looks out, and all the pastures dance with lambs,
> And when the flock, with warmer weather, climbs
> Higher and higher, him his office leads
> To watch their goings, whatsoever track
> The wanderers choose. For this he quits his home
> At day-spring, and no sooner doth the sun
> Begin to strike him with a fire-like heat,
> Than he lies down upon some shining rock,
> And breakfasts with his dog.
>
> Wordsworth, *Prelude*, 223–8[25]

In this, the hard pastoral, Wordsworth replaces the guardianship of Pan, the invisible God, with the selfless stewardship of the shepherd who lives a life of pain and pleasure – the "word 'office' surely chosen for its classical connotations of ethical responsibility".[26] And despite all his hard work, he has time to "lie down upon some shining rock, and breakfast with his dog". His enjoyment of nature, transforms what others might see as mundane agricultural slavery into a 'service' to higher powers. It is this perception that makes him a spiritual freeman:

> In those vast regions where his service lies,
> A freeman, wedded to his life of hope
> And hazard, and hard labour interchanged
> With that majestic indolence so dear
> To native man.
>
> Wordsworth, *Prelude*, 252–6[27]

Like all Romantics, Wordsworth was inspired by Rousseau's *Social Contract* and the idea that those who lived closest to nature would most likely, live lives of greater virtue. His essential point was that this "kind of hardship, independent, isolated, and above all, *natural*, ennobles", not just the shepherd but the spectator. In *The Prelude* Wordsworth turns the shepherd into an aesthetic object:

> His form hath flashed upon me, glorified
> By the deep radiance of the setting sun:
> Or him have I descried in distant sky,
> A solitary object and sublime,
> Above all height! like an aerial cross
> Stationed alone upon a spiry rock
> Of the Chartreuse, for worship. Thus was man
> Ennobled outwardly before my sight,

And thus my heart was early introduced
To an unconscious love and reverence
Of human nature;

Wordsworth, Prelude, 269–79²⁸

Michael – a pastoral poem

Nowhere is that reverence more evident than in Wordsworth's poem *Michael* – subtitled a pastoral poem, written around 1800. The poem begins with a description, a wordscape, of the landscape where Michael, an eighty-year-old shepherd lived and struggled with his wife Isabel, some twenty years his junior, and their son Luke:

If from the public way you turn your steps
Up the tumultuous brook of Greenhead Ghyll
You will suppose that with an upright path
Your feet must struggle; in such a bold ascent
The pastoral mountains front you, face to face you
But courage! for around the boisterous a brook
The mountains have all opened out themselves,
And made a hidden valley of their own.
No habitation can be seen; but they
Who journey thither find themselves alone
With a few sheep, with rocks and stones, and kites
That overhead are sailing in the sky.
In truth an utter solitude;

Wordsworth, Michael, 1–13²⁹

Michael had inherited the land many years before and learnt to understand the harsh weather of the fells; "the winds are now devising work for me". These experiences had etched themselves on his memory:

Fields, where with cheerful spirits he had breathed
The common air: which with vigorous step
He had so often climbed: which had impressed
So many incidents upon his mind
Of hardship. skill or courage, joy or fear:
Which like a book, preserved upon his memory
Of the dumb animals, whom he had saved,
Had fed or sheltered, linking such acts
The certainty of honourable gain;

Wordsworth, Michael, 66–73³⁰

By living close to nature, the family had been happy and content for many years, but when Luke turned eighteen, this harsh idyll came to an end. Luke was sent to work for a kinsman, a rich merchant in the city, to pay off a debt incurred by the son of Michael's brother. Like a good son Luke agrees readily to go. On the eve of his departure, Michael takes Luke to a place on the side of mountain where he had been intending to erect a sheepfold and attempts to give the boy advice that would keep his character pure. He instructs Luke to place the cornerstone, telling him he will finish the sheepfold while he is away. At first Luke prospers but later falls into bad company and becomes a criminal, fleeing "beyond the seas". Michael never finishes the sheepfold and goes there daily to mourn the loss of his son. Seven years later he dies and after his wife dies three years later, the farm is sold out of the family and the land ploughed over. All that remains is the oak that grew beside the door and the unfinished sheepfold by the brook.

Wordsworth's message is unequivocal; the pastoral life is pure, moral and happy. Like Virgil, Wordsworth saw the farmer and his family, living an uncomplicated, spiritual life devoted to hard toil, close to nature, as the ideal bringing its own rewards. And of course, the town and its industry corrupts; had Luke remained he would have retained his honest, moral life. However, Wordsworth's opinions were to change and by 1815 he admitted not only were the admirable, domestic emotions of the rural poor under siege but that he had sentimentalised the idea of rural labour.[31] In Book 8 of *The Excursion,* published that year, there is a formal lament for the disappearance of the georgic values, and as children are sucked into the urban vortices as prisoners of towns and factories they lose their birthright:

> Oh! where is now the character of peace,
> Sobriety and order, and chaste love,
> And honest dealing, and untainted speech,
> And pure good-will, and hospitable cheer:
> That made the very thought of country-life
> A thought of refuge.
>
> Wordsworth, *Excursion* bk 8, 239–44[32]

Today, though the sheep remain and the landscape is much as Wordsworth described it, you are more likely to meet a rambler than a shepherd in Greenhead Ghyll. It is the decedents of those urban children who have vicariously taken the place of the shepherd and it is the rambler who enjoys a sense of freedom in the fells. As folk singer/writer Ewan McColl expressed it after the infamous Peak District Kinder Trespass in the 1930s (see Chapter 16):

> I'm a rambler, I'm a rambler from Manchester way
> I get all my pleasure the hard moorland way
> I may be a wage slave on Monday
> But I am a freeman on Sunday
> I've been o'er Snowdon, I've slept upon Crowden
> I've camped by the Wain Stones as well
> I've sunbaked on Kinder, been burnt to a cinder
> And many more things I can tell
> My rucksack has oft been my pillow
> The heather has oft been my bed
> And sooner than part from the mountains
> I think I would rather be dead.
>
> Ewan McColl, *The Manchester Rambler*[33]

John Constable and the soft Pastoral

While Wordsworth was establishing the hard pastoral vision of England, a place close to Godliness and physically accessed by walking, his contemporary John Constable was creating a comparable, but equally important vision of the softer, lowland countryside. In contrast to Wordsworth, Constable was drawn to human landscapes, as Charles Leslie, his first biographer observed, "he required villages, churches, farmhouses and cottages". Constable himself said it was the Suffolk landscape, that made me a painter and I am grateful, "the sound of water escaping from mill dams etc., willows, old rotten planks, slimy posts and brickwork, I love such things". His vision of the soft georgic complements Wordsworth's hard georgic, and it has become accepted as the way we see the lowland, farmed landscape.

When Constable entered the Royal Academy school in 1799, at the late age of twenty-two, he was instructed to study human form and copy Old Masters, including paintings by Claude Lorrain, Jacob van Ruisdael and Thomas Gainsborough. These he found inimical to his true desire to paint landscapes, subjects the Academy considered unworthy for a serious artist:

> For the last two years I have been running after pictures, and seeking the truth at second hand. I have not endeavoured to represent nature with the same elevation of mind with which I set out, but have rather tried to make my performances look like the work of other men ...There is room enough for a natural painter. The great vice of the present day is bravura, an attempt to do something beyond the truth.[34]

He resolved to return home to East Bergholt, Suffolk and "spend time making some laborious studies from nature – and I shall endeavour to get a pure and unaffected representation of the scenes that may employ me with respect to colour particularly and anything else". That summer and for the next few years Constable made hundreds of sketches of the Stour valley, always aspiring to find the truth of nature.

His early paintings were, unsurprisingly, influenced by the Great Masters, with the addition of his own improvements. The painting of *Dedham Vale* (1802) derived its pictorial composition from Claude's *Hagar and the Angel,* which Constable had seen on a visit to his patron, Sir George Beaumont. He added an elaborate foreground with a wealth of naturalistic detail, not forgetting the picturesque principle of foreground roughness (Plate 44). The colour and tonality suggests he borrowed as much from Gainsborough as from Claude but an important difference which announced Constable's new conception of nature is apparent in his treatment of trees. For Gainsborough it was sufficient to show the generic distinction between trees, to differentiate oak from ash, but Constable not only wanted to render the appearance of the tree more accurately but to express the individuality of each tree.

After his early work in the Stour valley Constable's progress slowed and, failing to establish himself as a professional painter, he embarked on sketching tours. He first visited the Peak District, Derbyshire and then the Lake District

PLATE 44. John Constable (1776–1837): *Dedham Vale* c.1802.

where the landscape had a liberating effect. Despite appalling weather, Constable explored the fells both artistically and physically gaining a new sense of the organic structure of landscape, sketching details of plants, waterfalls, clouds and much besides. During the visit he met William Wordsworth and a friendship gradually developed, nurtured by Sir George Beaumont who was patron to them both. Constable used Wordsworth's poetry on the title page of *English landscapes* (1830) though none of the engravings was of the Lake District. On his return Constable was determined to concentrate on painting the scenes that had delighted him as boy; village lanes, the fields and meadows running down to the River Stour or boat traffic passing the locks at Flatford or Dedham (Plate 45).

The engravings show why Constable would become so universally accepted as

a natural painter. From Bellini to Claude landscape paintings had been built up of distinct zones, with a light and colour used to highlight what was important in the painting. As a result the eye passed through the landscape in a zig-zag fashion, moving along a path the feet might travel if the landscape were truly three-dimensional. The viewer being drawn ever further in by the presence of a river, a road, or the structure of the landscape itself. This hierarchical organisation facilitated movement through the picture. Claude had used such *coulisses* and subsequently the technique was applied to the eighteenth century landscape garden. Gently curving paths encouraged the visitor to move from one scene to another, each one separated and highlighted by alternating patterns of light and shade – an effect created by evergreen shrubs and trees. Constable rejected this artificial contrivance in his paintings, no one single element, whether in colour, tone, handling or subject, was allowed to dominate the landscape. The eye roamed freely over the painting, just as if the spectator was looking at the landscape with the artist. As Bermingham said "the 'artlessness' thus artfully managed in such landscapes convinces us of the realism of the representations, and the impenetrability imposes on us a feeling of nature's mysteriousness".[35]

His first exhibited oil painting *Dedham Vale: Morning* (1811) was his most ambitious depiction of his local scenery so far. It was a simple snapshot of the valley in the early morning light but its numerous vignette-like details go beyond the mere picturesque. It depicted a country scene of ordinary every day life; in the foreground are crossroads, but the road and lanes lead out to the sides of the painting not into the distance, and a boy brings cattle from their overnight pasture, a woman on the lane is going to market and a man is on the road above her. As Leslie Parris noted, the overall effect of the Claudian composition and a stone inscribed Dedham Vale in the foreground adds an Arcadian dimension to the picture. The foreground, containing all these naturalistic but disparate elements are in shade, and by comparison, the pastoral landscape beyond glows in the morning light. This ordered landscape with scattered churches seems to extend far beyond the lateral boundaries of the canvas, unifying the picture into a singular whole. In these paintings Constable, like Wordsworth, was redefining the pastoral, gone are the classical references and the georgic was appropriated as a genre to convey the essence and timeless quality of the English landscape.

It has been suggested that although Constable's paintings feature many elements of the pastoral, his landscapes are not Edenic nor do his figures, "blissfully rejoicing in their work", seem to be totally pastoral.[36] But in another sense his engravings, and the painting of *Dedham Vale: Morning*, expresses the very essence of pastoral. One of the definitions followed in this book has been that the pastoral achieves its significance by opposition – by contrasts, expressed or implied – to the existing order. That is to say, the values embodied in its world create conflict with other ways of life. The most traditional contrast is between a little world of natural simplicity and the great world of civilization, with its power, statecraft, ordered society, established codes of behaviour and artifice in general. In Constable's day the conflict between the two was tearing the countryside apart as the landscape of lowland England, including East Anglia, was subjected to Acts of Inclosure, between 1760 and 1820. Common Land was enclosed by hedges to make fields for cattle, in the process creating a landless generation who found themselves living off charity, often forced into industrial towns to seek work in the new factories. It was a scene described by the agricultural labourer John Clare,

> Thus came enclosure – ruin was its guide
> But freedom's clapping hands enjoyed the sight,
> Though comfort's cottage soon was thrust aside
> And workhouse prisons raised upon the site.
>
> John Clare, *Fallen Elm*[37]

Two years after this poem was published (1820) agrarian unrest and riots broke-out in Suffolk. Constable was aware of the very great changes taking place in the Suffolk landscape but there is no hint of this in *Dedham Vale: Morning*. At first glance it is a delightful scene, one Constable had known since childhood – but the landscape of Dedham Vale has been redrawn by Enclosure; hedges surround rectangular fields in which cattle graze or hay is to be cut for winter feed, and prosperous farmsteads sit at the centre of the new farms. In the centre and at either side of the painting are church towers spreading their anglican authority over the landscape. In contrast to this ordered, authoritarian world is the natural simplicity of the old world, described as Arcadia. Have the cows spent the night on perhaps the remnants of common land? The girl and the man make their way along old sunken lanes and tracks, while in the valley a new turnpike road speeds the movement of coaches. Constable makes no moral judgement; as a good churchman and son of a corn merchant he would have approved of the agricultural scene before him and the figures were just a picturesque element. But whether he intended to or not, Constable shows us the actuality of rural life at a time of great change; the passing of the old order and the emergence of the new. In his critique, Barrell in *The Dark Side of Landscape* suggests that unlike his contemporary artist George Morland, whose paintings are not ambiguous and "we know ... that raggedness is being shown as aesthetic *and* social interest" with Constable "we do not know as we study these figures whether we are discovering something about what Constable has seen, or about how he sees it".[38]

After Constable moved to London in 1816 he rarely returned to the Stour Valley. When he embarked on his most ambitious project, a series of six paintings showing the Stour valley, he relied on his memories and the many sketches he had made of landscape and clouds. Constable poured himself, and everything he knew and loved, into what he called his 'six-footers' – the colour of meadows and trees, clouds, the effect of light glistening on leaves and water, and everyday country scenes, as well as the feelings they evoked in him. The most famous of these paintings, was the *Hay Wain* (1821) whose charm lies in its very innocence (Plate 46). It depicts a pastoral scene of haymaking at noon, the empty cart is fording the river into the fields beyond where men are scything and a second haywain is being loaded.[39] These paintings were a culmination of Constable's craft; as he matured more emphasis was placed on the landscape

PLATE 46. John Constable: *The Hay Wain* – a full-scale study *c.*1821.

and the figures become sparse and indistinct. And as his interest in nature grew "the emphasis of his work becomes less social, and the figures carry less and less of the meaning of the pictures, which is displaced into the clouds" where said Constable, "the Student may daily watch her endless varieties of effect".[40] Constable's late paintings do not portray the real life of those who labour in the fields, rather in Barrell's words they "combine the Pastoral and the Georgic in a way now familiar to us: they attempt to reconcile, and to conceal, the gap between what we do and what our servants, do through the mediating term of nature".[41] In so doing, paintings like the *Hay Wain*, helped create an image of the ideal pastoral landscape; by avoiding any engagement with reality, the observer is free to escape and wallow in the warm Arcadian glow of the English countryside.

A national icon

In 1827 the *Times* called Constable "unquestionably the finest landscape painter of the day" and when he died 10 years later the press were unanimous in asserting that though "his mode of painting was peculiar", it did embody "much truth and sound principles of art which will render his works lasting, and far more valuable in years hence". Constable's landscapes were altogether more comforting for sedentary viewers; one did not really know where they were, and one certainly did not expect to walk into them, but they were, and remain, the abiding image of England. His move to the status of national icon began in 1866 when the Commons Preservation Society associated Debham and the Stour Valley with 'Englishness'. His reputation continued to grow and gained momentum with the rise of 'commodity patriotism' in the late 1880s. Growing concern over German militarism and foreign wars fanned the patriotic flames, and what better way could a citizen support England than by buying a painting of the heart of England by an Englishman? Constable's paintings fitted the bill and by 1900 the *Haywain* was well on its way to becoming a national icon. Admirers were not concerned with his brush work, fidelity to nature, nor did they praise his 'picturesque portrayal' or careful use of chiaroscuro – instead they began to search out rural areas that resembled the paintings. Nostalgia for a rural England fueled both the artist's popularity and a thriving tourist industry in the Stour valley, known today as 'Constable Country'. As English industrial supremacy gave way to German and American industrialisation, the association of England with old-fashioned agrarian scenes grew stronger and by 1925 the Stour valley was seen as a refuge from encroaching modernity. By the Second World War English nostalgia had decidedly classified Constable as a rural painter in the pastoral tradition. Today the pastoral image conveyed by Constable's paintings are what many people nostalgically regard as the countryside, even though it bears little resemblance to the modern agricultural scene.

Notes and References

1. Gilpin, W., *A dialogue upon the gardens of the Right Honourable the Lord Viscount Cobham at Stow*, 1748. www.faculty.bsc.edu/jtatter.gilpin.html

2. Gilpin was persuaded to publish accounts of his tours; *Observations on the River Wye and several parts of South Wales, etc, relative chiefly to Picturesque Beauty; made in the summer of 1770* (1782) was followed by *Observations on mountains and lakes of Cumberland and Westmorland and the west of England* (1786) and the *Scottish Highlands* (1789). The books were an instant success, both in Britain and America and quickly ran to three editions, with annotated versions appearing for several decades after his death.

3. Gilpin, W., *An essay on prints*. T. Cadell and W. Davies, London, 1768.

4. Quoted in Andrews, M., *The Search for the Picturesque*. Scolar Press, Aldershot, 1989, p. 64. George Stubbs was painter best known for his paintings of horses, most often fine race horses.

5. Gilpin, W., *Remarks on forest scenery & other woodland views* 1. Fraser & Co., Edinburgh, 1834, p. 53.

6. Price, U., *Essays on the Picturesque*. J. Mawman, London, 1810, p. 12.

7. Knight, R. P., *An analytical inquiry into the principles of Taste*. T. Payne, London, 1805, pp. 145–6. In *Essays on the Nature and Principles of Taste* (1790) Reverend Archibald Alison advanced his theory of Association. This denied the existence of objective qualities inherent in objects and claimed anything might be beautiful if it aroused pleasant and therefore beautiful ideas. Picturesque objects were those that reminded a person of pictures they had seen, and Alison suggested the art of gardening was akin to landscape painting and accordingly, the same principles could be applied to the improved landscape.

8. *Ibid.*, pp. 145–6.

9. Payne Knight, R. P., *The Landscape: A Didactic Poem*. W. Bulmer 1795. Republished 1972, Gregg International, Farnborough, pp. 31–2.

10. Savory, J. J., *Thomas Rowlandson's Dr Syntax*. Cygnus Arts, London, 1997, p. 20.

11. Hussey, C., *The Picturesque: studies in a point of view*. G. P. Putnam's Sons, London, 1927, p. 4.

12. Heaney, S., 'The triumph of spirit'. *Guardian* 11 February 2006.

13. quoted in Solnit, R., *Wanderlust*. Verso, London, 2001, pp. 105–6.

14. Wordsworth, W., *Preface to the Lyrical Ballads*, 1802.

15. *Lyrical Ballads*. J. & A. Arch, London, 1798. *Lines written a few miles above Tintern Abbey* was the terminal poem in the *Lyrical Ballads*.

16. *Home at Grasmere: the journal of Dorothy Wordsworth and the poems of William Wordsworth*. Penguin Classics, London, 1986, p. 234.

17. Wordsworth, W., *Home at Grasmere*, lines 145–50. www.bartleby.com /145/ww301htm.

18. Heaney, S., *op. cit.*

19. www.bartleby.com /145/ww301htm, lines 401–9.

20. www.bartleby.com /145/ww294htm.

21. Day Lewis, C. (trans.), *Virgil: The Eclogues, The Georgics*. Oxford University Press, London, 1983, p. 74.

22. *Ibid.*, p. 112.

23. www.bartleby.com /145/ww294htm.

24. *Ibid.*

25. *Ibid.*

26. Patterson, A., *op. cit.*, p. 280.

27. www.bartleby.com /145/ww294htm.
28. *Ibid.*
29. www.bartleby.com /41/372.htm.
30. *Ibid.*
31. Wordsworth, W., *Guide to the Lakes.* Frances Lincoln, London, 2004, pp. 92–3.
32. www.bartleby.com /145/ww294htm.
33. www.ntlworld.com/paul.thorp/lyrramb.htm.
34. Parris, L., *Constable: pictures from the exhibition.* Tate Gallery, London, 1991, p. 15.
35. Bermingham, A., *Landscape and Ideology.* University of California Press, Berkeley, 1986, p. 120.
36. Jorgensen, R., *The Evolution of the Signified in Constable's Landscape Paintings.* 2008, Oxford University, unpublished, p. 9.
37. www.poemhunter.com/poem/the-fallen-elm. Clare's inspiration to write poetry came after buying a copy of James Thomson's *Seasons,* with money he could ill-afford.
38. Barrell, J., *The Dark Side of the Landscape.* Cambridge University Press, Cambridge, 1980, p. 150.
39. Constable often made full-scale studies for large exhibition paintings using a broad painting style to establish the general balance of the composition and its colours.
40. Barrell, J., *op. cit.,* p. 162. Quote from *The Introduction to English Landscape Scene*ry.
41. *Ibid.,* p. 163.

CHAPTER ELEVEN

The Pastoral Vision
and the American Dream

When in 1524, the Italian explorer Giovanni da Verrazzano gave the name Arcadia to the coast north of Virginia on account of the beauty of the trees he little imagined that for over 300 years the Virgilian concept would influence cultural life and shape the making of America. In England there was every reason why Elizabethans should have seen the new continent as Arcadia for the exploration coincided with a time when the Court, its courtiers, musicians and poets were enthralled by pastoral ideas and ideals. There had never been a time when pastoral poetry enjoyed such popularity; in 1579 Spenser's Virgilian poem *The Shepheards Calendar* was published and eleven years later, Sidney's *Arcadia* (1590). What Elizabethans found particularly fascinating about the New World was the absence of anything like European society. It was a "landscape untouched by history, nature unmixed with art. The new continent looked, or so they thought, the way the world might have looked before the beginning of civilization". A Golden Age confirmed by the presence of the Indians and their simple ways; for the shepherds substitute Wanchese and Manteo, the two 'Savages' brought home by an early traveller Captain Arthur Barlowe. Leo Marx noted in *The Machine in the Garden*, they fitted perfectly into the picture of America as a mere landscape, remote and unspoiled, and a possible setting for pastoral retreat.[1] As Marx makes clear it is impossible to separate the taste for pastoral and the excitement felt throughout Europe, about the New World. The age was fascinated by the idea that the New World was or might become Arcadia, a realisation of the long-held dream of an idealised, imaginary world of perpetual spring that had held sway over mens' minds since Theocritus and Virgil.[2]

Early arrivals

From the late sixteenth century the English, Scots, French, Swedes, Germans and Dutch began to colonise eastern North America, and by 1700 there were British settlers living mainly as small town farmers. The most important and accurate history of the early life among these settlers was written Robert Beverley, a substantial planter and official in the colonial government. *The History and Present State of Virginia* (1705) reaffirmed the image of America as nature's garden, a new paradise of abundance; "all the Countries ... seated in or near the Latitude of Virginia, are esteemed the Fruitfullest, and Pleasantest of all Clymates ...these are reckoned the Gardens of the World ...".[3] Despite this fecundity of nature, or rather because of it, the European settlers were, in Beverly's opinion, lazy in contrast to the native Americans. The Indians, he wrote, "are an admirable people, gay, gentle, loving, generous, and faithful". The "natural Production of that Country", he says, "explains the ease of life, the fabulous freedom from care, hence the charm of the natives". And the reason for this state of bliss is obvious, they are:

> ... without the Curse of Industry, their Diversion alone, and not their labour, supplying their Necessities ... none of the Toils of Husbandry were exercised by this happy People; except the bare planting a little Corn, and Melons, which took up only a few Days in the Summer, the rest being wholly spent on the Pursuit of their Pleasures.[4]

"They are not", says Beverley:

> debauched nor corrupted with those Pomps and Vanities, which have enslaved the Rest of mankind; neither were their Hands hardened by Labour, nor their Minds corrupted by the Desire of hoarding up Treasure: They were without Boundaries to their Land: and without Property in Cattle; and seem'd to have escaped, or rather not to have been concern'd in the first Curse, *of getting their Bread by the sweat of their Brows*, for by their Pleasure alone, they supplied all their Necessities: namely by Fishing, Fowling and Hunting: Skins being their only clothing; and these, too, five-sixths of the year thrown by: living without labour, and only gathering the fruits of the earth when ripe, or fit for use: Neither fearing present want, nor solicitous for the future, but daily finding sufficient afresh for their subsistence.[5]

In contrast to the blissful lives of the Indians, the settlers, said Beverly, were dependent on England and unwilling to work:

> Thus, they depend altogether upon the liberality of nature, without endeavoring to improve its gifts by art or industry. They spunge upon the blessings of a warm sun, and a fruitful soil, and almost grudge the pains of gathering in the bounties of the earth. I should be ashamed to publish this slothful indolence of my countrymen, but that I hope it will sometime or other rouse them out of their lethargy, and excite them to make the most of those happy advantages which nature has given them: and if it does this, I am sure they will have the goodness to forgive me.[6]

In his direct and realistic observations Beverly exhorted his fellow countrymen to undertake the management of their landscape, to reconcile nature and art in ways that had been depicted since Virgil's time. In doing so Beverly's *The History and Present State of Virginia* anticipated the agricultural ideal that would be articulated by subsequent American writers, most prominently by Thomas Jefferson.

Thomas Jefferson

Jefferson (1743–1826) was born at Shadwell in the frontier county of Albermerle, Virginia. He loved this region of wooded and lavender hills and as a young boy roamed the woods, hunting and fishing, getting to know intimately the wild plants and animals. Despite coming from such a backwoods area, Jefferson received a reasonable classical education. He was able to read Greek and Roman authors in the original, something he continued to do throughout his long life and could recite the *Idylls* of Theocritus from memory. At sixteen he decided to further his classical studies by entering the William and Mary College in Williamsburg, enrolling in the Philosophy School to study mathematics, metaphysics and philosophy. There Jefferson was fortunate in being tutored and eventually befriended by Dr William Small, a member of the Scottish Enlightenment whose interests and scholarship ranged over many disciplines. He introduced Jefferson to the writings of British Empiricists, John Locke, Francis Bacon and Isaac Newton, who he came to regard as the three greatest men the world had produced.[7]

After graduating Jefferson studied law but as his *Garden Book* reveals he was already developing a keen interest in nature, gardening and garden design, alongside a growing interest in architecture. He had read the *Works of William Shenstone*, containing his essay *Unconnected Thoughts on Gardening* and purchased Dodsley's *Description of the Leasowes*, twenty years earlier. In 1786, Jefferson visited Europe to study English gardens and followed an itinerary set out by the landscape gardener, Thomas Whately, in his *Observations of English Gardens*. Jefferson wrote, "I always walked over the gardens with his (Whately's) book in my hand", noting carefully "the particular spots he described ... and saw with wonder, that his fine imagination had never been able to seduce him from the truth". "Nature", according to Whately, is always simple. It "employs but four materials in the composition of her scenes, ground, wood, water, and rock. The cultivation of nature has introduced a fifth species, the buildings requisite for the accommodation of men".[8] These were stimulating ideas for the young lawyer and planter who was evolving own plans for his picturesque estate on the edge of the American wilderness.

In 1768 Jefferson began building the house he called Monticello, levelling the mountain top across the river from Shadwell. Choosing an elevated position was a new departure in Virginia, as Fiske Kimball pointed out, it was gesture suggesting a romantic, unorthodox impulse without precedent in America or even in England.[9] However this was not strictly true, for as a classical scholar Jefferson would have been familiar with the writings of Leon Battista Alberti and his recommendation to Cosimo Medici:

> A villa should provide views to enjoy all of the Pleasures and Convenience of Air, Sun and fine prospects ... I would have it stand pretty high, but upon so easy an Ascent that it should hardly be perceptible to those that go to it, till they find themselves at the top, and the large prospect opens itself to their view.[10]

Echoing Alberti's words, Jefferson later described the location of Monticello in more poetic terms:

> Where has nature spread so rich a mantle under the eye? Mountains, rocks, rivers. With what majesty do we there ride above the storms! How sublime to look down

into the workhouse of nature, to see her clouds, hail, snow, rain, thunder, all fabricated at our feet! and the glorious Sun when rising as if out of a distant water, just gilding the top of the mountains and giving life to all nature![11]

With work underway on the house Jefferson turned his attention to the garden and estate. His youthful ideas of landscape had been fired not by "idyllic Claudian canvases or Rosa's romantic wildernesses of roaring torrents, twisted trees, and rock dells" but came direct from an appreciation of nature: first from the literary descriptions of Arcadia by Virgil and Homer and then from writers like Tasso, Shakespeare and Milton who "celebrated the same heroic scenes of glades, woods, streams and meadows, that could well have served as elevated descriptions of the Virginian countryside".[12] Jefferson wanted to integrate house, garden and landscape in ways that made Monticello self-sufficient in both amenities and the necessities of the good life (Plate 47). Following the example of Castell's plan of the *villa urbana,* (Chapter 8) structures were placed along the walks and drives surrounding a large open area and like the extensive tree planting, were all subordinated to the aesthetic considerations of the surrounding views (Figure 7).

PLATE 47. Monticello – Jefferson was constantly pulling down and rebuilding the house, accruing considerable debts in the process. Since 1923 it has been owned and managed by the Thomas Jefferson Foundation and is a National Historic Monument.

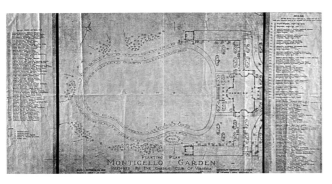

FIGURE 7. Monticello Garden restored by Garden Club of Virginia 1939. Six years after establishing the orchard, Jefferson laid-out the first vegetable garden on the terrace. Its large size, some 668 ft long with a width of 80 ft (*c.*204 × 25 m), was an indication of the scale of production required by the Monticello 'family'.

Jefferson had to spend more time than he desired in the urban centres of Williamsburg, Philadelphia, Paris, New York and Washington and at the end of his term as Secretary of State, he wrote to George Washington: "I return to farming with an ardour which I scarcely knew in my youth and which has got the better entirely of my study".[13] Jefferson was happiest in his garden and regarded his political activity as a temporary departure from the natural and proper pattern of his life. In a letter to the artist Charles Willson Peale he wrote:

> I have often thought that if heaven had given me a choice of my position and calling, it should have been on a rich spot on earth, well watered, and near a good market for the production of a garden. No occupation is so delightful to me as the culture of the earth and no culture comparable to that of a garden.

Visitors to Monticello noted that Jefferson's life was close to that of a Roman owner of a *villa urbana*; as Karl Lehmann pointed out, he was like the "good *paterfamilias*, who supervised his farms from his luxurious mansion and enjoyed the pleasures of physical exercise and intellectual life on their grounds" (Plate 47).[14] Working in his garden Jefferson was free from the anxieties of high political office and believed, that "if America could be transformed into a garden, a permanent rural republic, then its citizens might escape the terrible sequence of power struggles, wars and cruel repressions suffered by Europe".

Jefferson's Pastoral vision

Jefferson believed the American continent could become the site of a new Golden Age, a "land depicted as if it might become, the scene at long last, of a truly successful "pursuit of human happiness".[15] When Jefferson wrote *Notes on Virginia* (1785) he transferred the Pastoral ideal from the literary mode, were it traditionally lodged, and applied it to the shaping of a political manifesto. His concern was not some esoteric fantasy but rather the question of how rural America could hold-off forces that were transforming the economy of Europe, with such negative effects for both people and landscape. What policies would a government need to preserve a simple society of the middle landscape, and avoid the excesses he saw in Europe; and what were their chances of success when, with minor distinctions aside, the same sort of men coming to power in England were already busy in America?

The answer for Jefferson straightforward, and came direct form his personal experiences at Monticello:

> Those who labour the earth are the chosen people of God, if he ever had a chosen people, whose breasts he has made his peculiar deposits for substantial and genuine

fire, which might otherwise escape from the face of the earth. Corruption of morals in the mass of cultivators is a phenomenon of which no age nor nation has furnished an example. It is the mark set on those, who not looking up to heaven, to their own soil and industry, as does the husbandman, for their subsistence, depend for it on the casualties and caprice of customers. Dependence begets subservience and venality, suffocates the germ of virtue, and prepares fit tools for the designs of ambition. This, the natural progress and consequences of the arts, has sometimes perhaps been retarded by accidental circumstances: but, generally speaking, the proportion of which the aggregate of the other classes of citizens bears in any state to that of its husbandmen, is the proportion of its unsound to its healthy parts, and is a good-enough barometer whereby to measure its degree of corruption. While we have land to labour then, let us never wish to see our citizens occupied at a workbench, or twirling a distaff. Carpenters, masons, smiths, are wanting in husbandry: but, for the general operations of manufacture, let our work-shops remain in Europe. It is better to carry provisions and materials to workmen there, than to bring them to the provisions and materials, and with them their manner and principles. The loss by the transportation of commodities across the Atlantic will be made up in happiness and permanence of government. The mobs of great cities add just so much to the support of pure government, as do sores do to the strength of the human body. It is the manners and spirit of a people which preserve a republic in vigour. A degeneracy in these is a canker which soon eats to the heart of its laws and constitution.[16]

Jefferson's discounting of economic criteria in favour of agriculture and the small-scale farmer, in order to preserve rural society and manners, finds its truest parallel in Virgil's bucolics. In the *Georgics* Virgil extolled the virtues of the farmer both for his way of life and as bastion against the city, absentee landowners and those who wished to make war. Like the farmer in the *Georgics*, the Virginian farmer on his family-sized farm would produce everything his family needed, and a little more. In so doing, he would create happiness for his family and his dependents. By equating desires with needs, Jefferson turned his back on industry and trade, the husbandman would be free of the tyranny of the market. The absence of economic complexities made credible the absence of a class structure, and in Jefferson's eyes this happy state was grounded in the farmer's actual ownership of land. For Jefferson the landscape was no longer understood simply by its physical attributes, and as a place of toil, but it took on a metaphorical meaning; "its function as a landscape – as an image in the mind – represents aesthetic, moral, political and even religious values.[17] This idea would persist for the next century and half and become the foundation of both the parks and conservation movements.

In contrasting the American farmer with the European workman, Jefferson followed Virgil's example, setting the joy of independence against the misery of dependence. Like Meliboeus in the first *Eclogue*, access to the land had been blocked in Europe and the dispossessed driven from the land into the city. As a result they had become economically dependent, a condition which "begets subservience and venality" and so "suffocates the germ of virtue". This, warned Jefferson, is what will happen if America develops its own system of manufactures. The fresh, health-giving, sunlit atmosphere of Virginia will be replaced by the dark, foul air of European cities and the agricultural society Jefferson valued would disappear for ever. In Virgil's words what would be lost would be:

> Lads hardened to labour, inured to simple ways,
> Reverence for God, respect for the family. When Justice
> Left the earth, her latest footprints were stamped on folk like these.

Virgil, *Georgics* 2, 474–5[18]

From Jefferson's time the cardinal image of America was a rural landscape, a well ordered green garden magnified to continental size. For more than a century people held onto the version of the pastoral ideal Jefferson set-out investing it with a quality of thought and feeling that could only be called mythic.

However Jefferson's ideal could not be sustained in the face of inevitable mechanization and industrial progress. Even as *Notes from Virginia* was being published, others like Tenche Coxe, a young Philadelphia merchant, foresaw America could not survive as a Pastoral economy. He was convinced political independence would require a greater economic self-sufficiency, a balanced economy that would include home-based manufacturing. Otherwise the young nation's prosperity and security would remain precarious, but Coxe argued that industrialization was the means to achieve the pastoral ideal. He agreed that farmers and planters were the bulwark of the nation and that "rural life promotes health and morality by its active nature, keeping our people from the luxuries and vices of the town". But for Coxe the problem of industrialisation in Europe were the evils associated with it, whereas if it were undertaken within the pastoral framework, "it will save us immense expense for the wages, provisions, clothing and lodging of workmen, without diverting people from their farms".

In time Jefferson became resigned to the fact that manufacturing was inevitable, not because he accepted it, he continued to detest the factory system, but because he realised the emerging nation could no longer depend on Europe. The Napoleonic wars, the exclusion of American shipping from the seas, had prevented the export of raw materials and the import of manufactured goods. "Shall we", said Jefferson, "make our own comforts, or go without them, at the will of a foreign nation?" It was hoped, he said, that the New World environment would purify the European factory system and avoid the excesses and squalor of industrial towns. But within ten years all mention of the pastoral landscape was forgotten and industry was regarded as the key to national wealth, self-sufficiency and power.

Emerson and the Transcendentalists

Fifty years after Jefferson wrote *Notes from Virginia*, Ralph Waldo Emerson (1803–1882) was expressing concern over the landscape and settlements of New England. Referring to the New World as 'our garden' and the place Columbus was encouraged to seek, because the 'harmony of nature' required its existence,

Emerson asked, what had become of that initial yearning for harmony? When compared with Europe, the American scene in 1844 was not pleasing to the eye; "It includes few beautiful gardens, either public or private, and the countryside as a whole – land and buildings regarded as one – looks poverty-stricken, plain, and poor". Emerson, like Wordsworth and Jefferson, believed the cities were to blame. He told an audience in Boston "Cities drain the country of the flower of youth, the best part of the population, and leave the countryside (in the absence of a landed aristocracy) to be cultivated by an inferior, irresponsible class". He would arrest the growth of cities and urged support of "whatever events" that "shall go to disgust men with cities and infuse into them the passion for country life and country pleasures".[19]

Emerson's own attitude towards the city followed a pattern seen throughout this book. He enjoyed the society and intellectual stimulation of his native city, Boston, but moved to Concord, Massachusetts, to be closer to nature not only because "it was the quietest of farming towns" but because it lay "on the directest line of road from Boston to Montreal".[20]

Though Emerson took delight in farming and gardening, he did not adhere to the simple minded faith that a rural existence was inherently ennobling. He wrote that hard labour on the farm untunes the mind and in a letter to Thomas Carlyle (1847), he described his efforts to "lay out a patch of orchard near my house". "The works of the garden and orchard will eat up days and weeks, and a brave scholar should shun it like gambling, and take refuge in cities and hotels from these pernicious enchantments".[21] Though written in jest it suggests an urbane man whose life in Concord was insufficient in itself.

In September 1836 Emerson and other like-minded intellectuals had founded the Transcendental Club and in the same month he anonymously published his essay *Nature* which laid the foundations of its philosophy.[22] At its heart was a belief in the integrity of nature. Since the renaissance nature had been appreciated for its beauty, a beauty that lay in the eye of the beholder, now NATURE was to be regarded in its own right, with its own values. Beauty existed whether or not man was present.

Henry David Thoreau and Walden Pond

Emerson's friend and acolyte, Henry Thoreau (1817–1862) was born in Concord, Massachussetts, and in essence he was a country boy. From the age of six he roamed freely in the surrounding landscape of woodlands, streams and meadows and his father and mother, who knew the Concord woods thoroughly, took their children there to study birds and flowers. These early experiences did much to shape and determine the future course of his life. At Harvard University Thoreau read *Nature* but though he was influenced by Emerson's transcendental ideas, his own personal experiences of nature and a familiarity with English Romantic poets, in particular William Wordsworth, allowed him to formulate his own ideas. Soon after graduating in 1837 he met Emerson and they became close friends, though at times it was a turbulent relationship:

PLATE 48. Walden Pond
– Thoreau's Cove *c.*1908.

My good Henry Thoreau made this solitary afternoon sunny with his simplicity and clear perception. How comic is simplicity in this double-dealing, quacking world. Everything that boy says makes me merry with society, though nothing can be graver than his meaning.[23]

After working in the family's pencil business and as a teacher, Thoreau decided he wanted to set his time free, not for leisure as some suggested, but to undertake what he regarded as the more important human activities; reading, meditation and the observation of nature. He built a cabin in a woodland clearing by Walden pond – a small glacial lake two miles south of Concord – and stayed there for 2 years, from July 4, 1845 until September 6, 1847 (Plate 48). In *Walden or Life in the Woods*, Thoreau said, I took up this abode so as to "live deliberately, to front only the essential facts of life, and see if I could not learn what it had to teach, and not, when I came to die, discover that I had not lived".[24]

When Thoreau went into the woods at Walden Pond, armed with little more than his flute and classical texts including the poetry of Virgil, he took the notion of the Pastoral and Arcadia into another dimension. Until this time Arcadia had been used as a metaphor by writers and artists to describe the simple life. The shepherds' ability to reduce their material needs to a minimum had been an endearing and enduring trait but it was not assumed that the writer or artist would live such a life. As Leo Marx noted, those writers who took the felicity of shepherds in green pastures as their subject were careful to situate themselves near wealth and power. By contrast, Thoreau entered into the role if not of the shepherd then that of the poet in the landscape; he became the lute player in Giorgione's *Fete Champetre* (see Plate 12). But Thoreau did not claim to be harking back to some golden age nor was he deliberately acting out a pastoral fantasy, rather he wanted to confront nature in order to find himself. That is not to say he was unaware of the Arcadian symbolism of his retreat, how could he when the spirit of Virgil, his favourite author after Homer, was very much in the air. Thoreau even compared the Concord river to the Mincius on one occasion, and other people, including Emerson, called him Pan.

So though in *Walden,* Thoreau obscures all reference to the traditional, literary character of pastoral withdrawal, such a reference was unnecessary because he had adopted the role of the 'shepherd/poet' living in the landscape. And he had no need to establish the conceit of an artificial literary *locus amoenus* when the natural world at Walden Pond provided all the symbolism he required. The setting was as much a blend of myth and reality as Giorgione's painting *Fete Champetre*; as Marx said, the landscape "may not have been a land of fantasy like

Arcadia, yet neither is it Massachusetts".[25] His hut by the side of the pond was positioned, like the two youths and nymphs in the painting, between civilisation and wilderness in a cleared pastoral landscape. The village of Concord, where Thoreau would walk on Sundays to take lunch with his mother, was only a short distance away. On the other side were the woods which Thoreau chose to regard as the mysterious and untrammeled, a primal wilderness. In reality they had been hunted by native Americans since time immemorial and were already subject to predation by loggers. In this *locus amoenus* Thoreau could act out his fantasy, like Tityrus in the first *Eclogue*:

> Tityrus, here you loll, your slim reed-pipe serenading
> The woodland spirit beneath a spread of sheltering beech, ...
>
> Virgil, *Eclogue* i, 1–2[26]

The Pastoral always involves a criticism society, or its rulers, combined with a sense of loss, and it was Thoreau's belief that the true America had yet to be discovered and was in danger of being lost for ever. The materialism of his neighbours inhibited such discovery: "most of the luxuries, and many of the so-called comforts of life, are not only dispensable, but positive hinderances to the elevation of mankind. With respect to luxuries and comforts, the wisest have ever lived a more simple and meager life than the poor". Transcendentalists believed less in the self-made man than in the self-made soul and Thoreau's advice to his neighbours was to "Simplify, simplify. Instead of three meals a day, if it be necessary eat but one; instead of a hundred dishes, five and reduce other things in proportion".

Thoreau reserved his strongest criticism for farmers and their betrayal of the georgic ideal. In a reference to Virgil, and other ancient writers, Thoreau said:

> Ancient poetry and mythology suggest, at least that husbandry was once a sacred art: but it is pursued with irreverent haste and heedlessness by us, our object being to have large farms and large crops merely. We have no festival, nor procession, nor ceremony, not excepting our Cattle-shows and so called Thanksgiving, by which the farmer expresses a sense of the sacredness of his calling, or is reminded of its sacred origins. It is the premium and the feast which tempt him. He sacrifices not to Ceres and the Terrestrial Jove but the infernal Plutus (the personification of wealth) rather. By avarice and selfishness, and a grovelling habit, from which none of us is free, of regarding the soil as property, or the means of acquiring property chiefly, the landscape is deformed, husbandry is degraded with us, and the farmer leads the meanest of lives. He knows nature as a robber.[27]

Among Transcendentalists there was an aching desire to believe in the farmer as the bedrock of a Pastoral society. Emerson drew on Jeffersonian agrarianism and the nobility of the farmer when, in *Nature,* he said that farm life puts one in touch with the natural world and, by extension, the spirit, "what is a farm but a mute gospel?" And in *The American Scholar*, his address to Harvard students, he had said "the Young American, like the noble husbandman, will renounce the values of a commercial society; No longer driven by lust for wealth and power, he will adopt material sufficiency as his economic aim". However, the reality was very different and Thoreau's experience at Walden left him under no illusion about farming. The American farmer, he said was "so far from representing the pastoral life, a desirable alternative to the ways of Concord and the market economy, the typical farmer in Walden is narrow minded and greedy".

As a competent gardener, Thoreau undertook the task of growing his own food on an 11 acre (4.5 ha) field of light sandy soil, knowing full well, as one farmer said, it was "good for nothing but to raise cheeping squirrels on". Thoreau said, "For more than five years I maintained myself solely by the labor of my hands, and I found, that by working six weeks in a year, I could meet all the expenses of living. The whole of my winters, as well as as most of my summers, I had free and clear for study.[28] In writing of his time at Walden, Thoreau not only described the sensory, transcendental experience but also updated the Theocritan *Idyll*:

> I did not read books the first summer; I hoed beans. Nay, I often did better than this. There were times when I could not afford to sacrifice the bloom of the present to any work, whether the heads or hands. I love a broad margin to my life. Sometimes, in a summer morning, having taken my accustomed bath, I sat in my sunny doorway from sunrise till noon, rapt in revery, amidst the pines and hickories and sumachs, in undistilled solitude and stillness, while the birds sang around or flitted noiseless through the house, until the sun falling in at my west window, or the noise of some traveller's wagon on the distant highway, I was reminded of the lapse of time. I grew in those seasons like the corn in the night, and they were far better than any work of the hands would have been. They were not time subtracted from my life, but so much over and above my usual allowance.[29]

Thoreau and nature

Thoreau's response to nature and the landscape at Walden can best be understood through the three levels of aesthetic appreciation suggested by L. S. Reid in his book *The Aesthetics of Beauty*, namely the sensory, intellectual and spiritual – and while each can be experienced independently, taken together they enhance the intensity of experience. The popular definition of a transcendentalist is one who believes that all knowledge is acquired through the senses and that in order to attain the ultimate in knowledge one must transcend the senses. Thoreau possessed a detailed sensory interest in nature, and of the landscape, and this became a crucial factor in all his writing. He saw not only with the eye, for he "felt that sight alone was too remote for the kind of knowledge he wanted", and that "we do not learn things with our eyes; they introduce us, and we learn by converse with things". Scent, he held, was "a more primitive inquisition", "a more oracular and trustworthy". It showed what was concealed from the other senses: by it he detected earthiness. Taste meant less – though "eating became a kind of sacrament to him". Most acute was his sense of touch; "My body is all sentient. As I go here and there, I am tickled by this or that I come in contact with, as if I touched the wires of a battery". But Thoreau wanted more than contact with nature, he wanted the deepest immersion;

This delicious evening, when the whole body is one sense, and imbibes delight through every pore. I go and come with a strange liberty in Nature, a part of herself. As I walk along the stony shore of the pond in my shirt sleeves, though it is cool as well as cloudy and windy, and I see nothing special to attract me, all the elements are unusually congenial to me. The bullfrogs trump to usher in the night, and the note of the whippoorwill is borne on the rippling wind from over the water. Sympathy with the fluttering alder and poplar leaves almost takes away my breath; yet, like the lake my serenity is ruffled but not ruffled ...[30]

But Thoreau strongly disliked pure sensuality and the Theocritan image of lazing in the sun was not for him. His desire was for "no higher heaven than the pure senses can furnish, a purely sensuous life". Thoreau gave his most rapt attention to sounds, whether the simple joy in playing the flute, and how its echo lent a detachment, and so enchantment, to his life; or the good cheap music of nature, "the hum of insects, the booming of ice, the fall of distant trees, or the voice of a neighbor singing". The sweetness of the song of a wood thrush seemed to take him out of himself; "he leaves his body in a trance and has the freedom of all nature". Music, not the kind to be found in oratorios and opera – "only a man who has a poor ear for music must go to art for it" – but the simple pleasure of sound takes him to another level of experience. He wrote "the contact of sound with the human ear whose hearing is pure and unimpaired is coincident with an ecstasy".

The only sound Thoreau did not enjoy was that of the railroad. The railroad had been laid through the Walden woods a few years before Thoreau built his hut: "the Fitchburg railroad touches the pond about a hundred rods south of where I dwell. I usually go to the village along its causeway, and am, as it were, related to society by this link". But the whistle of locomotive penetrated the woods in:

> ... summer and winter, sounding like the scream of a hawk sailing over some farmer's yard, informing me that many restless city merchants are arriving within the circle of the town, or adventurous country traders from the other side .... Here come your groceries, country; your rations, countrymen! Nor is there any man so independent that he can say nay. And here's your pay for them! screams the countryman's whistle; ...[31]

Thoreau mistrusted all innovation, denouncing "the telegraph as well as the railroad and the steamboat" as instruments "by which the old subsistence farming was being disabused into commercial agriculture" with crops "produced for the market and for profit and thus (becoming) indistinguishable from trade". This is Thoreau's real sense of loss, the machine was destroying the land and landscape making country people servants of the city;

> And hark! here comes the cattle-train bearing the cattle of a thousand hills, sheepcots, stables and cow-yards in the air, drovers with their sticks, and shepherd boys in the midst of their flocks, all but the mountain pasture, whirled along like leaves blown from the mountains by September gales. The air is filled with the bleating of calves and sheep, and the hustling of oxen, as if a pastoral valley were going by.[32]

PLATE 49. George
Inness (1825–1894): *The
Lackawanna Valley c.*1855

But no sooner had Thoreau said this, than he retreated back into his arcadian world;

What's the railroad to me?
I never go to see
Where it ends,
It fills a few hollows,
And makes banks for swallows,
It sets the sand a-blowing,
And the blackberries a-growing.[33]

The answer to his question was, of course, that the railroad and its effects did matter a great deal to Thoreau; "all the Indian huckleberry hills are stripped, all the cranberry's are raked up into the city", but to preserve Walden's pastoral illusion he had to focus on his own perfect *locus amoenus*.

The railroad posed a real dilemma for the Transcendentalists. In Emerson's mind, the railroad was the means by which the American Pastoral would finally be achieved. "Go west young man (and grow up with the country)" had been penned by the Indiana journalist John B. L. Soule in 1851 and though different in tone to Emerson, the words summarised the latter's thoughts. Emerson was convinced the new power emerging in America, brought about by technological advances, could be made to serve the rural idea rather than subjugate the nation's people. He was confident that in "Young America" mechanical power would be matched by a new access of vitality, to the imaginative, utopian, transcendent, value-creating faculty, Reason. His hope arose from a conviction that men who confront raw nature will ask ultimate questions and he saw the virgin landscape as a source of spiritual therapy, a divine hieroglyph awaiting translation by Americans into aims worthy of their vast new powers. "The land", he explained:

> is the appointed remedy for whatever is false and fantastic in our culture. The continent we inhabit is to be the physic and food for our mind, as well as our body. Moving west meant casting off unwanted influences, rigid social forms and urban ways from England and Europe. The machine, appearing at a providential moment, provided access to a bare common of continental size where millions may find a new life. An American genius will arise. Sharing Jefferson's belief in the redeeming qualities of the land, Emerson believed the Young American, like the noble husbandman, will renounce the values of a commercial society. No longer driven by lust for wealth and power, he will adopt material sufficiency as his economic aim.[34]

The renunciation of worldly striving in favour of a simpler, more contemplative life had, as Leo Marx commented, always had been the core of the pastoral ethos; but here, in the New World, the beneficent influence of an unmodified landscape makes the act credible as never before. "How much better" said Emerson of the movement of men and machines into the West, "when the whole land is a garden, and the people have grown up in the bowers of a paradise".

The dilemma posed by the advance of the railroad was captured by George Innes, in his painting of *The Lackawanna Railway* (1855) (Plate 49), described by Barbara Novak, as one of the most puzzling pictures in American Art.[35] The Pastoral tone is set by the solitary figure in the foreground, relaxing in a classical Arcadian pose at the foot of tall trees, exactly as Claudian tradition dictates, whilst the cattle in the meadow continue to graze unruffled by the approaching train. The tree stumps indicate that the pasture has recently been reclaimed from the wilderness, an act that can be seen either as an indication of progress or the destruction of Arcadia. The engine roundhouse, with puffs of smoke adding to the picturesque scene, is merged into the landscape by the remaining trees and background hills. The painting on the one hand suggests the romantic, if misguided, ideal of how industry and farming could be harmonised, which is no doubt how the executives of the Delaware, Lackawanna and Western Railroad Company who had commissioned the painting, wished to see it. On the other hand, it is full of foreboding, an elegy for a world the artist knows is under threat from the railroad, and the industrial progress it represents. Innes was said to have been initially repelled when asked to paint a scene of the Railroads' operations for he could not see how such objects could be assimilated into "his habitual Virgilian mode". But like the Pastoral painters of earlier centuries, Inness gave his 'patrons' the painting they wanted but managed to convey an overall effect of nostalgia for a pastoral dream that was fast fading. In time, Emerson too came to share that view as he saw the damage the railroad brought in its wake.

At Walden Thoreau came to appreciate that the Pastoral was not to be found in reality: it does not reside in natural facts or in social institutions or anything 'out there' but in consciousness, it was a state of mind or a mode of thought. For Thoreau immersing oneself in Nature teaches man to know himself. Not as a macho exercise in survival, man pitted against the forces of nature, as the return to wilderness is often portrayed today, but a discovery of how far the "higher potentialities of a human being can be developed when one lives deliberately". Thoreau believed Mankind had reached a point in evolution that was scarcely developed from the savage state – "the civilised man is a more civilised and experienced savage". The higher life, Man had attained, was the highest point of our evolutionary development, but there was further yet to go. "Man's capacities have never been measured; nor are we to judge of what he can do by any precedents, so little has been tried". Walden calls for us to enter a new stage of conscious development, to act deliberately on problems we have hitherto tried to settle blunderingly. But before we can know where we are, we must first have the courage to lose ourselves deliberately, freeze in for a winter alone, investigate the state of our ignorance. Primitive nature, which "puts no questions and answers none which we mortals ask", can thus define the extent of our development and clarify the direction we may most profitably go.

John Muir and preservation of wilderness

By the end of the nineteenth century much of the wildness had been removed from the American wilderness. The railroad had helped transport settlers across the entire continent and Nature had been plundered for its resources; virgin forests had been cut, minerals mined, the soil ploughed and planted, its animals and birds slaughtered, often in the most wasteful manner. Many pioneers believed it was their Christian duty to inherit the cornucopia of God's munificence and it seemed as though "Americans were determined to have Arcadia and eat it, too".[36] One person who was acutely aware of this exploitation was the Scottish American, John Muir (1838–1914), naturalist, mountaineer, farmer and environmental campaigner. He had absorbed Transcendental ideas at the University of Wisconsin in the 1860s and became a great admirer of Thoreau, and was said to always carry a copy of Emerson's essays on his travels. Muir came to understand that Transcendentalism represented that aspect of man's spiritual make up which seeks to connect with a higher, non-physical reality but unlike Emerson, he believed such connectivity could only come from a direct and physical immersion in what he regarded as nature's most grand objects – the wild mountains of California – the place he regarded as 'home'. Whereas Emerson, when he exhorted students to commune with nature and engage in manual labour, was really interested in stimulating the mind, Muir wanted to experience nature with his whole being. He would travel alone in the wildness of Yosemite at all seasons; climbing, studying the rocks, the flora and fauna, often taking risks that would bring him close to death on several occasions. At night he would read Emerson under stars by the campfire. When the two met for a day in Yosemite, Muir tried to persuade Emerson to wander among the high peaks and meadows but the older man declined and refused even to sleep under the stars. Muir realised that Emerson was more of a philosopher of nature than an active participant. As one writer observed "Muir's glacial-daisy-gentian meadows lay forever beyond the perimeter of Emerson's world".

Muir became obsessed with the need to preserve the Yosemite and Sierra as pristine lands. The setting-up of National Parks in America had first been advocated by the artist George Catlin in 1832 after he witnessed the impact of westward expansion on Indian civilisation, wildlife and wilderness. But Muir understood that without State intervention the remaining wild places would be lost for ever and he campaigned for Yosemite to be declared a National Park (Plate 50).

> Government protection should be thrown around every wild grove and forest on the mountains, as it is around every private orchard, and the trees in public parks. To say nothing of their value as fountains of timber, they are worth infinitely more than all the gardens and parks of towns[37]

Through books, articles and lectures Muir stimulated an enthusiasm for wilderness and nature in a entirely new way. He drew attention not just to the beauty of nature but also its beneficial effects, rejecting the notion that "the earth had been made for humans and its resources had value only as commodities". In so doing Muir re-invoked the ancients meaning of Arcadia, as a wild unspoiled region, the home of spirituality, but not solely in poetry or prose, but as a reality of experience. Muir believed people of all ages, sex and income should not only have the right of access to the wild places but that they needed contact with wild nature. In *Our National Parks* (1901), written after Yosemite had become a National Park in 1890, Muir declared that:

> The tendency nowadays to wander in wildernesses is delightful to see. Thousands of tired, nerve-shaken, over-civilised people are beginning to find out that going to the mountains is going home; that wildness is a necessity; and that mountain parks and reservations are useful not only as fountains of timber and irrigating rivers, but as fountains of life. Awakening from the stupefying effects of the vice of over-industry and the deadly apathy of luxury, they are trying as best they can to mix and enrich their own little ongoings with those of Nature, and to get rid of rust and disease. Briskly venturing and roaming, some are washing off sins and cobweb cares of the devil's spinning in all-day storms on mountains; sauntering in rosiny pinewoods or in gentian meadows, brushing through chaparral, bending down and parting sweet, flowery sprays; tracing rivers to their sources, getting in touch with the nerves of Mother Earth; jumping from rock to rock, feeling the life of them, learning the songs of them, panting in whole-souled exercise, and rejoicing in deep, long-drawn breaths of pure wildness. This is fine and natural and full of promise. So also is the growing interest in the care and preservation of forests and wild places in general, and in the half wild parks and gardens of towns.[38]

In 1903 President Theodore Roosevelt met Muir in Yosemite. He had written to Muir expressing his desire "... to drop out of politics absolutely for four days and just be out in the open with you". During their time together Muir convinced Roosevelt, and the Governor of California, of the need for national parks to receive National status to prevent further environmental degradation and improve their management. The subsequent legislation established the National Parks system in the United States and during the twentieth century fifty-eight National Parks were created, with a presence in forty-nine of the fifty states. And the movement Muir did so much to instigate has extended world-wide to nearly 100 countries.

PLATE 50. The Yosemite National Park – a view of the el Capitan. Close to where John Muir met President Roosevelt in 1903.

Notes and references

1. Marx, L., *The Machine in the Garden*. Oxford University Press, Oxford, 2000, p. 36.
2. Marx, L., *op. cit.*, p. 38.
3. Beverly, R., *The history and present state of Virginia*. For R. Parker, London, 1705, p. 75.
4. *Ibid.*, p. 126.
5. *Ibid.*, p. 10.
6. *Ibid.*, p. 264.
7. Adams, W. H., *Jefferson's Monticello*. Abbeville Press, New York, 1983, p. 23.
8. *Ibid.*, p. 122.
9. Kimball, F., *Thomas Jefferson Architect: original designs in the Coolridge Collection of the Massachusetts Historical Society*. Da Capa Press, Boston, 1968.
10. Quoted in Bennis, E., *The Story of Gardens in Europe*. European Garden Heritage Network, 2006, p. 13.
11. Adams, W. H., *op. cit.*, p. 44.
12. *Ibid.*, pp. 150–1.
13. *Ibid.*, p. 153.
14. *Ibid.*, p. 161.
15. Marx, L., *op. cit.*, p. 76.
16. Jefferson, T., *Notes on the State of Virginia*. J. W. Randolph, Richmond VA, 1853, p. 176.
17. Marx, L., *op. cit.*, p. 128.
18. Day Lewis, C., trans. *Virgil: The Eclogues, The Georgics*. Oxford University Press, London, 1983, pp. 474–5.
19. Marx, L., *op. cit.*, p. 235.
20. Machor, J. L., *Pastoral Cities: urban ideals and the symbolic landscape of America*. University of Wisconsin Press, Madison Wisconsin, 1987, p. 158.
21. Emerson, W., *Letter to Thomas Carlyle. 31 December 1843*. His friend Henry Thoreau happily planted out Emerson's orchard.
22. Emerson, R. W., *Five Essays on Man and Nature,* edited by R. Spiller. AHM Publishing Corporation, Illinois, 1954. In a wider perspective Emerson and his fellow transcendentalists were seeking a way of thinking and writing that was different from anything found in England, France, Germany or any other European nation. It was many decades since the Americans had won independence from England and yet their outlook was still defined by the old world and they were anxious to establish their own voice. As Emerson expressed it "We will walk on our own feet; we will work with our own hands; we will speak our own minds .... A nation of men will for the first time exist, because each believes himself inspired by the Divine Soul which inspires all men".
23. Emerson, R. W., *Journal.* February 17, 1838.
24. Thoreau, H. D., *Walden or Life in the Woods*. Anchor Books, New York, 1973, p. 80.
25. Marx, L., *op. cit.*, p. 245.
26. Day Lewis, C., *op. cit.*, p. 3.
27. Thoreau, H. D., *op. cit.*, p. 141.
28. *Ibid.*, p. 97.
29. *Ibid.*, p. 62.
30. Thoreau, H. D. *op. cit.*, p. 112.
31. Thoreau, H. D., *op. cit.*, pp. 100–1.
32. *Ibid.*, p.106.
33. *Ibid.*
34. Emerson, R. W., *The Young American*. www.emersoncentral.com/youngam.
35. Novak, B., *Nature and Culture. American Landscape and Painting 1825–1875*. Thames

and Hudson, London, 1980, p. 172.

36. Macog, C., *Yellowstone: the creation and selling of an American Landscape 1870–1903*. University of New Mexico Press, Albuquerque, 1999.

37. Wolfe, L. M., *John of the Mountains: the unpublished journals of John Muir*. University of Wisconsin Press, Madison 1979, pp. 350–1.

38. Muir, J., *Our National Parks* (1901). www.sierraclub.org.

CHAPTER TWELVE

America and Religious Pastoral

A new aesthetic

During the first half of the nineteenth century a renaissance took place in the religious and cultural life of New England. Just as in fifteenth century Italy, it began with the lifting of the heavy hand of religious dogma which led to a renewed emphasis on the optimistic enjoyment of the world. The strict Puritan tradition had acted as a restraint on anything that was not utilitarian. Calvin had warned his followers that man must not use those creative abilities granted by God, to paint or carve anything that would diminish and insult God's majesty. As a result Puritans, though they may not have been indifferent to the beauty of nature and man's creativity, channeled their glorification of God into an enthusiasm for mundane work rather than the aesthetic. As a consequence the Puritans of New England had produced neither painting, music, architecture, stained glass nor sculpture which revealed their religious feelings. A change in this outlook meant Calvinism would have to be adjusted in ways that would allow creative thought and endeavor to flourish. This change was brought about by the transcendentalists, men like Emerson, who turned away from the hellfire and damnation of New England Calvinism and sort universal truths in Nature. They had been influenced greatly by the aesthetic principles of German romantic philosophy which believed a work of art exhibited the organic properties of a work of nature. It was argued that the growth and development of a work of art was analogous to the natural growth of a plant; as an organic form, it contained its own vital or germinal power by which it shaped and developed itself from within, outwards. It was this inner, vital, organising power that united the diverse component parts into an interrelated unity and determined its outward form – the beauty of a work of art stemming from the variety of its component parts drawn together into a unified whole. However, the American romantics impelled by their Puritan background, believed it was necessary to combine organic form with purpose or function in order to provide a complete aesthetic theory, one that would give moral or social intent to a work of art. Thus organic conception contained within it a functional aspect. In his essay *Fitness* Emerson described an aesthetic form in which art is the creation of beauty and beauty cannot exist without the useful.

By combining beauty in art with utility, or function with nature and describing the whole as an emanation of God, the aesthetic theorists of New England transcendentalism joined the ascetic aspect of Calvinism with an aesthetic appreciation of God the artist. In their view God could be glorified through beauty and artistic creativity rather than by self-denial. A new aesthetic sense inspired an expression of feelings, a sense of personal enjoyment in ones labour, pleasure in recreational activity and the tempering of ones duty with a feeling for humanity. With this came an acceptance of the ordered universe as an object of beauty created by God the artist, for man's pleasure and moral improvement and this renewed sensibility inspired new generation of artists and writers, among them the designer of parks, Frederick Law Olmsted and the artist, Frederic Edwin Church, both born in the small New England town of Hartford, Connecticut.

Frederick Law Olmsted and Frederick Church – the early years

Though not much is known about their early lives, it is evident from their later work that they spent many hours in the fields and woods around Hartford 'imbibing a romantic love for cultivated nature and rural life',[1] and acquiring an extensive knowledge of New England plants and animals. They came to love the landscape of the Connecticut River valley which was still in the "almost paradisal condition of the pre-industrial river valley".[2] When Olmsted was three his mother died:

> I was so young that I have but a tradition of memory rather than the faintest recollection of her. While I was a small school boy if I was asked if I could remember her I could say "Yes: I remember playing on the grass and looking up at her while she sat sewing under a tree", I now only remember that I did so remember her, but it has always been a delight to me to see a woman sitting under a tree, sewing and minding a child.[3]

Kalfus, in *Frederick Law Olmsted: the passion of a public artist*, observed that the scene is like a sentimental Victorian painting of an idealised domestic tableau, especially as it is placed in the ubiquitous pastoral setting of such paintings.[4] Olmsted's father took an intense interest in nature, landscape and its people, spending his leisure time seeking out places of natural beauty and, keen to pass on his enthusiasm, he took young Frederick on excursions around their home in Hartford. These short trips later became annual tours with the whole family, who would set-off on what Olmsted described as these youthful "tours in search of the picturesque":

> I can see my pleasure began to be affected by conditions of scenery at an early age, long before it could have been suspected by others from anything that I said and before I began to mentally connect the cause and effect of enjoyment in it.[5]

Olmsted loved the sheer beauty of these New England landscapes and they remained a life-long source of pleasure, as well as the ideal he would strive for as a landscape architect. The "root of all my good work" he said "is an early respect for, regard and enjoyment of scenery ... and extraordinary opportunities for cultivating susceptibility to the power of scenery".

Olmsted's father was keen that Frederick should have a firm, Puritanical upbringing and entrusted his education to a succession of Congregational ministers who had limited educational qualifications but they did not neglect to teach the harsher aspects of Calvinism. This had the opposite effect of what was intended and instead of becoming a stern puritan, Olmsted was left troubled by depression and grew to loathe classroom learning and cherished intellectual freedom. He would spend many hours on solitary rambles in the fields and woods of New England. On one occasion, when he was sixteen, Olmsted experienced sumac (*Rhus*) poisoning which so weakened his eye, he was prevented from joining his friends at Yale University. The next few years he was, in his own words, "given over to a decently restrained vagabond life, generally pursued under the guise of an angler, a fowler, or a dabbler on the shallowest shores of the natural sciences". Though he did attend a number of Emerson's lectures, after which he urged his Hartford friends to read the essay, *Nature*.

After showing considerable artistic ability at school, Frederic Church had enrolled with two local Hartford artists until his father, somewhat reluctantly, sent him to study with Thomas Cole, recognised as America's finest landscape painter.[6] From 1844 to 1846 Church studied at Cedar Grove, Cole's studio in the Catskills, where he learnt not just the masterly techniques of painting but also the moral imperatives that underpinned them. Cole's realistic and detailed portrayals of the American landscape were all painted with a deep, underlying moral message. "Nature", he argued, "in the form of the American landscape, was an ineffable manifestation of God". "The Fine Arts", he wrote in his diary, "are an imitation of the Creative Power" and he believed a close study of nature was essential to grasping unique underlying truths and their moral implications. His painting *View on the Catskill – Early Autumn* (Plate 51), was inspired by Claude and conveys the image of a perfect Pastoral Ideal – harmony in nature. Ten years later, the companion piece *River in the Catskills* (Plate 52), records the troubling transformation of the environment by human activities. In his *Essay on American Scenery* Cole described the process of creating an agrarian landscape out of the American wilderness as the "ravages of the axe".[7] So though the *River in the Catskills* embraces certain Pastoral conventions, depicting fields and cattle, it subverts this tradition by the signs of improvement or modernisation.

Within a year of leaving Cedar Grove, Frederic Church completed one of his earliest masterpieces *West Rock, New Haven* (Plate 53). It depicts with painstaking realism, a well known geological monument, fronted by men making hay. But this virtuous, pastoral scene was more than a simple pastoral, it resonates with a deeper moral meaning. Viewers would have known the site was associated with Connecticut's early colonial history and the painting suggests that todays peace and prosperity was only made possible by the struggles of the past.

Meanwhile Olmsted had still to settle to any career. He was driven by the Calvinist preoccupation that one's usefulness was measured through one's calling and perhaps that is why, in the mid-1840s, Olmsted considered life as

PLATE 51 *(opposite, above)*. Thomas Cole (1801–1848): *View on the Catskill – Early Autumn c.1837.*

PLATE 52 *(opposite, below)*. Thomas Cole: *River in the Catskills c.1844.* A bridge on the Canajoharie and Catskill Railroad cuts through the once tranquil landscape and a steam engine with billowing smoke crosses the river. The maple tree on the left in *A View on the Catskill* has been cut to a mere stump, while the framing trees on the right have completely disappeared. A lone man, axe in hand, surveys the scene amid branches he has recently cut from a tree. The dense foliage has been cleared to create a man-made pastoral landscape. Cole was working on this painting during the time Frederic Church was a pupil at the Cedar Grove studio.

PLATE 53 *(below)*. Frederic Church (1826–1900): *West Rock, New Haven, Connecticut, c.1849.*

a gentleman farmer: "an honourable and learned profession" but if farming was to be his calling it must be the vehicle through which he could participate in the reform of society. Like Jefferson, who he admired, Olmsted believed the farm was the nucleus of democracy. "Rural pursuits", he told his brother, "tend to elevate and enlarge the ideas, for all the proudest aims of Science are involved in them; they require a constant applications of the principals(sic) and objects of the Chemist, Naturalist, Geologist, Mechanic, *etc.* ... I believe our farmers are, and have cause to be, the most contented men in the world".[8] At last Olmsted felt he had discovered his true sense of vocation and envisioned himself as a "country squire" with a responsibility to educate farmers and improve their standards by disseminating scientific knowledge and rural taste. Encouraged by his son's enthusiasm, Olmstead's indulgent father purchased a farm in Connecticut and when that failed, he bought a second on Staten Island. There one of Olmsted's neighbours was Judge William Emerson, elder brother of Ralph Waldo, and where Thoreau had been a family tutor. There is no evidence to suggest Olmsted met Thoreau though they shared transcendental ideas and had many mutual friends.

Olmsted's aesthetics of landscape scenery

Olmsted was now beginning to form his own outlook on landscape. Like Jefferson, he did not confine his reading to farming or science and read the latest literature on art criticism, including Ruskin's *Modern Painters*, and the writings of late eighteenth century English landscape gardeners, travellers, and theorists of landscape art. Earlier he had read Gilpin's *Remarks on Forest Scenery, and Other Woodland Views (Related Chiefly to Picturesque Beauty), Illustrated in the Scenes of the New Forest* and *An Essay on the Picturesque* by Uvedale Price. He also admired Humphry Repton, and read his *Sketches and Hints on Landscape Gardening* (1795) and *The Theory and Practice of Landscape Gardening* (1803). From these sources Olmsted culled both an aesthetic theory and practical techniques for establishing a natural, romantic landscape. He was influenced also

by the eighteenth century Swiss physician, Johann Georg von Zimmermann and the Reverend Horace Bushnell, of the North Congregational Church in Hartford, a close family friend and mentor.[9] In *Ueber Die Einsamkeit*, or *Solitude Considered, with Respect to Its Influence on the Mind and the Heart* Zimmermann concluded that scenery worked its powerful effect through the imagination.[10] And whilst Bushnell's notion of the Organic Principles, mentioned earlier, was already an integral part of Olmsted's aesthetic theory, he added the Minister's theories concerning the importance of 'unconscious influence'. Bushnell believed the most important and constant influence people exert on each other was not verbal, but rather a silent emanation of their real character which showed in their habitual conduct, making itself felt at a level below that of consciousness.[11] Olmsted realised he had learnt much about scenery from his father's silent appreciation of the landscape.

In combining the two, Olmsted produced his own ideas about the effect of scenery on man. Scenery, he decided, worked by an unconscious process to produce a relaxing and 'unbending' of the faculties made tense by the strain, noise and artificial surroundings of urban life. The effect came not as a result of examination, analysis or comparison, nor of appreciation of particular parts of the scene; rather, it came in such a way that the viewer was unaware of its workings. The conditions necessary for such an experience were the absence of distractions and demands on the conscious mind.

A change in direction

As Olmsted was mulling over these ideas, his interest in farming was waning in the late 1840s. Perhaps he began to appreciate that farming was not profitable or that it did not match his reforming zeal, or like Thoreau, he had become disillusioned with farmers and farming practices. Whatever the reason Olmsted realised that the farm was no longer at the centre of the nation's well-being, "our country has entered upon a stage of progress in which its welfare is to depend on the convenience, safety, order and economy of life in its great cities".[12] The countryside, which had been Olmsted's ideal, had all but disappeared. Machines were replacing men and world markets were destroying the independence of farming communities. The farm was no longer the nucleus of American society: "Children born there", Olmsted noted, "were eager to leave ... and to abandon rural occupations" and "Women would run in to do a little shopping, intending to return by supper time to farms perhaps a hundred miles away". But cities had their own problems. Olmsted cited noxious air and overcrowding as the major "sources of morbid conditions of the body and mind, manifesting themselves in nervous feebleness ... and various functional derangements" among urban dwellers. Olmsted was aware also of the social ills – the absence of community and personal mistrust - that meant on "a stroll through the denser part of town" it was necessary "to merely avoid collision with those we meet and pass upon the sidewalks, we have constantly to watch, to foresee, and to guard against their movements".[13] Olmsted contrasted these conditions with his own experience growing-up in Hartford, which was then a small country town. He argued it was the responsibility of government to provide its urban citizens with those social and cultural advantages previously enjoyed in the countryside by only the privileged few. Olmsted believed the resolution to these problem was the provision of public parks and recreational greens. Planting public gardens and establishing a system of parks through cities would not only alleviate injurious conditions but also make the urban world more humane and civilised by promoting "harmonious co-operation of men in a community".

The campaign for public parks

By the middle of the nineteenth century the east coast cities were perceived to stand for all that was reprehensible and dangerous, and both Emerson and Thoreau expressed their contempt for them. However, a reform movement sprang-up which saw Jefferson's pastoralism as a guide to solving the social and physical problems of the eastern cities. Reformers argued for the restoration of nature to the city, a *rus in urb,* and Horace Bushnall, who was particularly interested in urban design, said in an essay, *City Plans,*[14] that the health and beauty of a city "depends to a considerable degree, on the right arrangement of and due multiplication of vacant spaces" as "so many breathing places for the inhabitants." He argued that the provision of urban parks should be the responsibility of the municipal authority and made the radicle suggestion that they should financed by public funds. These ideas were greeted with derision but in October 1853 Hartford City Council approved proposals for a park, making it the first municipal park in the United States to be conceived, built and paid for by citizens.

In New York the need for a centralised park was even more acute. William Cullen Bryant, editor of the *Evening Post,* was among the first to call for a new park and from 1844 promoted the idea in a series of editorials. Andrew Jackson Downing, the leading landscape gardener of the day, took the lead in a campaign to restore nature to the city.[15] Although the idea of a park attracted strong support, there were those critics who said American conditions made such a park in Manhattan unnecessary. They argued that whilst parks may be indispensable in dense European cities, "our circumstances are very different: surrounded by broad waters on all sides, open to sea breezes, we need no artificial breathing places". The campaign for parks was successful however and in 1853 land for what would become Central Park was privately purchased. The newly elected mayor, Ambrose Kingsland, put out a message saying the park would be especially useful to the city's well-being by providing an alternative to the "thousands who pass the day of rest among the idle and dissolute, in porter-houses, or in places more objectionable". Kingsland reflected the belief that parks had a value beyond just physical health and possessed a moral value. As the *American Journal of Science and the Arts* asserted, "placing in a town or city, a spot with spreading trees, and pleasant walks between" would allow, "the feelings of that people ... to flow in a kinder and smoother channel; there would be more cheerfulness and more happiness than there would otherwise have been". Offering opportunity for recreation and amusement in natural surroundings (parks) would lead to a more tranquil and contented society. By incorporating nature in the city, it was believed Americans' would improve society by making it more civilised.

In Emerson's opinion the Reformists were misdirecting their efforts and those attempting to make their cities more organic, by incorporating physical

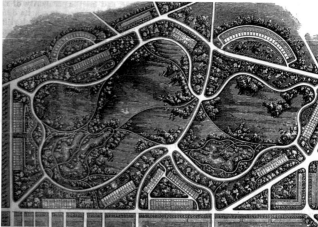

nature or advocating purer manners, were misguided. Such efforts, he believed, addressed themselves only to the surface of existence. By emphasising the material, institutional, and external at the expense of the internal, Reformers sought "to raise man by improving his circumstances" and failed to recognise that "society gains nothing whilst a man, not himself renovated, attempts to renovate things around him". If, Emerson continued, America seemed to lack unity and lie "broken and in heaps", if cities seemed to be separating from nature, ... it was "because man is disunited with himself".

PLATE 54 *(left).*
Birkenhead Park today.
The recently restored
Swiss Bridge is where
Olmsted is said to
sheltered from the rain.

FIGURE 8 *(right).* Map of
Birkenhead Park *c.*1879.

Central Park, New York

In the spring of 1850 Olmsted undertook a six month trip to England with the intention of pursuing a career in journalism, "to take up and keep a position as a recognised literateur, a man of influence in literary matters". The trip proved to be a life changing experience for Olmsted. In *Walks and Talks of an American Farmer in England* (1852) Olmsted described how, soon after his arrival in Liverpool, he was directed to the newly planned suburb of Birkenhead, 'a model town' built in accordance with the advanced science, taste, and enterprising spirit that are supposed to distinguish the nineteenth century. What followed was an enthusiastic description of Sir Joseph Paxton's Birkenhead Park (Plate 54) (Figure 8), the Peoples' Garden;

> ... five minutes of admiration, and a few more spent studying the manner in which art had been employed to obtain from nature so much beauty, and I was ready to admit that in democratic America there was nothing to be thought of as comparable with this Peoples' Garden.[16]

Olmsted also commented on the "perfection" of the gardening:

> I cannot undertake to describe the effect of so much taste and skill as had evidently been employed; I will only tell you, that we passed by winding paths, over acres and acres, with a constant varying surface, where on all sides were growing every variety

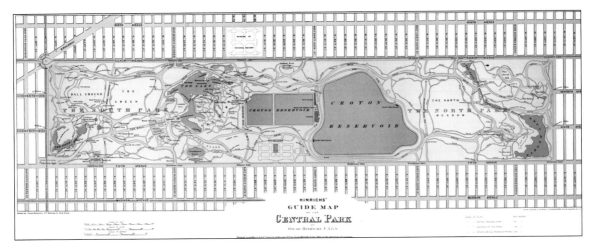

FIGURE 9 *(above)*. New York: Vaux and Olmsted's prize plan for Central Park *c*.1875.

PLATE 55 *(right)*. Autumn in Central Park, New York *c*.1980–2006.

of shrubs and flowers, with more than natural grace, all set in borders of greenest, closest turf, and all kept with consummate neatness.[17]

However this was "but a small part", of what Olmsted regarded as Birkenhead's greater significance:

> ... all this magnificent pleasure-ground is entirely, unreservedly, and for ever the peoples' own. The poorest peasant is as free to enjoy it in all its parts as the British queen. More than that, the baker in Birkenhead has a pride of an OWNER in it.[18]

On his return, the Scottish-born architect Calvert Vaux invited Olmsted to assist in preparing a designs for Central Park in Manhattan. Their entry, submitted under the name of Greensward, was finally accepted by the Park Commissioners in April 1858 (Figure 9). Though the *Greensward* plan was heavily influenced by Paxton's plan for Birkenhead Park and followed the principles laid out by

Gilpin, Price and Repton for the so-called natural, picturesque style of English garden, the underlying aesthetic differs radically from any previous venture in landscape art (Plate 55). It brought together all the strands of Olmsted's understanding of what might be termed, the New England moral aesthetic. In his Report to the Commissioners, Olmsted explained that creating Central park was not simply to make a place of amusement or gratification of curiosity or for gaining knowledge. The main object and justification was to produce a certain influence in the minds of people. Olmsted offered the spectator a new awareness of nature by which latent senses and feelings might be stimulated. The character of this influence was poetic and would be produced by means of scenes. Through the observation of these scenes, the onlookers' mind may be more or less lifted out of moods and habits into which it is, under the ordinary conditions of life in the city, likely to have fallen. Olmsted considered parks to have the same kind of effect upon the mind as the poetry of Wordsworth and shared Emerson's belief that the poet-scholar should reveal their spiritual significance. The aesthetic of the park leads the spectators' mind into musing or poetic mood. It induces contemplation. Olmsted believed the common people, for whom he created his parks, were not only able to appreciate good art, but were also capable of creative thought. There is, he said, a sensibility to poetic inspiration in every man of us. Though Wordsworth may have had greater poetic sensibility than others, he was neither differently constituted nor more affected than other men by the beauty of nature.

Olmsted called this sense of appreciation, 'Taste', and though it is instinctive, he believed, it was to be found among individuals in varying degrees. "The power of scenery to affect men is, in a large way, proportionate to the degree of their civilization and the degree in which their 'Taste' has been cultivated". Olmsted assumed there was a sense of appreciation for the beauty of nature in everyone and he employed his art to provide natural environments, what he called Pastorals, which were visually pleasurable:

> Olmsted used the style of the Beautiful – or as he usually called it, the Pastoral – to create a sense of the peacefulness of nature and to sooth and restore the spirit. The Pastoral style was the basic mode of his park designs, which he intended to serve as the setting for 'unconscious or indirect recreation.' The chief purpose of a park, he taught, was 'an effect on the human organism by an action of what it presents to view, which action, like that of music, is of a kind that goes back of thought, and cannot be fully given the form of words.'" In such designs there were broad spaces of greensward, broken occasionally by groves of trees. The boundary was indistinct, due to the 'obscurity of detail further away' produced by the uneven line and intricate foliage of the trees on the edge of the open space. In other parts the reflection of foliage by bodies of water introduced another element of intricacy and indistinctness. The effect was reminiscent of parks on estates that Olmsted had seen in England, and it was the image of the rich turf of that country, which he described as 'green, dripping, glistening, gorgeous' when he first saw it, that remained for him the model of the Pastoral style.[19]

Olmsted believed what distinguished his art from that of the gardener was what he called the "elegance of design" – the creation of a composition in which all the parts were subordinated to a single, coherent effect. There was no place in his work for details that were to be viewed as and admired as such. People should not, he warned, think "of trees as trees, of turf, water, rocks, bridges, as things of beauty in themselves". In his art they were " as little so as warp and woof in a brocade". All of this was in line with the organic aesthetic, mentioned earlier, in which "the beauty of a work of art stems from the variety of component parts drawn together into a unified whole". But in the New England aesthetic, beauty could not exist on its own, that is without utility, as Emerson had noted in his essay *Fitness*:

> Olmsted's emphasis on the 'sanitary' influence of his style of landscape design reflected his desire to have his designs produce an effect on the whole human organism. He believed that such service to human needs, and not simply the creation of decoration, should underlie all art. 'Service must precede art'. he declared, 'since all turf, trees, flowers, fences, walks, water, paint, plaster, posts and pillars in or under which there is not a purpose of direct utility or service are inartistic if not barbarous. … So long as considerations of utility are neglected or overridden by considerations of ornament, there will be not true art.[20]

In designing the parks Olmsted wanted to free the spectator from the visual limitations of the city, blank walls of high rise buildings, fences, and monotonous grid patterns of paved streets. Large expanses of greensward interwoven with varieties of vegetation, rocks ledges, water, "even the horizon to provoke the limitless sense of space" – would inculcate a sense of freedom. Olmsted's belief that, the natural scenery of his parks must induce a sense of freedom, was so strong that he opposed the use of any barriers that obtruded in the landscape:

> The faculties were to be freed from the rigidity and confinement into which they have been repressed by the routine convention, the daily grind of specialisation, and the city environment. The spectator can now realise himself to be with other men, unified into a total organic whole, living within the universal laws that determine all natural processes. The aesthetic experience offers the spectator the opportunity to contemplate the world as an interrelated whole. Exposed to the beauty and grandeur of nature, the casual park stroller is invited to participate in the creative reason of the artist (Plate 56).[21]

The design of the park was, as Olmsted described it, a landscape of "tranquil, open, pastoral scenes", incorporating many of the features he had seen at Birkenhead park. Gently curving paths leading through a series of openings and closing vistas, giving the visitor the impression they were in world set apart. Trees were planted around the periphery to conceal the houses on the surrounding streets and major roads cutting through the park were sunk below ground level to eliminate disruption from traffic in this idyllic landscape. The Park's romantic, pastoral, English quality was enhanced by a large open 15 acre (6 ha) field, the Sheep meadow, where 200 sheep could roam and people meet (Plate 57). Elsewhere, the Ramble was designed as a woodland walk through

highly varied topography, artificially created with dells and stream enhanced by natural planting. The planting replicated the vegetation of Adirondack mountains where Olmsted and his transcendental friends had a weekend retreat.

The final years

Olmsted's ideas were a manifestation of a way of thinking, both intellectual and popular, which persisted into the final decades of the the nineteenth century. After the Civil War an urban, pastoral park planning movement swept the country, with parks and park systems established in almost every city and town. Their importance lay in more than the parks physical beauties or the psychological balm they offered in providing urban dwellers easy access to natural landscapes. They served as a new token in continuing efforts to promote and define the special characteristics of American cities. Cities in which nature and nurture had been brought into confluence. But by the end of the 1890s the influence of Frederick Olmsted and Frederic Church, and the other Hudson River painters, had waned. Olmsted's notion of the park as a token of the continuing efforts to promote and define the special characteristics of American cities had serious shortcomings, most importantly, in simply glossing over the underlying social problems of the city. Church too, had been largely forgotten, and according to one visitor to his home at Olana, he felt "that his country has not known his value".[22] But it was more than aesthetic culture that had left him behind. His old hero, the naturalist Alexander von Humboldt, whose ideal notions of natural unity dovetailed so well with his own religious convictions, had long been overtaken by Darwin and the theory of natural selection. "If only", the artist opined in 1883, "that science had rested for ten years". But even though the notion of the natural city declined, the pastoral ideal remained, firmly embedded in American society. Even today there is continuing a belief

PLATE 56 *(left)*. Central Park. Olmsted said the park would be a check against the future when "New York will be built up" and no trace of nature would remain, "with the single exception of the few acres contained with the Park". He believed the park "could remain unchanged – a pastoral enclave removed, in effect from history". Today Olmsted's words have become reality – the park is surrounded by the skyscrapers of Manhattan.

PLATE 57 *(right)*. Central Park – the Sheep meadow at the heart of the park. *c.*1900.

that America was better when it was an agrarian society and life was more enjoyable when everyone lived on a farm and grew their own food. By the end of the twentieth century, however, the legacy of art and landscape left by Church and Olmsted had been recognised as among America's finest artistic achievements of the nineteenth century.

Notes and References

1. Machor, J. L., *Pastoral Cities: urban ideals and the symbolic landscape of America.* University of Wisconsin Press, Madison WI, 1987, p. 168.
2. Howat, J. K., *Frederic Church.* Yale University Press, New Haven, 2005, p. 5.
3. Quoted in Kalfus, M., *Frederick Law Olmsted: the passion of a public artist.* New York University, New York, 1990; first published 1931, p. 132.
4. *Ibid.*
5. Quoted on www.olmsteadlegacytrail.com. By the time he was sixteen, the family had toured the Connecticut Valley, the Hudson River and westwards to the Adirondack's and Niagara Falls. Olmsted Snr also took them to places made famous by New England writers and artists, like the locations in upstate New York mentioned by James Fenimore Cooper in his *Leatherstocking* novels, and those on the Hudson River featured by the artist Thomas Cole.
6. Thomas Cole, originally from Bolton in Lancashire had been inspired by Claude and Constable and shared the views of Emerson and Thoreau, in particular the notion that man and nature could co-exist in peaceful harmony.
7. Cole, T., 'Essay on American Scenery', *American Monthly Magazine*, January 1836, pp. 1–12
8. Hubbard, T. K., *Frederick Law Olmsted, Landscape Architect, 1822–1903: early years and experiences, together with biographical notes.* G. P. Putnam's Sons, New York, 1922, p. 75.
9. Central Park: the largest religious work in the city, Part 2. *God in the NYC gardens*, 2011.
10. In the book Zimmermann described how he had reluctantly left his mountain canton of Berne to minister to the ailing Frederick the Great. Separated from his home and family, he sank into deep melancholy only assuaged by daily walks in a garden "cultivated in the English taste". His curiosity aroused, Zimmermann began to search for the explanation of nature's ability to heal derangements of the mind. Olmsted had read the book as a boy and after rediscovering it when he was twenty-two, thereafter it became his constant companion.
11. Machor, J. K., *op. cit.*, p. 169.
12. *Ibid.*
13. *Ibid.*, p. 161.
14. Park History, Bushnell Park Foundation.
15. Andrew Jackson Downing, who had started as a nurseryman in the Hudson River Valley and rose to become "an oracle of picturesque and naturalistic landscape design" paralleling the aesthetic of the Hudson River painters. He became Olmsted's friend and mentor and would almost certainly have designed Central Park, New York if he had not drowned earlier in a river accident. From 1848 Downing began including letters and editorials advocating urban parks in his own magazine, *The Horticulturalist*. He advocated the creation of urban parks financed by private funds, for the enjoyment of a select group of people.

16. Olmsted, F. L. O., *Walks and Talks of an American Farmer in England*. G. P. Putnam, New York, 1852, p. 79.

17. *Ibid.*

18. *Ibid.*, p. 81.

19. Beveridge, C. E., *Olmsted – His Essential Theory*. National Association for Olmsted Parks.

20. *Ibid.*

21. Fein, A. (ed.), *Landscape into Cityscape: Frederick Law Omlsted's plans for a greater New York City*. Cornell University Press, Ithaca NY, 1968, p. 12.

22. Avery, K. J., *Treasures from Olana*. Cornell University Press, London, 2005, p. 65.

CHAPTER THIRTEEN

Ruskin, Morris and the Garden City

PLATE 58. Widnes, Lancashire: the chemical industry in the late nineteenth century.

By the 1860s it was evident that England had paid heavily for the industrial progress of the previous hundred years. The landscape around towns and villages was despoiled by factories and extractive processes, often creating dense pollution in the atmosphere, leaving the land derelict and scarred with waste and stinking pools of water. Natural vegetation and wildlife struggled to survive and the lives of factory workers were equally short and brutal. In the working class districts of industrial towns like Leeds and Manchester, sanitation was appalling and drinking water was no more than sooty rainwater (Plate 58). James Thomson's poem, written early in the 1870s, depicts the despair of nineteenth century London where:

> The open spaces yawn with gloom abysmal,
> The sombre mansions loom immense and dismal,
> The lanes as black as subterranean lairs...

James Thomson 3, 5–7[1]

In the countryside the collapse of agriculture in the 1870s, exacerbated by cheap imports from the Empire, forced farm labourers to seek work in the new factories and with no one to husband the land, the agricultural landscape deteriorated. Fields were abandoned and overgrown and villages fell into disrepair as landlords could no longer afford essential repairs.

The Middle Classes and the pastoral resurgence

This gloomy picture led to a resurgence of interest in the pastoral but there had been a change; in previous centuries the Pastoral world, that is to say the simple life in a green garden, had been the vision of a sophisticated, leisured individual and was the prerogative of the aristocracy, emperors, popes, and bankers. In the last quarter of the nineteenth century this luxury passed to the middle classes. Their numbers had grown rapidly as a result of economic expansion and it was the children of the new suburbs who took up the pastoral ideal most enthusiastically; the sons, and especially the daughters, of those who worked in the professions – the finance houses, the upper reaches of the civil services, the military or academia. They had no pressing need for employment, however their attitude towards the country had always been ambivalent; sometimes they saw it as the abode of joy but more often regarded it as dull. Now, with the traditional countryside of England apparently disappearing for ever, the middle classes reasserted the pastoral ideal with a renewed intensity, believing health and happiness could only be found in the country, in rural life and agricultural occupations.

There was no coherent movement among this new leisured class, no formal or dogmatic creed, indeed a large part of its appeal was its openness and flexibility. But a love of the countryside became an article of faith, as essential to their respectability as a belief in manners and morality. The words *Back to the Land, Back to Nature* and *The Simple Life* were often repeated and those subscribing to this ethos shared three specific ideals: a desire to return to the land, a revival of traditional handicrafts and a simplification of everyday life. This outpouring of nostalgia for rural life was stimulated in part by writers like Thomas Hardy, especially in his early novels, like *Under the Greenwood Tree* or *The Mellstock Quire: A Rural Painting of the Dutch School* (1872). This simple bucolic story was seized upon as an authentic portrayal of country life, though in reality it was based on the village life Hardy had experienced as a child, augmented by stories told by his grandmother. Hardy's later novels were darker and reflected the social decay and personal suffering caused by the agricultural decline and economic struggle but these were largely ignored by his urban readers.

The 1870s also saw an important shift in the Pastoral vision. In essence the Pastoral is a vision of the natural world set-in evaluative juxtaposition against the civilised world which threatens it. As previous chapters have shown, those threats were usually martial or economic, personified by a tyrannical landowner who often dispossessed the shepherd of his pastures. Romantic artists and writers, like Wordsworth, Emerson and Thoreau had begun the shift away from this conventional image towards a broader concern for the twin threats posed by urbanisation and industry. By the 1870s the threat had been firmly identified with the impersonal power of the machine which was destroying the natural environment, and the quality of life it symbolised. And this was not regarded as a passing phenomena, all sections of society assumed Britain's industrial and urban condition would persist, as Jan Marsh wrote in *Back to the Land*:

> It was a different response to look at the misery, squalor and brutality of the Victorian city and identify the cause not as a lack of compassion nor the effects of advanced capitalism, but as the urban industrial system itself, and to demand its removal. From this analysis, the solution was clear: the city must go, industry must be dismantled, the people must be resettled in villages and the economy return to craft workshops and guilds.[2]

The new Pastoral did not seek to wrest power from the machine but rather questioned its ability to sustain life. Neither did it eulogise the rural world at the expense of the wider civilisation or suggest an escape to the past, to primitive nature, but rather it set up a contrast between two sets of values: identifying those values of the civilised world that should be retained and the values of the rural world that were being lost. Its aim was to evaluate the possibilities of life within what one of the foremost pastoralists, William Morris, called a "more complete civilisation".

John Ruskin

Foremost in the crusade against the machine was the towering figure of John Ruskin (1819–1900), art critic and moral crusader, whose influence in the latter a half of the nineteenth century was omnipresent. Ruskin loved the earth, its seasons, and its labours with a passion that had begun in childhood but as he approached middle age he became increasingly frustrated by the destruction of the land and landscape. He saw England as a ruined garden, a subject pursued in his writings, its most pastoral expression coming in *Sesame and Lilies* (1865) and *The Crown of Wild Olive* (1866). In the conclusion of *Sesame and Lilies* Ruskin posed an open question to the nation's industrialists, especially the owners of coal mines:

> Suppose you had each ... a garden large enough for your children to play in ... no more – and that you could not change your abode, but that, if you chose, you could double your income, or quadruple it, by digging a coal shaft in the middle of the lawn, and turning the flower beds into heaps of coke. Would you do it? I hope not ....yet that is what you are doing with all England.[3]

The garden for Ruskin was the essence of all that was good in English country life and the mine signified the material idolatry and desecration of the earth. The sacred earth was being converted to a Cave of Mammon. In parallel with the destruction of the land was the loss of human dignity brought about by the machine and its use. The landscapes Ruskin admired were those that bore the mark of man's labour and it was the pastoral tasks he saw threatened by the machine. His basic complaint was not that the machine deprived man of an income but of dignified work that had kept him close to the earth. In the *The Crown of Wild Olive* he showed how agrarian labourers were prostituted to the machine; the farmer "has got his machine made, which goes creaking, screaming, and occasionally exploding, about modern Arcadia". Ruskin's vision was of a higher civilisation that recognised the necessity and dignity of human labour: "Hand labour on the earth, the work of the husbandman and of the shepherd; – to dress the earth and keep the flocks on it – the first task of man, and the final one ...". This Georgic vision, like that of Jefferson before him, was based on labour, and both hoped to redirect misguided energies back to the land. However, one cannot avoid the observation that the vision of both Ruskin and William Morris came from well-placed "townies", neither of whom had experienced the drudgery and hardship of the farm labourer.

PLATE 59. The Red House, Bexley Heath, designed by Philip Webb, where William and Jane Morris lived from 1860 to 1865.

William Morris and the Arts and Craft movement

The reaction of William Morris to the machine came in two separate ways, in two distinct phases of his life, one as an ardent medievalist, the other as a revolutionary socialist. The son of a financial broker in the City of London, Morris (1834–1896) had spent his childhood in "the security and pleasant ceremony of middle-class prosperity",[4] sheltered from the ugliness of the city. As a weak and sickly child, his early education was at home, giving him time to spend hours playing in Epping Forest, near London, learning the names of all the flora and fauna and often dressed in a suit of armour acting out the adventures of a gallant knight. His sensitive disposition accounts for Morris's reaction to the Great Exhibition of 1851 where the display of machinery offended his aesthetic sensibility. So horrified by the thought of the industrial society it heralded, he vowed to turn his back on the contemporary world and live, as far as possible, in the fourteenth century, espousing the values of Malory and Chaucer.[5] At Exeter College, Oxford, Morris met a kindred spirit, Edward Burne-Jones, who became his close friend and partner. Both were intended for the Church but they were influenced by Dante Gabriel Rossetti who encouraged them to become artists. The *Pre-Raphaelite Brotherhood* were heavily indebted to Ruskin who praised medieval craftsmen, sculptors and carvers who, he believed, were free to express their creative individualism. Unlike nineteenth century artists whom he accused of being servants of the industrial age.

Morris was never a great artist and after Oxford he spent a brief period as an architectural student, before forming a company of designers and decorators with Burne-Jones in 1861, *Morris, Marshall Faulkener & Co*, specialising in stained glass, carving, furniture, wallpaper, carpets, tapestries and more besides. During his time as an architectural student he had met Philip Webb[6] and after his marriage, Morris commissioned him to design the Red House at Bexley Heath (Plate 59). This became Morris's workshop and artistic sanctuary but after only 6 years ill-health, and the drudgery of the daily commute, compelled Morris to return to London.

The loss of the dream represented by Red House, and a growing sense of personal failure, soon became apparent in his writing. Painfully removed from a setting that epitomised his romantic idealism and surrounded by a civilisation and a world he was irrevocably committed to but regarded as "such a sordid, loathsome place" Morris began a process of evaluative contrast that would continue throughout his life. "Between these two worlds", as Calhoun said, "Morris was hardly a happy man, but for the first time in his life his situation was perfectly conducive to pastoral contemplation".[7] His first epic poem *The Earthly Paradise* (1868) was about a group of medieval norsemen setting out to search for a land of everlasting life, and it began by inviting readers to turn their back on the ugly modern world and think of London as it once was, a theme he would return to in the second phase of his life:

> Forget six counties overhung with smoke,
> Forget the snorting steam and piston stroke,
> Forget the spreading of the hideous town;
> Think rather of the packhorse on the down,
> And dream of London, small, and white and clean,
> The clear Thames bordered by its gardens green;[8]

PLATE 60 *(left)*. Kelmscott Manor, Oxfordshire.

PLATE 61 *(right)*. Blackberry pattern. Wallpaper Sample Book 1 – William Morris and Company – page 025.

Morris's love of nature and the English countryside is apparent in all his early poems, much of it in the tradition of pastoral poetry. He was heavily influenced by Virgil's poetry[9] however, *The Earthly Paradise* recalls the *Idylls* of Theocritus; many in Victorian England regarded the *Idylls* as more realistic than the images of the countryside found in Virgil's pastoral verse. Pastoral writers of this period were interested in the real, in particular those natural phenomenon under threat of destruction by industry. The idyllic landscape is most evident in Morris's description of the English countryside on a warm summer's day:

Within a lovely valley, watered well
With flowery streams, the July feast befell,
And there within the Chief-priest's fair abode
They cast their trouble's heavy load,
Scarce made aweary by the sultry day.
The earth no longer laboured; shaded lay
The sweet-breathed kine, across the sunny vale,
From hill to hill the wandering rook did sail,
Lazily croaking, midst dreams of spring,
No more awake the pink-foot dove did cling
Unto the beech-bough, murmuring now and then:
All rested but the restless sons of men
And the great sun that wrought this happiness,
And all the vale with fruitful hopes did bless.[10]

The Earthly Paradise brought Morris immediate fame and popularity, establishing him in the public's mind "as a poet of Arcadia".[11]

Morris had continued his search for a replacement to the Red House and a year after the publication of *The Earthly Paradise*, he discovered Kelmscott Manor, in Oxfordshire (Plate 60). It was "a heaven on earth: an old stone Elizabethan house ..., and such a garden! close down on the river, a boat house and all things handy ...". The house provided an important retreat for Morris and in his later years it became a symbol of the simple country life. There the ugly modern world might never have existed and Morris could enjoy being in nature, taking inspiration from the landscape, and finding ideas he would use in his design of wallpapers and fabrics (Plate 61). But Morris could not settle, no sooner was he at home in leafy Oxfordshire than he had a compulsion to return to London. Surrounded by the natural richness of Kelmscott Manor he would say, "I rather want to be in London again, for I feel as if my time were passing with too little done in the country: altogether I fear I am a London bird; its soot has been rubbed into me, and these autumn mornings can't wash me clean of restlessness".[12]

Morris and socialism

In middle age Morris faced a personal crisis, religious in its nature. He wrote simply: "nothing can argue me out of this feeling which I say plainly is a matter of religion to me: the contrasts of rich and poor are unendurable and ought not to be endured by either rich or poor". Morris was now entering the second phase of his life, having previously made a strenuous effort to avoid any political entanglement, he was being drawn increasingly and irrevocably towards socialism, which he saw as the only way to challenge the capitalist system he abhorred. In Socialism Morris saw the means to achieve his vision of an integrated, whole society. One in which the landscape was not damaged and the stark division between town and country was abolished. He repeated over and over again his hatred of the ugliness caused by rapid industrialisation, the poisoning of the atmosphere by sulphurous emissions from factories, pollution of rivers, cutting down of trees – in short the wholesale destruction of everything regarded today as the environment. In a lecture to the University College, Oxford, Morris set out a personal charter:

> a. To keep the air pure and the rivers clean, to take some pains to keep the meadows and tillage as pleasant as reasonable use will allow them to be; to allow peaceable citizens freedom to wander where they will, so they do no harm to garden or cornfield; nay, even to leave here and there some piece of waste or mountain sacredly free from fence or tillage as a memory of man's struggles with nature in his early days; is it too much to ask of civilisation to be so far thoughtful of man's pleasure and rest, and to help so far as this her children to whom she has most often set such heavy tasks of grinding labour? Surely not an unreasonable asking. But not a whit of it shall we get under the present system of society. That loss of the instinct for beauty which has involved us in the loss of popular art is also busy in depriving us of the only compensation possible for that loss, by surely and not slowly destroying the beauty of the very face of the earth. Not only have whole counties of England, and the heavens that hang over them, disappeared beneath a crust of unutterable grime, but the disease which, to a visitor coming from the times of art, reason and order, would seem to be a love of dirt and ugliness for its own sake, spreads all over the country ...
>
> *Art Under Plutocracy,* University College, Oxford, November 14, 1883.[13]

And the cause of this state of affairs was the machine; a year later Morris posed the question, "What are the necessaries for a good citizen?" The answer, he said, was "first, honourable and fitting work and the second was a decency of surroundings, including 1. Good Lodging. 2. Ample space. 3. General order and beauty":

> There must be abundant garden space in our towns, and our towns must not eat up the fields and natural features of the country. Nay, I demand even that there be left waste places and wilds in it, or romance and poetry, that is Art, will die out among us. 3. Order and beauty means that not only our houses must be stoutly and properly built, but also that they be ornamented duly; that the fields be not only left for cultivation, but also that they be not spoilt by it any more than a garden is spoilt; no-one for instance to be allowed to cut down, for mere profit, trees whose loss would spoil a landscape; neither on any pretext should people be allowed to darken the daylight with smoke, to befoul rivers, or to degrade any spot of earth with squalid litter and brutal wasteful disorder.
>
> *Art and Socialism,* Secular Society of Leicester, January 23, 1884.[14]

Morris was among the first to articulate the aims and concerns of the environmental movement which remain as relevant today as they were a century or more ago.

Morris realised that his earlier painting and poetry, with their romantic vision of the middle ages wherein humans lived in harmony with each other and with nature, was an inadequate response to the iniquities of the city and its inhabitants. Moreover, he felt Wordsworth's nature poems were merely an attempt to escape reality and the late Romantics, poets like Keats and

Shelley and artists like Samuel Palmer, were merely wallowing in nostalgia. Even his own ballads, which had become required reading amongst the new middle classes, were a kind of genteel retreat from the grubbiness of the world they had created.

News from Nowhere

Towards the end of his life Morris set out his vision of the future in *News from Nowhere* (1890), a utopian pastoral combining socialism and soft science fiction (Plate 62). It is an account of a dream journey, from Kelmscott House in Hammersmith, London to Kelmscott Manor, Oxford undertaken in AD 2102 by William Guest – an ironic self-portrait of Morris himself. The book opens with Guest waking after returning from a meeting of the Socialist League the previous night. The shortcomings of the present-day had been established by a description of Guest's journey home, by "the means of travelling which civilization has forced upon us" that, "vapour bath of hurried and discontented humanity, a carriage of the underground railway". It had

PLATE 62. William Morris (1834–1896): The frontispiece to *News from Nowhere* depicting Kelmscott Manor *c*.1893.

been a beautiful early winters night but when Guest awakes, he finds the sun shining brightly and, "by the evidence of the river-side trees, it was summer of early June", and the Thames was sparkling in the summer sun. The London Guest sees on leaving his house is free of mechanical fetters: the soap-works with their smoke-vomiting chimneys were gone; the engineers works gone; the lead-works gone; and "no sound or riveting and hammering came down the west wind from Thorney-crofts".[15] And the Thames flows through a city that is, "a continuous garden ... going down to the water's edge, in which the flowers were now blooming luxuriantly, and sending delicious waves of summer scent over the eddying stream".[16] Guest finds himself in a future society, one based on common ownership and democratic control over the means of production. This agrarian society functions simply because the people find pleasure in nature, and therefore they find pleasure in their work. The cities of Victorian England have been dismantled and the people live in villages or scattered houses surrounded by gardens:

> This is how we stand. England was once a country of clearings amongst woods and wastes, with a few towns interspersed, which were fortresses for the feudal army,

markets for the folk, gathering places for the craftsmen. It then became a country of huge and foul workshops and fouler gambling-dens, surrounded by ill-kept, poverty-stricken farms, pillaged by masters of the workshops. It is now a garden, where nothing is wasted and nothing is spoilt, with the necessary dwellings, sheds, and workshops scattered up and down the country, all trim and neat and pretty. For, indeed, we should be too much ashamed of ourselves if we allowed the making of goods, even on a larger scale, to carry with it the appearance, even of desolation and misery.[17]

As Guest is about to undertake the journey he asks an Old Man what these villages are like and in reply is asked, if he has seen a tolerable picture of these villages as they were before the end of the nineteenth century? After replying in the affirmative, he is told:

our villages are something of the best of such places, ... only note that there are no tokens of poverty about them: no tumbledown picturesque: which to, to tell you the truth, the artist usually availed himself of to veil his incapacity for drawing architecture. Such things do not please us, even when they indicate no misery. Like the medievals, we like everything trim and clean, and orderly and bright; as people always do when they have any sense of architectural power: because they know that they can have what they want, and they wont stand any nonsense from Nature in their dealings with her.[18]

Morris is speaking as a one time medievalist, architectural student as well a socialist commentator.

What was distinctive about Morris from a pastoral perspective was his conception of the human relationship with nature. Guest speaks of his young guides having a passionate love of the earth which was common to but few people at least, in the days he knew, in which the prevailing feeling amongst intellectual persons was a kind of sour distaste for the changing drama of the year, for the life of the earth and its dealing with men. Indeed in those days it was thought poetic and imaginative to look upon life as a thing to be borne, rather than enjoyed. In contrast, the people of 2102 were living a life not only in harmony with nature, but one which fulfills the natural in themselves. Once again the pastoral, in saying something about the country, is saying something about society too. As co-inhabitants of the natural world these Arcadians do not exploit nature so much as work with it and there is no urgency because everything is done with the care of a craft worker. Morris creates a sense of people not just at ease with their surroundings but managing their environment thoughtfully for mutual benefit. This is sometimes described in terms of aesthetics, which implies an anthropocentric criteria of management, but for Morris aesthetics also includes a consideration for the well-being of the material itself, whether it be stone, or fields, or tree:

One change I noticed amid the quiet beauty of the fields – to wit – that they were planted with trees here and there, often fruit trees, and that there was none of the niggardly begrudging of space to a handsome tree which I remember all too well; and though the willows were often polled (or shrowded, as they call it in that countryside), this was done with some regard to beauty: I mean that there were was no polling of rows on rows so as to destroy the pleasantness of half a mile of country, but a thoughtful sequence to the cutting, that prevented a sudden bareness anywhere. To be short, the fields were everywhere treated as a garden made for the pleasure as well as the livelihood of all.[19]

One thing, said Guest:

it seems to me does not go with your word of 'garden' for the country. You have spoken of wastes and forests, and I myself have seen the beginnings of your Middlesex and Essex forest. Why do you keep such things in a garden. Isn't it very wasteful to do so?[20]

To which his guide replies

we like these pieces of wild nature, and can afford them, so we have them: let alone. As to the land being a garden, I have once heard that they used to have shrubberies and rockeries in gardens once, and though I might not like artificial ones, I assure you some of the natural rockeries of our gardens are worth seeing.[21]

and Guest is advised to visit Cumberland and Westmorland. When Guest wakes finally from his dream, he is pleasantly surprised to find he is not overwhelmed by despair at returning to the present. Rather he has been inspired by what he has seen and is determined to work for a socialist future, and "if others can see it as I have seen it, then it may be called a vision rather than a dream".[22]

Ebenezer Howard and the Garden City

The person who sought to make Morris's vision a reality was Ebenezer Howard and though there is very little information about his early life, it is hard to avoid the conclusion on the the evidence of his later life, that he must have been aware of, if not influenced by *News from Nowhere* and the socialist debate. When, in 1871, Howard was twenty-one, he emigrated to America hoping to succeed as a farmer but when that failed he moved to Chicago and began work as a reporter for courts and newspapers. His time in Chicago was of profound influence:

giving me a fuller and wider outlook on religious and social questions than I should have gained in England. A professional confrère Alonzo M. Griffen of a Quaker family helped me greatly in the direction of perfect freedom of thought; and associated with this, a very deep sense of responsibility, and a clear perception that all values, to be rightly estimated must be assessed mainly by their influence on the spiritual elements in our nature. Thus only can material conditions be widely and permanently improved.[23]

Howard (1850–1928) did not have a privileged background and this is perhaps why he was already pondering ways to improve the quality of life. In Chicago he frequented the company of influential nonconformist churchmen, social reformers and enjoyed an acquaintance with Ralph Waldo Emerson and the poet Walt Whitman. Within this circle the conditions of the working poor would have been a frequent topic of discussion. Chicago had expanded rapidly and new arrivals often found themselves in sub-standard housing built by land speculators. In 1873 H. W. S. Cleveland, appalled by the living conditions of western towns, published in Chicago his treatise, *Landscape Architecture as Applied to the Wants of the West*, probably America's first urban planning textbook. Whilst nine miles west of Chicago, Frederick Law Olmsted had completed the suburban village Riverside (Figure 10).[24] which carefully preserved natural features and green spaces threading throughout the housing, making it unlike any other suburb in America at the time. It is not unreasonable to suggest that Howard, as a young reporter who enjoyed the company of social reformers, would have been aware of some of this activity at least.

Returning to England in 1876, Howard took a job reporting for Hansard which would have made him aware of parliamentary concerns over conditions in the industrial cities, especially the insanitary housing. Once again he joined intellectual circles of nonconformist churchmen, religious groups and anarchists who were revolutionary reformers, amongst whom the issues of land, land ownership and the problems of urban squalor and poverty were constant subjects of discussion. According to MacFayden, Howard was convinced "the City was no proper environment for the human body" and for the next twenty years he pondered ways in which the quality of urban life might be improved.

According to Howard his defining moment came in 1898 when he read Edward Bellamy's *Looking Backward*, a futuristic novel about Boston in the year 2000. Like *News from Nowhere* it was an account of a dream but Bellamy was not concerned with the planning of the physical or biological environment, so though the smoking chimneys and factories had gone, the novel was about a society in which money, bankers, armies and governments had become redundant as people took responsibility for their own lives. After reading the book at a single sitting Howard said the idea of the Garden City sprang into his head. He published his ideas in *Tomorrow: A Peaceful Path to Real Reform* (1898), reissued four years later as *Garden Cities of To-Morrow*[25] in which Howard proposed that society be reorganised as a network of garden cities that would break the stronghold of capitalism and lead to co-operative socialism.

In Howard's utopian vision the problems of land, work and the quality of peoples' lives could be solved by combining the advantages of the pastoral landscape with good urban planning and design. Using the powerful symbol of three magnets, Howard demonstrated how the inherent disadvantages of both town and country could be overcome by a new kind of town which combined the advantages of both (Figure 11). Howard's diagrammatic plan of a Garden City to be built outside existing urban centres showed a new town of 1000 acres (*c*.405 ha) which, he said, should be organised according to the needs of the people and the environment, surrounded by 5000 acres (*c*.2023 ha) of farmland, which included cow pastures, allotments, fruit farms and an agricultural college. In addition there were to be new forests, a farm for epileptics and asylums for the blind and deaf, convalescent homes and children's cottage homes.[26] Inside the circular city, ringed by a railway line, was a layer of industry and commerce around the concentric circles of houses and gardens, with radial avenues leading to a grand central park (Figure 12).

The garden cities were to be economically, politically and socially self-sufficient. They would attract residents from the overcrowded areas and as each new garden city reached its optimum size, with a population of 32,000, a new city would be started. Howard envisaged a cluster of such garden cities, growing up around London and when the population of the Capital had been rehoused, the city could be demolished and a garden city built in its place, finally realizing Morris's dream of a pastoral London. Describing this utopia Howard said:

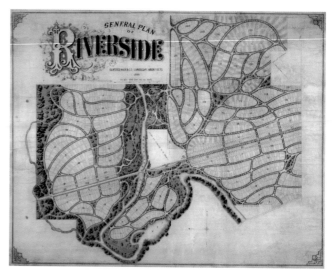

FIGURE 10. Frederick Law Olmsted: Plan for Riverside. A site of 11,600 acres (*c.*4700 ha) along the Des Plaines river, 9 miles (*c.*15 km) west of Chicago *c.*1869.

… nothing less than a vision of a transformed English industrial civilisation … There is no antagonism to any class. No abolition of anything in particular except slum dwellings and overcrowded industrial districts which disappear like a dissolving view … The migration of industrial population into the country takes places within the usual forms of law and by the usual methods of road and rail, motors and trains. Factories- no longer dark Satanic mills – have become sightly buildings, standing in gardens … A transvaluation of values has somehow been effected. Where foxes and partridges have been the principle occupiers of land in parks and preserves the land is carrying its complement of modest homes; red-cheeked children have taken the place of bright plumaged birds … England is looking sober, prosperous, thrifty – as though the bad dream of the industrial revolution had somehow no more permanence … the dream is broken, the ugly nineteenth century has been wiped off the slate …[27]

Letchworth Garden City

The idea of the Garden City received a mixed reaction but Howard had become a man with a mission and he toured the country lecturing and promoting its virtues. By 1902 a company had been formed with the aim of establishing garden cities, anywhere in the United Kingdom and it was looking to purchase 6000 acres (*c.*2428 ha) of agricultural land. The task was made easier by the agricultural depression which meant farmer's were keen to sell their unproductive land. Eventually a site was found at Letchworth, Hertfordshire (Figure 13).[28] Raymond Unwin and Barry Parker were appointed as consultant planners and architects for the project. Both were influenced strongly by Ruskin and Morris and had impeccable credentials but where Howard's garden city had looked to the future, they would take it back to an Arcadian vision of a traditional English village (Figure 14). They advocated working with the unique identity of the individual town or neighbourhood, using vernacular styles of architecture, respecting local landmarks and creating individual places and

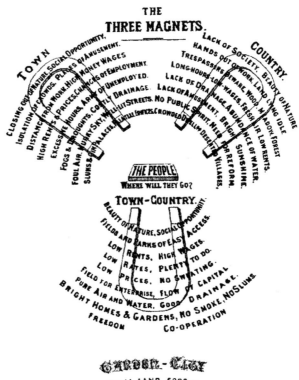

FIGURE 11. Howard: *Garden Cities of Tomorrow: The Three Magnets.*

FIGURE 12. Howard: *Garden Cities of Tomorrow: The plan for a new town.*

spaces. One of the most important spaces, said Unwin, was the village green where people could hold pageants and dance around the maypole,[29] a return to Merrie England. At the heart of Letchworth Garden City was an ornamental town garden, influenced strongly by Gertrude Jekyll:[30]

(the town garden) lies four square inside a belt of Lombardy poplars is a botanical garden and a flower show all summer. You can go there and learn the names and scents of new plants for your own herbaceous borders ... Letchworth came into existence just at the right time for herbaceous borders. Miss Jekyll had published her evangel which shattered the idea of the garden as a place which ought to be made to look like a dining room carpet. She had opened the gates of a garden of Eden where

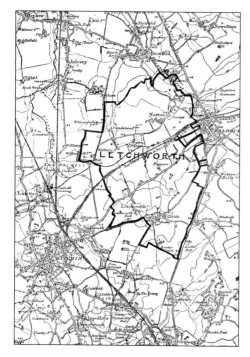

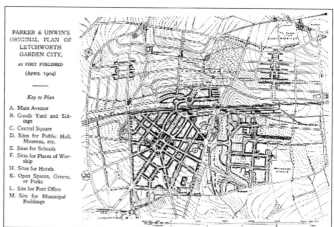

FIGURE 13 *(left)*. Letchworth and its environs 1903.

FIGURE 14 *(above)*. Parker and Unwin: plan for Letchworth Garden City 1904.

behind the borders of arabis, and forget-me-not, irises, and lupins, campanulas, montbretia, sweet sultan, verbena, gladiolus, dahlias, sweet peas, michaelmas daisies, anchusas, and paeonies, anemones and phloxes, delphiniums and chrysanthemums may in their season vie with one another in a friendly rivalry as to which can get the most sunshine ...[31]

Much of the private greenspace was intended to be productive rather than simply ornamental. There were allotments and smallholdings and every house had a garden, as did many factories and public buildings (Plate 63). Some residents came with the intention of being self-supporting but in practice self-sufficiency proved difficult and they had to supplement their income with crafts or casual work. For many the garden city was a new Arcadian utopia, a mecca for those seeking an alternative lifestyle; vegetarianism, dress reform and abstinence were commonplace. The pioneers also had progressive ideas for educational reform, and though the local education board was unwilling to finance what they regarded as experiments, the Letchworth School did have a radical approach to school life:

> Every effort is made to secure thoroughly hygienic conditions. Special attention is given to providing a suitable as well as liberal diet ... expert advice is followed in catering for vegetarians. Breathing exercises and Swedish drill are practiced regularly throughout the school and no two lessons follow one another without a short interval in the open air ... Further, in order to give maximum time in the fresh air, both lessons and meals are taken when ever possible out of doors ... [32]

Where possible woods, hedges, streams and fields were retained (Plate 64). One important area, Norton Common (63 acres/25.5 ha), to the north of the town, was kept intact (Plate 65). C. B. Purdom, the city's first estate manager, described this wild stretch of country, with its little stream, rich in birdlife and in wild flowers, with magnificent hawthorns and other trees, as being "of inestimable value to the town". Without the common, Letchworth "would lack a great deal of the peculiar rural atmosphere, which no gardens or even open fields, could bring to it ... it is part of the town and its influence pervades it. It is like a crown of untamed nature or, rather, like a heart of virgin sweetness which will ever keep the town pure...".

The development of the Garden Suburb

Parker and Unwin went on to prepare the master plan for Hampstead Garden Suburb, founded by Henrietta Barnett in 1906. Its aim was to be totally egalitarian, providing homes for all income groups, with houses separated by hedges not walls, gardens and roads that were wide and tree lined with good views of the countryside. Hampstead became the model for affluent estates around the country and by the time of the First World War there were at least fifty such projects underway, all with mock Tudor or neo-Georgian houses set in hedged gardens, along curving, tree lined streets. After the war garden suburb design became the accepted formula for middle-class housing developments across the country. Their location was often determined by the improving transport network and new suburbs proliferated at the end of the tramlines or metropolitan railways (Plate 66).

After the First World War Lloyd George declared that Britain would become "A land fit for heroes" which meant clearing slums and building new homes. The Tudor-Walters report on Housing (1918), and the Housing manual of the following year, adapted the architectural and landscape principles of Letchworth to municipal (public) housing establishing a style of council housing that endured until the 1950s. At its best, this resulted in small estates of detached

PLATE 63 *(left)*.
Letchworth Garden City: smallholders cottage.

PLATE 64 *(right)*.
Letchworth Garden City; the agricultural belt.

PLATE 65. Letchworth Garden City: Norton Common.

PLATE 66. Charles Sharland *c*.1910. One of the many London Underground posters depicting an Arcadian vision, minutes away from the city where 'garden city' housing estates would be developed.

and semi-detached houses with gardens, segregated traffic and pedestrians, cul-de-sacs, and public open spaces. At its worst, were the large estates with endless rows of houses, interspersed with acres of windswept grass, a pastoral landscape of little functional value. For all their fresh air and sunlight, these garden suburbs were the very antithesis of Howard's plan for self-contained settlements in which all the land was utilised. The very embodiment of all he was trying to prevent, "a debased version of the garden suburb ... a pseudo-Arcadian residential landscape of monotonous predictability".[33]

Notes and references

1. Thomson, J., *City of the Dreadful Night*. www.gutenberg.org.
2. Marsh, J., *Back to the Land*. Quartet Books, London, 1982, p. 3.
3. Calhoun, B., *The Pastoral Vision of William Morris*. University of Georgia, Athens, 1975, p. 16.
4. *Ibid.*, p. 29.
5. Chaucer, Geoffrey (1343–1400) regarded as the father of English literature whose *Canterbury Tales*, an account of fictitious pilgrims journeying to Canterbury provided the format for *The Earthly Paradise* by William Morris. Thomas Malory (d.1471) was the author of *Le Morte d'Arthur*.
6. Philip Webb (1831–1915) regarded as the father of Arts and Craft architecture who Morris met whilst they were both working for G. E. Street.
7. Calhoun, B., *op. cit.*, p. 29.
8. Morris, W., *The Earthly Paradise*. F. S. Ellis, London, 1878, p. 3.
9. Like Wordsworth, Morris undertook a translation of the *Aeneid*, with the important difference that he completed the task.
10. Morris, W., (1878) *op. cit.*, p. 529.
11. Marsh, J., *op. cit.*, p. 14.
12. Calhoun, B., *op. cit.*, p. 12.
13. www.marxist.org/archive/morris/works/1883/pluto.htm.
14. www.marxist.org/archive/morris/works/1884/as/as.htm.
15. Morris, W., *News From Nowhere and Other Writings*. ed. Wilmer, C. Penguin Classics, London, 1991, pp. 43–5.
16. *Ibid.*, p. 48.
17. *Ibid.*, p. 105.
18. *Ibid.*, p. 105–6.
19. *Ibid.*, p. 211.
20. *Ibid.*, p. 106.
21. *Ibid.*
22. *Ibid.*, p. 228.
23. MacFadyen, D., *Sir Ebenezer Howard and the Town Planning Movement*. Manchester University Press 1933, reprinted 1970, Massachusetts Institute of Technology.
24. Klaus, S. L., *A Modern Arcadia: Frederick Law Olmsted Jr. and the plan for Forest Hills Gardens*. University of Massachusetts Press, Amherst, 2004, p. 58.
25. Howard, E., *Garden Cities of To-morrow*. MIT Press, MA, 1965.
26. The philanthropist, Dr Thomas Barnado, was building children's villages with cottages arranged around a green at this time.
27. Howard, E., *op. cit.*, p. 230.
28. 3818 acres (1545 ha) were purchased at a cost of £155,587.

29. Unwin, R., *Town Planning in Practice.* Princeton Architectural Press, NY, 1996, p. 14.
30. Gertrude Jekyll was an important part of the *Back to the Land* ethos. As the daughter of retired Captain in the Grenadier Guards she was a woman of independent means who came under the influence of Ruskin and Morris, and the arts and craft movement. At Munstead Wood in Surrey, Jekyll created her own Arcadia, a green glade where no mechanical devices or noisy mowers disturbed the pastoral peace.
31. Quoted in Marsh, J., *op. cit.*, pp. 230–1.
32. *Ibid.*, p. 242.
33. Bunce, M., *The Countryside Ideal.* Routledge, London, 1994, p. 168.

CHAPTER FOURTEEN

Pastoral Visions of England and the First World War

By the end of the nineteenth century a sense of nostalgia for a longed-for countryside pervaded England. The country was now an urban society and just as in Alexandria, these circumstances brought forward writers whose "cultural function was to reconnect their newly urbanised readership with the countryside they or their family had recently left behind".[1] However, as Gifford in his discussion of the Pastoral points out, "the appetite for rural poetry, non-fiction and novels around the turn of the century was not only nostalgic but also, as Jeremy Hooker said of Richard Jefferies's novel *After London* (1885), about the wider crisis of modernity and modernism's challenge to Victorian values".[2] What had begun with Ruskin and Morris speaking out against the threat posed by machines and the industrial society had, by 1900, become a national crisis of confidence. Nature worship presented in the novel and poems seemed an attractive alternative, opposition even to the turmoil of the times. It was believed by many that only Nature could provide the spiritual recuperation they required. Regular visits to the country, rural or urban, were essential and to stay in the town for too long would, it was thought, lead to emotional atrophy and spiritual decline.[3]

Books about the country, nature lore and local tales appeared by the thousand. One of the most widely read authors of the day was Richard Jefferies (1848–1887) whose work went far beyond mere descriptive writing, and helped establish the mood of pantheist nostalgia. Born on a Wiltshire farm, he refused to work on the land and preferred to read or ramble through the woods and fields. In concluding *The Amateur Poacher*, Jefferies summed up the prevailing mood:

> Let us always be out of doors among trees and grass, and rain and wind and sun. There the breeze comes and strikes the cheek and sets it aglow: the gale increases and the trees creak and roar.
>
> Let us get out of these indoor narrow modern days, whose twelve hours have somehow become shortened, into the sunlight and pure wind. A something the ancients called divine can be found and felt there still.[4]

As faith in a conventional Creator decreased, many sensed a spiritual void in their lives, and found in nature and Nature poetry a quasi-religious experience, in transcendental terms. Nature became a substitute for religion and the Sunday

Upon the sabbath, sweet it is to walk
'Neath wood-side shelter of oaks spreading tree,
Or by a hedgerow track, or padded balk:
or stretch 'neath willow on the meadow
List'ning, delighted, hum of passing bee.

Joseph Cundell (1861) Bell and Daldy

Walk in the country became an alternative to church going (Plate 67). In words reminiscent of Emerson and Thoreau, Jefferies recalled in *The Story of My Heart* an experience he had had when he was seventeen, and his "heart was dusty". He had gone up a hill to a place where:

PLATE 67. Myles Birket Foster (1825–1899): a book illustration, for *SABBATH WALKS*, a pastoral scene of genteel sunday relaxation away from the city.

> I was utterly alone with the sun and the earth. Lying down on the grass, I spoke in my soul to the earth, the sun, the air, and the distant sea far beyond sight ... through the grassy couch there came an influence as if I could feel the great earth speaking to me.[5]

Thus prostrated, Jefferies prayed "that I might touch to the unutterable existence infinitely higher than deity". The book was a key text of the age and had many followers, including one young mother who took her baby to lie on the grass in the park, so fervently did she believe in Jefferies's words.

Kenneth Grahame was among those who rejected Christianity, replacing it with a vague sense of nature worship. His wife was even more pagan and appeared at their wedding dressed in an old muslin dress soaked in dew with a chain of daisies to show her communion with nature. In his classic children's pastoral book *Wind in the Willows* (1908) Pan, the overlord of Arcadia, makes a reappearance. Ratty and Mole, searching for a lost baby otter, hear a mysterious piping tune coming from a small island in the river. On the island they found themselves on "a little lawn of marvellous green, set round with Nature's own orchard trees – crab apple, wild cherry, sloe",[6] and were aware of the presence of Him. Mole "felt a great awe upon him that turned his muscles to water, bowed his head, and rooted his feet to the ground. It was no panic terror – indeed he felt wonderfully at peace and happy" ... he knew some august presence was very, very near:

Perhaps he would never have dared to raise his eyes, but that, though the piping was now hushed, the call and the summons seemed still dominant and imperious. He might not refuse, were Death himself waiting to strike him instantly, once he had looked with mortal eye on things rightly kept hidden. Trembling he obeyed, and raised his humble head; and then, in that utter clearness of the imminent dawn, while Nature, flushed with fulness of incredible colour, seemed to hold her breath for the event, he looked in the very eyes of the Friend and Helper; saw the backward sweep of the curved horns, gleaming in the growing daylight; saw the stern, hooked nose between the kindly eyes that were looking down on them humourously, while the bearded mouth broke into a half-smile at the corners; saw the rippling muscles on the arm that lay across the broad chest, the long supple hand still holding the pan-pipes only just fallen away from the parted lips; saw the splendid curves of the shaggy limbs disposed in majestic ease on the sward; saw, last of all, nestling between his very hooves, sleeping soundly in entire peace and contentment, the little, round, podgy, childish form of the baby otter. All this he saw, for one moment breathless and intense, vivid on the morning sky; and still, as he looked, he lived; and still, as he lived, he wondered.[7]

The book stimulated an interest in Pan as a figure who would save humanity from destructive progress and free people from outmoded and restrictive moral codes.

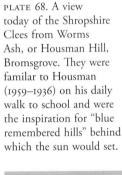

PLATE 68. A view today of the Shropshire Clees from Worms Ash, or Housman Hill, Bromsgrove. They were familar to Housman (1959–1936) on his daily walk to school and were the inspiration for "blue remembered hills" behind which the sun would set.

A. E. Housman

The poem most associated with the prevailing mood of nostalgic pastoralism was A. E. Housman's *A Shropshire Lad* (1896), written whilst he was living in Highgate, London. Housman had first seen the distant Clee hills – "those blue remembered hills" – as he walked across the fields to school in Bromsgrove, Worcestershire (Plate 68) but he later found himself, like many others in towns and cities, disassociated from his childhood landscape:

> Into my heart on air that kills
> From yon far country blows;
> What are those blue remembered hills,
> What spires, what farms are those ?
>
> That is the land of lost content,
> I see it shining plain,
> The happy highways where I went
> And cannot come again.[8]

A Shropshire Lad is a cycle of sixty-three very nostalgic poems expressing many of Housman's own feelings and emotions, centred around themes of Pastoral beauty, unrequited love, fleeting youth, grief, death and the patriotism of the common soldier.[9] The poems are not an accurate description of Shropshire for Housman rarely visited the county, nevertheless he presents it in an idealised Pastoral light. Local place names are used to evoke rusticity and conjure up nostalgia and though the poems have some awareness of the harsher realities of life, they are like Hardy's novels, recreating a sense of country life that has passed, even if it existed at all. The poems are not so much about the landscape as a place, but rather a location for feelings – of life, love, loyalty, friendships and death. As Richard North said:

> Housman used the Pastoral manner as it has always been used; to discuss very civilised people getting to grips with natures (their own) as yet untamed. So civilised people invent and reinvent Golden Age realities as waking dreams through which they can discuss what they have gained and lost, and in which to create sanctuaries from the modern.[10]

However, it was the sense of belonging to a place or region which made Housman's verse so popular, with its nostalgic evocation of lost lands and vanished friends. Evoking in the hearts of many who found themselves unwilling, rootless inhabitants of suburbia, memories of their own blue remembered hills.

Just about every English composer attempted to set Housman's poems to music. The most successful was George Butterworth (1885–1916)[11] whose eleven settings of *A Shropshire Lad* (1896) captured the essence of the poetry. Butterworth shared in the nostalgia for rural England believing it was vanishing fast, along with the loss of folk songs and dance he considered to be the countries true musical heritage. He joined his contemporaries, Vaughan Williams, Holst, Parry and others[12] in an urgent quest to find, collect and transcribe the folk songs and dance, they believed to be the true expression of pastoral England:

> As I rode out on a Midsummer's morning
> For to view the fields and to take the air,
> Down by the banks of sweet primroses
> There I beheld a most lovely fair.[13]

It had been widely believed that England had no national music, of the kind that was forming the basis of a cultural renaissance in other European countries. These early enthusiasts quickly showed this not to be the case and the publication of *English County Songs* in 1894 led to a revival of interest. Four years later the Folk Song Society was founded and when the composer Sir Hubert Parry gave the inaugural address to the Society, in the anti-urban, anti-industrial mood of the day, he declaimed "our terribly overgrown towns" of "pawnshops and flaming gin palaces", where "miserable piles of Covent Garden refuse which pass for vegetables are offered for food". From this environment came the modern song – "the enemy of folk music, which grew in the hearts of the people before they devoted themselves so assiduously to the making of quick returns".[14] A few years later the Women's Suffrage Movement asked Parry to compose music for the most patriotic of pastoral verses, Blake's *Jerusalem,* to aid recruitment in the First World War:

> And did those feet in ancient time.
> Walk upon Englands mountains green:

The Georgian poets

The folk song revival inspired a new generation of poets, like Walter de la Mare and John Masefield, to forsake the style and language of late Victorian verse and write in the manner of the folk lyric and ballad. They were part of a group known as the Georgian poets. Others included were Edmund Blunden, Robert Graves, D. H. Lawrence, Siegfried Sassoon and Rupert Brooke who first conceived the idea of a volume of new poetry.[15] The Georgian poets were reacting to the strict classicism of Victorian poetry, and wished to make poetry, like the folksongs, more accessible to people, Their poetry was essentially English and not aggressively imperialistic like the work of Rudyard Kipling. It was about the familiar, just as Wordsworth's poetry had been, but nature, which became an obsession, was not used for its own sake but as a way of exploring issues and a means of communication. The author and poet D. H. Lawrence expressed the negative mood out of which Georgian poetry was born:

> Poetry now-a-days seems to be a sort of plaster-cast craze, scraps sweetly moulded in easy Plaster of Paris sentiment. Nobody chips verses out of the living rock of his own feeling . ... Before everything I like sincerity, and a quickening spontaneous emotion.[16]
>
> letter to Blanche Jennings, 17 July 1908

In contrast, Georgian poetry placed a strong emphasis on describing emotional reality, as W. H. Davies said:

> We poets pride ourselves on what
> We feel, and not what we achieve;
> The world may call our children fools,
> Enough for us that we conceive.
>
> W. H. Davies, *In Hearing Mrs Woodhouse Play the Harpsichord*[17]

Realism was an early guiding principle of the Georgian poets. This meant the inclusion of details, however nasty or unpleasant, which "possessed a truth to reality as it was perceived by the five senses". The Georgian poets wanted to see the world with 'the innocent eye of childhood', not as an artistic mannerism or means.[18] Their fondness for pastoral settings was not a flight from reality but rather "in natural surroundings they felt themselves less distracted by contemporary and historical fashions, and thus better able to grasp and penetrate those endlessly recurring experiences most central and urgent to our humanity".[19] Hence the Georgians interest in nature, in love, birth and death both within the human and the natural world, along with the rhythm of the seasons.

However, much Georgian poetry was escapist; sunny flower-filled gardens with pretty country women and girls, conveniently overlooking the poverty and misery they concealed. It was a criticism applied to Rupert Brooke whose poems were considered to be too sentimental, even though they reflected the prevailing mood in England, among a certain class, in the years leading up to World War One. Typical was Brooke's popular poem *The Old Vicarage, Grantchester*:[20]

> Just now the lilac is in bloom,
> All before my little room
> And in my flower-beds, I think,
> Smile the carnation and the pink;
> And down the borders, well I know,
> The poppy and the pansy blow …
>
> Brooke, *The Old Vicarage, Grantchester*[21]

Edward Thomas

A more perceptive eye belonged to the Anglo-Welsh writer of prose and poetry, Edward Thomas (1878–1917). His poems, though never published in any of the Georgian anthologies, shared much with his contemporaries, in displaying a profound love of natural beauty but possessing an intensity of vision they never approached. Thomas wrote twenty-two books of prose and many articles, including a biography of Richard Jefferies (1909) whom he admired greatly: "as a child anything good or pleasant that I noticed seemed to belong by right to him".[22] He shared Jefferies's passion for the countryside and would leave his wife and children to spend months tramping around Wales and southern England. But Thomas was more than just a nature writer; he contrasted the beauty of the countryside and the simplicity of country life with what he saw the landscape becoming. The agricultural depression that led many farm workers to leave the land, had caused fields to remain fallow and become overgrown with weeds. Industry too, had ravaged the landscape and industrial towns were sprawling out into green fields.

In April 1914 Thomas visited the coterie of Georgian poets who had made their home near the village of Dymock, an unspoilt landscape of meadows, woods in the lea of the Malvern hills, on the borders of Herefordshire and Gloucestershire. He was there to meet the poet, Robert Frost, one of the few American poets respected by the Georgians. A deep friendship followed and they would spend many hours together, taking long walks and endlessly talking.[23]

During a second meeting in August, Frost persuaded Thomas to turn to poetry, though the outbreak of the First World War may have been an even greater imperative. The war intensified Thomas's love for England and in an essay *This England*, he expressed what England meant to him. He described in detail a hot summer spent in countryside around Hereford; and how he went for walks with an un-named friend (Frost); "If talk dwindled in the traversing of a big field, the pause at a gate or stile braced it again. Often we prolonged the pause whether we actually sat or not, and talked – of flowers, childhood, Shakespeare, women, England, the war". Nine months later the essay became the basis for his poem *The Sun Used to Shine* which, like the essay, contrasts the rural idyll with the threat of war and death.[24] After completing the essay *This England* he said, I was deluged by ... something that over powered thought. A deep love of England led to the patriotic thought:

> All I can tell is, it seemed to me that either I had never loved England, or I had loved it foolishly, aesthetically, like a slave, not having realised that it was not mine unless I were willing and prepared to die rather than leave it as Belgian women and old men and children had left their country. Something I had omitted. Something I felt had to be done before I could look again composedly at English landscape, at the elms and poplars about the houses, at the purple-headed wood betony with two pairs of dark leaves on a stiff stem, who stood sentinel among the grasses or bracken by hedge-side or wood's edge. What he stood sentinel for I did not know, any more than what I had got to do.[25]

Thomas's poems were not war poems. None were written in anticipation or experience of battle and he did not write at all during the few weeks he was in France.[26] His poems were about his beloved countryside; his subjects were not roses and nightingales but badgers, tramps, nettles, horse-drawn ploughs and sleeping under the rain, though often with the shadow of the war in the background. In his poems Thomas provides a vision of nature that is not Wordsworth's universal nature but a lovingly observed landscape of England. As Kirkham observes, his imagination:

> in his later prose and then in his poetry, ... was engaged with an idea of England: a pre-industrial rural England, both wild and cultivated, of prehistoric and historic foundations, a land of hills, valleys and streams, gardens, orchards, fields and woods, of farms and villages, possessed by a 'commonwealth' of wild creatures, labourers and wandering men. Almost all of Thomas's values are associated with this image of England.[27]

It is also an endangered England, one about to disappear from men's consciousness. Poems that affirm these values invariably present themselves in the context of imminent loss, as belonging to a dying order of life, a world coming to end. In the poem *As the Team's Head Brass* Thomas suggests that the rural order, represented by the plough-team is about to disappear, overtaken by agricultural change. Thomas knew it was a way of life that was disappearing.

The war, he realised "would be the final blow whether it was won or lost, but such certitude did not prevent him from rejoicing in those elements of ancient culture which remained".[28]

Thomas's poems stem from "his feelings about a spent England, sapped of vitality, living in the aftermath of its strength ... and on the other hand from his general awareness of the dark side of existence".[29] There is personal as well as a general loss: "a deterioration of a national character or loss of national identity. Frequently... personal and general loss are felt and presented as aspects of the same situation".[30] Thomas's feelings about the passing of England, and about war as "the culmination of a historical process of decline, are a particular expression of his general sensitivity to the transience of all things":

> The men leaned on their rakes, about to begin,
> But still. And all were silent. All was old,
> This morning time, with a great age untold,
> Older than Clare and Cobbett, Morland and Crome,
> Than, at the field's far edge, the farmer's home,
> A white house crouched at the foot of a great tree.
> Under the heavens that know not what years be
> The men, the beasts, the trees, the implements
> Uttered even what they will in times far hence -
> All of us gone out of the reach of change -
> Immortal in a picture of an old grange.
>
> Thomas, *Haymaking*[31]

Though under no pressure to enlist in the war, Thomas's sharpened feelings for England led him to enlist in the Artists Rifles in July 1915. He was commissioned into The Royal Garrison Artillery and killed shortly after arriving in France on Easter Monday, April 1917.

The First World War – a literary war

The outbreak of the First World War brought with it a wave of patriotism; entire cycling or rambling clubs, Morris sides, poets and musicians, the ranks of the new middle classes – teachers, clerks *etc.*, all rushed to enlist. Agricultural labourers eager to escape the boredom and hardship of working on the land, joined the colours. They all shared a common purpose: to protect the pastoral image of England, embedded in their consciousness. However, it was not just the image; it was the actual soil that embodied everything worth fighting for. When Thomas was asked why he was prepared to join-up, he bent down, picked up a clod of soil, held it out and said "literally for this".[32]

For Thomas's friend, Rupert Brooke, the outbreak of war was a quasi-mystical experience. He described his feelings on hearing the news in an essay *An Unusual Young Man*, in reality Brooke himself. After musing on his many pleasant memories of Germany, "he was awakened to a different one, by the thought that this day meant war and the change of all the things he knew".

He realised there might be a raid on the English coast and though he did not imagine any possibility of it succeeding, it was the thought of enemies and warfare on English soil. The idea sickened him. He was immensely surprised to perceive that the actual earth of England held for him a quality he found only in A— (female friend), and in a friend's honour, and scarcely anywhere else; a quality which, if he'd ever been sentimental enough to use the word, he would have called holiness:

> His astonishment grew as the full flood of 'England' swept him on from thought to thought. He felt the triumphant helplessness of a lover. Grey, uneven little fields, and small, ancient hedges rushed before him, wild flowers, elms and beeches, gentleness, sedate houses of red brick, proudly unassuming, a countryside of rambling hills and friendly copses. He seemed to be raised high, looking down on a landscape compounded of the western view from the Cotswolds, and the Weald, and the high land in Wiltshire, and the Midlands seen from the hills above Prince's Risborough. And all this to the accompaniment of tunes heard long ago, an intolerable number of them being hymns.[33]

In Margate, Kent, on the eve of war, the composer Ralph Vaughan Williams was walking along the cliff top when a tune came into his head which expressed his deepest love for the countryside and impending loss. He was responding to a poem by George Meredith, *The Lark Ascending*, written of few years before and the music remains one of most powerful and popular evocations of the English landscape:

> He rises and begins to round,
> He drops the silver chain of sound,
> Of many links without a break,
> In chirrup, whistle, slur and shake.
>
> For singing till his heaven fills,
> 'Tis love of earth that he instils,
> And ever winging up and up,
> Our valley is his golden cup
> And he the wine which overflows
> to lift us with him as he goes.
> Till lost on his aerial rings
> In light, and then the fancy sings.[34]

The men enlisting in the First World War took the Pastoral with them into the trenches. The war has been described as a literary war, not simply because poets like Edward Thomas joined the ranks, but as Fussell pointed out "it came at a special historical moment when it was possible for soldiers to be not merely literate but vigourously literate".[35] Two powerful, liberal forces had coincided; a time when the belief in the educative powers of classical and English literature was still strong and the appeal of popular education and "self-improvement" was at its peak. It was believed the study of literature at Workman's Institutes and schemes, such as the National Home Reading Union, actively assisted those of modest origins to rise in the class system. As Fussell puts it "the intersection of these two forces, the one aristocratic, the other democratic, established an atmosphere of public respect for literature unique in modern times". There were few of any rank who had not been assured that the greatest modern literature was English and who did not feel pleasure in that assurance. As they marched to war many soldiers carried anthologies of Pastoral verse, while everyone read Housman, and the novels of Thomas Hardy. At the Front the efficiency of the postal service meant books were commonplace and to counter the prevailing boredom literary discussions were not unusual, in all ranks, with no sense that literature belonged to the intellectuals, teachers or critics.[36]

In the stalemate that marked the first part of the war many men and officers took to writing to alleviate boredom. Forbidden from writing home about their experiences with any degree of truth or accuracy, some put their thoughts into diaries, others turned to poetry. For many Trench poets, Georgian poetry was the starting point,[37] the pastoral mode providing the opportunity to compare and contrast, to measure the horrors of war against rural places and objects they had left behind. Virgil's Golden Age became invested in 'home' and it was possible to both console oneself with thoughts of how 'it used to be' and to invoke "a code to hint by antithesis at the indescribable".[38] As the very things dear to the Georgian lovers of nature; fresh spring, red dawn, green trees, rain showers, the song of birds, the beauty of butterflies had suddenly become either false or deadly.[39] Typical was John William Streets's poem *Matthew Copse* which contrasts the pastoral beauty of spring with the horrors of war, and invokes the restorative powers of love and nature.[40] Streets was killed in the Battle of the Somme, along with nearly 500 other officers and men from the Sheffield Pals, killed or missing in a single day.

Once in thy secret close, now almost bare
Peace yielded up her bountiful largess;
The dawn dropp'd sunshine thro' thy leafy dress;
The sunset bathed thy glade with beauty rare.

Spring once wove here her tapestry of flowers,
The primrose sweet, the errant celandine;
The blue-bell and the wild rose that doth twine
Its beauty 'round the laughing summer hours.

Here lovers stole unseen at deep'ning eve,
High-tide within their hearts, love in their eyes,
And told a tale whose magic never dies
That only they who love can believe.

Now 'mid thy splinter'd trees the great shells crash,
The subterranean mines thy deeps divide;
And men from Death and Terror there do hide –
Hide in thy caves from shrapnel's deadly splash.

Yet 'mid thy ruins, shrine now desolate,
The Spring breaks thro' and visions many a spot
With promise of the wild-rose – tho belate –
And the eternal blue forget-me-not.

So Nature flourishes amid decay,
Defiant of the fate that laid her low;
So Man in triumph scorning Death below
Visions the springtide of a purer day.

Dreams of the day when rampant there will rise
The flowers of Truth and Freedom from the blood
Of noble youth who died: when there will bud
The flowers of Love from human sacrifice.

There by fallen youth, where heroes lie,
Close by each simple cross the flower will spring.
The *bonnes enfants* will wander in Spring,
And lovers dream those dreams that never die.

Streets, *Matthew Copse*

The Battle proved a turning point in attitudes towards the war and a poetic watershed. It no longer seemed appropriate to compare Flanders fields with those of pastoral England and a focus on nature detracted from the horror of war. As the poet David Jones explained, (the Somme) marked "a change in the character of our lives in the infantry on the West Front. From then onwards things hardened into a more relentless, mechanical affair, took on a sinister aspect".[41] Poetry came to reflect a sense of disillusionment, the senseless of war and the cost in human terms. Nature – birds, flowers, seasons, were all used to underline and reinforce the growing sense of despair. In Isaac Rosenbergs poem *Returning, We Hear the Larks*, the romantic symbolism of Shelley's, *To a Skylark* ("HAIL to thee, blithe spirit! / Bird thou never wert –/ That from heaven or near it / Pourest thy full heart/In profuse strains of unpremeditated art"),[42] is replaced by a more sinister imagery. The larks now appear as harbingers of death, their song showering down like death at uncertain moments upon blind soldiers who can no longer see the sky, any more than lovers can see the serpent hiding to destroy them.

Edmund Blunden

This change can be seen in the poetry of Edmund Blunden (1896–1974), the poet who most embodied the Pastoral. In *Undertones of War* (1928), his account of his wartime experiences, he described himself as a country boy: "a harmless young shepherd in a soldier's coat", words that could also apply to his care for the men he led. Blunden had grown-up in the Medway valley, Kent, where he developed a deep love of the countryside, its nature, the people who lived there and its ways. He said of his boyhood "it was hardly possible for any of us not to know hopfields and orchards and sheepfolds, and much else that was apparently eternal". The countryside was magical, prompting him to describe rural England as this "genuine Arcadia".[43] He later said "If I wrote of these things it was not because I was following ... 'The Georgians' but because my themes were daily experiences".[44] During the war his country upbringing, the classical education of a public school boy and "an extensive knowledge of literature ...". all furnished perspectives which enabled Blunden to cope "with the horrors in the trenches where each man developed his own strategy of self-preservation".[45] For Blunden the pastoral was not simply a verse form; he lived in a Pastoral world in which both the countryside and literature were alive and had feelings. Seeing the rich and fruitful land in Flanders, so much like his own Kentish landscape, laid waste was a torment. For it to be brutally torn up by shells was a scandal close to murder. In *Undertones of War* he returned repeatedly to the pathos and shock of it: "The greensward suited by nature for the raising of sheep, was all holes, and new ones appeared with great uproar as one passed".[46]

Blunden's survival in the trenches for nearly two years makes his poetry, and description of the war, especially graphic, conveying the sense in which initial innocence gave way to near despair, as the restorative powers of nature began to weaken. When he first joined the Royal Sussex Regiment on the front line, Blunden could not believe the Pastoral landscape was being violated: "In the afternoon, looking eastwards ..., I had seen nothing but green fields plumy grey-green trees and intervening tall roofs; it was as though in this part the line could be only a trifling interruption of a happy landscape". But going up that night into the battle zone, he became aware that he was entering a perverse pastoral: "several furious insect-like zips went past my ear". And daylight propelled him further towards the truth: although the morning light was "high and blue and inspiriting on the ground there were phenomena not at all like those of the benign bucolic world". Indeed, "at some points in the trench ... skulls appeared like mushrooms".[47] As time progresses Blunden became increasingly disillusioned:

> I begin to understand the drift of the war. It is a drift - nobody one wants it, no one is in charge - toward the insensate destruction conducted against the background of the unbearably beautiful. Over Coldstream Lane, the chief communication trench, deep red poppies, blue and white cornflowers, and darnel thronged the way to destruction; the yellow cabbage flowers thickened here and there in sickening brilliance ... Then the ground became torn and vile, the poisonous breath of fresh explosions skulked about, and the mud which choked the narrow passages stank as one pulled through it ... .[48]

After his battalion had suffered great losses, Blunden returned to Ypres late in 1916 but "it is not the same 'we' who in the golden dusty summer tramped down into the verdant valley, even then a haunt of every leafy spirit and the blue eyed ephydriads, now natures slimy wound with spikes of blackened bone". But worse came the following spring, when the battalion harboured "in readiness among the familiar woods", west of Vlamertinghe:

> but the woods are not the same as when the battalion lived in them during the relatively 'Arcadian' days of 1916. The wood-spirit has been shelled silly like everyone else, and the 'parting genius must have gone on a stretcher'. The rural roads are now made of greasy planks instead of earth, rails criss-cross the Salient, ammunition and stores are piled everywhere, and even the eels, bream, and jack, in the stream are dead. They have been shelled and gassed.[49]

Blunden saw the wood as being in a position as vulnerable as his own. War destroys man and nature alike. He was obsessed with "the growing intensity and sweep of destructive forces". Taking up the rations at night in a quiet sector used be something like a pastoral activity, but the scene is now a demonic anti-pastoral, dominated by such details as "slimy soil", a "swilling pool of dirty water", "tree-spikes", and the everlasting "plank road", to leave which, is to fall into a swamp up to the armpits, to remain on it is "to pass through accurate and ruthless shellfire".[50] The horrors of the battlefield, described by Blunden, were the subject of a painting by Paul Nash *The Menin Road* (Plate 69). The painting is ironic in that no road can be seen. The trees, a traditional symbol of strength and regeneration, have been transformed into black and burned stumps of destruction. Luxurious foliage has been replaced by forms which vaguely resembled floral elements but which are in fact barbed wire. Rays of light breaking through, a traditional element of a Romantic landscape painting, have been transformed into an additional threat to the last soldiers scattered in the rugged landscape. In the pools, the water is lifeless. The painting is very antithesis of a pastoral scene, it proclaims, as in Ivor Gurney's poem *Mist on the Meadows*, despair.[51]

War Graves – a pastoral setting

As the first mass casualty lists began to appear during 1915 the government was faced with the daunting challenge of how the vast army of the dead was to be decently interred. Rupert Brooke, in arguably the most famous of all English war poems, *The Soldier*, gave voice to the popular mood of the day;

> If I should die, think only this of me:
> That there's some corner of a foreign field
> That is for ever England. There shall be
> In that rich earth a richer dust concealed;
> A dust whom England bore, shaped, and made aware,
> Gave, once, her flowers to love, her ways to roam,
> A body of England's, breathing English air.
> Washed by the rivers, blest by suns of home.

Brooke, The Soldier[52]

The poem would often be quoted in newspapers and among those involved in the construction of war cemeteries. On the battlefield the situation was chaotic; the bodies of soldiers were being thrown into abandoned trenches, some were buried where they fell, their graves marked in the most rudimentary way, many others were never found. Grieving relatives who began to make their way to France and Belgium found many sites were just patches of mud, torn earth, bereft of vegetation or covered by rank grass. Some, who could afford it, began erecting ornate memorials, whilst others repatriated the bodies. Both practices were considered contrary to the notion of what the government and the country regarded as a national war. In previous wars the fallen were often buried on the battlefield, their graves marked by wooden crosses that soon weathered away, and the names of the men went unrecorded. Now the Victorian celebration of death and the large numbers of dead, over one million British deaths alone, meant a new approach was needed.

General Fabian Ware, commander of a mobile unit of the Red Cross, began to record and care for graves,[53] whilst the British Red Cross suggested the temporary graves would be less miserable if they were planted with grass and simple flowers. After consulting the Royal Botanic Gardens, Kew, the cemeteries came to resemble one of Helen Allingham's cottage gardens, as flowering annuals bloomed across the battlefield. Ware appreciated a more permanent solution was needed. At issue was how the English,[54] wished to be seen by itself and by other nations "at the end of its passage through an ordeal that tested the roots of its culture and identity to destruction".[55] In 1915 Fabian Ware successfully negotiated for a "perpetuity of sanction" on land paid for by France and maintained by a "properly constituted" British authority which, as Crane pointed out in his biography of Ware, "provided the framework for a collective and national memorial project on a scale the world had never seen".[56] This made possible the securing of a "corner of a foreign field that is for ever England" spoken of by Rupert Brooke. But not all were in favour,

Mist lies heavy on English meadows
As ever in Ypres, but the friendliness
Here is greater in full field and hedge shadow
And there is less menace and no dreadfulness
Dreadful green light baring the ruined trees,
As when the Very lights went up to show the
    land stark.

Gurney, *Mist on the Meadows*

PLATE 69. Paul Nash (1889–1946): *The Menin Road* c.1919.

the Countess of Selborne, regarded Ware's treaty it as "pure socialism of the advanced school". Ware's intention was to stop the private retrieval of the bodies of soldiers, mostly officers, by wealthy relatives. He believed that "if men of all classes were being asked to give up their lives in Kitchener's New Army, then men of all classes should lie together in death".[57] In May 1917 the Imperial War Graves Commission was established and after much debate, the architect Edwin Lutyens finally determined the major principles to be adopted in the design of all cemeteries – there would be no repatriation, offices and men would be buried together and each individual soldier was to be honoured individually in graves marked with a simple headstone rather than a cross.

Lutyens expressed the need for a permanent monument and proposed a memorial stone; "a great stone of fine proportion 12 feet [3.65 m] long, without undue ornamental trickery and elaborate carvings, looking to the west and facing the men who lie looking ever eastward towards the enemy". Lutyen's War Stone, inscribed with the words *Their name liveth for evermore* came to be placed in most cemeteries, in front of the headstones (Plate 71).

A monolithic stone was deliberately chosen as an ambiguous symbol which allows free association, however, its the form brings to mind an altar used in the religious gatherings of many faiths, places of sacrifice, metaphorical or real. Nor can the memorial stone's association with Poussin's pastoral painting *Et in Arcadia ego* be overlooked. As a classicist, Lutyens would have been familiar with Virgil's fifth *Eclogue* in which a tomb, with a memorial inscription is set amid the idyllic setting of Arcadia. In Poussin's painting the shepherd's have discovered the tomb and one points to the words, *Et in Arcadia ego*. In the first version of this painting a skull rests on the tomb, a typical *Memento mori,* but in the later version a shepherd's shadow becomes the symbol of death (Plate 71). The words, *Et in Arcadia ego,* have been variously translated but can be taken to mean either, And I (=in death) too (am) in Arcadia or 'the person buried in this tomb has lived in Arcadia', an interpretation widely accepted in the nineteenth century.

PLATE 70. Hooge Crater Cemetery, Belgium. A "corner of a foreign field that is for ever England". The French and Belgium governments passed a law deeding land for the cemeteries of foreign soldiers as a *sepulture perpetuelle*. The illusion of the cemetery as a corner of a foreign field, is strengthened by having only a low wall, hedge or both, delineating it from the surrounding landscape. The only visible evidence of war graves is Reginald Blomfield's celtic-inspired Cross of Sacrifice in front of Lutyen's memorial stone.

PLATE 71. Nicolas Poussin (1594–1665): *Et in Arcadia ego c.*1637–8

Both interpretations are relevant to the War Stone's place in the cemetery; either the soldiers now lie in Arcadia, or once they lived in Arcadia, an idyllic England "untouched by modernism, urbanism, or industrialism and therefore innocent enough to offer hope".[58]

After the war the shattered, traumatised landscapes throughout France and Belgium became tranquil Gardens of Rest. Some critics believed nature was used to mask the reality of war and the gardens fostered a popular acceptance of it.[59] And yet like all pastorals, the cemeteries speak out against the horrors of war. For the poet Edmund Blunden "the smoothing of battle-zones into cemeteries, of quagmires into lawns dotted with white headstones in part negated the horrors of war but in so doing brought the reality of war screaming to the surface":

> The beauty, the serenity, the inspiration of the Imperial cemeteries have been frequently acknowledged by more able eulogists; for my part, I venture to speak of these lovely, elegiac closes (which cause me to deny my own experiences in the acres they now grace) as being eloquent evidence against the war. Their very flowerfulness

and calm tell the lingerer that the men beneath that green coverlet should be there to enjoy such influence; the tyranny of war stands all the more revealed.[60]

A last hurrah for the Georgian poets

After the war the surviving Georgian poets returned to nature and pastoral images; as Gifford pointed out: "after the horrors of the First World War they sought refuge in rural images that did not disturb a sense of comfortable reassurance".[61] Edmund Blunden could still expresses his deep feeling for the countryside, but nature and the pastoral no longer offered rest;

> I saw the sunlit vale, and pastoral fairy-tale;
> The sweet and bitter scent of the may drifted by;
> And never have I seen such a bright bewildering green,
> But it looked like a lie.
> Like a kindly meant lie.
>
> Blunden, *A Sunlit Vale*[62]

A belief in nature as a permanent repository of goodness could not be recovered. A kind of religious disillusionment now pervaded:

> If the 'green' is a lie, it may be God's kindly invention, but we cannot make do with untruths. A belief in nature as an antidote for what men inflict upon one another is no longer tenable. It is the best nature can offer but it is not enough. Other facts undermine her. The pastoral framework has been shattered by contemporary experience. Nature may be consolatory now, but she is no longer man's preceptress.[63]

Vaughan Williams too, the master of nostalgic evocation, who had served in the medical corps in France, had undergone the same metamorphosis as Edmund Blunden. When he composed his symphony *Pastoral* in 1922, it was not about all things quaintly rustic, the imagined idyll of English landscape turned into sound, rather it was inspired by the scarred battlefields of France and was a requiem for the dead. He had turned the pastoral on its head and "so instead of being a source of comfort, this pastoral is a confrontation with loss, with lament, with death".[64]

Many considered the poems of rural scenes and village life to be out of touch and though Georgian poetry would be dismissed in pejorative terms by modernist poets, like T. S. Eliot and Ezra Pound, its pastoral imagery continues to have a lasting effect upon English culture. The Georgian poets reinforced a national love of the countryside and the nostalgic poems of Housman and Brooke remain among the most widely read and loved poems. And many people today would still echo the words Vita Sackville-West, in one of the last georgic poems, *The Land* (1927): "The country habit has me by the heart".[65]

Notes and References

1. Gifford, T., *Pastoral. The new critical idiom.* Routledge, London, 1999, p. 72. The 1901 census showed that 77% of the population lived in urban areas and only 12% of males were employed in agricultural work.

2. *Ibid.*

3. Marsh, J., *Back to the Land.* Quartet Books, London, 1982, p. 33.

4. Quoted in Marsh *op. cit.*, p. 34.

5. *Ibid.*, p. 36.

6. Grahame, K., *The Wind in the Willows.* Charles Scribner's Sons, New York, 1915, p. 7.

7. *Ibid.*, p. 155.

8. Housman, A. E., *A Shropshire Lad XL.* www.bartleby.com

9. Housman was deeply affected by the death of his mother when he was thirteen, news he received by telegram when he was away from home, and his unrequited love for another man. It was also the time of the Boer War in which his younger brother had been killed.

10. North, R. D., 'Walks: in search of the modern pastoral'. *Independent.* 27 December, 1997.

11. Butterworth was to die by sniper's bullet during the Battle of the Somme but long after his death he was described by a BBC presenter as 'Composer, Collector of Folk Songs, Morris dancer, Cricketer and Soldier'.

12. Thomas Sharp began collecting folk songs in 1903 and in claimed to have recorded 500 tunes in two years from ageing singers all over the country. He defined the folk song as, a song created by common people, by which Sharp meant "the remnants of the peasantry ... who resided in the country and subsisted on the land" and who were unlettered but not ignorant. He was of the opinion that such music evolved unconsciously over generations and was "transparently pure and truthful, simple and direct in its utterance", and "wholly free of the taint of manufacture, the canker of artificiality" – therefore possessing a virtue and value not found in composed music of however high a quality (quoted in Marsh *op. cit.*, p. 79). Sharp's songs were enthusiastically incorporated into school music teaching, aided by a government Education Act, where they remained a part of the school curriculum until the 1950s.

13. Anon, *The Sweet Primroses* (Roud 586; Ballad Index Sh51;trad.).

14. Quoted in Marsh, *op. cit.*, p. 76.

15. Simon, M., *The Georgian Poetic.* University of California, London, 1978, p. 14. The volumes of *Georgian Poetry* published between 1912–1915 are regarded as the most authentic voice of Georgian poetry and were the most influential.

16. *The Letters of D. H. Lawrence Vol 1 1901–13*, edited by Boulton, J. T. Cambridge University Press, Cambridge, 1997, p. 63.

17. Rogers, T. (ed.), *Georgian Poetry 1911–22.* Routledge, London, 1977, p. 244.

18. Simon, *op. cit.*, p. 53.

19. Simon, *op. cit.*, p. 55.

20. Brooks wrote the poem whilst travelling in Germany in May 1912, following a failed love affair.

21. www.bartleby. com

22. Quoted in Motion, A., *The Poetry of Edward Thomas.* Routledge and Kegan Paul, London, 1980, p. 100.

23. Friends of the Dymock Poets. www.dymockpoets.co.uk/Thomas.

24. Hollis, M., *Now All Roads Lead to France.* Faber and Faber, London, 2011, p. 283.

25. Quoted in Motion, A., *op. cit.*, p. 89.

26. Aged 37 and with diabetes Thomas could have avoided military service.

27. Kirkham, M., *The Imagination of Edward Thomas*. Cambridge University Press, Cambridge, 1986, p. 119.
28. Motion, A., *op. cit.*, p. 110.
29. Kirkham, M., *op. cit.*, p. 119.
30. *Ibid.*, p. 120.
31. www.thepoetryfoundation.org
32. Quoted in Barlow, A., *The Great War in British Literature*. Cambridge University Press, Cambridge, 2000, p. 18.
33. Brooke, R., 'An Unusual Young Man', *New Statesman,* 29 November 1999.
34. www.bartleby.com
35. Fussell, P., *The Great War and Modern Memory*. Oxford University Press, New York, 1997, p. 157.
36. *Ibid.,* p. 157.
37. In the 1930s Henry Newbolt estimated there were still at least 1000 active poets; the vast majority would be recognisably 'Georgian'. As many poems rely on interpretation as opposed to clear facts, the poets by-passed military censorship.
38. *Ibid.*, 164.
39. Two years before the war Georgian focus was appearing to narrow down to the red flowers, especially roses and poppies, whose blood colours would become an indispensable part of the symbolism of war.
40. www.greatwar.co.uk/poems/john-william-streets-matthew-copse.
41. Quoted in Barlow, A., *op. cit.*, p. 26.
42. Quiller-Couch, A. (ed.), *The Oxford Book of English Verse: 1250–1900*. Clarendon Press, Oxford, 1919.
43. *Poetry Society Bulletin* 14. Quoted in *Edmund Blunden,* edited by R. Marscak, Fyfield Books, Carcanet Press, Manchester, 1993 p. 12.
44. *Ibid.*, p. 13.
45. *Ibid.*
46. Blunden, E., *Undertones of War. www.*archive.org, p. 191.
47. Quoted in Fussell, P., *op. cit.*, p. 261.
48. Fussell, P., *op. cit.*, p. 263–4.
49. Fussell, P., *op. cit.*, p. 264.
50. Fussell, P., *op. cit.*, p. 268.
51. www.poemhunter.com/poem/mist-on-meadows.
52. Hardner, H. (ed.), *The New Oxford Book of Verse*. Book Club Associates Bungay, Suffolk, 1974, p. 863.
53. In 1915 General Ware's unit was incorporated into the army as the Graves Registration Commission, later the Imperial War Graves Commission (IWGC).
54. It is fully understood that the soldiers who died in the First World War were of many nationalities, from both the United Kingdom and the Commonwealth.
55. Geurst, J., *Cemeteries of the Great War by Sir Edwin Lutyens*. 010 Publishers, Rotterdam, 2010, p. 26.
56. Quoted in Laqueur, T., Empires of the dead: how one man's vision led to the the Creation of WWI's War Graves. *Guardian*, Friday 22 November, 2013.
57. *Ibid.*
58. Geurst, J., *op. cit.*, p. 20–1.
59. Mosse G. L., *Fallen Soldiers*. Oxford University Press, Oxford, 1991, p. 81.
60. Blunden, E., introduction to an account of the work of the Imperial War Graves Commission 1937.
61. Gifford, T., *op. cit.*, p. 71.

62. Marscak, R.,*op.cit.*, p. 92.

63. Silkin, J., *Out of Battle. The poetry of the Great War.* Macmillan, Basingstoke, 1998, p. 120.

64. www.theguardian.com/music/tomserviceblog/Aug/11/symphony-guide-vaughan-williams.

65. Sackville-West, V., *The Land.* www.poemhunter.com/victoria-sackville-west. Though widely read and highly influential at the time, the poem, if not the sentiment, has been largely forgotten today.

CHAPTER FIFTEEN

Modernism and the Anti-Pastoral Landscape

T. S. Eliot and the *Imagists*

Reaction to Georgian poetry was led by two expatriate American poets Ezra Pound and, most importantly for this narrative, T. S. Eliot. Artistic movements generally arise as a reaction against the immediate tradition and what members of a new movement, known as *Imagism*, disliked was the tradition that began with Wordsworth with its lyric emphasis, which often drew on the imagery of nature with the poet as narrator. The *Imagists* believed the Wordsworthian style, and Georgian poetry which followed, had become decadently mushy, rhythmically inert, predictable in its imagery, and emotionally dishonest. It had turned poetry from something vital into something merely decorative. So however passionate and innovative Wordsworth's own best poetry had been, poetry by the end of the nineteenth century had lost its vitality and degenerated into subjective posturing often wrapped in the cloudiness of nostalgia or dreams, presented in flaccid language. For Eliot the root of mediocre English poetry, as represented by the 1920 *Georgian Anthology,* was its pretense that England was a green and pleasant land when he saw himself inhabiting a corrupt, crumbling civilisation, one that was essentially urban. Besides which, in poetic terms, the idyllic harmony of the romantic pastoral landscape seemed dull in comparison to the energy, confusion and noise of the city.

From the opening lines of Eliot's anti-pastoral poem *The Waste Land* (1922) any idea of the fecundity of nature was shattered: "April is the cruelest month".[1] The imagery summons up a particular and startling image of spring; traditionally the time of renewal and optimism, to Eliot it had become something hostile to life because it "wakes us from our winter torpor". In places the language of *The Waste Land* hovers on the verge of "pastoral loveliness but is continually marred by the ugly and the uncouth":[2]

> The river's tent is broken; the last fingers of leaf
> Clutch and sink into the wet bank. The wind
> Crosses the brown land, unheard. The nymphs
>   are departed.
> Sweet Thames, run softly, till I end my song.
> The river bears no empty bottles, sandwich
>   papers,

Silk handkerchiefs, cardboard boxes, cigarette
   ends
Or other testimony of summer nights. The
nymphs are departed.
And their friends, the loitering heirs of City
   directors;
Departed, have left no addresses.

Eliot, The Waste Land iii. The Fire Sermon[3]

Mention of the sweet Thames is an evocation of past memories. From the time of Alexander Pope, it had been seen as the essence of pastoral England, now images of departing nymphs, a standard feature of elegiac Renaissance pastoral, are merged with the depiction of trash left behind by idle revellers engaged in debauchery on the river bank where "the rat drags its slimy belly".

Eliot's early poetic style, particularly in *The Waste Land,* really brings out the "sense of collapse of the past", and he deliberately invokes the past to insist upon this point. What once had meaning no longer does. These ancient visions of a life so much more passionately full and coherent than the present age are gone. They remain only as isolated bits, reminders of the inadequacy of our own times; Eros has become a tired mechanical ritual, the beautiful aspects of nature have filled up with cigarette butts and garbage or turned threatening, faith has become empty, the centres of the ancient civilisation (Jerusalem, Athens, Alexandria, Vienna, London) are being destroyed in the universal, technological chaos of war, and the world is filling up with refugees (an important element in the characters of the poem). It remains an all too familiar world.

The Modern movement

Eliot was part of a wider Modern movement encompassing the activities and output of those who felt the traditional forms of art, architecture, literature, religious faith, social organisation and daily life were becoming outdated in the new economic, social, and political conditions of an emergent, fully industrialised world. In all these fields something new and relevant was needed to replace the old order. They were wrestling with the questions: What faith could one place in a tradition which had led to the horrors of the Great War of 1914–1918? And was there something to be salvaged, or should the entire tradition be junked? The common ground between them all was that nature, and by inference the pastoral landscape, could no longer provide the answers. In the new order nature was the servant, the tool of man, and many shared the sentiments of Eliot, that nature was no longer to be trusted.

In the final quarter of the nineteenth century the certainties of man's superiority over nature, that had existed since the Renaissance, were undermined by two disruptive sources; in biology by Charles Darwin and in political science by Karl Marx. Modernist writers saw that humans were a part of nature "Homo Sapiens – mammals with superior cognitive functioning – affected by basic biology, and most of all by intelligence and emotion".[4] Writers like Virginia

Woolf, took it upon themselves to remind their readers that nature is the place from which we all come and to which we will all return. In her novel *Mrs Dalloway,* Woolf expressed this drastic new view through her character Clarissa: "we are biological beings and what we do by-and-large does not have a grandiose impact on the continuation of life". "Clarissa realised that, like the waves of water, the survival of species will rise and fall and that every living thing is just the part of a cycle of life and death: nothing more, nothing less."[5]

Among artists the notion emerged that art should not be contaminated by the real world and in future be practiced "within a closed formal sphere ... . Art stood separate from the materialistic world and the mundane affairs of ordinary people".[6] Some artists went in search of 'art', a search for the truth or essence of art, stripping away familiar objects which tended to conceal or distract from the real underlying truth. Art was not simply a matter of manipulating images, it was the 'art' behind the image that was deemed important. "Art can be many things and one example may look quite different from the next. But something called 'art' is common to all. Whatever this 'true' art was, it was universal; like the scientific "truth of the Enlightenment. All art obviously possessed it".[7] One artist who pursued this line of argument was the Dutch artist, Piet Mondrian in whose work it is possible to trace the development of these ideas, and the rejection of nature as a source of inspiration.

Piet Mondrian

In the late nineteenth century Dutch art had become a backwater, unaffected by developments elsewhere in Europe. Artists of the Hague School had renewed an interest in the landscape paintings of Ruisdael and Hobbema, and a preference for the *pasage intime*, scenes of the pastoral Dutch countryside and country life. At first Mondrian followed their example but his work soon began to change (Plate 72):

> I preferred to paint landscape and houses seen in grey, dark weather or very strong sunlight, when the density of atmosphere obscures the details and accentuated the large outlines of objects. I often sketched by moonlight – cows resting, flat Dutch meadows, or houses with dead, blank windows. I never painted these things romantically; but from the very beginning I was a realist. Even at this time, I disliked movement, such as people in action. I enjoyed flower, not bouquets, but a single flower at a time, in order that I might better express its plastic structure.
>
> After several years, my work unconsciously began to deviate more and more from the natural aspects of reality. Experience was my only teacher; I knew little of the modern art movement When I first saw the work of the Impressionists, Van Gogh,Van Dongen and the Fauves,[8] I admired it. But I had to seek the true way alone.[9]

In 1908 Mondrian became interested in the theosophical movement launched by Helena Petrovna Blavatsky (HPB) and he joined the Theosophical Society a year later. Blavatsky believed it was possible to attain a more profound knowledge of nature than that provided by empirical means and for the rest of his life much of Mondrian's work was inspired by a search for spiritual knowledge. It was the genius of HPB, wrote the historian James Webb in *The Occult Underground,* to apply Darwin's theory to produce a hopeful resolution to the human condition".[10] Webb continues: "Whereas others saw only the destruction of the sustaining myth of man's divine origins, HPB discovered that evolution could apply also to the 'spiritual' aspects of existence. But as Kramer pointed out 'an art born of an alliance of aesthetics and mysticism was still obliged to traffic in material objects and thus remain accessible to visual perception, if its spiritual function was to be realised. It could not – or not yet anyway – so completely dematerialise itself as to become invisible if it were to continue as art'".[11]

After seeing just a few paintings by Braque and Picasso in the new Cubist style, at an exhibition in Amsterdam, Mondrian moved to Paris where he soon mastered the cubist technique. In the *Gray Tree* the last remnants of naturalistic detail were still be discerned but overlain "in favour of pure painting'.[12] It would be a further two years before he finally expunged the last traces of realism from his paintings.

Mondrian returned reluctantly to the Netherlands on the eve of the First World War and found himself trapped there for the duration of the war. During this time he came to know others who shared his ideas, among them the painters, Theo van Doesburg and Bart van Leck, the architects J. J. P. Oud and Robert van't Hoff, the designers Vilmos Huszar and Gerrit Rietveld and the Belgium sculptor Georges Vantongerloo. In 1917 Mondrian and van Doesburg founded a movement they called *de Stijl* (the Style). This was to have an immense influence not only on the future of abstract art but also on the theory and practice of modern architecture and design. But *de Stijl* was more than an art movement:

> It was a social and cultural program, based on a visionary amalgam of idealist aesthetics, industrial mechanics, and utopian politics. Its ambition was to redesign the world by imposing straight lines, primary colours, and geometric form – and thus an ideal of impersonal order and rationality – upon the production of every man-made object essential to the modern human environment. Rejecting tradition, it envisioned the rebirth of the world as a kind of technological Eden from which all trace of individualism and the conflicts it generates would be permanently banished. its goal was to liberate European culture from the 'archaistic confusion' of the past in order to create an entirely new and completely harmonious civilization.[13]

By September 1917 Mondrian was painting his first geometrical abstractions. He wrote "(they) cannot be cloaked in what is characteristic of the particular, natural form and colour, but must be expressed by the abstraction of form and colour – by means of straight line and determinate primary colour". In his personal manifesto *The New Plastic in Painting,* Mondrian not only triumphantly affirms pure abstraction as an aesthetic absolute but repeats the need to emancipate painting from the thralldom of what is variously called 'nature's appearance', 'naturalistic representation', 'naturalistic form', 'naturalistic colour' and so on. Green was the one colour that could never be used because of its association with nature. It is said that Mondrian had such a revulsion against green and growth (that) when seated at a table beside a window through which trees were visible he would switch places. He believed abstract beauty was superior to natural beauty, he claimed that if you depict nature you must include "whatever is capricious and twisted in nature". Natural beauty contains emotional components that distract from visual harmony and order". Harmony can only be found when painting is stripped of representation. The cycles of life and death in the natural world lend it beauty but distract from 'pure' beauty present in lines and elementary shapes. For Mondrian, this meant that the harmony one could feel with the city was fundamentally different and superior to that of the country.

PLATE 72. Pieter Mondriaan (1872–1944): *East Zuider Sea windmill by moonlight c.*1903.

Cornelis van Eesteren

Closely associated with *de Stijl* was the architect and urban planner, Cornelius van Eesteren. As a student he collaborated with van Doesburg on an exhibition, *Les Architecture du groupe De Stijl* (1923) which stimulated much discussion in France. After his appointment as Head of Urban Development in Amsterdam (1929) Van Eesteren saw the opportunity to achieve the de Stijl goal of "creating an entirely new and completely harmonious civilization" through the planned extension of the city. Rejecting tradition and "adopting a more scientific approach to planning based on the collection and analysis of physical and social data".[14] Forecasts of population growth were used to determine requirements for housing, leisure facilities, employment and traffic. These distinct functions, along with nature and natural areas, were strictly separated in what he called the 'Functional City'. This concept, that would come to determine urban planning worldwide for the rest of the twentieth century, was first seen in the 1935 General Extension Plan for Amsterdam (Figure 15). New suburbs and other areas of development were arranged in fingers or lobes, separated by green wedges.

The Amsterdam Bos Park

One of those wedges was be a new park, which in practice became an urban forest, the Amsterdam Woods (Bos Park). This would be the size of Haussmann's Bois de Boulogne in Paris and arguably "the largest urban park created in the anywhere in the world during the twentieth century".[15] The designers of the Bos Park took three essentials ideas from de Stijl and van Eesteren's planning

ALGEMEEN UITBREIDINGSPLAN VAN AMSTERDAM. SCHAAL 1 : 50000

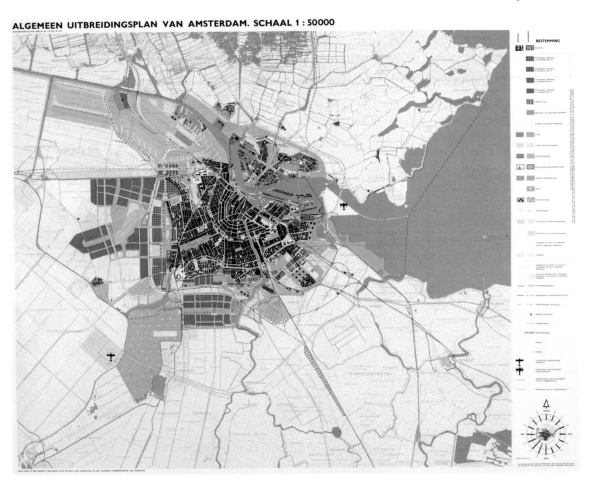

FIGURE 15. General
Extension plan for
Amsterdam (1935). The
new residential areas are
coloured red and the Bos
park is the large green
area projecting south.

principles, firstly, social function, secondly, separation of functions and thirdly,
a scientific approach. The official brief for the park stated that:

1. the woodland for the most part should have a social character, no part of the
   woodland should be for decoration or exploitation, but woodland to be enjoyed
   by everyone.
2. the layout and planting are to meet the requirements arising from the different
   needs of all sorts and conditions of the Amsterdam population.[16]

Though the Dutch had been making forests for many centuries, the Bos Park
was different in two important respects, firstly it was not a commercial forest
rather it was to have the character of a natural forest of north-west europe;
and secondly the design of the park was to be modernist. Ninety years before,
Frederick Law Olmsted argued that the park offered an escape from the pressures
of urban life. "Extensive woods", he said in *Public Parks and the Enlargement
of Towns,* ought "to surround the park deep enough to completely shut out the
city from our landscapes and achieve the greatest possible contrast with the
restraining and confining condition of the town".[17] However the Modernist

vision was of a city were such escape was no longer necessary, and the park should be integral to invigorating city life. Though in its arrangement, *city–countryside–nature*, remained pastoral, no overt or covert message was intended. The sylvan glades would not be the haunt of fauns, Pan was not hidden among the trees, and this was no Arcadia. Nor did Nature offers any self knowledge, understanding or have a deeper meaning, as Thoreau believed.

The Bos Park was perhaps the first example of an anti-pastoral landscape; in the words of Berrizbeita:

> The park is stripped of its metaphorical and spiritual intention it is demystified. The emphasis on materiality and the unveiling of the technical means of construction eliminate the transcendental in the park and invalidate the conceptual separateness of the park from the city. Rather than being presented as isolated and protected from technology and capitalism and, in turn, offering the individual shelter from these forces, the park is understood as one of many productive entities within the metropolis. Like the subway system or the stock exchange, the park is a piece of a system that contributes to and strives for maximum productive efficiency. In its multiplicity of functions, organised rationally according to function and production, the park is akin to an overlay of activities of the city. It no longer stands against the world but is one thing worldly thing among others.[18]

Berrizbeita further argued that what the modernist vanguard repudiated was any assumption of the importance of the individual designer, just as Mondrian had eliminated the presence of the artist in his paintings. The individual designer was replaced by hydrologists, social scientists, foresters, planners and landscape architects, all adopting a scientific approach to the design. Jakoba Mulder, had overall responsibility and was known affectionately as *Mejuvrouw van het Bos* (Miss of the Forest) because of her dedication to the park throughout her life.[19] The basic elements of wood, water and meadow were arranged in roughly a 1:1:1 ratio (Figure 16). As Berrizbeita observed this "even but intermingled distribution of landscape conditions recalls the spatial distribution in *de Stijl* paintings, which typically gives even weight to all elements of the painting while filling the space of the canvas evenly all the way to the edges".[20] (Plate 73).

Le Corbusier and the Villa Savoie

The Modernist architect who had perhaps the most profound influence on twentieth century architecture and planning was the Swiss born, le Corbusier, a visionary who shared *de Stijl's* deep mistrust of the natural world. The Dutch landscape architect Mien Ruys thought Corbusier even misunderstood the meaning of nature.[21] He envisaged a brave new world in which man would transcend his dependence on nature with all its unpleasantness; of rain, wet grass, scorching sun, falling leaves. Nature in future would be a green abstraction represented by sun, sky, and vegetation, viewed from a house that would become a 'machine for living'. One his most seminal works is the Villa Savoie at Poissy, near Paris, built between 1928 and 1931. This best expresses the Corbusian relationship between architecture and nature; the villa "was placed unobtrusively on a softly crowned pasture and orchard", ... "conveying the image of a modernist fabrique set in a Virgilian landscape".[22] Corbusier's reference to Virgil recalls the way in which the renaissance architect Palladio described his Rotunda near Vicenza (Plate 74). Set in a bucolic, Georgic landscape, Palladio described the ideal life of the villa, a *villa urbana*, in which:

> its owner from within a fragment of created order, will watch the maturing of his possessions and savour the piquancy of contrast between his fields and his gardens; reflecting on, contemplating throughout the years the antique virtues of a simpler race, and the harmonious ordering of his life and his estate will be a paradise.[23]

At Poissy Le Corbusier played the pastoral cliche to the extreme. With painterly vision, he described how the villa was sited so: "the view is very beautiful, grass is a beautiful thing, and so is the forest – to be barely touched. The house will be placed on the grass, like an object, disturbing nothing".[24] For Corbusier the Virgilian landscape needed little shaping, the greater landscape was left untouched, as a stage on which sun, air and rain were the principal actors.

The villa was raised above the ground on thin concrete pillars, or pilotis, which were the only apparent points of contact between the raised white form and the earth. The receding core of the ground floor was originally painted green so the house appeared to hover above the grass dome. The facade, uniformly divided, its surfaces flat and without texture, appeared as a pristine shell detached from its surroundings. Corbusier believed any vegetal composition might detract from the impact of the pure "architectural volumes", while the white facades constituted a "trellis against which the tree branches (were) advantageously silhouetted".[25] Because the grass was considered unhealthy and damp, the garden was elevated 11 feet (3.5 m) onto a roof terrace, where it could be protected from harsh sunlight and rain. Corbusier argued that the terrace transformed the usually inert apartment building into a breathing sponge integrating air and greenery within its concrete structure.[26] The roof terrace also afforded "distant views on the horizon" unavailable from the ground: "Immersed in nature and isolated from other buildings, the Villa Savoie needed only to frame the landscape to compose a most picturesque tableau"[27] of the agrarian landscape of Poissy (Plate 75).

Le Corbusier proposed that villas, like the Villa Savoie, should be placed on columns in a beautiful corners of the countryside, and in his book *Precisions,* he criticised what he saw as the failings of the Garden City:

> We shall have twenty houses rising above the tall long grass of a meadow where the cows will continue to graze. Instead of the superfluous and detestable clothing of garden city roads and byways, the effect of which is always to destroy the site, we shall have a fine arterial system running in concrete through the grass itself, and in the open country. Grass will border the roads; nothing will be disturbed - neither trees, flowers, nor the flocks and herds. The dwellers in these houses, drawn hence through a love of of the life of the countryside, will be able to see it maintained intact from their hanging gardens or their ample windows. Their domestic lives will be set in a Virgilian dream.[28]

Christopher Tunnard and Bentley Wood

Not everyone shared the Corbusian vision. The young Canadian landscape architect, Christopher Tunnard, criticised the architect for failing to appreciate the significance of the garden, both to the architecture and the occupants of the house. After observing at first hand some of le Corbusier's houses and gardens, he stated they were "adaptations rather than pure creative works". "Corbusier should", he said, "be congratulated for whole-heartedly adopting the cult of nature worship but he has failed to appreciate the significance of the surrounds". The dreams of Virgil, said Tunnard, can never be said to have included a vision of a modern woman getting her feet wet in the long grass. "Le Corbusier must be congratulated on extending the natural garden to its logical conclusion" but:

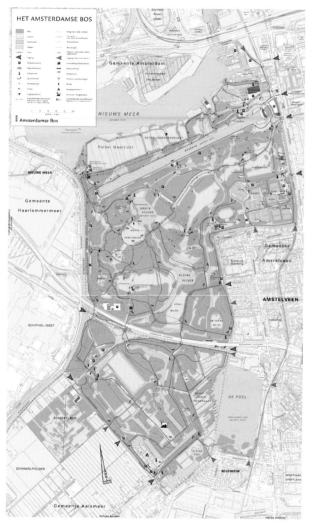

> Few people want to be condemned to languish at a window and exercise exclusively on a roof garden. Yet, to the author quoted, the levelling of a space for recreation in the long grass of the meadows and the banishment of the flocks and herds would seem to be a sacrilege and certainly a desecration of the contours of the virgin soil. The sportsman can with his gun take pleasure in purely agricultural country, but most of us soon find that Nature unadorned (even with the alternative of a roof garden by Le Corbusier) is not enough: that the landscape or at any rate the surroundings of the house must be planned in accordance with human needs. Certainly the old conception of garden designed as a series of pretty pictures must be put aside and a new and economical technique be used. The garden as an organization, whether that organization be only a path and a plant, must exist and can be ordered into a perfect and satisfying relationship with the house and landscape.[29]

FIGURE 16. Plan of The Amsterdam Bos (Woods).

The functional garden, said Tunnard, avoids "the extremes of the wild garden and the intellectual classicism of the 'formal' garden; it embodies rather a spirit of rationalism and through an aesthetic and practical ordering of its units, provides a friendly and hospitable milieu for rest and recreation. It is in effect, the social conception of a garden".

Tunnard demonstrated this concept at Bentley Wood at Halland, East Sussex. The controversial, modernist house, designed by Serge Chermeyeff, "was a two-story flat roofed rectangular building made of brick and concrete with shingle

PLATE 73. The Amsterdam Wood – the 'unintended' pastoral nature of this scene was enhanced by Amsterdam City Council's decision to use highland cattle to graze the grass.

PLATE 74. Palladio (1508–1580): Villa Rotunda, near Vicenza.

PLATE 75. Le Corbusier: the Villa Savoie *c.*1929

clad sides"[30] set in a secluded setting on an 84 acre (34 ha) plot, most of which was left untouched (see Figure 10). Tunnard's plan carefully maintained the natural appearance of the site, planting only groups of birch trees to create a natural passage from the geometry of the house to the wilderness beyond. A nearby coppice was thinned to highlight a single oak, and under planted with spring bulbs. The natural contours of the land were emphasised with a closely mown lawn around the house giving way to uncut grass. And by borrowing the landscape in the eighteenth century manner, views were created beyond the boundary to give the impression of a vast park (Plate 76).[31]

In harmonizsing the traditional English landscape with the stark modernism of Chermeyeff's architecture, Bentley Wood marked a new naturalism in twentieth century design. With its slender white columns and recessed facade, Bentley Wood resembles a Greek temple presiding over the pastoral landscape of a rugged hill, with the Sussex Downs spreading before it. The serene austerity,

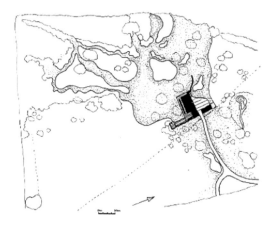

FIGURE 17. Plan of Bentley Wood

PLATE 76. Bentley Wood.

the subtle deployment of colour and texture, the harmonising of contemporary architecture and timeless countryside suggested a way forward for landscape design. But shortly after working at Bentley Wood, Tunnard joined the flow of modernists to America and took no further part in developing the modernist landscape, in theory or practice. It has been suggested that he was frustrated by entrenched conservatism prevailing in English gardening circles that remained gripped by the arts and craft, under the influence of Lutyens and in particular, the flower garden traditions of Gertrude Jekyll. These would continue to retain their hold for decades to come. Only after the Second World War would architects and planners influenced by modernist ideas, take centre stage as cities across Britain, as well as those in Europe and America, were transformed, some would say today disfigured, by Corbusian-inspired architecture and minimalist landscapes. In England, where Nicholas Pevsner, an early advocate of modernism, had once said, "the English dislike revolution, innovation and even logical thought", a typically British compromise was found, welding the new ideas of modernist planning onto the discredited garden city. In the post-war New Towns of Harlow, Hemel Hempstead and the others that followed, a new generation of landscape architects, among them Geoffrey Jellicoe, Sylvia Crowe and Brenda Colvin were able to take forward the ideas first advanced by Christopher Tunnard.

Notes and References

1. It is possible Eliot had in mind his close friend Jean Verdenal who he had met in Paris during his year at the Sorbonne 1910–11. He was killed at Gallipoli in 1915, though not in April as Eliot believed but in May. Bloom, H., *The Waste Land*. Infobase Publishing, New York, 2007, p. 69.
2. Young, R. V. 'Withered stumps of time: *The Waste Land* and mythic disillusion'. *Intercollegiate Review*, Spring 2003, 30.
3. Johnston, I., *T. S. Eliot's* The Love Song of J. Alfred Prufrock *and* The Waste Land. Vancouver Island University, Vancouver, 1996.
4. Skumautz, K., 'How natural images convey modernist concepts in Virginia Woolf's *Mrs Dalloway* and Erich Maria Remarque's *All Quiet on the Western Front*'. *Coastline Journal,* July 3 2010.
5. *Ibid.*
6. Witcombe, C., *Art for Art's Sake*. www.arthistoryresources.net.
7. *Ibid.*
8. Cornelis van Dongen (1877–1968) was a Dutch painter and one of the Fauves (wild beasts) artists, a short-lived group in the early twentieth century whose work emphasised painterly qualities and strong colour over representational values retained by the impressionists.
9. *Mondrian and the Hague School*. Whitworth Art Gallery, University of Manchester, Manchester, 1980, p. 18.
10. Quoted in Kramer, J., *Mondrian: positive mysticism and plastic mathematics*. www.redbubble.com.
11. *Ibid.*
12. Kramer, J., *op. cit.* Mondrian changed his name from Mondriaan while studying in Paris.

13. *Ibid*. Mondrian and other members of *de Stijl* were influenced the mathematician and theosophist M. H. J. Shoenmaekers who formulated the plastic and philosophical principles of the movement. In 1915 he published *The New Image of the World*, followed in 1916 by *Principles of Plastic Mathematics*.

14. Mumford, E. P. *The CIAM Discourse on Urbanism, 1928–1960*. Massachusetts Institute of Technology, MA, 2000, p. 59.

15. Tate, A., *Great City Parks*. Spon Press, London, 2001, p. 168.

16. *Dienst der Publieke Werken, Amsterdam Het Amsterdamse Bos 1973*. Quoted in A. Ruff, *Holland and the Ecological Landscape*, Deanwater Press, Stockport, 1979, p. 11.

17. Olmsted, F. L., *Public Parks and the Enlargement of Towns*. American Social Science Association 1870. Hathi Digital Library.

18. Berrizbeitia, A., 'The Amsterdam Bos: the modern public park and the construction of collective experience', in *Recovering Landscape: essays on contemporary landscape architecture*, edited by J. Corner. Princeton, Architectural Press, New York, 1999, p. 181.

19. Jakoba Mulder (1900–1988) was an architect, planner and landscape architect in Amsterdam's Office of Public Works.

20. Berrizbeitia, A., *op. cit.*, p. 193.

21. Quoted in *Garden History* 28(1) Summer 2000. Woudstra, J., *The Corbusian Landscape* p. 136.

22. Le Corbusier, Jenneret, P., *Ouvre Complet 1910–1929*, p. 186; quoted in D. Imbert, *The Modernist Garden in France*. Yale University Press, Princeton, 1993, p. 163.

23. *Ibid.*, p. 163.

24. *Ibid.*

25. *Ibid.*

26. *Ibid.*

27. *Ibid.*, p. 164.

28. Gideon, S., *Space, Time and Architecture*. Harvard. University Press, Cambridge MA, 1974, p. 24.

29. Campbell, K., *Icons of Twentieth-Century Design*. Frances Lincoln, London, 2007, p. 49.

30. Trieb, M. (ed.), *Modern Landscape Architecture: a critical review*. MIT Press, Cambridge MA., 1998, p.15.

31. Tunnard, C., *Gardens in the Modern Landscape*. Architectural Press, London, 1950. Tunnard was equally influenced by Japanese philosophy, something he probably acquired during his youth on the west coast of Canada where there was a large Japanese population and their gardens, an interest he shared with Percy Cane. In particular he applauded the oriental integration with nature and advised designers to adjust their style to suit the site rather than trying to adapt the site to a preconceived plan.

CHAPTER SIXTEEN

The Workers' Pastoral

At the end of the nineteenth century the Pastoral ideal in England ceased to be the sole preserve of artists and poets, or even the leisured middle classes. Rather, it became a potent force for those Ewan McColl described as wage slaves – those young people forced by economic necessity to spend their working week tied to the machine or anchored to a desk. The countryside was perceived as a pre-industrial, pastoral haven and a place where, according to Octavia Hill: "the silence of the heather-clad hills offered a spiritual counterbalance to the strains of urban existence". The idealised rural imagery of Wordsworth and the other Lake poets, together with the critique of industrialism spearheaded by Ruskin, Arnold and Morris, evolved into a reinterpretation of the countryside as the authentic, unadulterated England. And for those young men and women who poured into the countryside for recreation there was a sense of liberation, a feeling of a new world. This was especially true for the inhabitants of the northern industrial towns and cities for whom the countryside offered a combination of fresh air, physical activity and informal self-education. Many of the pioneering organizations of ramblers and cyclists were founded during this period; the Cyclists Touring Club in 1878, the Manchester YMCA Rambling Club in 1880, the Polytechnic Rambling Club in 1885 and the London Federation of Rambling Clubs in 1885.

In the aftermath of the Great War returning soldiers were in no mood to accept the *status quo*; having fought for the land, working men wanted to assert their rights to the land. In 1918 the prime minister, David Lloyd George, in an eloquent electioneering speech, had spoken of creating "a land fit for heroes" but he could not deliver on his rhetoric. Many working people faced bleak economic conditions; by 1921 two million were unemployed and others were on extremely low wages. Appalling living conditions fostered many diseases; tuberculosis was rife and ailments caused by malnutrition, such as rickets, were common. As conditions worsened and unemployment rose, people flocked to the countryside in their thousands – by train, charabanc, bicycle and a fleet of buses – to seek solace in the countryside. But those seeking escape from towns and cities found access to the countryside was severely curtailed. A succession of Enclosure Acts in the eighteenth and nineteenth centuries had allowed landowners to appropriate what was once common land to protect their shooting interests. In the Peak District, close to the industrial conurbations of Manchester and Sheffield, there were just 12 legal footpaths and only 1200 acres

(458 ha), less than 1% of the 150,000 acres (60,702 ha) of moorland, was open for public access. The demand by ramblers for access to the mountains, and the longing for a home in the country in what Hardy and Ward called *Arcadia for All*,[1] would have widespread repercussions for town and country, especially on how the landscape was, and continues to be, seen, used and controlled. For it was the response of the middle classes to these developments that shaped the pastoral framework of today's countryside legislation.

T. A. Leonard and the Co-operative Holiday Association

Rambling was particularly popular in northeast Lancashire where rambling clubs were commonly a part of the leisure activities at non-conformist churches.[2] However, a scarcity of affordable accommodation meant working class ramblers had no option but return to the smoke and grime of the town after a day in the hills. Rural holidays remained the preserve of the higher social classes and cheap accommodation was only to be found in commercial seaside resorts, like Blackpool. This was a popular destinations during Wakes Week for workers in Lancashire and surrounding counties.[3] As the one occasion in the year when workers could leave behind the drudgery of the mills and factories, for many this was a time of unbridled, hedonistic pleasure. However, not everyone approved of the dissipations and frivolities of Blackpool. One of the most vociferous critics was a young Congregational minister in Colne, Lancashire, the Rev. T. A. Leonard (1864–1948), a Christian Socialist and disciple of Morris, Arnold and Ruskin, all of whom he quoted in his sermons. Leonard favoured the restorative calm of a holiday in the countryside and told his congregation in 1891 that he would be organising walking holidays in the Lake District for his church's Social Guild Walking Club. The contrast between this holiday and those to which young working-class men were accustomed could hardly have been more distinct:

> ... in the long 'day-tramps' over the hills and moors many a young fellow learned for the first time the real wholesome pleasure of a mountain holiday, and found that such a holiday was not only healthier, but less expensive than the usual 'Blackpool bust'.[4]

Three years later Leonard formed the Co-operative Holidays Association (CHA) with John Paton, another prominent Congregationalist and social reformer. Paton was founder of the National Home Reading Union which aimed to improve the standard of working class leisure reading but it failed to become a national movement. Seeing Leonard's successful venture, he invited him to expand his walking holidays on a national basis by working in co-operation with the Union. The CHA blended socialism with the romantic construct of the pastoral endowing it with a unique leisure ideology and appeal. Not simply a holiday organisation, it was, as Leonard (*c*.1900) stated, one with:

> a definite ethical mission to fulfill – namely the cultivation of character, and we seek to achieve this at a season when men and women are most susceptible to better

influences... Comradeship, simplicity, reverence may perhaps be regarded as the watchwords of our movement.[5]

Snape suggests, the CHA was an expression, within a leisure context, of the contemporary yearning for the pastoral, discussed in Chapter 14:

> Their critique of industrialism's obsession with material progress at the expense of quality of life gave impetus to the CHA's negation of the economic and social structures of urban capitalism and its attempt to replicate a pastoral mode of existence in which complexity was superseded by simplicity and competition was replaced by co-operation. The choice of the countryside as the location for Leonard's project in communal leisure was highly symbolic. Not only did it affirm a mode of leisure grounded upon an appreciation of nature and the pastoral as inherently superior to the hedonism of urban leisure culture but it also reflected a contemporary view of the rural as the locus for a post-industrial socialist utopia. (Morris 1915; 1962). The idealised pastoral vision of Ruskin and Morris and the rural imagery of the Lakes poets were the foundations for the CHA's guiding principles of fellowship and commonwealth and the model for its holidays.[6]

A typical CHA holiday, of a weeks duration, comprised non-optional daily rambles, not uncommonly 18–20 miles (*c.*29–32 km) in length. Walking was considered superior to cycling because its slower pace encouraged a reflective appreciation of one's surroundings, and as a result, a cultural understanding of the countryside traversed. Ramblers were accompanied by a lecturer, often provided through the National Home Reading Union, who gave wayside talks on the natural history and literary associations of the area. In a popular guidebook of the period Burnett (1889) noted that there was an expanding class of people who wished to acquire a knowledge of the historic and artistic connections of the areas through which they rambled:

> We are of the opinion that for a walk to be thoroughly enjoyable there should be some object, other than the desire to cover a certain distance, to engage the mind or charm the fancy ... we purpose on our peregrinations to pick up as we go along any bit of folk-lore, any inconsiderable trifle of history, any forgotten incident which long ago absorbed the mind of a former generation and present it to the reader at the time and place when and where it will be most likely to interest him.[7]

Central to the cultural meaning of the countryside was a symbolic interpretation of the landscape. To some extent this was implicit in the CHA's Christian morality. Wayside breaks provided opportunities for sermons and prayers in communion with God's creation and Paton noted how clear skies and heather-clad moors enhanced the outdoor services and sermons with which the early rambles were liberally sprinkled. In time the religious dimension of the countryside came to embrace a wider spiritual relationship with the landscape and Nature, inspired largely by Ruskin. The CHA's ideological outlook clearly reflected Ruskin's contrast of the materialistic nature of urban leisure with the potential of the countryside as an alternative leisure space:

The delights of horse-racing and hunting, of assemblies in the night instead of the day, of costly and wearisome music, of costly and burdensome dress, of chagrined contention for place or power, or wealth, or the eyes of the multitude; and all the endless occupations without purpose and idleness without rest, of our vulgar world, are not, it seems to me, enjoyments we need to be ambitious to communicate. And all real and wholesome enjoyments possible to man have been just as possible to him since first he was made of the earth, as they are now; and they are possible to him chiefly in peace. To watch the corn grow and the blossoms set, to draw hard breath over ploughshare or spade; to read, to think, to love, to pray, – these are that make men happy; they have always had the power of doing these; they never will have the power to do more. The world's prosperity or adversity depends on our knowing or teaching these few things: but upon iron, or glass, or electricity, or steam, in no wise.[8]

PLATE 77. The first CHA holiday group, Ambleside 1891 (T. A. Leonard is in the second row, fourth man from the right).

The early CHA parties were addressed by Canon Rawnsley, joint founder of the National Trust. He introduced ramblers to the poetry of Wordsworth and the teachings of Ruskin, and taught them to see "the wonder and beauty of the countryside". The spiritual element was further emphasised through music, in particular the singing of hymns on rambles, however, it was necessary to reconcile the practice of singing *en route* with quiet enjoyment and unobtrusiveness. Rawnsley pointed out that if not properly controlled, the "sing-song nuisance" detracted from the spirituality of the outdoors. Rules were imposed not only on what could be sung but on how it was sung, Leonard determined the tone the CHA was to adopt, often dismissing popular songs in favour of hymns, traditional ballads and recently collected folk songs.

For a week the collective nature of a CHA holiday offered an opportunity to re-create Wordsworth's vision of a pre-industrial mountain republic and live in an utopian socialist microcosm. One observer noted, "each party was a commune to itself, with every class of society represented from the mechanic to the university professor" (Plate 77). One group included teachers, shop assistants, warehousemen and weavers, another comprised a cotton mill holiday club, clerks, a carpenter, a dressmaker and two university lecturers. The groups also included a high proportion of women. Financially independent women were beginning to seek a greater freedom of movement and unaccompanied travel but frequently experienced difficulties. As a female teacher and CHA member remarked, it was all too common to discover on seaside holidays that fellow lodgers were not the right "sort". CHA holidays pioneered an equality of opportunity as well as opportunities for an intermingling of the sexes, within a context of respectability. In the relaxed atmosphere of a CHA holiday women were encouraged to wear walking boots, short woollen skirts with woollen underwear but jewellery had to be left at home.[9] Holiday practices of this nature represented a daring breach of convention for the young adults of the Victorian-Edwardian era:

I think I can best describe it [the CHA] by the name of Bohemia for all its inhabitants lived the life of the free. All the ladies pinned up their skirts, wore stout-soled boots, carried sticks, went without headgear or wore men's caps. One woman (I hardly like to call her lady) wore men's leather leggings, but then she was a suffragette. The men are fairly prim, contenting themselves by wearing soft collars and going about very often without coats or waistcoats... a more heterodox wild crew I never saw. This wild retreat is known to the world as the [CHA] Guest House, Newlands Vale, Keswick.

CHA, 1909[10]

The Influence of the CHA

Leonard was a major influence on outdoor recreation in the twentieth century and together with Paton, the CHA established the philosophical and cultural framework for countryside leisure and recreation which continues to the present day.[11] It established the practice of providing simple, affordable and non-exclusive accommodation, promoting greater access to the countryside and laid the foundations of the spirit of fellowship that characterises walking and rambling today. In terms of countryside leisure practice, its legacy lay not in footpath preservation nor in increased land access, but in its promotion of a cultural context, a phenomenon widely acknowledged as a powerful determinant of people's attitudes to the countryside as a leisure space. From the beginning the countryside was formulated as a place which was socially inclusive, free of access and a celebration of the moral and cultural symbolism of the pastoral landscape. This distinguishes countryside recreation in Britain from approaches adopted in other countries, as Snape points out, "its ideology and behavioural code reflected (an) approach to the countryside not as an untamed wilderness, as in North America, nor as a pre-romantic uncivilised remote place", nor, it must be added as the place for commercial, hedonistic pleasure. Rather it was a place of quiet and reflective leisure antithetical to and opposite to the city, material consumption and commercialism. The type of leisure promoted was thereby grounded upon a rejection of materialism, conspicuous consumption and rowdy behaviour, in favour of simplicity, affordability and sober, interpretative and quiet enjoyment of the countryside. This pastoral approach heavily influenced mid-twentieth century legislation on access and recreation which aimed to make the countryside more accessible to urban populations, so its so-called 'natural' beauty might be enjoyed by all.

The right to roam

Henry Thoreau highlighted the importance of walking in his essay *Walking* published posthumously in 1862 and today it stands alongside Emerson's *Nature* in importance to the environmental movement. From it comes one of the most memorable conservation quotes "In wilderness is the salvation of the world". Walking for Thoreau was more than recreation, it was an experience that stimulates sensitivity towards the existence of nature and the spirituality it beholds. There is not a walker who does not share Thoreau's sentiments on returning from a day in the hills:

> ... in the distant woods or fields, in unpretending sprout-lands or pastures tracked by rabbits, even in a bleak and, to most, cheerless day, like this, when a villager would be thinking of his inn, I come to myself, I once more feel myself grandly related, and that cold and solitude are friends of mine. I suppose that this value, in my case, is equivalent to what others get by churchgoing and prayer. I come home to my solitary woodland walk as the homesick go home. I thus dispose of the superfluous and see things as they are, grand and beautiful. I have told many that I walk every day about half the daylight, but I think they do not believe it. I wish to get the Concord, the Massachusetts, the America, out of my head and be sane a part of every day.[12]

The publication of Thoreau's *Walden* (1886), along with a biography of Thoreau written by Henry Salt, a leading British Fabian, stimulated considerable interest among British socialists and by the turn of the century he aroused a greater interest in England than he did in his own country. Some members of the newly formed Labour party even called their local chapters, Walden Clubs. Many shared Thoreau's desire to escape from the city into the sanity of the pastoral landscape. As unemployment rose and conditions worsened, people flocked to the countryside in their thousands to enjoy the delights of walking in the country. By 1932 it was estimated that some 15,000 working class ramblers left Manchester every sunday, many dressed in improvised rambling clothes – old army tops and old work shoes for boots. Not surprisingly, landowners and their game keepers loathed this ragged army walking over their land. The ramblers were met with a plethora of notices prohibiting entry onto the moors and open land "in many of the most beautiful parts of their native land".[13] 'The right to roam', was becoming a major issue and the flashpoint came when the Lancashire branch of the British Workers' Sports Federation (BWSF), a communist-inspired working class movement, tried to take their London comrades on an illicit exploration of Bleaklow (Plate 78). The walkers were turned back by gamekeepers with many threats and abuse, much to the astonishment of their comrades from London. Out of a sense of humiliation came a resolve to undertake a mass trespass of Kinder Scout, a wild place that was both an obsession and an icon for Sheffield and Manchester walkers. On Sunday 24 April 1932 400 or so young, working men, led unofficially by Benny Rothman, set-off towards Kinder singing the *Red Flag* and the *Internationale*. Halfway to their objective they were met by the Duke of Devonshire's gamekeepers and a brief skirmish took place between, as the *Manchester Guardian* reported, eight keepers and 40 or so ramblers. Six ramblers were arrested, including Rothman, and at the ensuing trial he spoke of the frustration and anger that had led to the trespass:

> We ramblers after a hard week's work, and life in smoky towns and cities, go out rambling on weekends for relaxation, for a breath of fresh air, and for a little

PLATE 78. The Peak District – Glossop, Doctors Gate. A popular destination for walkers from Manchester and Sheffield giving access to Bleaklow, a wild and desolate moorland plateau in the Dark Peak of Derbyshire. This old roman road was closed to walkers when owned by the Dukes of Norfolk, to protect the grouse moors.

sunshine. And we find when we go out that the finest rambling country is closed to us. Because certain individuals wish to shoot for about ten days per annum, we are forced to walk on muddy crowded paths, and denied the pleasure of enjoying to the utmost the countryside.

"Our request, or demand", said Rothman, "of access to all peaks and uncultivated moorland is nothing unreasonable ..."[14]

The arrests and subsequent imprisonment divided opinion amongst ramblers.[15] The National Council of Rambling Federations believed the mass trespass would set back negotiations for access legislation, while one branch of the CHA declared its utter disgust at what they regarded as organised hooliganism,[16] though many of the trespassers were well-read and regarded themselves as much part of a political movement rather than a recreational organization. The (BWSF) played no further part in the campaign and the struggle for access was taken on by the Ramblers' Association (1935), under the chairmanship of the Reverend T. A. Leonard. Their aim was to keep rambling and the countryside – with its emphasis on freedom, beauty and relief from everyday life – distinct from what the BWSF regarded as a political class struggle.

Legislation for access and national parks

The Ramblers' Association began to lobby for national parks, as well as for access to the hills and the protection of existing rights of way. National Parks had been first mooted in England by William Wordsworth when he described the lake district as a "sort of national property in which every man has a right and interest who has an eye to perceive and heart to enjoy".[17] In the United States National Parks were first established during the 1860s and wilderness areas, like Yellowstone and Yosemite, were regarded with a spiritual reverence by John Muir, Frederick Olmsted, Frederic Church and other Hudson River artists (Chapter 11). England and Wales lacked any comparable areas of true wilderness and the pastoral, natural beauty, so admired and cherished by the Romantic poets, had been created, maintained and managed by human activity. An alternative to the American model was required – one that would protect the land-use, preserve the landscape and allow access to the land. In 1931 the Addison Report established the principle purpose of a National Park was to:

(i) safeguard areas of exceptional natural interest against (a) disorderly development and (b) spoilation (ii) to improve means of access to areas of natural beauty; and (iii) to promote measures for the protection of flora and flora.[18]

The Report also recommended the creation of a National Park Authority to select areas for designation but no further action was taken. Five years later the Council for the Preservation for Rural England (CPRE)[19] established a Standing Committee on National Parks (SCNP) which included Members of Parliament alongside representatives with interests in the countryside and recreation[20] as a campaigning body. The first *Access to the Mountains Bill* was presented to Parliament in 1939 but this simple Bill, "was mauled, mangled and amended ... so as to become a monstrous, unrecognizable changeling, not an access to the mountains bill, but a landowners protection bill".[21] With the Bill's dismissal there was little hope of legislation before the looming Second World War and on the eve of war the Ramblers' Association issued a manifesto setting out the importance of access to the countryside in a time of war:

> It will be in the national interest that those citizens who can do so should get into the countryside at regular intervals. There is nothing so beneficial to health, nerves, and general well-being as a good walk in the country, especially to people who live in towns and cities and whose work imposes a great strain on them. The Ramblers' Association there fore hopes that every effort will be made by government and local authorities and by owners and occupiers of land to maintain rights of way and to provide reasonable freedom to roam over uncultivated land.[22]

The Second World War proved to be a time of serious introspection in Britain examining the kind of society needed after the war. There was a renewed political determination to succeed where Lloyd George had failed in achieving social reform for the working classes. Among the reforms identified were the right of access to the mountains and the establishment of National Parks. The war-time Government appointed architect and rambler John Dower to consider National Parks and how they should be selected, administered and planned. The subsequent Dower report (1945) defined National Parks as:

> an extensive area of beautiful and relatively wild country in which, for the nation's benefit and by appropriate national decision and action:
> a. the characteristic landscape beauty is strictly preserved
> b. access and facilities for public open-air enjoyment are amply provided
> c. wildlife and buildings and places of architectural and historical interest are suitably protected, while
> d. established farming use is effectively maintained.[23]

Dower did not see any conflict between rambling and agriculture and believed that if the insistent claims of the ramblers' organisations were to be met "there must be a right to wander at will over the whole extent of uncultivated land, such as mountains, moors, hill grazing and heath".[24] As for grouse shooting, Dower said in a ringing declaration "when the issue is seen as a broad question of principle – whether the recreation needs of the many should or should not outweigh the sporting pleasures of a few – there can be little doubt of the answer; that walkers should, and sooner or later will, be given the freedom of access over grouse moors".[25]

When Lewis Silkin, Minister of Town and Country Planning in the new Labour Government, presented the National Parks and Access to the Countryside Bill to Parliament in 1945, he described it as a "peoples' charter for the open air":

> Now at last we shall be able to see that the mountains of Snowdonia, the Lakes and waters of the Broads, the moors and dales of the Peak, the South Downs and tors of the West Country belong to the people as a right and not as a concession. This is not just a Bill. It is a peoples' charter – a peoples' charter for the open air, for the hikers and the ramblers, for everyone who loves to get out into the open air and enjoy the countryside. Without it they are fettered, deprived of their powers of access and facilities needed to make holidays enjoyable. With it the countryside is theirs to preserve, to cherish, to enjoy and to make their own.[26]

There was little or no opposition to the Bill and the first National Park was established, appropriately, in the Peak District on 17 April 1951, followed by the Lake District, Wordsworth's 'national property'. Eight more followed in the 1950s and three others were created in England thirty or so years later, the South Downs finally completing the task in 2010 (Figure 18). The *National Parks and Access to the Countryside Act 1949* marked a radicle new beginning for access to open country but Silkin avoided the much vaunted issue of a "freedom to roam over all extensive open or cultivated tracts of land" fearing that such a measure would trigger too much resistance from land owners. Instead he opted for a more limited measure, allowing local authorities to negotiate Access Agreements with landowners.[27] It would be the year 2000 before the Countryside and Rights of Way Act finally allowed the public to walk freely in areas of downland, moorland and heathland.

The Act establishing National Parks, and the Areas of Outstanding Natural Beauty that followed a year later, effectively identified and protected most of the most attractive, picturesque and cherished hard and soft pastoral landscapes in England and Wales (Plate 79). But unlike National Parks in many other countries, the parks do not belong to the people and are national only in the sense they are of special value because of their beauty and the recreational value they offer to all. As might have been anticipated though not fully expected, the National Parks have become the nation's playground, 'Britains breathing spaces', with an estimated 110 million people visitors a year.[28] On a fine weekend the Peak District is far busier than many urban parks and visitors join with hundreds of others walking, running, cycling, hang-gliding, driving, picnicing or simply enjoying the landscape. The numbers have led to inevitable problems of over-use, conflicts of interest and environmental issues. The Environment Act (1995) instructed the National Park Authorities to manage these conflicting interests; protecting and enhancing the natural beauty, wildlife and cultural interests whilst promoting public enjoyment; and understanding and fostering the social and economic well-being of the local communities.

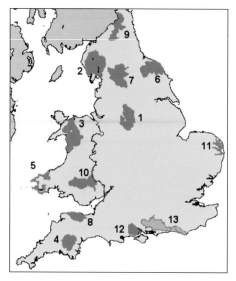

	National Park	Year	km²	m²
1	Peak District	1951	1438	555
2	Lake District	1951	2292	885
3	Snowdonia	1951	2142	827
4	Dartmoor	1951	956	369
5	Pembrokeshire Coast	1952	620	240
6	North York Moors	1952	1436	554
7	Yorkshire Dales	1954	1769	683
8	Exmoor	1954	693	268
9	Northumberland	1956	1483	555
10	Brecon Beacons	1957	1351	522
11	The Broads	1988	303	117
12	New Forest	2005	580	220
13	South Downs	2010	1641	634
	Total		16,270	6680

FIGURE 18. National Parks in England and Wales.

Arcadia for all

The desire for escape to Arcadia was shared by people in the towns and cities whose low incomes, and an absence of private transport, meant they were unable travel to the countryside. Their feelings were so strong that many literally took matters into their own hands and a makeshift world of railway carriages, old bus bodies, former world war one army huts, even in one instance, a disbanded aircraft fuselage emerged in the countryside. These could found around towns and cities throughout the country in the 1920s and '30s but mostly in the environs of London and the south-east of England, where the population was greatest. These were followed by more permanent wooden shanties and shacks built on land bought cheaply, or acquired at no cost, by squatting. Many were built close to home, offering an easy escape from the city, but they were considered "so much the better if they could be combined with a special landscape feature such as lake, some hills, a river or woodland".[29] At first they were used as summer and weekend retreats but later they became more permanent residences, as people established smallholdings and tried to become self-sufficient.[30] Plotholders spoke of wanting a place of their own and a desire to move out of smoky cities to these settlements, often by the sea, with more healthy air and fresh food from nearby farms:

> Owning a place of one's own acquired the appeal of a panacea, to cure all known afflictions. For the plot-owner, it was the promise of freedom, of independence and an opportunity to assert one's individuality. There was status to be won, security and a chance of financial returns. In contact with the land, souls would be purified, bodies rejuvenated and family life cemented.[31]

Following Lloyd George's 'peoples' budget' of 1909, which introduced a land tax, a quarter of England changed hands in the 5 years from 1918 to 1922. Farmers experiencing financial difficulties due to declining agricultural prices, were willing to sell marginal land cheaply to speculators for housing development. Any remaining land – liable to flooding or with steep slopes, shingle banks and wind-swept sand dunes, heavy clays or dry chalky uplands – was sold off as tiny building plots resulting in the shanty explosion. These so-called 'plotlands'[32] "offered a place in the sun for the enterprising, if not the rich".[33] The plotlands lacked any overall planning or services, such as mains water supply, sewage systems, electricity, and roads were little more than lines on a map; tracks rutted in summer, muddy and waterlogged in winter. Undeveloped plots, left unsold or forgotten by their owners reverted to a semi-wild state forming a diverse ecological mix, which Hardy and Ward termed "a makeshift landscape".

Shacks were often single story houses constructed of wood or what other materials were to hand – "a product of design rather than of conscious Arcadian design".[34] The challenges posed by the marginal sites, the pressing need for economy and the involvement of unskilled builders produced a brand of architecture that was unique:

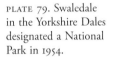

PLATE 79. Swaledale in the Yorkshire Dales designated a National Park in 1954.

> Starting with basic materials and plenty of ingenuity, a plotland house (could) grow into an amalgam of just about any architectural style imaginable. Pebble dash meets pirate ship, via gnomes, palm tree, and corinthian columns. Outsider architecture, their random chaos is the very antithesis of the controlled and manicured English landscape.[35]

The expansion of plotlands

Housing speculators, in general, had no interest in plotland, but one or two had a more philanthropic streak. Foremost among them was Charles Neville who took an active, if paternal interest, in the development of Peacehaven, near Lewes in East Sussex which became *cause célèbre* in the nineteen thirties. Neville began to purchase land in 1915 from the Cavendish Land Company and eventually he acquired a 5 mile (8 km) strip along the cliff top, extending a mile (1.6 km) inland. Neville divided the area into a myriad of small plots and offered them for sale in national newspapers. *Peacehaven*, as he called the development, was promoted as an 'Arcadia by the sea' and his greatest success was in selling the dream. What plot holders were buying was not just a few square feet of real estate but a stake in what was described as the 'Land of Romance', a *locus amoenus,* where the soft sea breezes and sunshine were evidence of its health-inducing qualities. It was the place where the "twelve component parts of a serene and desirable state of life" – health, happiness, contentment, recreation, satisfaction, freedom, hope, rejuvenation, home-life, prosperity, peace, and a haven – could all be enjoyed (Plate 80).[36] What was on offer was nothing less than the opportunity of *villeggiatura* for the working classes. An article in the *Daily Chronicle* (1923) described the rapid progress and extolled the successful development of the town:

> Yes, Peacehaven, the garden city by the sea, is one of the most remarkable places in England ... As a piece of town planning I have no hesitation in saying it is the finest thing we have in England, and if I were not afraid of using extravagant language I would say the world ... I found Peacehaveners a happy, jolly community, very proud of their infant prodigy of a garden city.[37]

Unfortunately Peacehaven was not the ordered development Neville intended; he could not control the sale of the plots and far from filling in the massive grid in a systematic way, the process became distinctly haphazard (Plate 81). Many plot holders never took possession of their land and others had no intention of developing their holdings.

The response

While the tumbledown shacks, converted coaches and self-build bungalows may have created Arcadia for some, for others it threatened to destroy it. The very disorder and personal freedom sought by the newcomers was an anathema to the self appointed guardians of a more traditional landscape. Critics of Peacehaven saw:

> mile upon mile of unmade roads, building plots more often derelict than not, half-finished bungalows and temporary caravans and sheds, a two mile frontage of shops – many of which were closed – and a prestigious seafront that was really no more than an untended belt of crumbling cliff-top.

Thomas Sharp, a highly influential inter-war planner and landscape architect, regarded Peacehaven as the failure of the whole Garden City concept:

> The *reuductio ad absurbum* of the garden-city is extension to absurdity, and of this, unfortunately, innumerable examples exist. The worst in England is Peacehaven, which has rightly become a national laughing stock ... It is indeed a disgusting blot on the landscape.[38]

PLATE 80 *(right).* Peacehaven – Cripps Avenue. Mrs Cripps Silver Wedding – as contented Peacehaveners they were anxious to uphold solid middle class standards.

PLATE 81 *(below).* Peacehaven – Seaview Avenue. Plot holders could purchase building materials from the neigbouring military camp after the First World War.

The author and broadcaster S. P. B. Mais, an ardent campaigner for the British countryside and traditions, saw Peacehaven as the personification of all the unplanned developments along the south coast of England . "The poison", he said:

> begins at Peacehaven, which until thirteen or fourteen years ago was a piece of unspoilt downland open to the sea. It is now a colony of shacks, a long ungainly street of houses that all seemed ashamed of themselves.[39]

These words came from *The Plain Man Looks at England*, a chapter in *Britain and the Beast* (1938)[40] edited by the largely self-taught architect Clough Williams-Ellis, one of the most outspoken critics of plotlands and of unplanned development in general.[41] His earlier book *England and the Octopus* (1928) had been part of the counter attack that grew in pressure during the 1930s. It underlined the sense of betrayal felt by a generation who believed they had fought World War One to save the physical countryside of England, 'the Land', only to see a surrender to short-term political gains. This included the selling-off of land to plot holders, unchecked by protective legislation. Each new encampment, with a promise of a measure of freedom for its proud owners, was a spur to action by an emerging preservationist lobby. But their concerns were not just about landscape deterioration; they believed it was part of a wider social decline. The old hierarchy of the countryside was changing and what the preservationists saw in the plotlands was the relentless spread of an urban way of life, and with it, the rise of the working classes. For some like C. E. M. Joad the whole idea of people from the towns enjoying the countryside at all was distasteful:

> ... the hordes of hikers cackling insanely in the woods, or singing raucous songs as they walk arm in arm at midnight down the quiet village street. There are people wherever there is water, upon sea-shores or upon river banks, lying in every attitude of undressed and inelegant squalor, grilling themselves, for all the world as if they were steaks, in the sun. There are tents in meadows and girls in pyjamas dancing beside them to the strains of the gramophone, while stinking disorderly dumps of tins, bags, and cartons bear witness to the tide of invasion for weeks after it has ebbed; there are fat girls in shorts, youths in gaudy ties and plus-fours, and a roadhouse round every corner and a cafe on top of every hill for their accommodation.[42]

Williams-Ellis was the unofficial leader of a campaign seeking to preserve an elitest vision of Arcadia. A survivor of pre-war Georgian England, Williams-Ellis had absorbed his aesthetic sensibility from his artist mother Annabel, née Strachey, a member of the Bloomsbury Group, friend of Ralph Waldo Emerson and admirer of Ruskin;

> It was my mother, too, as a second stage of my keying down of the picturesque, who revealed to me the almost 'natural' beauty of the old Welsh cottages that she was so fond of sketching. To begin with, I could not allow that they had any merit or interest at all. How could a mere hovel of only two rooms with no upstairs, no stone-mullioned windows, no arched doorways even, be called beautiful or even interesting?[43]

He learnt from his mother the importance of a sense of order within the countryside: "I shared my mother's dynastic views and regarded everything ancestral with a reverence almost superstitious, if not indeed religious". This view, widely shared by his mother's generation of painters, like Helen Allingham and Birkett Foster, harked back to the eighteenth century concept of *concordia discors*. Country people were regarded as quaint, a lower form of life, and were assumed to have a dignity within their natural state, akin to other fauna. This pseudo-respect was not extended to the lower type of humanity who lived in towns and were regarded as a dangerous rabble or at worse, a mob. Williams-Ellis believed there were two types of working class people. Those who took on the values of the dominant culture and became cultivated and those who did not and stayed vulgar, 'mean and perky' and insensitive to beauty. These people were, he said, probably at the root of the trouble:

> ... it is chiefly the spate of mean building all over the country that is shrivelling up the old England – mean and perky little houses that surely none but mean and perky little souls could inhabit with satisfaction ... .Cultivated people of all classes must deplore what is happening.[44]

Williams-Ellis and his contemporaries believed ordinary men and women were incapable of making the right decisions about matters of taste and beauty and that the time had come for a new professional elite, one who had absorbed the lessons of Ruskin and Morris, and could bring order out of the chaos.

The battle for the countryside

PLATE 82. Derek Jarman's cottage at Dungeness – one of the most famous remaining shantys. The shingle bank at Dungeness did not attract interest from those developing seaside towns and in the 1920s it was abandoned to fishermen and squatters.

In the 1930s the plotlands became part of a much wider debate concerning the individual's rights of property and his/her freedom of action, set against a growing clamour for the State to act in the wider public interest. As a battle it was inevitably one-sided; the plotlanders, blissfully unaware of the war of words ranging around them, were intent on quietly enjoying their place in the sun – by the sea, in woods or fields. While the preservationists, what Williams-Ellis referred to as the 'Amenity Brigade' – a loose association of architects, journalists, civic leaders, industrialists and other activists – were using all the means of the media to articulate their views and offer alternative visions of the future. Resistance to change in the countryside came from an influential network of voluntary bodies; like the National Trust, who concentrated on acquiring and holding property of beauty or historic interest for the benefit of the public, and the Council for the Preservation of Rural England (CPRE) who sought to protect the rural heritage, in places under threat, and arouse public opinion on the question of beauty in the countryside. The CPRE was not simply trying to prevent the despoilation of the landscape by unplanned development but was lobbying for the preservation/defence of the countryside; its landscape, its class structure and its general way of life against the ravages of the expanding town and its inhabitants.[45] These national organisations, along with specific local groups, all shared the belief that "if Arcadia was to survive then it could not be for all".

The preservationists realised that voluntary action alone was not enough and that greater government control over the use of land was needed – ranging in scope from an extension of local bye-laws to a complete nationalisation of land. In the House of Commons Lady Cynthia Mosley said in 1930: "the time has come when we must definantly choose between the end of *laissez faire* or the end of rural England". The central issue occupying the minds of politicians and preservationists alike was the question of what rights the State should have over land and property. The Town and Country Planning Act (1932), signified a move from a traditional urban and suburban bias towards a recognition of the need for countryside planning, but in practice the Act changed very little. The best means of protection remained the public acquisition of land. In 1929 Eastbourne Urban District Council purchased the celebrated beauty spot, Beachy Head to save it from development and in 1935 the London County Council went a stage further with a Green Belt scheme aimed at retaining an accessible reserve of open countryside for Londoners. But in spite of these efforts and local authority attempts at using local bye laws and enforcement officers, as well as new *Public Health Acts*, the problem of the plotlands and indiscriminate building in the countryside, remained unresolved by the end of the 1930s. The outbreak of World War Two brought a temporary lull, halting all further developments, whilst the military coastal defence strategy removed many seaside retreats along miles of coastline.

The introspection of the wartime years already mentioned, acknowledged that a substantial increase in State involvement over a wide range of activities, including land-use planning was needed. Post-war there was a political climate in which radical steps towards controlling the use and ownership of land could be taken, alongside a renewed sense of optimism that believed a more beautiful Britain could be achieved through planned development. The 1947 *Town and Country Planning Act* effectively controlled and prevented new plotland developments but proved less effective in removing those already in existence. With few exceptions a direct confrontation, involving the removal of a plotland settlements and restoring the land to its natural state, did not prove possible. In most instances the costs of compensation and land restoration were too high and some plotlands remained, even into the twenty-first century. However, the Act (1947) reinforced local byelaws and the use of these powers ensured much higher building standards than before, and the incremental process of enlargement and improvement has seen many existing properties change out all recognition (Plate 82).

The effects of the legislation

These two movements, one led by ramblers for access to the countryside and the other, an Arcadian quest for a place in the countryside, resulted in legislation that has had far reaching consequences for people and the pastoral landscape. Overall the legislation helped fix the notion of the 'goodness' of pastoral landscape firmly in the nation's psyche, whilst the Town and Country Planning Acts reinforced the separation between town and country. The 1947 Town and Country Planning Act effectively controlled urbanisation of the countryside and nationalised the development of land, preventing individuals from undertaking any form of development without planning consent, whether in town or country. In so doing, as Hardy and Ward pointed out, it prevented any further creative expression by the working classes.

Notes and References

1. Hardy, D. and Ward, C., *Arcadia for All*. Mansell, London, 1984, p. vii.
2. Snape, R., 'The Co-operative Holidays Association and the cultural formation of countryside leisure practice'. *Social Sciences: Journal Articles*. Paper 2, 2004. University of Bolton Institutional Repository, p. 3.
3. Wakes weeks originated as a celebration of a religious anniversary, but had morphed into a week's unpaid holiday.
4. Snape. R., *op. cit.*, p. 4.
5. *Ibid.*, p. 11
6. *Ibid.*, pp. 7– 8. The influence of Morris is observable in the adoption of the term 'guest house' from *News from Nowhere*, of Wordsworth in the Association's motto *Joy in widest commonalty spread* and the title of its journal, *Comradeship*.
7. *Ibid.*, p. 16.
8. *Ibid.*, pp. 10–11; Ruskin, *The Moral of Landscape* 1856, p. 310.
9. *Ibid.*, p. 11. Enthusiasm for the increased freedom did not extend to a greater sexual liberty, and the implicit moral dangers of mixed groups of single people were assiduously addressed. Sleeping outdoors by unmarried members was forbidden outright and flirting was roundly condemned.
10. *Ibid.*, p. 30.
11. In 1913 Leonard, believing the CHA had become to 'middle class', set-up the Holiday Fellowship which had a simpler ethos and a greater emphasis on internationalism. The HF continues to the present day.
12. Thoreau's *Journal*, January 7, 1857.
13. Stephenson, T., *Forbidden Land*. Manchester University Press, Manchester, 1989, p. 154.
14. *Ibid.*
15. Five men, including Rothman, were jailed for between two years and six months.
16. The trespassers were far from hooligans and saw access to the mountains as much part of a wider class struggle. Many of the trespassers were familiar with the working class literature of the day; including Tressell's *The Ragged Trousered Philanthropists* which provided a a comprehensive picture of social, political, economic and cultural life in Britain as a time when socialism was coming to the fore; others could quote the American socialist, Upton Sinclair.
17. Wordsworth, W., *Guide Through the District of the Lakes in the North of England*, 5th edition. Hudson and Nicholson, London, 1835, p. 88.

18. Stephenson, T., *op. cit.*, p. 165.

19. Now the Campaign to Protect Rural England.

20. The Standing Committee on National Parks included other groups representing leisure and nature conservation, among them the Ramblers' Association, the Youth Hostels' Association (YHA), and the Council for the Protection of Rural Wales (CPRW).

21. Stephenson, T., *op. cit.*, p. 198.

22. *Ibid.*, p. 86.

23. Dower report.

24. Stephenson, T., *op. cit.*, p. 198.

25. *Ibid.*, p. 199.

26. *Ibid.*, p. 208.

27. Shoard, M., *This Land is Our Land.* Gaia Books, London, 1997, p. 308.

28. www.countrysideinfo.co.uk/habitats.

29. Hardy, D. and Ward, C., *op. cit.*, p. 2.

30. William Morris, Prince Kropotkin and Leo Tolstoy, had created powerful images of future societies organised free from central government, based on voluntary co-operation between workers, and were said to be an influence on the plotholders. George Landsbury, Leader of the Labour Party in the 1930s, declared "I just long to see a start made on this job of reclaiming, recreating, rural England".

31. Hardy, D. and Ward, C., *op. cit.*, p. 2.

32. Plotlands was the term used by the local authorities.

33. Hardy, D. and Ward, C., *op. cit.*, p. 2.

34. Hardy, D. and Ward, C., *op. cit.*, p. 2.

35. *The Dabbler*, 2 June, 2011.

36. Hardy, D. and Ward, C., *op. cit.*, p. 80.

37. Quoted in Hardy, D. and Ward, C., *op. cit.*, p. 84.

38. Quoted in Gardiner, J., *The Thirties.* Harper Press, London, 2011, pp. 235–6. In the years between 1921 and 1926, the population of Peacehaven rose rapidly from 24 to 3000 inhabitants.

39. *Ibid.*, p. 235.

40. Williams-Ellis, C. (ed.), *Britain and the Beast.* Dent. London, 1937.

41. Though this did not prevent him from having his own, tasteful, country weekend bolt hole, shielded from public view, rented on the Bray estate, near Guildford in Surrey, where neighbours included a number of Labour Cabinet ministers.

42. Hardy, D. and Ward, C., *op. cit.,* p. 40.

43. Williams-Ellis, C., *Architect Errant: The autobiography of Clough Williams-Ellis.* Constable, London, 1971.

44. *Ibid.*

45. Quoted in CPRE 2026 *A Vision for the Countryside 2009.* The CPRE was formed in 1926 by Patrick Abercrombie to limit urban sprawl and ribbon development. It changed its name to the Council for the Protection of Rural England in the 1960s. According to Howard Newby, the CPRE was "a strange amalgam of patrician landowners, for whom the preservation of the countryside was closely linked to their conception of 'stewardship', and socially-concerned Fabians (Hampstead dwellers, but keen hikers on the Downs) who believed in the pursuit of social justice through national planning".

CHAPTER SEVENTEEN

Arcadia Revisited: the ecological landscape

PLATE 83. London County Council housing c.1960

Thoreau warned of the dangers of wild nature being eroded by civilisation: "if we do not look out we shall find our fine school house standing in a cow yard at last". He proposed that every town should have a park, or rather a "primitive forest ... where a stick should never be cut ... but stand and decay for higher uses – a common possession forever, for instruction and recreation". Post-war redevelopment and expansion of towns and cities had excluded nature and the landscape was often no more than a field of close mown grass, decorated with the occasional tree (Plate 83). These conditions prompted an increasing number of architects, landscape architects, teachers, sociologists, as well as members of the public, throughout Europe and Scandinavia in the 1970s to express their concerns about the urban landscape. They shared the belief of Roland Ranier, the Austrian architect, that:

the public green zone has only become necessary in the unhealthy conditions of the densely mechanised cities of the industrial age. They are a substitute for private open-space and the natural landscape that has been encroached upon by the city. They are intended to compensate the mass of urban dwellers for unnatural, unliveable environments ... the great mass of urban dwellers do not need a few paths and benches in a green plot but a highly varied recreation area where they can move about freely made into a natural environment.[1]

In the Netherlands landscape architects, parks managers and eco-artists were already developing alternative ways of designing and managing the urban landscape, bringing nature back to the city, and these developments were to have a far reaching influence. Appropriately the changes were first observed in the Amsterdam suburb of Bijlmermeer, the most Corbusian of all developments.

Amsterdam: the Bijlmermeer

The Bijlmermeer, to the south-east of Amsterdam, was inspired by Corbusier's concept of the *Villa Radieuse* (the Radiant City). In this futuristic vision of the city nature was to be enjoyed, or had been reduced to sky, grass and trees.[2] This vision had reached its apotheosis at CIAM (Congrès internationaux d'architecture moderne) in 1930. Corbusier described a new city of high rise buildings, 15–20 storeys high, in which living, work, recreation and transport were segregated and eighty percent of the land was released for recreation.[3] These ideas were very popular among young Dutch architects and their influence was still to the fore when the design of Bijlmermeer began in 1962. The suburb was to be a new, utopian concept in urban living, the very antithesis of the garden city (Figure 19). The white monolithic blocks, ten-storeys high,[4] would house 100,000 residents making it the largest project of its kind undertaken anywhere in the world. Among the critics of the proposals was Jakoba Mulder (*Mejuvrouw van het Bos:* Chapter 15), a senior architect in Amsterdam's Office of

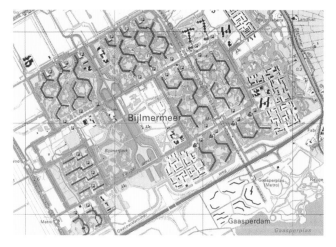

FIGURE 19 *(left)*. Amsterdam, The Bijlmermeer – the blocks marked in red have since been demolished.

PLATE 84 *(below left)*. The Bijlmermeer, Amsterdam *c.*1976. The ten-storey housing blocks surround the green space bisected by the metro and, at a lower level, the pedestrian and cycleways. The apartments were not on pilotis as Corbusier envisioned due to the weak load-bearing capacity of the soil.

PLATE 85 *(below right)*. Corbusier: The Villa Radieuse.

FIGURE 20 *(below)*.
Amsterdam, The
Bijlmermeer: internal
courtyard zoning.
Consideration of
climate, function and
activities resulted in a
clear framework for the
residential courts.

Public Works, who spoke out for a more humanist approach, but to no avail.[5] Its architects and planners believed the Biljmermeer, with its high-rise living, freedom from traffic, communal gardens for leisure and recreation, nightingales in the trees and children playing on the green, would offer a futuristic lifestyle for Dutch middle class families, far more comfortable than Amsterdam's city centre (Plate 84). However, Amsterdam's landscape architects recognised that the Corbusian ideal of the pastoral landscape, with its sinuous paths winding their way through endless swathes of mown lawn, punctuated only by a few wispy trees, would be totally inadequate. (Plate 85) The inhuman scale of the architecture and the incessant North Sea wind would cause social problems and physical discomfort and, as the official *Landscape Report* stated; "it would be unthinkable to force residents to live for many years with the earliest stages of

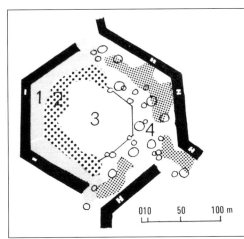

1. Access zone. The gallery side of the court subject to the full force of downward winds which make conditions unpleasant and prolonged stays improbable This area was zoned for pedestrian and cyclists.

2. Transition zone. A short distance from the flats the wind begins to eddy and planting is used to breakup the turbulence and filter-out dust.

3. Play meadow. This lies half in sun and half in shade and was designated for football, netball *etc*.

4. Sun zone. On the sunny side of the court play spaces and sitting areas were arranged in interconnected spaces.

PLATE 86 *(below)*.
Amsterdam, Bijlmermeer:
the inner court – zone 3
the play meadow. *c.*1975

PLATE 87 *(right)*.
Amsterdam, Bijlmermeer:
a more natural waters
edge *c.*1978

cultivation because of the use of conventional methods".[6] Influenced no doubt by Mulder, they saw the answer was in adopting and adapting the techniques pioneered at the Amsterdam Woods, which had largely been overlooked in the intervening years. The biophysical conditions in and around the inner courts, that ranged in size from 5 to 12 acres (2–5 ha) were identified and the appropriate function and planting was allocated to each zone (Figure 20) (Plate 86). The *Official Guide to Green Space* also spoke of returning nature to Bijlmermeer:

> In laying out the open spaces in Bijlmermeer, attention was mainly focussed on the inhabitants. That is why the bundled green space is again divided into smaller sheltered compartments for the residents to feel protected, and give prominence to all facets of recreation. Tall screens of greenery were placed along the facades so that their height is broken and their overpowering effect is mitigated for people outside. Particular emphasis was laid on trees. Instead of pretty gardens there will be natural-looking wooded areas and shrubbery. The landscape architects have gone out of their way to try and imitate nature as much as possible. That's why plants such as cornflowers and bramble, poppy, clover, dandelion and dogs tooth mercury are allowed to grow wild. This calls for a new kind of upkeep.
>
> The green in Bijlmermeer has a specific function. Rows of trees planted in certain ways and placed near the facades in the right position have to break the winds and prevent them from beating down on the flats. Trees and shrubs temper the elements and offer protection. The aged residents as well as children have their sunny, wind sheltered spots. Everything in this district is an experiment in living.[7]

However, the use of native species did not give the landscape a natural appearance, for as in the Amsterdam Woods, there was a strict demarcation between wood and meadow. The designers began to appreciate that in natural areas, such as coastal dunes, woodlands and urban wastelands, these artificial barriers did not exist; tree, shrub and herb communities would merge and people could interact freely with their natural surroundings. In the late 1960s a more natural landscape emerged at Bijlmermeer with the inner courts resembling woodland glades and at the water's edge, aquatic plants merged into the longer grass (Plate 87).[8] Lying by the waterside on a warm, sunny summer afternoon, as dragonflies skimmed the water, it was possible for a brief moment to experience the sense of idyllic pleasure described by Theocritus, even to forget the overwhelming presence of the architecture.[9]

Louis Le Roy

In this milieu of change one man stood out as the catalyst, Louis Le Roy, art teacher and 'wild gardener' from the northern town of Heereveen. Born in 1924, Le Roy's childhood was influenced by his elder brother whose natural history workshop was full of pinned butterflies, beetles, pressed flowers and botanical drawings. Le Roy described it as the "office of a humanist scholar desperately searching for the origin of life".[10] After the family moved to the The Hague in the 1930s Le Roy may have been influenced by Jac. P. Thijsse, teacher and pioneer environmentalist. Thijsse's concern was that the old rural, polder landscape was undergoing an irrevocable change before people were aware of its beauty and significance and he campaigned tirelessly to make people aware of the great variety and beauty of the native flora and fauna. He wrote books that ranged from scientific studies, such as the *Birds of the Netherlands,* to more popular books describing the native flora seen in and around the town, and even contributed to school reading books. Thijsse also transformed an old potato field into an Instructive Garden (Plate 88), as a place where teachers and school children could learn about the countryside's fast vanishing habitats. It is possible Le Roy was among the many children who visited *Thijsse's Hof,* he certainly absorbed Thijsse's philosophy that "Those who live for what grows, flowers, crawls, breathes should be better and richer. They get interested in music, painting, sculpture, religion. Grow themselves. Be better". Thijsse was highly critical of public parks which he believed had turned their backs on nature and he wanted to see a new kind of park:

> I dream of a garden where the public, young and old, ignorant and informed can witness and experience the whole season of our native plants, from the first of January to the thirty first of December. A garden where the town dweller can surrender himself to the flora and fauna.[11]

Le Roy's own ideas about art and environment began to develop in 1949 when he became an art teacher in Heerenveen. "I was looking", he said "for a relationship, first with the city and then the nature in the vicinity; My point is, that man is rooted in culture and in nature. These two work together and it is unfortunate that we no longer experience this. Biologists and artists are usually strangers to each other. I now consciously aim to stand on both 'legs'. I am a realist. The reality is my power".[12] Le Roy began to experiment with the construction of his garden which in fact was no garden, but a garden-like habitat in which ecological motifs played the main role. Le Roy saw the dynamics of plant communities as a key element in a much more complex event, namely the coherent dynamics of organisms (including ourselves) on which these communities depend. In other words, a dynamic ecosystem in which man is an integral part. Le Roy said of this time:

> As a painter the realisation grew in me that I actually created nothing, gave no result. Until then I had just personally interpreted images of reality. [...] As I was building my building (the farmhouse) I became increasingly aware of that gift becoming more developed, and an urge grew in me to me to actually build the landscape – nature – ... . This would at once enable my spatial awareness to develop stronger in another way. And the result would again be that my interpretive possibilities for painting reality, could be expanded. In this way, a never-ending interaction can be launched between making and interpreting an increasingly innovative and complex reality![13]

The natural city

Le Roy developed his own, highly original theories over the next 20 years and as the environmental debate raged in the Netherlands, he presented his ideas of town planning, design and gardening in *Natuur uitschakelen; natuur inschakelen*[14]

(Switch on nature, switch off nature) (1973). Le Roy criticised man's alienation from nature, and how the interweaving of culture and nature had disappeared in the post-war period. Rising prosperity, he said, had resulted in "explosive urban developments with districts of monotonous housing" in which the city dweller had lost touch with his environment. Development and construction had become an institutionalised process, conceived and run by dedicated and technically, highly qualified staff, the architects and planners, who had lost touch with the people for whom they planned and the land they managed. Le Roy, like Morris earlier, believed people were "desperately seeking to find a compromise between the technology necessary for survival in the present day and those former values that had been lost, or were in the process of being lost, by too much technology".[15]

PLATE 88. Thijsse's Hof Bloemendaal *c.*1985 A natural landscape. Thijsse used native plants to re-create the habitats of the Dutch countryside on 5 acres (2 ha) of a former potato field.

Le Roy's plan for the Natural City was an alternative to the garden suburb which had done much to alienate people from nature (Figure 21). Like Howard's original plan it sought to achieve a continuum between town and country. The landscape, he argued, was divided between two vast monocultures; the rural environment with such activities as agriculture "a production area for food we cannot do without", forestry and water catchment; and the urban environment with housing and industry. Sandwiched between them was a growing extent of land in public ownership, some in parks both urban and country, but much, like motorway verges, inaccessible. Le Roy's plan respected the existing patterns of monocultures but returned the land in between to individual use; some divided into parcels for allotments, screened from alien monoculture by dense woodlands, and in other places given over to peoples' gardens. Nature reserves (*natuur gebied*) outside the city were to act as reservoirs for wildlife and be linked to the city by new, artificial ecosystems. Peoples' involvement in making the ecosystems, rather than their being designed and maintained by municipal services, was an essential part of this plan. Le Roy believed residents who had created natural gardens in public parks and green spaces would share in the ecological process and renew their contact with the environment.

In 1966 Le Roy was invited to try out his ecosystem theories on a central road verge in a nondescript, garden suburb of Heerenveen (Figure 22). Beginning without a detailed plan, as Le Roy believed its absence "would free people from its inhibiting influence and dubious aesthetic values", use was made of discarded building materials and over 1000 species and varieties of trees, shrubs, herbs, ferns bulbs, fungi and mosses were randomly planted. Le Roy's observation of spontaneous, wasteland communities had led him to the conclusion that nature

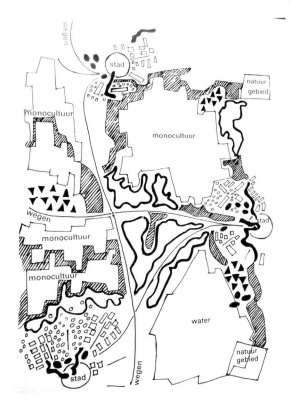

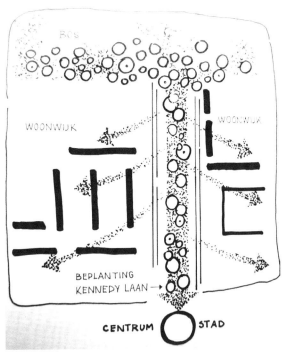

FIGURE 21. Le Roy's visionary plan for the Natural City.

FIGURE 22. Le Roy: The Kennedylaan. Initially this was a boring grass strip, 18 m wide and just over a kilometre in length, running from an area of woodland into the centre of the town.

PLATE 89. Kennedylaan, Heerenveen *c.*1975 informal plant identification.

PLATE 90. Kennedylaan, Heerenveen *c.*1985

would always creates variety, and therefore a beautiful scene. All that was required was a rich provision of plant material and within 7 years a rich and diverse habitat would emerge (Plate 89). By 1975 as Le Roy predicted, the Kennedylaan had a quality rarely found in more conventional municipal parks (Plate 90):

> As one enters, all the stress of the surrounding town falls away and is replaced by the sound of birds, the flight of dragonflies, the sight of snails on the hogweed stems. In the shelter of the trees the sun's warmth is pleasant and free from glare while the trees make pleasing patterns on the path. The senses come alive. At weekends the Kennedylaan is full of people though not in an overcrowded way, for many of them are pursuing activities not associated with the urban landscape – children gathering seed heads for winter display, or a family group botanizing with a Keble Martin. As Le Roy had said, harmony in nature brings a closeness too nature and between people, so that people stop to talk in a way that would never happen on the pavements to either side.[16]

Although Le Roy's ideas met with opposition amongst those landscape designers and parks officials who believed he sought to replace design with anarchy, there was widespread acceptance among residents of the Randstad suburbs[17] and many Le Roy gardens were made by parents, teachers, and local authorities. Today Le Roy is recognised as one of the most significant innovators in ecological art, design and a pioneer in public participation, "encouraging the questioning of the conventional planning process, and providing a model in which citizens are an integral part of the process rather than an adjunct or hindrance to it".[18]

Delft: the Gilles estate

One of the first city parks departments to challenge the conventional design of urban landscapes was Delft where the Director, Henk Bos, in an unpublished report asked the question: "How did we design our new cities in the post-war period?" To which he answered: "by standards based on tidiness and order; the parks and open spaces could be looked at but scarcely used. In different cities the new urban landscape is very much alike, everything is complete but monotonous".[19] This posed a particular problem for children whose only freedom "was that which adults allow" but "children ignore architects good intentions and are delighted to play in other areas – water ditches or buildings under construction" (Plate 91). He added:

> People want more adventure near their homes; they prefer narrow and winding paths to the straight ones and wild flowers to cut lawns. They like hilly grounds with little swamps rather than flat gardens. Some people say leave the site as it is when the contractors have gone away and let nature have its own way. Although for many designers this slogan goes too far, the whole idea is a reaction to the concrete world we live in.[20]

He asked whether designers were willing to see and translate the needs of the population instead of pressing their own ideas. It was very important that both designer and executor consult the public, teachers and children ... the

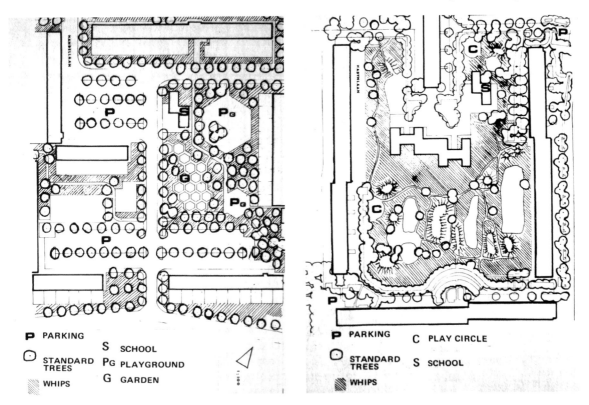

P PARKING

⊙ STANDARD TREES

▨ WHIPS

S SCHOOL

Pg PLAYGROUND

G GARDEN

P PARKING

⊙ STANDARD TREES

▨ WHIPS

C PLAY CIRCLE

S SCHOOL

FIGURE 23 *(left)*. Delft, Buitenhof: the standard treatment of the external spaces around the apartment blocks.

FIGURE 24 *(right)*. Delft, Gilles estate: the experimental landscape.

people have to be educated not to be afraid of city offices but defend their own interests. In conclusion, he asked whether:

> ... it was possible to bring nature into towns? Of course it was impossible to copy a piece of nature reserve in the city but for all that it was worth trying and with good co-operation among town planners, landscape architects, civil engineers it must be possible to break through the current trend of tidyness.[21]

The opportunity to break through this trend of tidyness and came on the Gilles estate, a soulless 1970s' housing scheme on the edge of the city. There an entirely new experimental landscape would be created with the appearance of a spontaneous, urban common, what John Muir described as "half wild parks" Comparisons with the conventional approach shows the radical nature of the new approach (Figures 23 and 24). Conventionally car parking was placed as close to the front entrance of the apartment block as possible, an example of what one critic called "the storage of private property on public ground". As a result children had to cross roads to reach the formal play facilities and in these circumstances many stayed close to the door and waited for their mothers to carry them across. This lack of connection between the physical and social environment was an obvious cause of failure in the urban landscape.[22] In the new approach cars were removed to the periphery and the space between the housing blocks was mounded and planted with native trees and shrubs before being left to develop spontaneously.

Where possible "existing vegetation was retained along with low-lying areas subject to flooding, former ditches and walls and those places where children had already begun to play, so a 'sense of place' could be continued".[23] Young children were encouraged to explore and experiment in their home landscape, building camps, lighting fires, planting seeds, with a member of the Parks staff on hand to provide tools (Plate 92). Later, when the child progressed to the school located at the centre of the 'common', experiential teaching methods were used to explain the physical and biological phenomena the children had already experienced whilst introducing man-made laws of the social environment. After 7 years the Netherlands Institute for Preventive Medicine, University of Leiden, reported

PLATE 91. Delft: The unplanned play of children.

that the new design had been a success; it was attractive to children, an efficient use of space and successfully integrated the environments of home and landscape, landscape and school[24] (Plate 93). The report recommended the experiment should be tried in other Ranstadt cities, and similar approaches were followed in Haarlem and The Hague, often with greater ecological and silvicultural knowledge.

In the late 1970s Corbusian-inspired high-rise living fell from favour, rejected by architects, planners and people who wanted a return to more conventional housing in a natural setting. One successful initiative was at Bloemendaal, a suburb of Gouda. Planned on an old, established polder landscape, much of the former landscape

PLATE 92. Delft, Gillis estate *c.*1975. Building dens was one of many informal activities taking place in the new landscape. Rather than being regarded as an eyesore the materials were left and constantly re-used.

PLATE 93. Delft, Gillis estate *c.*1984. People had trodden out the paths which were later surfaced with shell. Some thinning of the trees had taken place to encourage the understory but in a way that would not disturb the natural appearance of the landscape.

was retained, including the old farm road along the dyke for cyclists and pedestrians, creating a scene reminiscent of Hobbema's *Avenue at Middlemaar*. Old farmsteads were converted to community use, pre-existing canals were lined with large pollarded willows and wooden bridges, designed in a traditional style, led onto pastoral play meadows (Plates 94 and 95).

This naturalistic approach to the urban landscape which placed people at the forefront of consideration, prompted Dr J. Smidt, of the Institute for Systematic Botany at the State University of Utrecht, to inform the European Association of Landscape Contractors (1977) that by:

> paying attention to the desires and needs of users in landscape areas - human, plants and animals, it has proved possible to create quality. To design spaces where it is possible to live and exist, instead of increasing estrangement with the natural environment.[25]

England: Oakwood, Warrington New Town

In England the new nature-like approach was pioneered in the Oakwood district of Warrington New Town, Cheshire during the 1980s, by Robert Tregay. Up till then the New Town's landscape architects had adopted a typical garden city approach, with tree lined streets, mown grass verges and borders filled with exotic shrubs. Having seen the developments in the Netherlands and reacting to the 'concrete jungle' of the post-war years, Tregay wanted to bring "nature to the doorstep" and encourage natural play. His ideas were further influenced by urban forestry and the vision expressed by Nan Fairbrother in *New Lives New Landscapes* (1972):

PLATE 94 *(below left)*. Gouda, Bloemendaal *c.*1986. The old road along the dyke for pedestrians and cyclists.

PLATE 95 *(below right)*. Gouda, Bloemendaal *c.*1986. A play meadow for informal games, camping *etc.*

... tree belts framing self-contained urban landscapes ... within the tree belts ... the different environments, and here the trees provide not mass but the organization of space; the thinning out to enclose open areas of scenery, and framing in a leafy background, the individual settings for human beings.[26]

The opportunity to adopt a radical, ecological approach[27] came in the Oakwood District, formerly a wartime Ordnance factory (Plate 96), where the task was to re-establish a totally new landscape, not simply in aesthetic terms, but in restoring the total ecosystem: In Tregay's words:

> We did not use top soil. We researched and designed shelter belts to reduce heat loss from buildings, established meadows and wetlands, experimented with tree seeding and natural regeneration, and used what are now called swales instead of piping water underground. We set up a wildflower nursery and established flower-rich areas in the new woodlands and in wetlands and meadows. We wrote about the approach and tried to influence policy at a national level.[28]

Inspired by the English pastoral landscape (Plate 97), the plan for Oakwood established linear belts of native woodland to create 'cells' for new housing shops, schools and factories and provide corridors for wildlife and pedestrians (Figure 25). Gently curving internal roads were lined with trees and wild flowers and small ponds and wetlands were established on inaccessible land along the main feeder roads. Decorative, but otherwise functionless, grass verges and

PLATE 96 *(above).* The former Ordnance factory, Risley.

PLATE 97 *(left).* The English pastoral landscape with its arrangement of woodlands, individual trees, and small fields.

other extraneous open spaces were 'bundled' into small but meaningful areas for play and other uses . A pre-existing wetland, Risley Moss, was designated a local nature reserve and linked to the housing by a wildlife corridor along Birchwood Brook. These areas provided the focus for environmental education provided by the country's first urban ranger service, both in and out of school, as well as a location for informal play. In this way nature was restored to peoples' lives (Plate 98).[29]

The ecological landscapes at Warrington were described by Kathy Stansfield in the *Architects Journal* as "the quiet revolution in design",[30] and the enviromentalist Nicholson Lord observed that:

> ecological design, design with nature, is a fundamental principle of land management and by extension management of the earth, its landscape and its resources. It seeks to rejoin functions and identities disjointed by industrialism and treats human beings as a vital element on the ecological mosaic.[31]

The ecological approach pioneered in the Netherlands, and adopted and developed further at Warrington, and elsewhere in Sweden, Switzerland and Canada, is acknowledged today as the precursor to the present interest in environmental sustainability[32] and which has been developed further by artists, environmentalists and landscape architects in many countries.

PLATE 98 *(above)*. Warrington New Town Oakwood: The new housing approached through woodland, the paths followed desire lines initially trodden by residents.

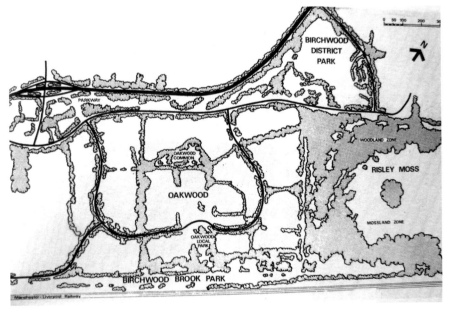

FIGURE 25 *(right)*. Warrington New Town; the linked woodland belts and surrounding parks.

Notes and References

1. Ranier, R., *Liveable Environments.* Artemis, Zurich, 1972, p. 10.
2. Le Corbousier, *Unité*, pp. 27–28. Quoted in Imbert, D., *The Modernist Garden in France.* Yale University Press, Princeton, 1993, p. 180.
3. The 1932 Athens congress in dealt with the concept of Functional City; three years later came van Eesteren's the General Extension Plan for Amsterdam.
4. One of Corbusier's followers, Walter Gropius, who was conscious of the psychological and social demands as well as economic, suggested the height should be reduced to 10–12 storeys.
5. Vandewalle, J., *The Story of Bijlmermeer.* Research paper for the course: Planned Communities University of Cincinnati ISSU.
6. *Dienst der Publeike Werken, Amsterdam. Het Groen in de Bijlmermeer.* 1971.
7. Public Works Department, Amsterdam Living with Greenery 1972.
8. Ruff, A., 'Holland and the alternative landscape', in *Landscape Design with Plants*, edited by B. Clouston. Heinemann, London, 1977, p. 117.
9. Ruff, A., *Holland the Ecological Landscapes.* Deanwater Press, Stockport, 1979, p. 21.
10. Le Roy, L., *Retourje Mondrian.* Heerenveen, 2003, pp. 12–13. Quoted in *Environmental Art: operation of ecology as environmental art.*
11. Thijsse. J., De Levende Natuur 1940 in Landwehr en Sipkes, *Wildeplantentuin*, Instituut voor Naturrbeschermingseducatie, Amsterdam, 1974. Quoted in Ruff, *op. cit.*, p. 8 Thijsse had an important influence on the natural form and habitats in the Bos park.
12. Le Roy, L., *op. cit.*, pp. 12–13 quoted in *Environmental Art: operation of ecology as environmental art.*
13. *Ibid.*
14. Le Roy, L., *Natuur uitschakelen; natuur inschakelen.* Ankh-Hermes, Deventer, 1973.
15. *Ibid.*
16. Ruff, A., *op. cit.*, p. 32.
17. The Randstad towns were the the main cities of the Netherlands – Amsterdam, The Hague, Rotterdam and Utrecht – that form a horseshoe around the central green heart of Holland.
18. Woudstra, J., 'The Eco Cathedral Louis Le Roy's Expression of a "Free Landscape Architecture"'. *Die Gartenkunst* 20(1), pp. 185–202.
19. Bos, H., *What About the Future of Urban Parks and Open Spaces?* 1973 (unpublished). Quoted in Ruff, A., *op. cit.*, pp. 36–7.
20. *Ibid.*
21. *Ibid.*
22. The Netherlands Institute for Preventive Medicine, University of Leiden.Unpublished report.
23. Ruff, A., *op. cit.*, pp. 36–7.
24. The Netherlands Institute for Preventative Medicine, *op. cit.*
25. Smidt, J. T., *Ecology in Physical Planning*, Papers of the European Landscape Contractors Association 1977. By the 1980s is was evident that the Bijlmermeer and other developments like the Gilles estate had failed. In Amsterdam people were reluctant to move to the new suburbs and as the radical mood of the 1970s evaporated, the taste of the Dutch middle class, for whom the suburbs were originally intended, changed. People wanted family houses with a garden front and back, not the utopian vision Corbusier intended. In the 1980s the Dutch government allocated the empty flats at both estates to the under-privileged, and in particular to immigrants from former

colonies, and by the end of the decade it was known as a poor black neighbourhood (Sterk, B. and Zahirovic, S., 'The Bijlmer: a Dutch approach to multiculturalism', in *Humanity in Action*). The design of the architecture was also causing problems; many it felt it was huge and impersonal and the external landscape, by then incredulously referred to as "the surroundings of an English landscape", was said to contribute to the impersonal atmosphere, giving the whole environment a desolate and eerie touch. Many saw the woodland as threatening and a refuge for antisocial activities. In the 1980s the experimental, natural landscapes in Amsterdam and Delft were removed and in 1995 a decision was taken to clear the high-rise flats at Bijlmermeer and build low-rise family houses in their place, much closer to the humanistic development Mulder had advocated earlier (Vandewalle, J., *The Story of Bijlmermeer*).

26. Fairbrother, N., *New Lives New Landscapes*. Architectural Press, London, 1970, p. 335.

27. Ruff, A., 'Holland and the ecological landscapes', *Garden History* 30(2) Winter 2002, p. 245. When describing the developments taking place in the Netherlands, the choice of the title for the book *Holland and the Ecological Landscape* was a matter of considerable concern. For the developments taking place in the Netherlands were not simply concerned with the use of native plants, rather what was emerging was an ecological approach to urban landscape that concerned man's relationship to nature and his interaction with the landscape in the social community; as well as the dynamic landscape processes involved in the use and management of native plant communities. The term 'ecological landscape', though not widely used in the Netherlands at that time, seemed to sum up the new approach and assist in establishing the conceptual idea in the minds of landscape architects.

28. Pers. comm. Robert Tregay.

29. Tregay. R. J. and Moffatt, J. D., 'An ecological approach to landscape design and management in Oakwood, Warrington'. *Landscape Design* 132, pp. 33–36.

30. Stansfield, K., 'Landscape design – the quiet revolution', *Architects Journal* 52, 1983, pp. 1232–3.

31. Nicholson-Lord, D., *The Greening of the Cities*. Routledge and Kegan Paul, London, 1987, p. 222.

32. Thompson, I., *Ecology, Community and Delight*. E. & F. N. Spon, London, 1999, p. 152.

CHAPTER EIGHTEEN

Eco-Pastoral – the pastoral redefined

Nearly a century ago the Irish poet W. B. Yeats suggested that "The Woods of Arcady are dead" and though by the end of the twentieth century Virgil was largely forgotten, dreams of Arcadia and the Pastoral, remain deeply embedded in western culture, fundamental to the way we see and comprehend the world around us. Echoing the words Buell used at the beginning of his book *The Environmental Imagination*:

> Insofar as some form of pastoralism is part of the conceptual apparatus of all persons with western educations interested in leading more nature-sensitive lives, it is to be expected that pastoralism will be a part of the unavoidable ground-condition of most who read this book.[1]

In his book *What is Pastoral* (1996), Alpers said, that if he had anything new to say, it was that the pastoral survives into the modern age:

> Pastoral is actually around us, every day. It is simply different in the modern era, and this is to say that many antique ideas articulated by Theocritus, Virgil, Spencer, Shakespeare, are no longer typical. We no longer think about shepherds in the green hills of Sicily, for example, probably because the subject no longer interests us any more.[2]

And Donald Worster said:

> Pastoralism is sure to remain a luminous ideal and to retain the capacity to assume oppositional forms for some time to come". It retains the capacity to demonstrate a critique to individuals, communities, governments and institutions on a scale ranging from the local to the global.[3]

The revitalising of the pastoral has been brought about by an increasing ecological awareness. In many ways Arcadia and ecology, and more particularly the ecosystem, share a great deal in common; both are human concepts that are a state of mind, defining man's relationship to the natural world. Living today, in what Worster described as the Age of Ecology, man no longer sees himself as the centre around which the rest of creation revolves. We are no more or less than part of a complex web of relationships, involving both the biotic (living) and abiotic (non-living) components (see Figure 26). And in both Arcadia and the ecosystem it is understood that human actions are responsible for disrupting those relationships.

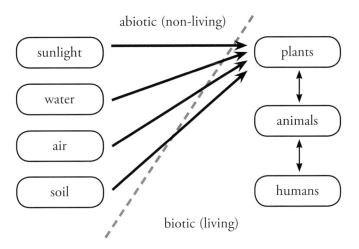

FIGURE 26. The ecosystem.

The age of ecology

In *Nature's Economy, a history of ecological ideas,* Worster describes how the eighteenth century Age of Reason gave rise to two major traditions in ecology: the first was the Christian-inspired Imperial tradition, best represented in the work of Carl Linnaeus and his desire to order and classify. Its aim was to establish through the exercise of reason and by hard work, man's dominion over nature. Opposing this was the pagan-inspired Arcadian view that advocated a simple, humble life aimed at restoring man to a peaceful co-existence with other organisms. This Arcadian stance was epitomised by Gilbert White, the parson-naturalist of Selborne, Hampshire, whose personal concept of ecology[4] was enhanced by the compelling idyll of contentment and peace he found in Virgil's *Eclogues* and *Georgics.* Like his contemporary, James Thomson author of *The Seasons,* White believed he had found the exact counterpart to the Virgilian ideal in the English countryside. White's desire was to see and study nature as a single integrated unity, held together by some rather mysterious organizing force. This holistic doctrine was used to attack the emerging industrial society and the new methods of scientific analysis, adopted since the time of Frances Bacon, which, it was believed, had removed the scientist from contact with both nature and society.

In the nineteenth century Charles Darwin's revolutionary book *The Origin of the Species* shattered the notion of the organising force being the Godhead and a century later the mysterious, organising force was identified as the ecosystem. As an objective science, ecology offers an insight, some would say a partial insight, into the workings of planet earth, as a result 'ecologists' as Worster explained, have always "found themselves not only marching in the vanguard of anti-technology forces, but also serving as teachers for each new generation of artists, writers, and designers, 'intent on recovering a sense of the sacred in nature'". Paul Sears, the American ecologist, calls ecology the subversive science[5] and for that reason alone, ecology for many people "has come to represent the arcadian mood that would return man back to a garden of natural peace and piety".[6]

Technology versus ecology

Since the seventeenth century increasing scientific knowledge has underpinned advances in human well-being and the extraction and utilisation of resources, with little regard to the consequences of exploding populations, depletion of stocks, species extinction and waste. Only recently have governments, societies and individuals come slowly, to appreciate the need to rethink our approach to the environment in more sustainable terms. David W. Orr defined two approaches to sustainability, both share a similar awareness of the problem but offer fundamentally different solutions. The first, technological sustainability, stems from previous knowledge and understanding adapted to new circumstances and assumes that:

> every problem has either a technological answer or a market solution. It is about expert interventions, in which the planet's ailments are identified and carefully stabilised through high-profile international agreements and sophisticated management techniques.[7]

However recent experiences, such as the failure of successive United Nation's Earth Summits, cast serious doubts on the ability of nations to resolve global problems in this way. Achim Steiner, director of the United Nations Environment Programme (UNEP) warned that pollution is killing millions of people a year, that ecosystem decline is increasing, that climate change is speeding up, and soil and ocean degradation is worsening. "If [the] trends continue … governments will preside over unprecedented levels of damage and degradation. Earth systems are being pushed towards their biophysical limits".[8] The alternative approach, ecological sustainability, seeks to confront the present situation and has "the task of finding alternatives to practices that got us into the trouble in the first place" making "it is necessary to rethink, agriculture, shelter, energy use, urban design, transportations, economics, community patterns, resource use, forestry, the importance of wilderness, and our central values".[9]

But the dilemma faced today is more than a choice between alternatives, there is a wider ethical question to answer. As nature has receded from our daily lives, it has receded from our ethics. In the *Living Landscape*, Harrison pointed out that it is a moral, rather than intellectual failing:

> All of us, not just conservationists, are suffering from a lack of values: we face a moral, no less than an ecological crisis. And because we no longer know what kind of world we should be constructing for the future, we are slow to resist the damage being done in the present, and we turn to the past for consolation; because we do not know what we are conserving the countryside for, our campaigns are fraught with confusion and indecision.[10]

Harrison refers to the countryside but in the twenty-first century this failing encompasses the Earth as a whole. Many argue that changes to our present attitudes will only succeed if we collectively develop an environmental conscience that assumes responsibility for our behavior towards other species and for the global ecosystem. Consciousness, that for centuries appeared to set us apart from nature, can, from a biocentric point of view, be seen as the species opportunity to take responsibility for ecological relationships and our ultimate survival. For this to happen we have to develop a conscience to a guide our environmental actions. In the twentieth century there were a number of individuals who did much to foster, and prick, that conscience.

Aldo Leopold

One of the first to articulate what an environmental conscience means was Aldo Leopold. Born in Burlington, Iowa in 1887, Leopold's boyhood years were spent exploring, hunting and sketching in the woods, swamps and fields around his home. These experiences influenced his decision to pursue a Forestry degree at Yale University, then the leading academic centre for the 'productivity outlook' to natural resources, as advocated by Gifford Pinchot.[11] Leopold's intellectual development would see him progress from what was earlier termed an Imperial tradition to a more Arcadian outlook. After publishing *Game Management* (1933) Leopold became uneasy with the economic attitude towards land use and began to question the agricultural 'crop' bias of conservation with its man-centred perspective. He believed there was a "need to re-establish a personal, co-existing relationship with nature, rather than the large-scale, impersonal management of resources by a professional elite".[12] By 1935 Leopold was fully converted to an ecological outlook and, reminiscent of Thoreau at Walden Pond, he began to spend more time at his cabin on the Wisconsin river, observing nature and restoring a small farm. His experiences there "sharpened his thinking about the relationship of people to the land and their moral obligation to take better care of it".[13] These observations were distilled into a set of natural history sketches, published posthumously as *Sand County Almanac* (1949).[14] Disillusioned with the overly managed world, Leopold declared that "perhaps a shift in values can be achieved by reappraising things unnatural, tame, and confined in terms of things natural, wild and free". Echoing Thoreau, Leopold criticised farmers and farming practice; in the American Midwest, land was falling into the hands of scientifically-minded farmers who had been trained by State Colleges and farm agents to maximise agricultural output. The prehistoric prairie with its diversity of plants and wildlife was being replaced by a monoculture of corn, wheat or soybeans, in so-called clean farming. His disillusionment with the too strictly managed landscape also affected his scientific belief; "science" he wrote "was in cahoots with the technological mentality that was regimenting the world in pursuit of mere material advancement".[15] In an essay *Natural History – The Forgotten Science* Leopold pleaded for a return to outdoor, holistic education, and a style of science open to amateurs and sober minded nature lovers, who were sensitive to "the pleasure to be had in wild things".

The final essay in the *Sand County Almanac* had the most lasting effect. In *The Land Ethic*, Leopold sought to redefine man's place in nature, arguing that

Man's own well-being requires the circle of cooperative, communal relatedness be extended to encompass all beings. Such an ecological ethic would, he argued, change man's role from that of master of the earth to "plain member and citizen of it".[16] And with this new ecocentricity came the "stirrings of an ecological conscience", as Donald Worster explained:

> Ecology revealed to Leopold a new dimension in the very old notion of natural rights. This idea … had historically been used (as in the American Declaration of Independence) to legitimise self-assertion by individuals or nations against a controlling power. By the very order of nature, it was argued, certain inalienable rights belong to all men, but natural rights had never included the rights of nature. The ecological conscience, however would extend these concepts to all species, even to the earth itself. The rights of life and liberty-perhaps even the pursuit of happiness-must belong to all beings, for all are members of the biotic community. But in contrast to previous appeals for natural rights, this was not a demand made and forced on the ruling classes by an excluded minority, rather, it required a moral decision by that powerful elite on behalf of the inarticulate lower orders. To invest the ruling order with the power to determine the justice of its own deeds is always an act of faith, and for that reason alone, the rights of nature must always remain in jeopardy. But in a sense this new doctrine had its own compelling force, apart from human whim. Unless man recognised the rights of the entire earth household, Leopold warned, he might find his own survival threatened by environmental collapse. It had happened before, as recently as the Dust Bowl years.[17]

Publication of Leopold's *Sand County Almanac* was followed by a new branch of moral philosophy, environmental ethics, that sought to incorporate environmental obligations into a value system concerning social benefit, amenity and aesthetics.

Rachel Carson

The nature writer and scientist who, more than anyone, took on board the environmental ethic and helped launch the ecology movement as a political and cultural force was Rachel Carson. Carson's early writing derived from rambles along the shore of her coastal home in Maine and were in the Gilbert White tradition, but it was the publication of *Silent Spring* (1962) that launched the aggressive ecology movement. Carson had long been aware of the dangers of chemical pesticides and in *Silent Spring* she argued that uncontrolled and unexamined pesticide use was harming, even killing, not just animals and birds, but also humans. Its title evoked the apocalyptic image of a spring in which no bird songs could be heard because they had all vanished as a result of pesticide use. The book was, and remains, highly controversial, but a Professor of History, Gary Kroll, has said it was "Rachel Carson who played a large role in articulating ecology as a 'subversive study' – as a perspective that cuts against the grain of materialism, scientism, and the technologically engineered control of nature".[18]

Laura Sayre, in *A Georgic Apocalypse: From Virgil to Silent Spring*,[19] drew chilling parallels between Carson's apocalyptic image and its counterpart in Virgil's *Georgics*. Both authors portray a powerful, even gut wrenching account of death and devastation in the midst of otherwise familiar scenes of rural harmony and plenty. In the *Georgics*, Virgil's plague arrives in a mysterious and indiscriminate fashion; the signs of sickness among sheep and cattle have to be vigilantly watched for because livestock diseases come suddenly and require swift action:

> Thicker and faster than squalls of wind that tear at the sea's face
> Come many diseases of cattle,
> Killing not one here and there, but a whole summer pasture –
> The lambs, the dams, the whole lot of them root and branch.

Virgil *Georgics* 3, 470–3[20]

Virgil describes an event that occurred in the long deserted hills and valleys, to the north of the Adriatic:

> It happened long ago here, but you'd see derelict ranches
> of Sheep, old grazings empty up to the far horizon.
> For here it was that once the sky fell sick and a doleful
> Season came, all hectic with the close heat of autumn, ...

Virgil *Georgics* 3, 376–9

All the animals, tame and wild were killed, and the sickness seemed to be everywhere – in the air, in the water, in feed and food. Nothing escaped the contagion which brought a gruesome death and without their animals the farmers were forced to work the land themselves:

> Painfully men scratched at the soil with mattocks, used their
> Own nails to cover the seed corn, harnessed their necks
> To tug the creaking wagons over a towering hillside.

Virgil *Georgics* 3, 534–5

But the pestilence spread to water and the air:

> Now the deepwater tribes, yes all the swimming creatures
> Lie on on the shores edge, washed by the waves like shipwrecked bodies
> And seals take refuge in rivers they never swam before.
> The viper perishes too, in vain defence of her winding
> Lair; and the startled snake, his scales standing on end.
> The air is precarious for birds; they plunge down dead,
> Leaving their life in the clouds.

Virgil *Georgics* 3, 540–6

Virgil piles horror on horror until suddenly he breaks off, leaving readers at the end of the book with these frightening images seared into their minds.

Carson begins *Silent Spring* with a *Fable for Tomorrow* in which she describes "a town in the heart of America where all life seemed to live in harmony with its surroundings":

The town lay in the midst of a checkerboard of prosperous farms, with fields of grain and hillsides of orchards where, in spring, white clouds of bloom drifted above the green fields. In autumn, oak and maple and birch set up a blaze of colour that flamed and flickered across a backdrop of pines. Then foxes barked in the hills and deer silently crossed fields, half hidden in the mists of the fall mornings.[21]

In a few short sentences, writes Sayre, Carson "mobilises a long cultural heritage of georgic imagery (even I am tempted to call it pastoral in this instance), peaceful and reassuring: a small town in a rural landscape, where wildlife and farm life co-exist, where each season brings its own aesthetic delights, at once new and familiar; where 'laurel, viburnum and alder, great ferns and wildflowers' fringe the roads". The town's natural beauty is an attraction for visitors, who come to see the bird migrations in the spring and fall, and "to fish the streams, which flowed clear and cold out of the hills and contained shady pools where trout lay". Into this idyllic countryside comes contagion, like Virgil's, mysterious, sudden and indiscriminate:

Then a strange blight crept over the area and everything began to change. Some evil spell had settled on the community: mysterious maladies swept the flocks of chickens; the cattle and sheep sickened and died. Everywhere was a shadow of death. The farmers spoke of much illness among their families. In the town the doctors had become more and more puzzled by new kinds of sickness appearing among their patients. There had been several sudden and unexplained deaths, not only among adults but even among children, who would be stricken suddenly while at play and die within a few hours.[22]

And just as in Virgil's plague scene, doctors and healers are powerless. Children succumb alongside their parents; livestock of every variety sicken and die and those who survive lose their fertility. The orchards come into bloom, but the bees have all disappeared, "so there was no pollination and there would be no fruit". Though Carson's account is severely pared-down in comparison to Virgil's, it emphasises the gruesome, unnatural mode of this strange plague. But Carson differs from Virgil in one important detail; whereas the origins of the *Georgic* plague are unknown, the final lines of the *Fable* state explicitly that this was no act of a wrathful god or other external force. "No witchcraft, no enemy action had silenced the rebirth of new life in this stricken world. The people had done it themselves".[23]

Environmentalism

Rachel Carson's critique helped develop a broad philosophy, ideology and social movement, loosely termed environmentalism, that sought to balance relations between humans and the various natural systems on which life depends, in a way that ensure all components are accorded the proper degree of respect. Like Orr, O'Riordan classified environmentalism into two categories, *ecocentrism* and *technocentrism* (Figure 27).[24] The Ecocentric ethic, as conceived by Leopold, was defined by O'Riordan in the 1960s:

ENVIRONMENTALISM

Ecocentrism		Technocentrism	
Deep ecologists	*Self-reliance Soft technologists*	*Environmental managers*	*Cornucopians*
Intrinsic importance of nature for the humanity of man	(1) Emphasis on smallness of scale and hence community identity in settlement, work, and leisure	(1) Belief that economic growth and resource exploitation can continue ties assuming: (a) suitable economic adjustments to taxes, fees, *etc.* (b) improvements in the legal rights to a minimum level of environmental quality (c) compensation arrangements satisfactory to those who experience adverse environmental and/or social effects	(1) Belief that man can always find a way out of any difficulty either political, scientific, or technological
Ecological (and other natural) laws dictate human morality	(2) Integration of concepts of work and and leisure through a process of personal and communal improvement	(2) Acceptance of a new project appraisal techniques and decision review arrangements to allow for wider discussion or genuine search for consensus among representative groups of interested parties	(2) Acceptance that pro-growth goals define the rationality of project appraisal and policy formulation
	(3) Importance of participation in community affairs, and of guarantees of the rights of minority interests. Participation seen both as a continuing education and political function		(3) Optimism about the ability of man to improve the lot of the world's people
Biorights – the right of endangered species or unique landscapes to remain unmolested	(4) Lack of faith in modern large-scale technology and its associated demandson elitest expertise, central state authority and inherently anti-democratic institutions		(4) Faith that scientific expertise provides the basic foundation for advice onmatters pertaining to economic growth, public health and safety
	(5) Implication that materialism for its own sake is wrong and that economic growth can be geared to providing for the basic needs of those below subsistence levels		(5) Suspicion of attempts to widen basis for participation and lengthy discussion in project appraisal and policy review
			(6) Belief that all im-pediments can be overcome given a will, ingenuity and sufficient resources arising out of growth

FIGURE 27. The pattern of environmental ideologies.

Ecocentrism preaches the virtues of reverence, humility, responsibility, and care: it argues for low impact technology (but is not anti-technological); it decries bigness and impersonality in all forms (but especially in the city; and demands a code of behaviour that seeks permanence and stability based upon ecological principles of diversity and homeostasis.[25]

Responses – Eco Art

In the 1990s ecocentric approaches to environmentalism had a powerful impact on the creative arts. A new sense of awareness brought an ongoing reappraisal of the way in which artists, writers and designers saw the world around them and how they approached their work. Ecological artists joined with scientists and conservationists in addressing more directly the issues raised by environmentalism: sustainability, pollution, politics, the condition of the ecosystem at local and global scales, along with our relationship to it. In general they subscribed to one or more of the following principles:

Attention to the web of interrelationships in our environment – to the physical, biological, cultural, political, and historical aspects of ecological systems.
Create works that employ natural materials, or engage with environmental forces such as wind, water, or sunlight.
Reclaim, restore, and remediate damaged environments.
Inform the public about ecological dynamics and the environmental problems.
Re-envision ecological relationships, creatively proposing new possibilities for co-existence, sustainability, and healing.

An example of how Eco Art can redefine the pastoral message was Agnes Denes's *Wheatfield – A Confrontation* (1982) which involved the planting and harvesting of a 2 acre (0.8 ha) wheatfield on a vacant lot in downtown Manhattan (Plate 99). A thousand pounds of healthy wheat, worth $158, was harvested from land valued at $4.5 billion. It was a powerful restatement of Virgil's Georgic didactic message of the simple farmer as a critique to the wealthy and the powerful, in Denes's words:

PLATE 99. Agnes Denes, *Wheatfield – A Confrontation, Battery Park Landfill, New York* c.1982.

Manhattan is the richest, most professional, most congested and, without doubt, most fascinating island in the world. To attempt to plant, sustain and harvest 2 acres of wheat here, wasting valuable real estate and obstructing the 'machinery' by going against the system, was an effrontery that made it the powerful paradox I had sought for the calling to account. It was insane. It was impossible. But it did call people's attention to having to rethink their priorities and realise that unless human values were reassessed, the quality of life, even life itself, was in danger. ... Wheatfield was a symbol, a universal concept.[26]

Elaine King, Professor of the History of Art, Carnegie Mellon University, believes Eco artists have raised awareness and challenged the anthropocentricism of a culture based on the objectification and exploitation of nature:

> Without a doubt artists are noticeably reacting to news about climatic disaster, the extinction of threatened species, or the depletion of natural resources and confront us with their subjective response. Undeniably nature even today offers artists refuge and guidance, but with real estate developers, oil spills, toxic waste and nuclear disasters and with beer cans proliferating in Serengeti grass and Himalayan snow, it is hard not to feel that nature needs refuge and defence. In order to make influential art about the natural world, it's necessary to take into account both the crisis facing nature and the crisis in the definition of nature. Today it ever more becomes hard to arrive at any clear sense of what 'nature' is, especially in an era of new technology, instantaneous gratification and countless individuals only experiencing nature virtually through the Internet or television. The artistic representation of nature is closely linked with the social perception of the natural world. This is a two-way process: society draws its ideas about how to view and experience nature from the mediated conventions of visual culture, whilst artists react to current societal attitudes and governmental policy about the environment.[27]

King believes in future Eco artists should be involved in solving environmental problems:

> the complexities of the environmental problems we now face, can only be resolved by interdisciplinary approaches, involving all professions and disciplines working together from dissimilar perspectives for a similar goal. Each participant brings with him/her a varied solution, thus as a consequence the whole process receives broader dimensions and gains in richness:
>
> Even the most proficient scientist would not succeed in communicating the severity of an environmental problem to the larger public, because she/he would not know how to evoke a mixed response from the audience, or provoke a deep sense of belonging or familiarity and responsibility on a more regional and local level. This can be the role of an artist, a director or a writer. Art has the power to impact the environment, as well as raising awareness of environmental issues beyond charts and statistics. Perhaps artists and humanists should increasingly be incorporated into decision-making processes, at the highest level. Planning committees on environmental policy should include environmentally concerned artists, philosophers, historians, *etc.* as an inseparable part of the team.[28]

The post-Pastoral literature

For a long time poets and writers were burdened by the discredited, sentimental nature poetry of the Georgian poets. To remove such sentimentality Terry Gifford argued for redefinition of the Pastoral in a manner that takes account of the urgent need for responsibility and, indeed, advocacy for, the welfare of Arden (The Forest of Arden, Shakespeare's English *Arcadia* in *As You Like It*). Gifford believes that ecocentrism, in effect, brings about "a reversal of focus in the elements of the pastoral":

Now there is as much an interest in the welfare of Arden as in that of its exiled inhabitants, as much interest in their interaction with Arden as in what they take back from it, as much interest in how they represent their interaction with it as in how their representations of themselves as its inhabitants have changed.[29]

Gifford proposed the new term of 'post-pastoral' for literature which addresses the problems of human accommodation with nature, because:

The debasement of the tool considered essential since the beginnings of Western literature – the rich and long tradition of pastoral poetry – calls for a rediscovery of what I have called 'post-pastoral' poetry. This is not 'post' in the sense of postcolonial, for it was present in the work of some writers even as some of their other work was part of the decline of pastoral. It is more conceptual than temporal. It is 'post' in the sense of being beyond the traps of the pastoral, of being aware of some of the problematics of the pastoral, of pushing into the complexities of celebration and responsibility, of being a part of nature and yet uneasy with relationships of ownership and exploitation.[30]

To this end Gifford proposed that post-pastoral texts should be a response to some or all of the following six propositions:

A sense of awe in nature that comes with the re-positioning from anthropocentric pastoral to ecocentric post-pastoral.
A celebration of both constructive and destructive forces and an understanding that nature is not merely a pleasant idyll.
Acknowledgement of a link between human and external nature, where the landscape can affect our ideas, perception and well-being.
The recognition that culture is nature, because they are both ultimately the result of natural processes, i.e. nature and culture do not stand in opposition.
The transition from consciousness to conscience, so that observation of landscape gives rise to ecological concern or sympathy for nature.
A sense that exploitation of nature resembles human exploitation, as in various works of ecofeminism.[31]

New Nature poetry is more than merely descriptive:

it deals with tensions between us and our environment, our intense and often destructive relationship with it, our struggle to come to terms with the fact that we're part of the world out there and not simply observers and manipulators. Poets are trying to write about the ways in which nature is destroyed, its needs, or how it can be fixed/healed.[32]

For this reason, Hilary Llewellyn-Williams argued that "poets need no longer apologise for writing about Nature".

Margaret Atwood's nature poetry typifies the post-pastoral perspective. Her poetry frequently expresses an awe for nature whilst pitting civilisation against the surrounding wilderness, and society against the savagery from which it arose. Modern civilisation is often depicted as being afraid of the land, with individuals cutting themselves off from natural forces, the Corbusian ideal of the city as a bastion against nature. However, in Canada wilderness is always close at hand and people fear wilderness because it is something that denies them their own existence; Atwood pushes towards the recognition that in Canada the natural world is not something that can be easily incorporated into the human domain, and create a seamless unified field. Even where the stumps of trees reveal man once tried to farm the land, nature returns to reclaim it as her own. And where the natural world has been dominated, nature undermines the social order; in the poem *The City Planners* Atwood suggests that the houses will eventually "slide/obliquely into the clay seas, gradual as glaciers".[33]

Atwood regards this as "a more mature, modern view than the Wordsworthian tradition of 'nature's benignity'". In comparison to Wordsworth's Michael who lived in harmony with nature, as forceful as it was, the Pioneer in Atwood's poem *The Progressive Insanities of a Pioneer,* becomes increasingly insane as he attempts to assert his centrality in a wilderness wholly indifferent to him. At the poem's opening, the pioneer is armed with his land holding; "He stood at a point / on a sheet of green paper / proclaiming himself the centre".[34] Atwood implies this is how we think of ourselves; as the centre of the universe and everything must revolve around us. But the poem goes on to describes the futility of attempting to control natural forces: "in the darkness the fields / defend themselves with fences / in vain: / everything / is getting in". And though the pioneer tries to assert his importance, he fears he is not central but random. Looking around him, he sees the wilderness as "the absence / of order", he looks at "the swamps clamourings and outburst / of rocks, and finds he is disgusted". To the settler, "raw land" is merely swampy waste or rocky bush until it is transformed by the "civilised developer", a viewpoint shared by many today. What the pioneer wants is some grand narrative or vision that will allow him to stand back and comprehend his relation to the land. But farming is unequal to the force and extent of the wilderness and finally, the pioneer is defeated by the power of nature. Even though he lives in a world "with no walls, no borders", in his insane despair he screams "Let me Out"! The question Atwood poses is whether in trying to destroy nature we are not truly defeating ourselves.

In *Backdrop addresses cowboy*[35] Atwood sees the land possessing it own language and in the final lines of the poem the landscape answers back: "I am also what surrounds you: / my brain / scattered with your tin cans, bones, empty shell, / the litter of your invasions. / I am the the space you desecrate/as you pass through". The reader is encouraged to view the land as a sentient, existing being and, in Hatch's opinion, Atwood, comes close to creating an ecocentric or ecological view of the land: "yet one hesitates to use the term ecocentric in this case, since she does not recreate the landscape".[36] Writers and poets like Atwood cannot literally repair the biosphere, nor directly do anything to the environment but as Buell said, they try to practice a conceptual restorationism in reorienting the partially denaturised reader not to a primordial nature, which cannot be recovered either in fact or fantasy, but to an artifactual version of the environment designed to provoke place-sense.[37] Perhaps more specifically, they enable the individual to make sense of the place we are at.

The urban question and ecological design

Many environmentalists from Jefferson to Wendell Berry today, have believed in 'the good life' – one in which healthy communities, and in turn healthy cultures "informed by such ideals as hard work, neighbourliness, thrift and love" – are only possible in a rural, agrarian setting – the pastoral life. However, the vast majority of people in America, Europe and increasingly worldwide, live in urban and suburban areas and, as Mark Mitchell said: "are quite content to purchase their pasteurised milk from the supermarket" along with "their chickens nicely cleaned and plucked". This raises what might be described as the fundamental urban question: whether it is possible to re-create an urban environment that has a healthy community and is ecologically sustainable, or:

> Does something about the modern, urbanised world militate against the formation and sustenance of robust local communities? And if so, are there ways healthy communities can be realised apart from an agrarian context? If not, then it would seem that, given current demographic realities and trends, the possibility for cultivating strong local communities is correspondingly dim. If, on the other hand, there are possibilities latent in the fundamental structure of urban life itself, then the kind of community that humans naturally seek may be possible without abandoning the cities in favor of the farm. Indeed, far from denigrating cities as less suitable for human flourishing, Aristotle, for instance, argues that the best kind of human life is only possible in the context of a city. The city is the proper end (telos) of humans and to flee the city signals something the either seriously wrong with the person or the city. Perhaps, then, the present maladies of our cities are not intrinsic to cities but, rather, are the result of modern notions of cities that have seriously misunderstood the purpose and possibilities of urban existence.[38]

In her seminal book on urban design *The Death and Life of the Great American City*, Jane Jacobs pointed out that the scientific methodology employed by modern town planners had contributed to the problems facing the city and its inhabitants. Statistical forecasting, advocated by Van Eesteren and his CIAM colleagues that resulted in the Functional City, failed to appreciate the complex nature of cities. The result of modern planning has been to destroy, or more often failed to create, communities leaving "a cultural vacuum that is filled with a homogeneous culture that is bland as it is broad ... which leads to boredom, apathy and a diminished sense of care or responsibility".[39] In order to "to understand cities", according to Jacobs, "we have to deal outright with combinations of mixtures of uses, not separate uses, as essential phenomena". If towns are to be revitalised, that is to say given back life, in "which human lives can be lived with dignity and joy, then we must turn our attention to preserving local culture, local customs, local beauty, local economies, families and memories".

In the late 1980s designers in America and Canada, including architects, engineers, landscape architects began to examine ways in which separate activities in green architecture, sustainable agriculture, ecological engineering, ecological restoration and ecological landscape design could be used to create healthy urban communities. "Success", said Sim Van der Ryan and Stuart Cowan in their seminal book *Ecological Design* (1996), will "depend upon the adoption of an ecocentric approach" which can be defined as "any form of design that minimises environmentally destructive impacts by integrating itself with living processes".[40] At present, argued Van der Ryan and Sim, we live in two interpenetrating worlds:

> The first is the living world, which has been forged in an evolutionary crucible over a period of four billion years. The second is the world of roads and cities, farms and artifacts, that people have been designing for themselves over the last few millennia. The condition that threatens both worlds – unsustainability – results from a lack of integration between them. (What was needed were) skills to effectively interweave human and natural design. The designed mess we have made of our neighbourhoods, cities and ecosystems owes much to the lack of a coherent philosophy, vision, and practice of design that is grounded in a rich understanding of ecology. Unfortunately, the guiding metaphors of those who shape the built environment still reflect a nineteenth-century epistemology. Until our everyday activities preserve ecological integrity by design, their cumulative impact will continue to be devastating.[41]

Ecological design involves three critical strategies: conservation, regeneration, and stewardship:

> *Conservation* slows the rate at which things are getting worse by allowing scarce resources to be stretched further. But it assumes damage must be done, resources are still being used.
> *Regeneration* seeks to repair a world deeply wounded by environmentally insensitive design or inappropriate management. Regeneration is the expansion of natural capital through the active restoration of degraded ecosystems and communities. It is a form of healing and renewal that embodies the richest possibilities of culture to harmonise with nature.
> *Stewardship* is a particular quality of care in our relationships with other living creatures and with the landscape. It maintains natural capital by spending frugally and investing wisely.

In the book *Ecological Design*, Van der Ryan and Sim set out ways in which Ecological Design contrasted with Conventional Design (Figure 28).[42]

New approaches

Among those landscape architects whose work demonstrates how the concerns and objectives of artists, writers and designers are coalescing in a new ecological approach to environmental issues is George Hargreaves. Like the eighteenth century Romantic poets, Hargreaves refers back to certain critical experiences in Nature as the touchstone of his aesthetic development. He has recounted how, at the age of 18, he saw the spectacular view from Flat Top mountain in the Rockies: "It wasn't just the mountains or the trees or any of the individual elements. It was something about the sense of space itself". He mentions witnessing the force of Hurricane Gloria in 1982:

Issue	Conventional Design	Ecological Design
Energy source	Usually non-renewable, destructive relying on fossil fuels or nuclear power.	Where feasible, renewables: solar, wind small-scale hydro or biomass.
Materials use	High-quality materials; resulting in discarded toxic and low quality materials in soil, air, water.	Restorative materials; cyclical – waste becomes food for the next. Design for reuse, recycling, flexibility, ease of repair durability.
Pollution	Copious and endemic.	Minimised: scale and composition of waste related to ability of ecosystems to absorb it.
Toxic substances	Common and destructive – from pesticides to paint.	Used sparingly in very special circumstances.
Ecological accounting	Limited to mandatory requirements, *e.g.* environmental impact assessments.	Sophisticated and built-in. Covering wide range of ecological impacts over entire life of the project.
Ecology and economics	Perceived as being in opposition; in short-term perspective.	Perceived as compatible; long-term perspective.
Sensitivity to ecological context	Standard solutions replicated over the planet with little regard to place or culture.	Response to bioregion; solutions grow from place – design integrated with local soils, vegetation, materials, culture, climate, topography.
Sensitivity to cultural context	Tendency towards a homogeneous global culture – destroys localism.	Respects and nurtures traditional knowledge of place and local materials and technologies.
Biological, cultural and economic diversity	Standardised designs with high energy and materials, eroding biological, cultural and economic diversity.	Maintains diversity and locally adopted cultures and economies that support it.
Knowledge base	Narrow disciplinary focus.	Integrates multiple design principles and wide range of arts and sciences.
Whole systems	Divides systems along boundaries that do not reflect underlying natural processes.	Works with whole systems; produces designs that provide greatest possible degree of internal integrity and coherence.
Role of nature	Design imposed on nature to provide control and predicability so as to meet narrowly defined human needs.	Includes nature as a partner.
Level of participation	Reliance on jargon and experts who are unwilling to communicate with public, limits community involvement in critical design decisions.	Commitment to clear discussion and debate; everyone empowered to join design process.
Types of learning	Nature and Technology are hidden; the design does not teach over time.	Nature and technology made visible; the design draws people closer to systems that ultimately sustain us.
Response to sustainability crisis	Views culture and nature as inimical; tries to slow rate of decline by implementing minor conservation efforts without questioning underlying assumptions.	Views culture and nature as potentially symbiotic; searches for practices that actively regenerate human and ecosystem health.

I had studied geology and I always thought of change as a slow process but in Hawaii I was reminded of the power of immediate change, brought by a thirty foot wall of water. An awareness that nature is not merely a pleasant idyll but an understanding that it is both a constructive and destructive force.

FIGURE 28 Characteristics of conventional and ecological design.

This, said Hargreaves, "made me wonder, how could we imbue a project with the notion that the environment is not static, but is always changing?"[43] The desire to take account of Nature's dynamic qualities has led Hargreaves to a unique and intuitive method for approaching the process of landscape design. "Convention is easy to slip into, to keep making the same pictures. What I try to find are those magic moments of clarity when you hear the site is whispering to you". The link Terry Gifford spoke of between human and external nature, wherein the landscape can affect our ideas, perception and well-being. At the centre of Hargreaves philosophy is a recognition that culture is nature, that nature and culture do not stand in opposition. At the core of his practice there is a single overriding concern:

> connection – between culture and the environment, connection between the land and its people, Civilisations have long sought dominance over the landscape, pursuing agrarian and industrial wealth. In reaction, the last twenty-five years have brought about the emergence of an ecological approach to planning, the preservation and restoration of natural systems, and the notion of sustainable landscape. Our own built landscapes eschew these polarised approaches to the land – one potentially damaging to the balance of natural systems, the other blind to culture and remote from peoples' lives – seeking the in-between.[44]

The whispers Hargreaves listens for come, not from sites that embody the undisturbed beauty of Nature, but rather from those ruined and degraded landscapes created as an unfortunate by-product of the industrial world's activities. His design practice has specialised in the regeneration of these sites, of which Crissy Fields in San Francisco and the London Olympic Park are good examples.

Crissy Fields, on the San Francisco waterfront, was once an ancient 130 acre (52 ha) salt-marsh and estuary whose archeological history stretches back to a

PLATE 100 *(left)*. Crissy Fields, San Francisco – the restored tidal marsh. Storm water that used to go directly into the bay was directed into the marsh to extract the sediments and nutrients before releasing the water into the bay. The marsh was over-excavated and allowed to backfill naturally creating its own channels. Native grasses were chosen for their tolerance of the harsher conditions, minimising pesticide applications. The restored tidal marsh serves as a wildlife habitat, an educational facility, a scenic attraction, a recreational resource, a 'sacred place', and an ongoing scientific experiment.

PLATE 101 *(below)*. The London Olympic Park – one of the Swales.

time when native Americans harvested the sea and later the Spanish grazed cattle and cultivated the land. It was filled-in during the 1870s for the Panama Pacific Exhibition and any remnants of its history and ecology were eroded finally by the Army when creating an airfield. When the National Parks Service inherited the site, 70 acres (28 ha) were covered with asphalt and hard packed dirt whilst rubble lined much of the 6000 ft (1830 m) shoreline. Hargreaves's ecological approach, included the preservation and restoration of natural systems and the making of a sustainable landscape (Plate 100). Meetings with the public and local communities throughout the design and construction stages helped foster community involvement and responsibility. Community groups and individuals played an important role in restoring the tidal marsh and dunes and many continued their stewardship role after completion of the restoration helping to monitor and protect native plantings and an program helped young adults develop leadership skills.

A similar approach was adopted at the London Olympic Park where Hargreaves worked in collaboration with LDA Design, Britain's leading design, environment and sustainability consultancy.[45] The Lea Valley, like Crissy Fields, had been derelict since the 1990s and restoration involved creating two zones; one around the main stadium as a busy paved world of concourses and entertainment plazas while at the northern end a more natural landscape of meadows and woodlands was re-created. An important sustainable innovation in the Olympic Park was to reveal the water;

> We pulled back the landform and sculpted mounds out of the displaced soil, which allowed us to reuse all of the material on site. Instead of near vertical walls meeting the rivers, the land slopes down, via meandering pathways and bushy banks, to naturalised, reed planted edges. The result was largest urban river and wetland scheme in the UK involving the planting of more than 300,000 plants, including reeds, rushes, grasses, sedges and wildflowers.[46]

Instead of rainwater being fed into drains, some of the water was absorbed into a series of planted swales and rain gardens creating two wet woodland areas offering unique habitats for insects, amphibians and birds (Plate 101) and by allowing the remaining water to return slowly to the river system, the flood risk to 5000 homes was removed. Robert Tregay described this approach as simply "putting the pieces together" and regards the achievement of these ecological goals as one of the biggest challenges facing the Landscape profession today.[47]

Aesthetics and ecological design

Ecological approaches to sustainable design, construction and management, like Crissy Fields and the London Olympic Park, present a challenge to those landscape architects who have traditionally depended on picturesque aesthetics to communicate the idea of nature. Michael Boland regards eco-landscapes, like Crissy Fields, as "part of an expanded field of landscape aesthetics":

They are an example of what I call fourth nature landscapes that express that they are made and yet have ecological value. This notion of fourth nature is important, because it allows us to conceive of ecological value in landscapes that we traditionally thought of as cultural.[48]

Elizabeth Meyer, Associate Professor of Landscape Architecture at the University of Virginia, in a most thoughtful article *Sustaining Beauty. The performance of appearance,* observed that "rarely do aesthetics factor into the sustainability discourse". Meyer argued that designed landscapes, like Crissy Fields, should "provoke those who experience them to become more aware of how their actions affect the environment, and to care enough to make changes." The important role of such aesthetic, environmental experiences is to "re-centre human consciousness from an egocentric to a more bio-centric perspective":

> Beautiful landscape design involves the design of experiences as well as the design of form and the design of ecosystems. These experiences are vehicles for connecting with, and caring for, the world around us.[49]

"Designed landscapes", said Meyer, "can provide such landscapes if they afford experiences of the wild, when the abundance, the excessiveness, and the tenacious persistence of plants, wild life and water are uncovered in the most unexpected places ...".

Landscape of this kind have been called eco-revelatory because they reveal the endemic ecological process whilst affording a more direct connection between fundamental ecological processes and the experience of landscape. What Hargreaves described as an awareness and understanding of the structural components of natural systems by direct interaction. This contrasts with the typical urban landscape where ecological processes have been hidden, supplanted by the anthropomorphic, often technological, process. The new ecocentric ethic supplants this old self-interested and human-centred ethic. "Through conscious design, ecology not only guides but is revealed through education and direct experience of the result"; Meyer suggests it is through the experience of different types of beauty that we come to notice, to care, to deliberate about our place in the world:

> humanity can to listen to nature's language as revealed through ecological principles, ethics, poetry, and reverence for our nonhuman partner. Although, as partner, nature's language differs from our own, we still have the possibility of working co-operatively with it. This entails respecting both nature's needs and human needs. It means that other species, women and minorities are represented at the the decision making table and in the design process. The result is a healthier, more aesthetically pleasing environment for our own and future generations.[50]

Where is Arcadia today?

Finally, in an article *Ecological Turbulence and the Hadean Arcadia,* written after the first "Eco-Revelatory Design" exhibition,[51] Frederick Turner, Founders Professor of Arts and Humanities at the University of Texas, Dallas, answered the question that has been pursued throughout this book: *Where is Arcadia today?*:

> Ancient poets always found it in the countryside, in a pastoral place where the cultivated mingled with the uncultivated, or in sacred groves that were uninhabited but managed unobtrusively by eccentric sibyls or priests. In 18th-century America, the Founding Fathers found it in the agrarian archetype of the virtuous small town, with its meetinghouse and gentleman farmers with thumbed copies of Plato and the Bible on their shelves. This is an enduring ideal for Americans, as the work of late-20th-century writers such as Wendell Berry show. In the nineteenth century, the poets and painters found Arcadia in what they thought were wild landscapes – the Alps, the Lake District, the exotic lands of Abyssinia or Xanadu, the Rocky Mountains of Albert Bierstadt, the prairies of Frederic Remington. They did not realise that such landscapes were the product of the careful work of Swiss and Cumbrian farmers, of a continent full of Native American hunter-gatherers and gardeners of considerable ecological sophistication. To the Romantics, the human impact on nature was always a loss of innocence, a violation. Thus their attitude to it was elegiac, as they foresaw the encroachments of the city, the dark satanic mills. In the twentieth century poets such as T. S. Eliot and Ezra Pound found Arcadia, by sardonic reversal, found it in the city, where the evening is laid out on the sky "like a patient etherised upon a table". In the twenty-first century we will find Arcadia a *Rus* that is both suburban and subrural, not so far away from the arcadia of the bucolic poets, of Virgil and Horace, Tu Fu and Li Po, Kalidasa and Hafez, Radnoti and Pasternak.
>
> But it is a post-, not a pre-technological landscape, one in which the technology is perfecting itself into invisibility, and where form has ceased to follow function but rather elaborates itself into new, delicate, intelligible structures that create new functions – functions that we suddenly recognise from the cultural past. There are times when the present breaks the shackles of the past to create the future – the modern age, now was one of those. But there are also times, like the Renaissance and our own coming twenty-first century, when it is the past that creates the future, by breaking the shackles of the present. The environmental restorationists are recreating extinct ecosystems–prairies, oak openings, dry tropical forests – on land once apparently claimed forever for the city or the farm.[52]

There is no way of knowing how the fundamental changes inspired by Arcadian ecology, in poetry and literature, art and design will develop in future years. Perhaps, as Worster suggests, there will be no change in our present technocentric approach to nature but one thing is certain, the pastoral will remain the means to our seeing, understanding and commenting on the world around us. As the art critic Peter Fuller wrote, the Pastoral is "one of the few symbolic ideas in our culture from which we can draw some hope. It stands for a continuing, secular image of man's relationship to himself, of reconciliation between man and man, and, indeed, between man and nature".[53] Today the vision of Arcadia remains as alluring and satisfying as ever.

Notes and References

1. Buell, L., *The Environmental Imagination.* Belnap Press of Harvard University Press, Cambridge, MA, 1995, p. 32.
2. Alpers, P., *What is Pastoral?,* University of Chicago Press, London, 1996. Quoted in Joachim, M., *Ecological Code: a collage of quantum informatics in living automata cities,* Archinode Studio, New York.
3. Worster, D., *Nature's Economy.* Cambridge University Press, Cambridge, 1985, p. 2.
4. The term ecology itself is of recent origin having been coined by the German biologist Ernst Haeckel in 1866. The term ecosystem was first defined by the English ecologist Arthur Tansley, in reference to the plant communities, later it was developed in America by the Odum brothers into the systems approach, which allowed the study of the flow of energy and materials through ecological systems.
5. Worster, D., *op. cit.,* pp. 22–3.
6. Sean, P. B., 'Ecology – a subversive subject', *Bioscience* 14(7), 11–13, 1964.
7. Orr, D. W., *Ecological Literacy: education and the transition to a postmodern world.* SUNY Press, Albany, 1992, p. 24.
8. June 2012 on occasion of release of *Global Environmental Outlook.* 5th edition, UNEP.
9. Orr, D. W., *op. cit.,* p. 24.
10. Harrison, F., *The Living Landscape.* Mandarin, London, 1991, p. 13.
11. Worster, D., *op. cit.,* p. 267. Pinchot believed passionately that the world was "badly in need of managing, and was convinced that science could teach man to improve on nature, to make its processes more efficient and its crops more abundant". His aim was to maximise the productivity of those major resources in which man had a direct and immediate interest. His outlook on nature paid little attention to ecological considerations emerging at the time and he was strongly opposed to the preservation of nature simply for the sake of wilderness or scenery. An outlook that brought him into conflict with John Muir, founder of the Sierra Club.
12. Worster, D., *op. cit.,* p. 285.
13. www.thewildernesssociety.org.
14. Leopold, A., *A Sand County Almanac.* Oxford University Press, Oxford, 1949.
15. Worster, D., *op. cit.,* p. 286.
16. *Ibid.,* p. 287.
17. *Ibid.,* pp. 288–9.
18. Kroll, G., *Rachel Carson – Silent Spring: a brief history of ecology as a subversive subject.* *www.*onlineethics.org: National Academy of Engineering. Retrieved November 4, 2007.
19. Sayre, L., *Georgic Apocalypse: from Virgil to Silent Spring.* www.yale.edu/agrarianstudies/colloqpapers/24sayre.pdf
20. Day Lewis, C. (trans.), *Virgil: the Eclogues, the Georgics.* Oxford University Press, London, 1983, p. 104. This is the source of all quotations from the Georgics in this Chapter.
21. Sayre, L., *op. cit.,* p. 15.
22. *Ibid.,* p. 16.
23. *Ibid.,* p. 16.
24. *Ibid.,* p. 3.
25. O'Riordan, T., *Environmentalism.* Pion, London, 1976, p. 1.
26. www.agnesdenesstudio.com/writings.html. For 3 years, from 1987 to 1990, the harvested grain was taken to 28 cities world wide in *The International Show for the End of World Hunger,* organised by the Minnesota Museum of Modern Art, visitors were invited to take the Wheatfield seeds and plant them across the world.

27. King, E. A., 'The landscape in art: nature in the crosshairs of an age-old debate'. *Artes Magazine* 16, November 2010.

28. *Ibid.*

29. Gifford, T., *Pastoral.* Routledge, London, 1999, p. 148.

30. Gifford, T., 'Judith Wright's Poetry and the turn to the post-pastoral'. *Australian Humanities Review* issue 48, Australian National University Press, 2010, p. 75.

31. Gifford, T., *Green Voices.* Manchester University Press, Manchester, 1995, p. 121.

32. Bush, B., *Nature explored in pastoral and anti-pastoral poetry.* www.helium.com/items/369908.

33. www.poemhunter.com/poem/the-city-planners.

34. Hatch, R. B., 'Margaret Atwood, The Land, and Ecology', in *Margaret Atwood: works and impact*, edited by R. M. Nischik, Camden House, 2000, p. 184. Atwood came to appreciate this phenomenon during her childhood when the family spent the summer vacation in the woods of Ontario and Quebec.

35. www.poemfoundation.org/poem177290.

36. Hatch, R. B., *op. cit.,* p. 182.

37. Buell L., *op. cit.,* p. 267.

38. www.frontporchrepublic.com/2011/03/wendell-berrys-new-agrarian-remedies-urbanprospects/.

39. Jacobs, J., *The Death and Life of Great American Cities.* Vintage Books, New York, p. 144.

40. Van der Ryn, S. and Cowan, S., *Ecological Design.* Island Press, Washington DC, 2007, p. 33.

41. *Ibid.,* p. 33.

42. *Ibid.,* p. 25.

43. Gewertz, K., Landscape Alchemist. *The Harvard Gazette,* 6 February, 1997.

44. www.hargreaves.com

45. LDA Design was established in the 1980s by Professor Robert Tregay.

46. Neil Mattinson, senior partner at LDA Design. Quoted in Wainwright, O., *London 2012 Olympic Park.* www.bdonline.co.uk. Accessed 25 July 2012.

47. Tregay, R., *The Enterprising Community*, Landscape Institute Conference, 2008.

48. Boland, M., 'Crissy Field: a new model for managing urban parklands'. *Places,* July 2003.

49. Meyer. E., 'Sustaining beauty. The performance of appearance'. *Journal of Landscape Architecture,* Spring 2008, pp. 6–23.

50. *Ibid.,* p. 18.

51. 'Eco-Revelatory Design: Nature Constructed/Nature Revealed'. originated at the Department of Landscape Architecture, University of Illinois.

52. Turner, F., 'The landscape of disturbance', *Wilson Quarterly* Spring, 1998. *Ecological Turbulence and the Hadean Arcadia.* Frederick Turner's blog.

53. Quoted in Harrison, F., *op. cit.* pp. 17–18.

CHAPTER NINETEEN

Final Thoughts

This book has shown that there is an alternative landscape history and though for many Virgil would be regarded as among the 'dead white European males', Arcadia and the pastoral remain deeply embedded in western culture. It remains fundamental to the way we see and comprehend the world around us and for that reason this 'landscape tradition' can provide understanding and inspiration for all those who design, manage or simply enjoy landscape. As well as tracing the historical development of the Arcadian Vision the book has shown how those artists, writers, poets, designers, teachers and many others who have contributed to the advance of the pastoral tradition were strongly influenced by childhood experiences of the natural world. Olmsted's understanding of the importance of the 'unconscious influence' remains highly relevant. A recent study of creative designers showed many spent a lot of time during their childhood years, playing on vacant lots, where "Away from the all-too-carefully designed order, they could experience in the left-over spaces, weeds, bugs, and the cycle of unmanicured seasons. Here they had space to watch and dream." These experiences of nature sowed the seeds of a personal vision of Arcadia which later as writers, artists, and designers they sought to recapture in their own creative way.

Many of us share similar childhood experiences in the countryside as well as on the vacant lot but in modern society those experiences are becoming less and less possible. In the twenty-first century most people live in an urban environment that has become denaturised and, in these circumstances, they too are likely to develop denaturised imaginations. Many hours are spent in homes, schools, offices and work places sealed from the elements and natural processes; where there are few clues about climate, the sun's position or seasonal change. It is an artificial world in which the pipes and cables that bring fuel, electricity and water to the city are hidden from view, waste is transported away and rainwater drains into sewers. Food is produced in an unknown place and appears on supermarket shelves processed and wrapped. And as these life support systems of food, water, energy, waste and sewage become ever more intricate and hidden, it has become more difficult to understand or question them. Whilst nature is increasingly experienced on the television or as a computor visualisation. Living and working in this disconnected environment, it is to be expected that some sensitivity towards nature is lost – we have learnt detachment. This sense of detachment, and its consequences, was described by John Tallmadge in article entitled *Resistance to Nature*:

... urban landscapes serve as a constant reminder. And this reveals a more sinister form of resistance. Every time I walk past the unmowed lot with its blue chicory, dandelions, and thickets of amur honeysuckle, I am reminded of how severely we humans have mauled the local ecology, driving away the animals, tearing up the ground, introducing all sorts of aggressive alien species. Once started down this path, it's hard to stop, hard not to think of the extermination of the buffalo, the decimation of prairie flora, the shaving and burning of ancient forests. The landscape begins to look like a world of wounds, and its history begins to look like a pattern of war, enslavement, and genocide, where all creatures are reduced to means for human ends regardless of their own ultimate concerns. These are not happy thoughts, nor are the feelings they evoke. It helps me repress them to think of this urban land as somehow less natural because it has been 'impacted' or 'spoiled'. Maybe it's not really nature at all, not a real ecosystem, just a bunch of weeds and exotics mixed up with human junk. It doesn't count; it's not worth dealing with. I can ignore it. Such thinking makes urban nature invisible ... . Beneath it lies the old desire to escape from history and avoid responsibility for our sins.[1]

But does this matter? Should we not accept that as an urban society our experience of nature will be confined to an occasional trip to the countryside, a walk in the park, or somewhere to be viewed through the window of a car or train? Instead of nature being the life force that shapes our development, can it be reduced to an incidental experience? In *The Living Landscape* Fraser Harrison foresaw a world in which this had happened, and with it came a nightmarish vision of a landscape drained of its magic;

> ... inhabited by a population which sees only what *is* there and responds only to nature's shadows transmitted onto screens and traced in books. I foresee a countryside stripped of poetry and supervised by a society which prefers the geometry of agriculture to the wayward tangle on its shrinking margins. I see a countryside impervious to symbolic suggestion and dead even to sentimentality, a blank landscape confronting a blind nation. Then nature will be meaningless, a mere perpetration of animal and vegetable energy ... fatuously working out its botanical process.[2]

Childhood experiences

Harrison's concern was that nature could disappear and no one will be alarmed because they are not be aware its existence, a fear shared by Jac. Thijsse in the Netherlands at the beginning of the last century. It is fanciful to suppose this could really happen but there are reasons to fear that we are already on the way to such a nightmare. There is a generation of children today who have had only a limited experience of nature. A recent report by The National Trust, *Natural Childhood*, (2012)[3] confirmed the widespread perception that our nation's children have a largely screen-based lifestyle and the growth of virtual, as opposed to reality-based, play, has had a profound effect on children's lives; indeed, it has been called by Pyle "the extinction of experience".[4] In many peoples' opinion, this screen-based lifestyle is the reasons why today's children no longer engage with the natural world. It is a strange paradox that at a time when television has delivered a greater knowledge of plants, animals, habitats and ecological systems than at any previous time in human history, we have a generation who no longer know how to respond emotionally and philosophically to nature. And whilst it is easy to draw the conclusion that the lure of this screen-based entertainment is the main reason why children rarely go outdoors, the National Trust report points out it could also be a symptom of what Richard Louv refers to as "well-meaning, protective house arrest".[5] For a variety of reasons, not least a fear of dangers imagined or real, children wait to be taken to the park or woods by their parents in the car for an hour or two's experience of the natural world, an interlude quickly forgotten under the welter of other distractions at home. As a result children are suffering from what Louv termed Nature Deficit Disorder, a condition that describes the human costs of alienation from nature, among them a diminished use of the senses, attention difficulties, and higher rates of physical and emotional illnesses. Sound scientific evidence indicates that contact with nature in urban areas plays an essential part in improving mental health and restoring psychological well-being.[6] In Harrison's words;

> ... we, as a species, have an indispensable need of an intimate and harmonious relationship with nature , and that if we are deprived of that relationship we will be quite unable to achieve the level of personal and communal wellbeing which is necessary for a a civilised life.[7]

Given that it was Ruskin who believed the character of a people was determined by their experience of their part of the earth, it is appropriate the National Trust[8] should be highlighting the problems of sensory deprivation in children. They have listed 50 experiences all children should have before they are 11½ – unsurprisingly a generation ago these would have been an unwritten description of spontaneous play. But are these isolated experiences likely to instill a feeling for, and a response to the landscape? We learn about our world, and our place within it, by constant exposure to nature. In the early years children are not aware of the landscape in its totality: "the child's mind does not readily deal in generalities and abstractions, their world is made up of the singular and unique. Their eyes grasp only one thing at a time and have no facility for unifying the bits of land and sky into the single sweep that is landscape".[9] It is only after constant experience of the natural world, that as the child grows to maturity, a coherent vision of landscape forms. This is part of an evolutionary process that has been continuous since the time of our earliest ancestors;

> The annual cycle of plant life, the variety of behaviour and appearance in animals, the vicissitudes of the weather, the motion of the stars and planets, the power and regularity of the sun, the mysterious variability of the moon – all these natural features provided material for the symbolic systems, the mythologies, which primitive humans invented in order to shape their understanding of the world and their place in it.[10]

Without these experiences a complete and fulsome life is not possible and the individual must inevitably be impoverished. Taking the simple example of rain falling on his study window, Terry Gifford, in his book on the Pastoral, asked what images this conjured up in the mind of the reader.[11] For many rain is considered a nuisance, experienced only fleetingly as one runs from house to car, school or office, and they cannot appreciate the complexity of the smell, taste, feel, sight and sound of rain in its many moods and expressions. Gifford's point was that without a direct experience of nature it is not possible to empathise with those artists, composers and writers who have sought to explore, interpret and understand the natural world. How can one relate to the pastoral delights of Shelley's *Ode To a Sky Lark* or Vaughan Williams's *The Lark Ascending* if one has not absorbed, subliminally, the magic of the bird as it soars above the fields of one's childhood? Without those experiences, poetry, music, painting, for all their beauty, remain mere words, sounds or images.

We are at a critical time. As H. G. Wells once said "we are in a race between education and catastrophe". "The race", said David Orr, "will be decided in all the places, including the classrooms, that foster ecological imagination, critical thinking, awareness of connections, independent thought, and good heart'.

Like Henry Thoreau, Orr believes the most important classroom is nature itself and "if we hope to be educating the Rachel Carsons and Aldo Leopolds of the twenty-first century, we must design our schools and curricula accordingly".[12] Thoreau's description of those natural features and vegetation that make a city beautiful carry a truth that is even more relevant today and his warning that those who do not foresee the use of these things: "but legislates chiefly for oxen, as it were ..."[13] should be heeded by those involved in "both urban planning and the creation of new settlements", such as those "planned in the Thames Gateway area of the United Kingdom".[14]

Conclusion

This book has shown how our evolving perspective of nature has constantly altered our Arcadian vision, resulting in changes to art, literature and the design of landscape. Nature was once feared. Then, as the kaleidoscope changed, it became something to be tamed. Later it was viewed with pleasure. Today there is a responsibility, increasingly shared by society at large, to ensure that nature does not recede from our lives as we begin to recognise that the natural world is a vital partner in our survival. Those examples of pioneering innovations in the Netherlands, at Warrington New Town and more recently at Crissy Fields and the London Olympic Park show how it is possible to recreate and restore nature to the urban environment providing, in Robert Tregay's words, "Nature on the doorstep". Such eco-revelatory design involves ecologically sound practice, in planning, design, organic agriculture and involves many other spheres of poetry, literature and art, whilst not forgetting the involvement of local communities. It challenges, in the best pastoral tradition, conventional design which seeks to cover-up our dependence on nature with bland solutions, and it provides an alternative to the way we manage our human habitat. So where once Virgil offered us two visions of Arcadia, one looking back at a golden age in a land of perpetual spring; the other, the happy life of the farmer content to work the land and bring in the harvest, today there is a new vision of Arcadia, one that looks to the future. An Arcadia in which we work in harmony with nature to create a sustainable human habitat, only when that happens will William Morris's ideal of "a life lived, not only in harmony with nature but one that fulfills the natural in [our]selves" be realised.

Notes and References

1. Tallmadge, J., 'Resistance to nature', *Michigan Quarterly Review* 40(1), Winter 2001, Issue: Re-imagining Place. University of Michigan Library, Ann Arbor MI.
2. Harrison, F., *The Living Landscape*. Mandarin, London 1991 p. 42.
3. Moss. S., *Natural Childhood*. National Trust, 2012.
4. Pyle, R., 'Nature matrix: reconnecting people and nature', *Oryx* 37(2), 2003, 206–14. Quoted in *Natural Childhood*, National Trust, 2012.
5. Louv, R., *Last Child in the Woods*, 2005. Quoted in *Natural Childhood*, National Trust, 2012.
6. Douglas, I. 'Urban greenspace and mental health' (prepared for UK MAB Urban Forum), May 2004, pp. 1–14. Mass, J., *et al.* 'Green space, urbanity, and health: how strong is the relation?', *Journal of Epidemiology and Community Health* 60(7), 2006, 587–92.
7. Harrison, F., *op. cit.* p. 111.
8. Ruskin was a guiding influenced for Octavia Hill and Canon Hardwicke Rawnsley, two of the founders of the National Trust, intensifying their love nature and a belief in its restorative powers.
9. Harrison, F., *op. cit.*, p. 11.
10. *Ibid.*, p. 38.
11. Gifford, T., *Green Voices: understanding contemporary nature poetry*. Manchester University Press, Manchester, 1999, p. 9.
12. Orr, D. W., 'Teaching Ecological Imagination'. *New Dimensions* 12 March 2006.
13. in Dreiser, T., *The Living Thoughts of Thoreau*. Premier Printing, New York, 1958, p. 145.
14. Douglas, I., *op. cit.*, p. 10.

Timeline

Origins of Arcadia and the Pastoral	Theocritus born Syracuse, Sicily. The pastoral poems, the *Idylls* written in Alexandria(?), Egypt.
The Arcadia defined and refined	Virgil born near Mantua in Cisalpine Gaul. Began writing the *Eclogues* in 42 BC; and the *Georgics* between 37–29 BC. Dies of fever 19 BC. in Brundisium harbour.
Pastoral living	Pliny the Younger, AD 62(?)–113 lawyer, author, magistrate in Rome. Describes his villa urbana in *letters to Domitius Apollinaris*.
Nature becomes evil	AD 387 Augustine of Hippo converts to christianity; influences the development of western Christianity – Nature is regarded as morally corrupt. The Messianic *Eclogue* ensures Virgil's survival.
Rediscovery of Nature and Virgil	Petrach born in Tuscan city of Arezzo. 1336 first to climb a mountain for pleasure – Mont Ventoux. Commissions a copy of Virgil's poetry with a bucolic frontispiece by Simone Martine.
The Renaissance. Florence becomes the cultural centre of Europe	Cosimo de Medici rules Florence from 1434 to his death in 1464. Establishes Academy for the arts and sciences at the Villa Careggi in 1462. Succeeded by grandson, Lorenzo the Magnificent (1449–92). Mystic cult of Pan Medicus derived from Virgil.
AD 1450–1600 Venetian School Venice becomes a centre for Renaissance culture	Giovanni Bellini *St. Francis in Ecstasy* (1475–80). Jacopo Sannazarro *Arcadia* (1480). Francesco Colonna *Hypnerotomachia Poliphili* (1499). Giorgione *Fete Champetre?* (1510). Titian Noli me Tangere (1576); Landscape with a milkmaid (1530–50).
Arcadia in the new world	European colonization of eastern North America in late 16th century. 1524 di Verrazzano names coast of north Virginia Arcadia.
1605 Camillo Borghese elected Pope Paul V	1605 Cardinal Scipione, the cardinal-nephew commissions architect Flaminio Ponzio to build the Villa Borghese, Rome. 1613 purchases 80 ha estate Villa Mondragone in the Frascati hills; enlarged to 8094 ha of vineyards, forests and pastures by 1620. Estate arranged and managed as an embodiment of the Arcadian Pastoral to establish the Borgheses' ancestral pedigree. Pope Paul dies 1621.
Treaty of Utrecht (1579) and the beginnings of the Dutch Golden Age (1581–1715)	Carel van Mander Het Schilderboek (1604) encourages artists to combine antique pastoral with contemporary details. Frans Hals *Isaak Abraham Massa and Beatreix van der Lean* (1622). Early 17th century Country houses and pastoral *hofdichten* poetry.

Realism in Dutch painting	Claus Visscher *Pleasant Places* (1611). Jan Van Goyen *View of Haarlem and Haarlemmer Meer* (1646); paintings of ordinary Dutch scenes. Paulus Potter *Young Bull* (1647) symbol of patriotic and and economic pride. Rembrandt combines pastoral vision with real and imaginary scenes of Dutch landscape.
The Ideal Pastoral Landscape	1625 Claude (Gellée) Lorrain arrives in Rome. Sketches *en plein air* with Nicolas Poussin developing his landscape style. From 1637 until his death in 1682 paints his highly influential paintings of the Ideal Arcadian landscape.
America as Nature's garden	Robert Beverley *History and Present State of Virginia* (1705).
England – changing attitudes to Nature and the landscape	Thomas Burnett *The Sacred Theory of the Earth* (1681). Isaac Newton *Principia* (1685/6). Anthony Cooper (Earl of Shaftesbury) *The Characteristics, The Moralists* (1711). 1709–11 Joseph Addison, essayist, produces *The Tatler* (with Richard Steele); *The Spectator* 1711–12. Essays on Gardens influence debate on natural gardens. 1699–1712 Charles Howard, 3rd Earl of Carlisle commissions John Vanbrugh to design and build Castle Howard; estate laid out in a classical, landscape style.
The Arcadian landscape	Lord Burlington Chiswick House (1729) in neo-palladian style, earliest example of English landscape garden, designed by William Kent. James Thomson *The Seasons* (1730). 1737 William Kent designs Rousham, Oxfordshire.
The English country gentleman and landscape garden	Thomas Gainsborough *Mr and Mrs Andrews* (1750). William Shenstone The Leasowes 1743–63. *Unconnected Thoughts On Gardening* (1764). Escape to Arcadia *From* 1751 to 1784 Lancelot 'Capability' Brown 'improves' over 170 landscape gardens. Blenheim Palace (1764). Thomas Whately *Observations on Modern Gardening* (1770).
The Picturesque – tours of the British Isles	William Gilpin; *Observations on the River Wye and several parts of South Wales, etc., relative chiefly to Picturesque Beauty; made in the summer of 1770* (1782); *Observations on Mountains and Lakes of Cumberland and Westmorland and the West of England* (1786); *Scottish Highlands* (1789). Herefordshire landowners: Uvedale Price-Foxley. *Essay on the Picturesque* (1794) – and Richard Payne Knight – Downton Castle. *The Landscape* (1794), *Analytical Inquiry into the Principles of Taste* (1806). Humphry Repton writings on Landscape Gardening (1795, 1803, 1816).
The American Pastoral Dream	Thomas Jefferson starts Monticello (1768); *Notes on Virginia* (1785) 1786 Jefferson tours English gardens.
The Romantic movement	William Wordsworth – the 'hard pastoral'. 1798 Moves to Dove Cottage with sister Dorothy. *Lines written a few miles above Tintern Abbey* (1798); *The Prelude* (1798); *Michael* (1800); *Home at Grasmere* (1810). John Constable – the soft pastoral. 1799 enters Royal Academy. First painting exhibited – *Dedham Vale Morning* 1811. Moves permanently to London 1816. *Haywain* (1821).

The New England Transcendentalists	1836 Ralph Waldo Emerson – the Transcendental Club; publishes essay *Nature*. 1845 Henry David Thoreau moves to Walden Pond. *Walden; or, Life in the Woods* (1854). George Innes *Lackawanna Railway* (1855). 1868 John Muir arrives Sierra Nevada mountains. Campaigns to protect Yosemite and wilderness. 1871 Muir meets Emerson in Yosemite. *Our National Parks* (1901). 1903 Muir with President Theodore Roosevelt in Yosemite National Park. 1906 National Park legislation.
Pastoral painting and parks	1826 Thomas Cole begins to summer in Catskills. *View on the Catskill – Early Autumn* (1837); *River in the Catskills* (1844). Founder Hudson River School of landscape painting. 1844–6 mentors Frederic Church. *West Rock, New Haven, Connecticut* (1849). 1850 Frederick Law Olmsted visits England, Birkenhead Park. *Walks and Talks of an American Farmer in England* (1852). 1858 Central Park, New York (designed with Calvert Vaux). 1872–1895 Olmsted's firm carries out 550 projects, including many parks and parkways in the pastoral style. Olmsted Important early leader of conservation movement in US. Active in preservation of Yosemite and Niagara Falls. 1898 One of the founders of the American Society of Landscape Architects.
Utopian Pastoral and the Garden City	John Ruskin leads reaction to machine. *Sesame and Lilies* (1865); *Crown of Wild Olive* (1866). William Morris trains as an architect before forming a company with Edward Burne-Jones in 1861. Leading figure in 'arts and crafts' movement. 1859 commissions Philip Webb to design Red House, Bexleyheath, Kent. *The Earthly Paradise* (1868). 1869 Morris purchases Kelmscott Manor. 1884 Helps form the Socialist League and writes its manifesto. 1890 *News from Nowhere*. Ebenezer Howard *Tomorrow: A Peaceful Path to Real Reform* (1898), reissued as *Garden Cities of To-Morrow* (1902). 1903 Letchworth Garden City. Parker and Unwin appointed architects. 1906 Hampstead Garden Suburb followed by widespread suburban development.
First World War: Pastoral *in memoriam*	Nostalgia for nature. A. E. Housman *A Shropshire Lad* (1896); Richard Jeffries; Kenneth Grahame *Wind in the Willows* (1908). The Georgian Poets include Walter de la Mare, John Masefield and Rupert Brooke *Georgian Poetry Vols 1–3* published between 1912–17. Ralph Vaughan Williams *A Lark Ascending* (1914). Edward Thomas *The Sun Used to Shine. As the team's head brass* (1916). John William Street *Matthew Copse* (1916). Paul Nash *The Menin Road* (1919). Edmund Blunden *Undertones of War* (1928). Imperial War graves Commission 1917 Lutyens designs the War Stone. Vita Sackville-West *The Land* (1927).

Modern movements	1917 de Stijl; Pieter Mondrian geometrical abstract paintings 1917–1944. T. S. Eliot *The Waste Land* (1922). Le Corbusier *Villa Savoie* (1929). Van Eesteren – the Functional City; *Extension Plan for Amsterdam* (1935). 1937 Amsterdam Bos Park. Christopher Tunnard *Bentley Wood* (1928) – a functional garden; *Gardens in the Modern Landscape* (1938).
Battle for the Countryside and Legislation	1891 T. A. Leonard walks in the lake district; Co-operative Holiday Association (1889). Plotlands; Peacehaven 1915. 1926 Campaign for Preservation of Rural England. Clough William Ellis *England the Octopus* (1928). 1932 Kinder trespass. 1947 Town and Country Planning act. 1949 National Parks and Access to the Countryside Act. 1951 Peak District National Park. 1955 Environment Act.
Ecological Landscapes	Corbusier Villa Radieuse (1924); Amsterdam Bijlmermeer re-adoption of Bos park techniques. Louis Le Roy The Natural City – experimental wild landscapes; Heerenveen (1966); *Natuur uitschakelen; natuur inschakelen (Switch on nature, switch off nature)* (1973). Nature-like landscapes, Delft, Haarlem, The Hague and Gouda. Nan Fairbrother *New Lives New Landscapes* (1972). Allan Ruff. *Holland and the Ecological Landscape* (1979). 1980s Ecological landscapes; Warrington New Town. Robert Tregay and Roland Gustavsson *Oakwood's New Landscape* (1983).
New Directions, New Visions	Aldo Leopold *Sand County Almanac* (1949); Rachel Carson *Silent Spring* (1962); T. O'Riordan *Environmentalism* (1976). Eco-Art; Agnes Denes *The Wheatfield* (1982). Terry Gifford post-pastoral 1995 *Pastoral* (1999); Van der Ryan and S. Cowan *Ecological Design* (1996). 1998 Eco-Revelatory Design, University of Illinois. Hargreaves, Crissy Fields, San Francisco reopened 2001. LDA. London Olympic Park 2012.

Bibliography

Adams, W. H. (1983) *Jefferson's Monticello*. Abbeville Press, New York.

Addison, J. (1709) Essay no. 161. *Tatler*. Thursday, April 20, p. 157.

Addison, J. (1711) *The Spectator*. 5 and 6 March.

Addison, J. (1712) *The Spectator*. No. 414. Wednesday, June 25.

Addison, J. (1712) *The Spectator*. No. 477. 6 September.

Allinson, K. (2008) *Architects and Architecture of London*. Architectural Press, London.

Andrews, M. (1989) *The Search for the Picturesque*. Scolar Press, Aldershot.

Avery, K. J. (2005) *Treasures from Olana*. Cornell University Press, London.

Bacon, F. (1626) [1901] 'New Atlantis'. In *Ideal Commonwealths*, rev. edn by H. Morley. P. F. Collier & Son, New York.

Barlow, A. (2000) *The Great War in British Literature*. Cambridge University Press, Cambridge.

Barrell, J. (1980) *The Dark Side of the Landscape*. Cambridge University Press, Cambridge.

Benes, M. and Harris, D. S. (2001) *Villas and Gardens in Early Modern Italy and France*. Cambridge University Press, Cambridge.

Beveridge, C. E. (n.d.) *Olmsted – His Essential Theory*. National Association for Olmsted Parks.

Beverly, R. (1705) *The History and Present State of Virginia*. R. Parker, London.

Blunden, E. (1928) *Undertones of War*. www.archive.org.

Boland, M. (2003) Crissy Field: A new model for managing urban parklands. *Places*, July.

Boulton, J. T. (ed.) (1997) *The Letters of D. H. Lawrence. Vol. 1 1901–13*. Cambridge University Press, Cambridge.

Brett, R. L. (1951) *The Third Earl of Shaftesbury*. Hutchinson University Press, London.

Brooke, R. (1999) 'An Unusual Young Man'. *New Statesman*. 29 November.

Brown, C. (1986) *Dutch Landscape: the early years*. The National Gallery, London.

Brown, J. (1990) *Eminent Gardeners*. Viking, London.

Buell, L. (1995) *The Environmental Imagination*. The Belnap Press, Harvard University Press, Cambridge MA.

Bunce, M. (1994) *The Countryside Ideal*. Routledge, London.

Bush, B. *Nature Explored in Pastoral and Anti-pastoral Poetry*. www.helium.com/items/369908.

Butterfield, D. (n.d.) *Classical Manuscripts at St Gall and Reichenau*. The Carolingian Libraries of St Gall and Reichenau. www.stgallplan.org.

Cafritz, R. C., Gowing, L. and Rosand, D. (eds) (1988) *Places of Delight: the Pastoral Landscape*. The Phillips Collection and Weidenfeld & Nicolson, London.

Calhoun, B. (1975) *The Pastoral Vision of William Morris*. University of Georgia, Athens.

Campbell, K. (2007) *Icons of 20th Century Design*. Frances Lincoln, London.

Carré. J. (ed.) (1994) *The Crisis of Courtesy: studies in the conduct-book in Britain, 1600–1900*. E. J. Brill, New York.

Clark, H. F. (1980) *The English Landscape Garden*. Alan Sutton, Gloucester.

Clark, K. (1952) *Landscape into Art*. John Murray, London.

Clifford, D. (1962) *A History of Garden Design*. Faber and Faber, London.

Clouston, B. (ed.) (1977) *Landscape Design with Plants*. Heinemann London.

Cole, T. (1836) Essay on American scenery. *The American Monthly Magazine*, January.

Constant., Nieuw Urbanisme. *Provo* no. 9, 12 May 1966.

Corner, J. (ed.) (1999) *Recovering Landscape: essays on contemporary landscape architecture*. Princeton, Architectural Press, New York.

Day Lewis, C. (1983) (trans.) *Virgil: The Eclogues, The Georgics*. Oxford University Press, London.

Dodsley, J. (1765) *The Works and Prose of William Shenstone, esq.* (2 vols) Vol. 1. London.

Douglas, I. (2004) *Urban Greenspace and Mental Health* (prepared for UK MAB Urban Forum).

Drabble, M. (1984) *A Writer's Britain*. Thames and Hudson, London.

Dreiser, T. (1958) *The Living Thoughts of Thoreau*. Premier printing, New York.

Ehrlich, T. L. (2002) *Landscape and Identity in Early Rome: villa culture at Frascati in the Borghese era*. Cambridge University Press, Cambridge in association with American Academy, Rome.

Emerson, R. W. (1954) *Five Essays on Man and Nature*. Edited by R. Spiller. AHM Publishing Corporation, Illinois.

Evelyn-White, H. G. (1914) *Hesiod: The Homeric Hymns and Homerica*. Loeb Classical Library: revised edn. Harvard University Press, Cambridge, Massachusetts.

Fairbrother, N. (1970) *New Lives New Landscapes*. Architectural Press, London.

Falconer, R. Sir (1936) St Paul at the Tomb of Virgil, *University of Toronto Quarterly* 6(1), October.

Farrell, J. and Putnam, M. (eds) (2010) *A Companion to Virgil's Aeneid and its Tradition*. Wiley-Blackwell, Chichester.

Fein, A. (ed.) (1968) *Landscape into Cityscape: Frederick Law Omlsted's plans for a greater New York City*. Cornell University Press, Ithaca NY.

Fielding, H. (1751) *An Enquiry into the Causes of the Late Increase of Robbers*. A. Millar, London.

Frazer, A. (ed.) (1998) *The Villa Urbana*. University of Pennsylvania Museum, Philadelphia.

Fussell, P. (1997) *The Great War and Modern Memory*. Oxford University Press, New York.

Gardiner, J. (2011) *The Thirties*. Harper Press, London.

Geurst, J. (2010) *Cemeteries of the Great War by Sir Edwin Lutyens*. 010 Publishers, Rotterdam.

Gewertz, K. (1997) Landscape alchemist. *The Harvard Gazette*, 6 February.

Gibson, W. S. (2000) *Pleasant Places*. University of California Press, London.

Gideon, S. (1974) *Space, Time and Architecture*. Harvard. University Press, Cambridge MA.

Gifford, T. (1995) *Green Voices*. Manchester University Press, Manchester.

Gifford, T. (1999) *Pastoral*. Routledge, London.

Gifford, T. (2010) *Judith Wright's Poetry and the Turn to the Post-Pastoral*. Australian National University E Press.

Gilpin, W. (1748) *A Dialogue Upon the Gardens of the Right Honourable the Lord Viscount Cobham at Stow*. www.faculty.bsc.edu/jtatter.gilpin.html

Gilpin, W. (1768) *An Essay on Prints*. T. Cadell and W. Davies, London.

Gilpin, W. (1834) *Remarks on Forest Scenery and other Woodland Views*. Vol. 1. Fraser & Co., Edinburgh.

Grahame, K. (1915) *Wind in the Willows*. Charles Scribner's Sons, New York.

Grant, D. (1951) *James Thomson: poet of* The Seasons. Cresset Press, London.

Gombrich, E. H. (1971) *Norm and Form*. Phaidon, Oxford.

Griffin, J. *Virgil*. (1986) Oxford University Press, Oxford.

Halperin, D. (1954) *Before Pastoral*. Yale University, London.

Hardner, H. (ed.) (1974) *The New Oxford Book of Verse*. Book Club Associates, Bungay, Suffolk.

Hardy, D. and Ward, C. (1984) *Arcadia for All*. Mansell, London.

Harrington, R. (1994) *Nature Dressed and Redressed: William Shenstone, the Leasowes and the English landscape garden in transition c.1740–c.1763*. Lincoln College, University of Oxford, Oxford.

Harrison, F. (1986) *The Living Landscape*. Mandarin, London.

Heaney, S. (2006) The triumph of spirit. *The Guardian*. 11 February.

Heely, J. (1982) *Letters on the Beauties of Hagley, Envil, and The Leasowes*. Garland Publishers, New York.

Hillman, J. (1992) *Revisioning Psychology*. Harper Row, New York.

Hook, J. (1984) *Lorenzo de Medici: a historical biography*. H. Hamilton, London.

Housman, A. E. (1919) *A Shropshire Lad XL*. Bartleby. com.

Howard, E. (1965) *Garden Cities of To-Morrow*. MIT Press, Massachusetts.

Howat, J. K. (2005) *Frederic Church*. Yale University Press, New Haven.

Hubbard, T. K. (1922) *Frederick Law Olmsted, Landscape Architect, 1822–1903: Early Years and experiences, together with biographical notes*. G. P. Putnam's Sons, New York.

Hunt, J. D. and Willis, P. (eds) (1975) *The Genius of the Place: The English Landscape Garden, 1620–1820*. Paul Elek, London.

Hunt, J. D. (1976) *The Figure in the Landscape*. John Hopkins University Press, London.

Hunt, J. D. (1987) *William Kent Landscape Garden Designer*. W. Zwemmer, London.

Hunt, J. D. and de Jong, E. (eds) (1988) The Anglo-

Dutch garden in the age of William and Mary. *Journal of Garden History* 8(2 and 3) April–September.

Hunt, J. D. (1994) *Gardens and the Picturesque: Studies in the History of Landscape Architecture.* MIT Press Cambridge, Massachusetts.

Hussey, C. (1927) *The Picturesque: studies in a point of view.* G. P. Putnam's Sons, London.

Hussey, C. (2004) *The Picturesque.* Routledge, London.

Imbert, D. (1993) *The Modernist Garden in France.* Yale University Press, Princeton.

Jefferson, T. (1853) *Notes on the State of Virginia.* J. W. Randolph, Richmond VA.

Johnston, I. (1996) *T. S. Eliot's* The Love Song of J. Alfred Prufrock *and* The Waste Land. Vancouver Island University, Vancouver.

Jones, F. (2011) *Virgil's Garden.* Bristol Classical Press, London.

Kettering, A. (1983) *The Dutch Arcadia.* Boydell Press, Ipswich.

Kimball, F. (1968) *Thomas Jefferson Architect: original designs in the Coolridge Collection of the Massachusetts Historical Society.* Da Capa Press, New York.

King, E. A. (2010) The landscape in art: nature in the crosshairs of an age-old debate. *Artes Magazine* 16, November.

Kirkham, M. (1986) *The Imagination of Edward Thomas.* Cambridge University Press, Cambridge.

Klaus, S. I. (2004) *A Modern Arcadia: Frederick Law Olmsted Jr. and the Plan for Forest Hills Gardens.* University of Massachusetts Press, Amherst.

Knight, R. P. (1795) *The Landscape: a didactic poem.* Publ. W. Bulmer. Repub. 1972 by Gregg International, Farnborough.

Knight, R. P. (1805) *An Analytical Inquiry into the Principles of Taste.* T. Payne, London.

Knight, W. (1944) *Roman Vergil.* Faber and Faber, London.

Kroes, R. (1968) Recalling the Netherlands in 1968: trendsetter or follower? *European Journal of American Studies* 2000, May.

Kroll, G. (2007) *Rachel Carson – Silent Spring: a brief history of ecology as a subversive subject.* www.onlineethics.org. National Academy of Engineering. Retrieved November 4.

Landwehr en Sipkes (1974) *Wildeplantentuin,* Instituut voor Naturrbeschermingseducatie, Amsterdam.

Le Roy, L. (1973) *Natuur uitschakelen; natuur inschakelen.* Ankh-Hermes, Deventer.

Levesque, C. (1955) *Journey Through Landscape in Seventeenth Century Holland.* Pennsylvania State University, Philadelphia.

MacFadyen, D. (1933) *Sir Ebenezer Howard and the Town Planning Movement.* Manchester University Press, reprinted 1970, Massachusetts Institute of Technology.

Machor, J. L. (1987) *Pastoral Cities: urban ideals and the symbolic landscape of America.* University of Wisconsin Press, Madison WI.

Marscak, R. (ed.) (1993) *Edmund Blunden.* Fyfield Books, Carcanet Press, Manchester.

Marsh, J. (1982) *Back to the Land.* Quartet Books, London.

Martin, P. (1984) *Pursing Innocent Pleasures: the gardening world of Alexander Pope.* Archon Books, Hamden, Connecticut.

Marx, L. (1964) *The Machine in the Garden.* Oxford University Press, Oxford.

McKenzie, J. (2007) *The Architecture of Alexandria and Egypt c.300 BC to AD 700.* Yale University Press, Princeton.

Meyer, E. (2008) Sustaining beauty. The performance of appearance. *Journal of Landscape Architecture* Spring.

Millar, F. J. (2008) (trans.) *Ovid: Metamorphoses.* Loeb Classical Library, London.

Morris, W. (1991) *News From Nowhere and Other Writings.* edited by C. Wilmer. Penguin Classics, London.

Moss, S. (2012) *Natural Childhood.* National Trust

Mosse, G. L. (1991) *Fallen Soldiers.* Oxford University Press, Oxford.

Motion, A. (1980) *The Poetry of Edward Thomas.* Routledge and Kegan Paul, London.

Mumford, E. P. (2000) *The CIAM Discourse on Urbanism, 1928–1960.* Massachusetts Institute of Technology, Massachusetts.

Nash, R. (1966) (trans.) *Sannazaro, J.: Arcadia and Piscatorial Eclogues.* Wayne State University Press, Detroit.

Neufeldt, T. (2004) Italian Pastoral Opera and Pastoral Politics in England, 1705–1712 *Discourses in Music* 5(2) Fall.

Nicholson, A. (2008) *Arcadia.* Harper Perennial, London.

Nicholson-Lord, D. (1987) *The Greening of the Cities.* Routledge and Kegan Paul, London.

Nischik, R. M. (ed.) (2000) *Margaret Atwood: works and impact.* Camden House, Rochester, NY.

Novak, B. (1980) *Nature and Culture – American Landscape and Painting 1825–1875.* Thames and Hudson, London.

Olmsted, F. L. O. (1852) *Walks and Talks of an American Farmer in England.* G. P. Putnam, New York.

Olmsted, F. L. (1870) *Public Parks and the Enlargement of Towns*. American Social Science Association. Hathi Digital Library.

Orr, D. W. (1992) *Ecological Literacy: education and the transition to a postmodern world*. SUNY Press, Albany.

Orr, D. W. (2006) Teaching Ecological Imagination. *New Dimensions*. 12 March.

O'Riordan, T. (1976) *Environmentalism*. Pion, London.

Panofsky, E. (1955) *Meaning in the Visual Arts*. Anchor Books, New York.

Patterson, A. (1987) *Pastoral and Ideology*. University of California Press, Berkeley.

Pepper, D. (1984) *The Roots of Modern Environmentalism*. Croom Helm, London.

Petrarch *Epistolae familiares* iv. i. Trans. Robinson, J. H. (1898) The First Modern Scholar and Man of Letters. G. P. Putnam, New York.

Pliny the Younger (1904) *Letter To Domitius Apollinaris*. Harvard Classics 14. www.bartleby.com.

Plumb, J. H. (1961) *The Italian Renaissance*. American Heritage New York.

Pope, A. (1709) *Spring*. The First Pastoral lines 1–4. www.humanitiesweb.org

Price, U. (1810) *Essays on the Picturesque*. J. Mawman, London.

Pugh, S. (1988) *Garden, Nature and Language*, Manchester University Press, Manchester,.

Pugh, S. (1998) *Garden Nature Language*. Manchester University Press, Manchester.

Pyle, R. (2003) Nature Matrix: reconnecting people and nature. *Oryx* 37(2).

Quiller-Couch, A. (ed.) (1919) *The Oxford Book of English Verse: 1250–1900*, Clarendon Press, Oxford.

Ranier, R. (1972) *Liveable Environments*. Artemis, Zurich.

Robinson,W. (1997) *The Wild Garden*. Scolar Press, Ilkley.

Robinson, W. (1895) *The English Flower Garden*. 4th edn. John Murray, London.

Rogers, T. (ed.) (1977) *Georgian Poetry 1911–1922*. Routledge, London.

Ruff, A. (1979) *Holland and the Ecological Landscape*, Deanwater Press, Stockport.

Sackville-West, V. (1926) The Land. www.poemhunter.com/victoria-sackville-west.

Sargent, T. (1986) (trans.) *Theocritus*. W. W. Norton, New York.

Saumerez Smith, C. (1997) *The Building of Castle Howard*. Pimlico, London.

Savory, J. J. (1997) *Thomas Rowlandson's Dr Syntax*. Cygnus Arts, London.

Sayre, L. (n.d.) *Georgic Apocalypse: From Virgil to Silent Spring*. www.yale.edu/agrarianstudies/colloqpapers/24sayre.pdf.

Schama, S. (1987) *The Embarrassment of Riches: an interpretation of Dutch Culture in the Golden Age*. University of California Press, Berkeley.

Schama, S. (1995) *Landscape and Memory*. Harper Collins, London.

Shoard, M. (1997) *This Land is Our Land*. Gaia Books, London.

Silkin, J. (1998) *Out of Battle The Poetry of the Great War*. Macmillan Press, Basingstoke, Hampshire.

Simon, M. (1978) *The Georgian Poetic*. University of California, London.

Skumautz, K. (2010) How natural images convey Modernist concepts in Virginia Woolf's *Mrs Dalloway* and Erich Maria Remarque's *All Quiet on the Western Front*. *Coastline Journal*. July 3.

Smithers, P. (1968) *The Life of Joseph Addison*. Oxford University Press, London.

Snape, R. (2004) The Co-operative Holidays Association and the cultural formation of countryside leisure practice. *Social Sciences: Journal Articles*. Paper 2. University of Bolton Institutional Repository.

Solkin, D. (1982) *Richard Wilson. The landscape of Reaction*. The Tate Gallery, London.

Solkin, D. (1993) *Painting for Money The visual arts and the Public Sphere in Eighteenth Century England*. Yale University, London.

Solnit, R. (2001) *Wanderlust*. Verso, London.

Stansfield, K. (1983) Landscape Design – the quiet revolution. *Architects' Journal* 52.

Stephenson, T. (1989) *Forbidden Land*. Manchester University Press, Manchester.

Sutton, P. C. (1987) *Masters of 17th Century Dutch Landscape Painting*. The Herbert Press, London.

Tallmadge, J. (2001) Resistance to Nature. *Michigan Quarterly Review* 40(1), Winter Issue, *Re-imagining Place*. University of Michigan Library, Ann Arbor, MI.

Tandy, D. W. and Neale, W. C. (1997) *Work and Days*. University of California Press, Berkeley.

Tate, A. (2001) *Great City Parks*. Spon Press, London.

Thacker, C. (1985) *The History of Gardens*. University of California Press, Berkeley.

Thames Landscape Strategy (n.d.) *The meaning of Arcadia*. www.thames-landscape-strategy.org.uk

Thompson, I. (1999) *Ecology, Community and Delight*. E. & F. N .Spon, London.

Thompson, I. (2010) *The English Lakes*. University of Newcastle Press, Newcastle.

Thomson, J. (1981) *The Seasons: Spring*. Clarendon Press, Oxford.

Thoreau, H. D. (1973) *Walden or Life in the Woods*. Anchor Books, New York.

Tickell, T. (1713) *The Guardian* 30, 15 April.

Tregay, R. and Gustavsson, R. (1983) *Oakwood's New Landscape*. University of Alnarp, Alnarp, Sweden.

Tregay, R. (2008) *The Enterprising Community*. Landscape Institute Conference.

Trieb, M. (ed.) (1998) *Modern Landscape Architecture: a critical review*. MIT Press, Cambridge MA.

Tunnard, C. (1950) *Gardens in the Modern Landscape*. The Architectural Press, London.

Turner, F. (1998) The Landscape of Disturbance. *Wilson Quarterly*, Spring.

Turner, F. (n.d.) blog: *Ecological Turbulence and the Hadean Arcadia*.

Unwin. R. (1996) *Town Planning in Practice*. Princeton Architectural Press, NY.

Valentine, T. W. (1931) The Medieval Church and Vergil. *Classical Weekly* 25.

Van der Ryn, S. and Cowan, S. (2007) *Ecological Design*. Island Press, Washington DC.

Wainwright, O. (2012) *London 2012 Olympic Park*. www.bdonline.co.uk. 25 July.

Waites, I. (2012) *Common Land in English Painting, 1700–1850*. Boydell Press, Woodbridge.

Whately, T. (1790) *Observations on Modern Gardening*. 2nd edn. London.

Wilkinson, L. P. (1969) *The Georgics of Virgil*. Cambridge University Press, Cambridge.

Williams-Ellis, C. (ed.) (1937) *Britain and the Beast*. Dent, London.

Williams-Ellis, C. (1971) *Architect Errant: The Autobiography of Clough Williams-Ellis*. Constable, London.

Wine, H. (1994) *Claude the Poetic Landscape*. National Gallery Publications, London.

Witcombe, C. (DATE?) *Art for Art's Sake*. www.arthistory resources.net.

Wordsworth, D. and Wordsworth W. (1986) *Home at Grasmere: the journal of Dorothy Wordsworth and the poems of William Wordsworth*. Penguin Classics, London.

Wordsworth, W. (1798) *Lyrical Ballads*. J. & A. Arch, London.

Wordsworth, W. (2004) *Guide to the Lakes*. Frances Lincoln, London.

Worster, D. (1985) *Nature's Economy*. Cambridge University Press, Cambridge.

Woudstra, J. (2000) The Corbusian Landscape *Garden History* 28(1) Summer.

Woudstra, J. (2007) The Eco Cathedral Louis Le Roy's Expression of a 'Free Landscape Architecture'. *Die Gartenkunst* 20(1), 185–202.

Index